China Academic Library

AF822695

Academic Advisory Board:
Researcher Geng, Yunzhi, Institute of Modern History, Chinese Academy of Social Sciences, China
Professor Han, Zhen, Beijing Foreign Studies University, China
Researcher Hao, Shiyuan, Institute of Ethnology and Anthropology, Chinese Academy of Social Sciences, China
Professor Li, Xueqin, Department of History, Tsinghua University, China
Professor Li, Yining, Guanghua School of Management, Peking University, China
Researcher Lu, Xueyi, Institute of Sociology, Chinese Academy of Social Sciences, China
Professor Wong, Young-tsu, Department of History, Virginia Polytechnic Institute and State University, USA
Professor Yu Keping, Central Compilation and Translation Bureau, China
Professor Yue, Daiyun, Department of Chinese Language and Literature, Peking University, China
Zhu, Yinghuang, China Daily Press, China

Series Coordinator:
Zitong Wu, Foreign Language Teaching and Research Press, China
Yan Li, Springer

More information about this series at http://www.springer.com/series/11562

Suli Zhu

Sending Law to the Countryside

Research on China's Basic-level Judicial System

外语教学与研究出版社
FOREIGN LANGUAGE TEACHING AND RESEARCH PRESS

Springer

Suli Zhu
Law School
Peking University
Beijing
China

Sponsored by Chinese Fund for the Humanities and Social Sciences（本书获中华社会科学基金资助）

ISSN 2195-1853 ISSN 2195-1861 (electronic)
China Academic Library
ISBN 978-981-10-9340-1 ISBN 978-981-10-1142-9 (eBook)
DOI 10.1007/978-981-10-1142-9

Jointly published with Foreign Language Teaching and Research Publishing Co., Ltd.

© Foreign Language Teaching and Research Publishing Co., Ltd
Softcover reprint of the hardcover 1st edition 2016
and Springer Science+Business Media Singapore 2016
This work is subject to copyright. All rights are reserved by the Publishers, whether the whole or part of the material is concerned, specifically the rights of translation, reprinting, reuse of illustrations, recitation, broadcasting, reproduction on microfilms or in any other physical way, and transmission or information storage and retrieval, electronic adaptation, computer software, or by similar or dissimilar methodology now known or hereafter developed.
The use of general descriptive names, registered names, trademarks, service marks, etc. in this publication does not imply, even in the absence of a specific statement, that such names are exempt from the relevant protective laws and regulations and therefore free for general use.
The publishers, the authors and the editors are safe to assume that the advice and information in this book are believed to be true and accurate at the date of publication. Neither the publishers nor the authors or the editors give a warranty, express or implied, with respect to the material contained herein or for any errors or omissions that may have been made.

Printed on acid-free paper

This Springer imprint is published by Springer Nature
The registered company is Springer Science+Business Media Singapore Pte Ltd.

…

Do not move forward!
Ahead lies boundless forest,
With old trees displaying stripes from wild animals,
And lifeless vines intertwining with each other like pythons.
No star lights could shed through those heavy leaves.
When you hear the empty echoes from your first step,
You wouldn't dare to take another step.
…

He Qifang: Prophecy

For my classmate and friend Zou Bing
who has forever gone,
This is in memory of our friendship
that has turned into history.

Preface to the New Edition

I

It can be both good and bad to re-publish this book, which I wrote 10 years ago.

It may be a positive reflection on the author, since Peking University Press sees this book as valuable in terms of business and benefitting others. If this is the right judgment, then it shows that the book is of some value to today's China. But what does this value stand for? Is the book well written? And furthermore, what does it mean to be "well written"?

After revision, I began to realize that the main value for re-publishing this book is that the problems regarding China's judicial system that this book focuses on and discusses till exist to some extent or in some other adapted form. Some have been improved, but others have gotten more severe. Some questions are not limited to courts of basic levels and are even no longer limited to central and western regions or rural areas of China. My basic approach during my research at that time—analysis and theory pursuit based on China's problems and experiences—may still remain pioneering, especially in face of the rampant spread of conceptualist jurisprudence and ideological jurisprudence. With China's peaceful rise, the focus on China's problems and academic research demonstrated by this book has turned out to be even more imperative. This book,[1] which used to arouse intensive discussions and controversies, remains updated and even more targeted only because it used to be inappropriate at that time.

[1]Book reviews which are rather long are as follows:
Wang Mingming: "Ah Q and Qiu Ju, The Story Goes On…", *Wenhui Reading Weekly*, 2001/4/21;
Heng Fang: "China's Basic-level Judicial System Upon Three Fractures," *Twenty-First Century*, June Issue, 2002;
Xiao Han: "Reading *Sending Law to the Countryside*," *Social Sciences in China*;
Zhang Zhimei: "*Sending Law to the Countryside*: A Reader," *Social Sciences in China*, Issue 3, 2002;

For an ordinary person who makes living by doing academic research, this seems to be a success and a comfort. However, the significance of any texts, including literary texts, is always determined by social needs. It is ultimately a failure and a tragedy for a person who wishes to participate in or promote China's social development through academic research.

I yawn for rapid decay.

II

It has been 10 years, after all. The rapid development of China's society, including the judicial reform of last 10 years, has indeed brought many changes to China's basic-level judiciary. During these 10 years, I have written on subjects related to these changes and problems.[2] In general, these subjects are as follows:

Footnote 1 (continued)

Liu Xing: "Steping into Real Life with Law—On *Sending Law to the Countryside*," *Social Sciences in China*, Issue 3, 2002;

Feng Xiang: "*Sending Law to the Countryside* and Teaching Fish to Swim," *DUSHU*, Issue 2, 2003;

Wu Yuzhang: "Reading *Sending Law to the Countrysude*," *DUSHU* , Issue 2, 2003;

Ding Wei: "Book Review of *Sending Law to the Countryside*," *Hong Kong Journal of Social Sciences*, Spring Issue, vol. 27, 2004;

Zhao Xiaoli: "Anti-Judicial Theory in the Basic-level Justice?—Reviewing Su Li's *Sending Law to the Countryside*," *Sociological Studies*, Issue 2, 2005;

Frank K. Upham, "Who Will Find the Defendant if He Stays with His Sheep? Justice in Rural China," Book Review of *Song fa xiaxiang: Zhongguo jiceng sifazhidu yanjiu* by Zhu suli, *Yale Law Journal*, vol. 114, 1675–1718 (2005);

Huang Tao: "Sending Law to the Countryside—Research on China's Basic-level Judicial System," *Hong Kong Journal of Social Sciences*, Issue 32, Spring and Summer Volume, 2007;

Zhao Ming: "Law Philosophy Criticism of Local Knowledge—Taking *Sending Law to the Countryside* as focus of analysis," *Journal of Central South University of Forestry (Social Science Edition)*, Issue 2, 2007;

Jiang Zhiru: "On China's Judicial Road," *Law Book Review 6*, Peking University Press, 2008;

Zhang Qi: "China's Basic-level Justice from the perspective of State Social Relations—Thoughts on Mr. Su Li's *Sending Law to the Countryside*," *Legal System and Society*, Issue 17, 2009.

[2]Those directly or indirectly related are:

"Observation on Selection of Judges," *Legal Science*, Issue 3, 2004;

"Quality of Judges and Education of Law Colleges," *Studies in Law and Business*; Issue 3, 2004;

"There Is No Real Estate," *Journal of Law Application*, Issue 8, 2005;

"Perspective on Judicial Demands in China's Rural Areas," *How Systems Are Formed* (Revised), 2007 (originally as "Demands for Rule of Law In China's Rural Areas and Response of Legal Systems," *China Court*, March 27, 2006, B1–2);

"Parties in China's Judiciary," *Law and Social Science*, Inaugural Issue, Law Press, 2006;

"Courthouse on the Horseback and Rule of Law in China," *Tsinghua Law Review*, vol. 3, 2008;

"On *Judicial Picture of Rural China*," *Legal Review*, vol. 7, October, 2008.

"Being Prudent, but not Rejecting," *Journal of Law Application*, Issue 1, 2010;

"Active Judiciaries and Big Mediation," *China Legal Science*, Issue 1, 2010;

"About Active Judiciaries," *Journal of Law Application*, Issue 2–3, 2010;

"Image-Building of China's Judges—On Chen Yanping's Working Methods," *Tsinghua Law Review*, vol. 3, 2010.

1. China's basic-level judiciary has become increasingly important, particularly in rural areas. Due to many factors, including legislation and judiciary themselves, China is now entering into a period in which social conflicts happen more frequently and turn out to be sharp, and more and more people turn to the courts for settling disputes. People have greater expectations from the judicial system, but they are getting increasingly disappointed. The rapid development of China's economic society has brought great changes to disputes. With improved social mobility, the objects that people engage with are more diversified and disputes increase. The changes in interpersonal relations have reduced the applicability and efficiency of mediation, even in the rural areas. The cases in rural areas are no longer simple. Urban lives have more bearings on disputes, especially in areas on China's coast. Even in remote rural areas, divorce cases are more likely to be put forward by females. Personal injuries caused by vehicles, machines, and electrical appliances have completely changed the type of tort disputes. Issues involving lawsuit petitions have become common.
2. Although rule-based governance remains to be one of the key issues in the entire judicial system, dispute settlement with finality is still a key issue and pursuit of the basic-level judges.
3. The position of institutional functions (different from social functions) of basic-level courts in the court system, the trial system, and the administrative system inside the court, including internal and external supervision and prevention mechanisms to prevent miscarriage of justice, is not clear. These problems remain unchanged.
4. In the 1990s, the trial method and judicial reform started from the point of "the burden of proof lies upon he who affirms," which emphasized an adversary system, handling cases in court, and in-court procedures. This system has achieved a lot in urban areas, but still falls short of the practical needs and system support of the courts. Due to the severe lack of formalized conditions (including lawyers acting as agents and evidence documentation), the basic-level courts, especially those involving civil cases in the people's courts, have always been "active judiciaries," in which case, mediation usually comes first.
5. Generally speaking, there is still a severe lack of legal professionals in the courts. Even in the rural areas of developed and relatively developed regions in eastern China, there are occasionally lawyers with formal legal education in the basic-level judiciary, but civil lawyers at the local level are still rarely seen in most of the central and western regions. The uniform judicial examination has raised the standards for junior judges and thus brought about a flow of judges from central and western regions to the coastal areas of eastern regions and from local level to high-level courts. In addition, a large number of old judges have retired or are forced to retire in the name of raising the so-called standard of professionalism, and law-school graduates prefer not to work in basic-level courts due to meager payment, which results in the lack of judges in basic-level courts in central and western China. The total number of civil courts is on the decrease. There is severe short of judges with a law-school education in basic-level courts.

6. Since the 1990s, there has been huge improvement of judges' overall competence and professionalism. However, there is still not enough, or even less, attention in the legal, judicial, and jurisprudence circles paid to the specialized and comprehensive knowledge needed by basic-level judges. With insufficient emphasis on specific social conditions, there is neither enough attention to, nor adequate summary or improvement of effective judicial experience under such circumstances, which gives rise to a tendency toward rigid legalism.
7. Social reform has brought about recohesion and formation of legal and moral consensus in Chinese society. However, formal legal knowledge and belief have quite a few conflicts with customs that are rather stable and prevalent in Chinese society.

The society and the situations have changed, but some key issues remain unchanged.

III

As for this new edition, I have not made any substantial modifications to the content, even though there are new data and materials available to enrich and amend related chapters. My research has always been guided by fundamental issues. If the update of details does not affect the fundamental conclusion of the analysis, then it is superfluous.

I have made some adjustments to the language. Apart from correcting some misspellings, I have tried my best to simplify my expressions, abandoning or playing down the translated elements of original texts. There are certain areas in this book to which not enough reasons and explanations are given from today's point of view—I therefore add a few words to them.

Here is my explanation for reediting this book. I do believe that it is not necessary for readers who already have the previous edition to spend more money on this book, but there is one wish outweighing all other considerations, which is to leave a fossil for the history—about China's society, judiciary, and jurisprudence at the end of the twentieth century, which we have lived through.

August 2010 Suli Zhu

Confessions on the Last Day of the Twentieth Century (Preface)

I

In 1996, I published my first book of collected papers—*The Rule of Law and Its Native Resources*, which led to some discussion in the circle of jurisprudence. Apart from many compliments, there were also many doubts and criticisms. I gave my heartfelt thanks to both compliments and criticisms alike, even though some criticisms were strongly worded and determined to act on impulses and raised to a higher plane of principle and two-line struggle. In a somewhat snobbish line of thought, criticizing means respect. It means that the ideas and arguments made caused critics to be nervous and feel the urge to speak out, and even feel the need to fight. These debates would force me to review whether I had done anything wrong or imperfect and help me to understand how others view these issues, and from which angle and based on what presumption they draw such conclusions. It is actually a kind of encouragement to me, although I have no intention to change my views till my last breath. The only thing that I find it difficult to forgive is that a few individuals confess that they have not even seen the book, but have already begun to demonstrate (show off?) based solely on the name of the book. This method and writing style should not be tolerated in any academic circles.

I am still somewhat disappointed—I feel that many criticisms and even some praises are based on misunderstandings caused by carelessness. They often pay attention only to terms like "native resources." During this process, my views have been labeled as "conservatism," "postmodernism," "in support of localization of rule of law," and even been regarded as "dangerous thoughts." Some scholars believe I stand for rebuilding China's rule of law based on China's traditional culture. From their perspectives, China's culture itself does not provide any basis for modern rule of law, and my statement is therefore only a kind of sweet dream. There are other scholars who think that I refuse to learn from foreign experiences regarding rule of law and jurisprudence and that my emphasis that law is a kind of local knowledge will lead to dead ends. These misunderstandings are probably destined, since even those brand-new, historically pioneering works are doomed to be misunderstood. That is to say, as long as this kind of pioneering work shares some kind of similarities with those antiquated lifestyles, it will be misunderstood as opposition to those social lifestyles.[3] Not to mention my opinions which are neither brand-new nor historically pioneering enough.

However, I still want to illustrate these issues, as a confession to and a mark of respect to my friends, colleagues, and peers—since it is impolite to ignore such remarks. I determined to quote from my original book, including page numbers, in case people think that I have changed my words.

About whether native resources equate to tradition or if there is any basis for modern rule of law in contemporary Chinese society:

> To look for native resources and to focus on traditions of this country are usually understood as to look through the history, especially history books and rules. Those kinds of resources are important for sure, but what matters more is that we need to look for native resources from all kinds of informal legal systems of social lives. Historical research is only one way to get help from local resources. However, native resources do not exist in history only. Informal systems already being formed or developed in the social activities of people nowadays are even more important.
>
> With the reform of production methods, as well as migration of people, it is fair to say that the basic economic institutions to strengthen the traditional patriarchal system or a different form of the patriarchal system have been increasingly weakened. My emphasis of getting help from China's native resources to establish modern rule of law is exactly based on this fundamental precondition of economic system reform. (pp. 14–15)

As for legal transplant, I really do not think it is possible. My views are based on the difference in meanings of laws both literally and practically, or even broader as the difference between jurisprudence and rule of law. From my perspective,

> Even the influence of legal research on modern legal systems is also a justification process, which can only have some impact on the form, structure, and justification argument of the legal system at most. However, the legal system grows from the society, and its practice may, but not necessarily, apply to certain research results or some research results of jurisprudence.
>
> ... The life of a nation creates its own legal system, but academic jurists create only theories about legal system. (p. 287, 289; Marks of emphasis are left out.)

I prefer not to quote any more, incase I will be blamed for earning royalties by quoting my previous books. What I want to say is that my views or ideas were consistent throughout that book and in all other articles afterward, which serve as main clues and boundaries, although I do not think there is any particular significance in singling these views out. From my perspective, the most important thing is not how to express one's opinions, but whether the attitude and manner of analysis demonstrated by an article is in line with the author's words in terms of logic and mentality, or whether there is a coherent development. If it is not,

[3]Karl Marx: The Civil War in France, *Selected Works of Marx and Engles*, vol. 3, People's Publishing House, 1994, p. 54.

what are the reasons and factors? They should be explained at an appropriate time. Otherwise, there will be suspicion of being "opportunistic" and "jumping on the bandwagon." There is also a situation that the author themselves does not fully understand the topic under discussion, which is often seen in China's community of jurisprudence.

II

There is another issue that I need to clarify: It is about the issue of "local knowledge." It is true that there is no thorough discussion on this issue in this book, except one sentence that "A large part of the knowledge needed in our social life is specific and local". I think it is very clear and people will understand it once it is mentioned. But it seems this is not the case. Why? The question is that many people have a kind of foresight or prejudice (which is not necessarily negative in the sense of Gadamer, who believes that there is no knowledge that is complete, and therefore, it is prejudice which constitutes the basis and necessity for learners to seek knowledge) and an unnecessary feeling that knowledge is myth. To these people, it stands that only knowledge printed in textbooks, especially textbooks of university students and postgraduates, is knowledge and that only information which is becoming common propositions or those wrapped up in some exciting or "big" words is knowledge. But knowledge is shown in all kinds of forms. There are many kinds of knowledge that cannot be expressed (but can be done) or are awkward when expressed by language or common propositions in our social lives. Consider your feelings when you are in love. You may use the word "happiness" (which is based on your knowledge) to express your feeling. But happiness itself is different. It is not like the happiness you felt when you got an "A" or your mom bought you an ice cream when you were young. It is the same in terms of legal knowledge. Apart from the many propositions, principles, rules, standards, and other knowledge that can be generalized abstractly, the operation of law needs all kinds of other knowledge, such as so-called practical reasons and skills, or "common knowledge" and specific knowledge about the parties concerned (please refer to Chap. 1 of this book).

Another issue related to the notion that law is local knowledge is whether paying attention to and giving emphasis to this local knowledge will result in knowledge inclusiveness. I don't think this will be the case. I consider myself to be concerned very much with local knowledge, and I pay great attention to many of those details. I try to find out the theoretical significance in such knowledge. However, I do not think it leads to self-imposed enclosure. Frankly speaking, as far as the books I reference in this book are concerned, the legal sciences, as well as many other subjects, all demonstrate that paying attention to local knowledge does not necessarily lead to enclosure or obsolescence of knowledge. In addition, I have emphasized in this book many times that since the science of law is not a self-sufficient subject, openness of mind shall be directed not only to knowledge coming from foreign countries and marked as jurisprudence, but also to the knowledge and experience of oneself, as well as of other ordinary people, and to knowledge and research findings of related subjects. If you pay attention only to writings and opinions of certain foreign scholars from the subject (even within your academic field) of your own interests, and regard yourself as having true learning while resisting or ignoring research results of other subjects, you will likely have neither an open attitude nor the manner of a scholar—and will be acting as an apologist.

Even from a logical point of view, to build legality based on local knowledge is not meant and will not lead to supremacy of local knowledge. From my personal experience, if I want to pay attention to local knowledge, I must open my mind since only in this way can I possibly understand, feel, discover, and even find local knowledge. To understand local knowledge is and must be based on the premise of understanding many other kinds of knowledge (which, too, are local knowledge). If a person stays in a certain place for too long and fails to absorb others' points of view, he will think that everyday is the same and "only the world outside is exciting." If one has an open mind and keeps changing and enriching their frame of reference through understanding view points and knowledge of other people and subjects, the seemingly bland and mundane world is also full of energy and magnificence. There are many interesting questions that make your heart sensitive and young once more, and you will feel "a day that [your] heart beat finally comes" (written by He Qifang). You will feel—as described in my old poem—"All are familiar but newly met; All are understood but require new understanding." To rephrase it in a candid way which may lack academic tastes, you can understand yourself only by seeing others. To make it more academic, but perhaps more awkward, locality is one of the qualities of the knowledge demonstrated by inter-relations of all kinds of local knowledge.

III

Because I use the term "native resources," there are quite a few people trying to connect me with "localization of rule of law." This is a kind of misunderstanding based on "native" which takes my words only literally. As a matter of fact, attentive readers will notice that I have never talked about localization of rule of law. There was only one article in my book *Native Resources* in which I did mention the localization of legal studies, mainly because the whole academic circle was then discussing the standardization and localization of academic studies. My article was expected to focus on this main theme naturally. I do stand for localization of legal research. That is to say, Chinese scholars who have studied overseas, like me, must (but not only) study issues related to China. They should have their own visions and pursue their own findings (with or without achievement). They should not behave as the overseas students criticized by Chairman Mao as "having returned from Europe, North America, and Japan… only to talk about superficial knowledge of foreign countries. They act only as a phonograph and forget completely about their responsibilities of getting to know and creating new things."[4]

I myself don't stand for localization of rule of law; I don't think the way it is put is of any actual significance, but I suspect it as showing off without keeping one's feet on the ground. Why is it so? My reasons are as follows. First of all, to keep in line with the self-cited words in the previous section, I believe that it is not for the jurists to decide whether a country's rule of law is good or not. It is the life of a whole nation that has created its own rule of law. What the jurists have created is theory justification of a certain rule of law. Therefore, for those people who think highly of themselves only because what they have said has become popular or adopted by the government, and those who believe that slogans will determine the results of rule of law, they are taking themselves too seriously while being contemptuous toward others. If there is localization of the rule of law as a matter of fact, it cannot be westernized even if desired. However, if it is geared to international standards, it will not work out even if all jurists stand for localization. I myself understand this theoretical limitation very well. Just think of the following question: Can jurists order judges to listen to them? Or can they order citizens to listen to them? You may be unable to manage a stowaway (who is perhaps also trying to get in touch with the world in his own way?)!

These words are too realistic to be of any theoretical value—at least some people will think this way. As a matter of fact, I have further theoretical analysis. That is to say, I believe that there is such a hidden precondition in the slogan of the localization of rule of law that China is born to be and will forever be different from foreign countries (mainly Western countries). This theory gives emphasis to cultural type, which stands that due to the difference of cultural types between the East and the West, whatever (the rule of law included) comes from the West will not become effective until localized in China and that this situation will go on forever (the precondition of this theory is a metaphor borrowed from the genes of the biology). I respect this theory as well as the scholars that accept and stand for this theory (they might be right since we cannot test and verify who is right and who is wrong at the moment). However, respect does not mean that I am convinced or accept this. I still believe more in the historical materialism of Marx as well as related sociological and economic theories. I believe that a so-called cultural difference is not the reason for differences, but more the result of a difference in natural environment, modes of production, and other physical factors. The weak point of the cultural theory is to find out the reasons for historic cultural differences, and accurately tracking and attributing this difference to overall results. As far as I'm concerned, there is a hidden danger (which might be too strong a word) that all kinds of differences are made consolidated and eternal, and sometimes alleged only by a certain group of people. As far as the historical development of China

[4]Reviewing and Improving Our Studies, *Selected Works of Mao Zedong*, People's Press, 1966, p. 756.

since modern times is concerned, it seems that the Chinese do not adhere to traditional culture all that much. If a kind of new invention or foreign object can bring actual interests, people are ready to accept it, no matter if it is Marxism, democracy, science, TV, or pirated discs (I think that the original pirated disc surely came from outside China). In addition, with international economic and information exchanges getting increasingly frequent, today's China is converging with developed countries while diverging from traditional Chinese society. This has already become fact. It is therefore not necessary to accept a theory of localization of the rule of law that emphasizes difference as a purpose only for reducing transaction fees and increasing social wealth.

This does not deny the difference in individuals, ethics, the economic development level of different countries, or the major conflicts in interests of different countries. I believe that laws of different countries have their own features to some extent. However, this feature is the result not of how loudly the slogan of localization is being shouted, but the actions taken by people (not only jurists or law makers) to tackle detailed issues they face in their own lives. That is to say, a slogan itself does not solve problems—problems can only be solved by detailed research and actions. The law should be tailored according to specific issues. I believe that due to the secularity and practicality of law itself, what the law needs to consider truly and firstly is whether it is "feasible" (whether is it can be accepted practically by people), but not whether it is "local" (whether it is different from others). No matter whether it is local or international, if a law is unable to solve problems, it is not a good law. If it is localized during the process of solving actual problems, then it is a result, not necessarily a purpose. It is in this sense that I believe that the discourse regarding the localization and internationalization of the rule of law is a signboard rather than a true or meaningful issue. This kind of slogan bears the trace of an ideology—it emphasizes the political and directional correctness of the concept without paying much attention to its real meaning, not to mention caring about its actual effects. In this sense, I oppose either the internationalization or the localization of the rule of law, because either of them ignores the issues of the actual laws or systems in question. It is not pragmatic to approach first the terms or the cultural and political standards of an issue. I am a pragmatist myself who emphasize the institutional function of law, but not its external claims.

It is due to the above reason that I don't care much about the cultural label given to all kinds of materials or opinions by the current intellectual system. Neither do I pay any attention to the "true" or "core" thought of scholars, Chinese or foreign, ancient or modern. What I care about is whether materials and opinions—after my careful reading—can extend my understanding of the issues related to legal systems of modern China and give me new inspirations (I therefore do not force others to understand these materials and opinions). I will not read traditional Chinese documents only because my research is about contemporary Chinese issues. Neither will I forget about the wisdom hidden in what Confucius says about being "unwilling to comment on something which is not one's own concern" only because the concepts of judicial independence and professionalism come from the West. It is actually not that important to identify the academic tradition. What is more important is whether one can understand the issue and elicit a wise response. Academic research is a highly individual practice. It will not increase a person's wisdom to identify academic tradition. On the contrary, real wisdom can actually create and change academic tradition.

IV

I was urged to say the above words a long time ago. A law magazine used to suggest hosting an academic symposium on this subject and then publishing a special issue—but I don't think it is worth the efforts. There is another paper that consecutively carried a series of articles criticizing me and sent those papers to me. Seeing that I had no reactions at all, they asked me to write something to respond to those criticisms. I refused politely because I am afraid of being used by the media or by critics. There is a possibility that I might be led by those people to their directions. I felt it was better to keep my distance, continuing reading worthwhile books, doing my own research, and writing my own articles. However, the more important reason is that I don't think this kind of argument is meaningful. In a reply to one of my students,[5] I mentioned that the concept of native resource itself does not matter much. There is somewhat of a contingency related to its invention. What matters is the study of China's actual issues, answering China's questions, and putting forward specific ways to solve problems. It is meaningless to argue about the specific meaning of native resource (which is also the biggest misunderstanding against me). When we argue, the word that is supposed to express a certain view in a specific context might be substantiated and become "something" outside the context. As a result, people are fighting for this word, just as Liu Huan sings in his song "Retribution": "We almost forgot our intention that used to be unchanged. We almost lost our sincerity that we were born with." This is the result that I want to see least (Pragmatism again!). This phenomenon is called alienation in philosophy: It seems as if everybody is talking about this word, but the word is actually speaking on behalf of everybody. I wouldn't do such silly things, would I? Our ancestor Confucius already understood this principle long time ago, that's why he "did not talk about extraordinary things, feats of strength, disorder, or spiritual beings," and "as to what is beyond the physical world, the sage master leaves not discussed." Why did Confucius not talk or discuss about such topics? It does not mean that Confucius agreed to those "things," but that he was wise enough to know that when such issues are discussed, there will be no result (Just think about it, who in this world can actually accept defeat in debate?) because there is no definite reference. You cannot get back what is said, and opposite of the wishes,

[5]Suli: Few Explanations on "Native Resource," *Graduate Students' Journal of Peking University*, Issue 3, 1997.

extraordinary things, feats of strength, disorders, or spiritual beings would be materialized in people's minds. People can only say something when they remain silent. People cannot really say anything at any time. Speech is silver, while silence is gold. All these are words of wisdom.

Most importantly, argument does not solve any practical problems. Even if I won this argument and became somewhat "famous" because of this, I would only be given an undeserved reputation of a voice of "native resource," wouldn't I? Even Qin Wen in *A Dream in Red Mansions* knew that bearing an undeserved reputation is no good. If you really want to persuade people into having less doubt, you need to have something to show to the people. In China, as long as you are serious, smart, and capable, you can still present good and real things on research of seemingly trivial things. Chinese people are smart enough to recognize good things. Then, they will try to imitate (there will certainly be piracy involved) and then create. Thus, it is important not to argue too much (but it is OK to argue a little bit when necessary) or construct the issues such as how is "native resource" possible, whether "native resource" actually exists, and whether "native resource" is necessary. It is important that Chinese scholars present something truly academic from their research on China that foreigners are unable to present.

It has been three years since I have been able to present this book. It appears to me that this could have only been written by a Chinese author; it is a book in which I have explored "native resource" systematically and it has included, demonstrated, and pushed forward my previous thoughts. It comes from discussions and thoughts on some common phenomena in China's justice, from a person who lives on this soil. It also contains summaries and generalizations of experiences of a common Chinese judge at the local level. It does not simply demonstrate or enumerate Chinese phenomena, but has a theoretical pursuit. It does not only get deep into this field of judicial practice in courts to which the legal science circle has paid not enough attention to, but also makes issues which jurists seldom or hardly pay attention to under the current framework of legal knowledge more prevalent. Moreover, in terms of theoretical analysis, it does not refer to a theoretical framework which stresses cultural incommensurability, but makes efforts to analyze and explain empirical materials inside a theoretical framework which even common people can understand and exchange ideas about. It may not be perfect and may even have some errors, but it can only be produced by a Chinese person in this land that I am so deeply in love with. In this sense, it is original and irreplaceable.

V

This is the last dawn of the twentieth century.

I couldn't help feeling touched when finishing this book—at such a symbolic moment! Although I know clearly that the date is only a symbol without much true meaning, I can still feel the magnificence of this moment! (Modernization has certainly trained us to be so.)

At this moment, my students, colleagues, and compatriots on the other side of the ocean are gathering together to enjoy New Year's Eve dinner. They are bracing for the new year, new century, and new millennium with all kinds of complicated but forward-looking emotions. Within a few hours, there will be jubilation everywhere. But as a stranger all alone in a strange land far away, I have spent this moment in my office.

I miss my motherland.

It reminds me of a line written by a poet:

> Why there are always tears in my eyes?
> It is because I am so deeply in love with this land...[6]

Suli Zhu
Written at 6 o'clock on the last day of the twentieth century
Cambridge

[6]Ai Qing: "I Love This Land," *Ai Qing Selected Poems*, People's Literature Publishing House, 1979.

Contents

Part II Judicial Knowledge and Technology

Part III Judges and Legal Personnel

Part IV Reflection on Research Method

Introduction: Research on China's Justice at the Basic Level

This book is supposed to study China's judicial system at the basic, local level. But for what reason? This introduction will provide preliminary analysis and elaboration on some related basic issues in general. These issues are, namely Why do we study the judiciary? Secondly, why do we study judiciary at the basic level? Thirdly, why do we study China? And fourthly, what kind of practical and academic significance does this research have? I will address the first 3 issues in the following sections, as well as address the first half of the fourth question in later discussion. The discussion on the second half of the fourth question will form a separate chapter. At last, I will explain the theoretical framework, methods, and approaches of this book and finally present the structure of the book to aid readers.

Why Do We Study Judiciary?

China is expected to carry out a system of rule of law, and China is heading toward such a system. No matter what kind of review or forecast modern Chinese have on the current situation and direction of politics and laws in Chinese society, "rule of law" has become a public belief, just as the belief that the Chinese in the past had for "evolution" and belief that the today's Chinese have for "reform." Although there might be some superstition involved,[7] this belief and pursuit has certain reasons and justifications, and in terms of historical development, it seems to be a case for this trend.[8]

---

[7]Please refer to review made by Feng Xiang in *Wooden-Legged Justice*, Zhongshan University Press, 1999, especially articles like "Foreword," "Law and Literature (Preface)," "Puzzle of Qiu Ju and Civilization of Vega" and etc.

[8]Suli: "China's Modernization and Rule of Law in the 20th Century," *Legal Research*, Issue 1, 1998.

However, the ideal of rule of law shall be implemented into specific systems and techniques. Without guarantee of specific systems and techniques, we are not only unable to realize any grand ideals, but will likely make major errors. Even though such basic principles of rule of law that have been widely recognized are remembered by heart—such as universality of legal application, impartial treatment under the law, and non-retroactive laws—we cannot guarantee that the expected result of rule of law will come out. This is not only because that "principle is not the starting point of research, but its final conclusion,"[9] but also because that "general principle cannot decide specific cases."[10] I will make some detailed analysis on this point.

First of all, all these basic principles are not a priori principle, but a generalization and a summary of practical experiences from both positive and negative aspects in practice. In other words, these principles were not principles at first, but were gradually acknowledged as principles by people in their social practice. For example, the principle that law gives the same protection to the same group of people, or the principle of all people are equal before the law, was not commonly recognized in the actual history of human beings. The reason that all forms of slavery and feudal hierarchy were carried out for long periods of time in different parts of the world was not only because of the economic conditions of society at that time, but also because of the superstructures and ideologies adapted. Aristotle believed that the rule of law was the rule of good laws in his views. He believed that slaves were not people and that women were imperfect people.[11] Thomas Jefferson, who claimed in The United States Declaration of Independence that "all men are created equal," owned a large number of slaves himself.[12] These facts have been pointed out not to belittle those great thinkers or politicians, blame them for not being honest and deceiving people deliberately, or claim that "they had limitations due to their age or class." I just want to point out that all principles we recognize today are only summaries of history, representing the recognition of the choices made in our current age regarding previous knowledge. At least from a historical point of view, all principles are the product of experiences of people, but not an existence a priori.

Because these principles are a posteriori and empirical, it is difficult to say whether they are final truths. Even though we, in general, can be, and many times "have to" be, sure that our generation has a wider vision, more extensive knowledge and a better command of "truth" compared to our ancestors, we still cannot convincingly prove logically that we have arrived at the final truth. This is even

[9]Engles: Anti-Duhring, *Selected Works of Marx and Engles*, vol. 3, People's Publishing House, 1994, p. 374.

[10]Lochner v. New York, 198 U.S. (1905), dissenting, in *The Mind and Faith of Justice Holmes, His Speeches, Essays, Letters and Judicial Opinion*, sel. and ed. by Max Lerner, The Modern Library, 1943, p. 149.

[11]Aristotle: *Politics*, trans. Wu Shoupeng, the Commercial Press, 1965.

[12]The more accurate translation should be "Males are created equal," it is therefore excluded all women and minors.

true for those principles that we regard as unshakable truths today. Now that we have much time to live on beyond our imagination, how could we imagine that people have generalized and determined all principles of rule of law up till now?! We must presume that our lives and knowledge are just "as thin as a thread," as Zhuangzi has mentioned and are just a link in the chain of the timeline of the human being. Then, how could we presume that society in the future will be a continuation of today and remain unchanged, that no major social changes beyond our imagination will take place, and that all principles today will be adequate for people in the future or even our future life?! If history is really non-repeatable, as we usually say, then we must accept the following conclusion: Principles extracted from history will never be adequate in the future.

The more important thing is that due to its abstraction, general principle might be forever correct, but therefore useless. A general principle can never tell us when we can use it to verify a certain law, or which law we should verify. We have quite a lot of principles. Sometimes, these principles clash with each other. We cannot provide a structure table (actually another kind of principle) about the force of principles to solve these conflicts effectively. For example, apart from normal legal protection, should we give any certain kind of special protection to women, children, seniors, the disabled, ethnic minorities, overseas Chinese, foreign merchants, or people of other classifications? On the one hand, we have the principle of "all people are equal before law" (difference among people is not recognized literally); on the other hand, we have the principle of "the same group of people are given same protections" (difference among people is recognized literally). These two principles conflict with each other on such issues, but problems are not limited to the conflict. When these concepts are brought into practice, they can possibly cause trouble. For instance, if I lost my little finger due to work injury, would I be a disabled person? What if I lost my index finger, thumb, or even my whole hand (the left or the right)? All these questions cannot be answered by principle itself or principle deduction. Neither can they be answered by the concept itself or its definition. People must have case-specific judgment to provide justice (as judge as an occupation is the same word as judge as a verb). It is therefore fair to say that justice has a special role to play in rule of law. It is the bridge to bring law from the books into our real life to transfer principle to actual rules.

Another important significance of justice is that it is, at least sometimes, a kind of activity with a sense of legislation as well. Although people today are accustomed to the strict division of legislation from justice, this division is not clear either in terms of logics or in terms of practice. It is only a conventional formula and its dividing line is arbitrary. If legislation is regarded to set or establish rules for practical social life and not only as laws and stipulations produced by institutions labeled as legislature, according to so-called legislative proceedings, justice is inevitably a component of legislation in a broader sense. From the practices of different countries, judicial application and interpretation are always regarded as supplementary to legislature, or the so-called interstitial legislation. In common-law countries, the majority of laws are created, modified, and developed by judges in the field of common law, while in the field of statute law, it is the territory and responsibility of the court (but not limited to the court) to determine its meaning since Marshall.[13] Even in countries with a continental law system, justice is actually a supplement to legislation. Related law books in many countries stipulate clearly that when there is no express stipulation in law, the judge is expected to return a verdict according to law that may be stipulated by legislators under such circumstances, or prudent discretion, or the ambiguous principle of natural law.[14] A judicial verdict, whether it is intended to be legislation or a supplement to legislation, forms a restriction or guidance to justice concerning similar dispute in the future and thus plays the role of law in this sense.[15]

Justice is of more important significance to the formation and development of the rule of law in modern China. China is a big country with imbalanced political, economic, and cultural development in different regions. I believe that the basic judgment of Chairman Mao 70 years ago[16] still remains to be the most fundamental reality that all social scientists who study China's problems shall face directly. Today's China is in a dazzling period of reform. In such a country and during such a period, you can employ such grand concepts as "China," "transforming time" or "rule of law" to eliminate all specific differences, but you cannot solve any problems with the concepts themselves. It is necessary to ensure that legal rules are uniform, universal, and forward-looking and at the same time flexible, abundant, and realistic. Justice enjoys advantages that cannot be replaced by legislation.

Judges and others working in justice directly face tremendous and variable realities that involve living people and novel occurrences. They often find voids

---

[13]Marbury v. Madison, 1 Cranch 137 (1803).

[14]For example, Section 2 of Article 1 in the Swiss Civil Code of 1807 stipulates that "in the absence of customary law, the court shall decide in accordance with the rule that it would make as a legislator." German Civil Code stipulates that if there is a blank in the law that cannot be solved by analogy, then the judge shall determine applicable rules in accordance with "prudent discretion." Italian laws stipulate that when there is a lack specific legal rules or regulations to adjust similar issues, the judge shall return a verdict in accordance with general principle of modified positive law. Article 16 of the Portuguese Civil Code of 1867 emphasizes that "if issues of rights and duties cannot be solved in accordance with legal texts or spirit or analogy, they will be solved in accordance with natural law in line with specific situations." Although Article 5 of the French Civil Code stipulates that judges are forbidden to decide cases submitted to them by general or regulatory provisions, it stipulates in Article 4 that a judge "who refuses to give judgment on the pretext of legislation being silent, obscure or insufficient, may be prosecuted for being guilty of a denial of justice." Just like what Mr. You Rong says, this actually forces "the judge to apply law according to their own understanding of legislative spirit and impartiality, … and put forward the solution that has not been stipulated by law or with obscure stipulation, in order to fill the blank of law." You Rong (chief editor): *Foreign Legal History*, Peking University Press, 1992, p. 277.

[15]The famous jurist Ulpianus in Rome once pointed out that "anything that has been adopted by law can be explained or ruled to be extended to apply for other cases with similar social purposes," quoted from Edgar Bodenheime: *Jurisprudence—The Philosophy and Method of the Law*, translated by Deng Zhenglai and Ji Jinwu, Huaxia Publishing House, 1987, pp. 506–507.

[16]Mao Zedong: "Why Is It That Red Political Power Can Exist in China," "The Struggle in The Chingkang Mountains," and "A Single Spark Can Start A Prairie Fire." *Selected Works of Mao Zedong*, vol. 1, Edition 2, People's Publishing House, 1991.

and blind spots of legislation. Due to legitimate duties, they have to make specific decisions. No matter how we describe or stipulate a judge's behavior in theory, judges, in reality, have to make judgments and adjust related laws to seek what they think to be the best result (supposing that judges don't have any partiality). In areas where there are no legal regulations, desired judges will make practical and reasonable decisions based on customary practice, related policies, rules or principles, and previous judicial experience, thus filling in legal gaps. In areas that laws are not clear enough, they will give explanations with practical wisdom, completing and refining them. In areas when laws are in conflict, they will choose laws which they think have better reasons or will have the best results. Under the circumstance that legal language has flexibility, coverage, and extension of meaning (and this cannot be avoided), they will seek a legal explanation they think to be more reasonable. We can refer to the above situations as explanations, but they are, to some level, natural processes of legislation for social life. Through this kind of judicial practice, statute law is given its vitality and ability to be regenerated and created, in order to keep close to and remain synchronized with the whole society and specific social lives.

Although the above analysis has an implied meaning of expanding judicial right, my main purpose is not to assert the expansion of judicial discretion or the transformation of legislation through justice. My analysis is of empirical phenomenon and not standard. It has only pointed out features that justice actually has, and tries to break the conceptual separation of justice and legislation established by the "rule of law" claimed by legalism, and to recognize the reality of justice. This kind of reflection can help us to avoid unrealistic, empty talks and try to pursue the best possible results within the limits of practicality. This kind of denial of people's unlimited creativity is actually the confirmation of people's limited creativity. As for a transforming China, judicial research has exceptionally important significance for a country under rule of law with Chinese features.

Why at the Basic Level?

There are factors, both practical and academic, that influence my choice to focus my research on basic-level courts. Academic factors will be addressed in the 4th section. Practical factors are mainly considered here.

First of all, I have a judgment that China's fundamental problems remain agricultural problems. The majority of the Chinese population still lives in rural areas, and one of the most important tasks of the modernization of China's society is modernization of its agricultural society. A person who really cares about the happiness and sorrows of the Chinese people (not only Chinese intellectuals) cannot ignore the lives of normal people in China at the most basic level. I remember one of my classmates went to the south of Jiangsu Province for research. When he came back, he told me that a rural entrepreneur once spoke to them with the general idea that no intellectuals are speaking on behalf of us farmers, and only Mr.

Fei Xiaotong speaks for us. He may be a bit too extreme, but this is indeed reasonable to some extent. We intellectuals of this generation always think that we are speaking on behalf of people, but as a matter of fact, we are usually thinking of questions from our life experience, self-branded as enlightenment. We often speak according to a certain universal principle, without truly understanding what ordinary people living at the basic level of society actually need. I once carried out a basic-level judicial research project in a certain place; I used to see the *Booklet for Promotion of Legal Knowledge in Rural Areas* edited and printed by the Judicial Bureau of that province, which distributed the booklet to farmers or required them to purchase it. The first section in the collection was the Constitution of the People's Republic of China, and the second was Law of the People's Republic of China against Unfair Competition. This not only shocked me and other researchers, but also gave me a sting from my conscience. During the chaotic waves of the so-called rule-of-law construction and judicial reform, what on earth are our laws servicing? In all kinds of language about "rights," does the "rights" we are implementing still try to pursue grander benefits in the legal sector and the circle of law science? Is it acceptable to give our fellow countrymen these kinds of "fake and poor-quality" products? If it is true that knowledge still is something useful, then "for what kind of people" will be a question that we cannot avoid, at least for legal workers. As Cardozo once said, "the ultimate goal of the law is social welfare," and all laws have to demonstrate their reason for existence in social life.[17] If we do not know about the happiness and sorrows of ordinary people, do not observe the demands from their ordinary lives, and only create based on principles and the concept of rule of law, then laws and justice will be not only forged, but also fake.

Modern laws, to a large extent, mainly apply to urban society, industrial and commercial society, and society of strangers. Due to economic, social, and cultural reasons, it is difficult for modern laws and related systems to enter agricultural society and society of acquaintances, or to function effectively in such social environments in many countries around the world.[18] Judging from the current situation of law science research in China, a large number of scholars pay more attention to normative legal research and emphasize studying demands of urban industrial and commercial development; even the reform of the judicial system basically takes modern urban life as its background, including the research on the adversary system and reform in the mode of court hearings for examples. This is certainly good, as well as necessary for modernization, the development of market economy, and the opening up of Chinese society. However, a sound general structure of legal research must maintain the diversity of research and consider providing different citizens with different services. Much research in this regard, including many judicial research projects, is irrelevant or only remotely related to China's basic-level society. In places where lawyers are scarce or too expensive,[19] how can parties

[17]Cardozo: *Nature of the Judicial Process*, trans. Su Li, the Commercial Press, 1998.

[18]Donald Black, *The Behavior of Law*, Academic Press, 1976.

[19]Please refer to Chap. 9 of this book: Legal Personnel in Rural Society.

involved plead? If the parties concerned do not know what an argument is about, how can they possibly understand the processes of disclosure of evidence or cross-examination? If a large number of parties concerned expect or demand a judge to speak on behalf of them due to differing levels of knowledge, abilities, or financial capabilities, and if you happen to be the judge, how can you reconcile this role in terms of trial techniques or professional ethics? It is true that that those most major cases in China are mostly held above intermediate courts, but cases closely related to ordinary lives of ordinary people in China are tried in basic-level courts. Whether Lu Jun received bribes or not might be of concern of many football fans in China. Whether the singer Mao A'min evaded taxes or not might have garnered attention from lots of fans or entertainers. Chen Xitong's trial might have aroused the doubts of Chinese people, and even foreigners, on the determination of the Chinese government to fight against corruption. These cases are not Chinese justice as a whole. They are not even the main parts of Chinese justice, nor the key parts of Chinese justice in modern times.

The basic-level courts are the most important parts of the Chinese court. We can read the following figures from 1986 (which is on hand).[20] There are altogether 3404 people's courts of all levels around China, among which, there are 3007 basic-level courts, 15,000–18,000 people's tribunals (figures of 1994),[21] and the people's courts above the intermediate level take up only a tiny fraction of the total number. The total number of judges is less than 150,000,[22] while judges at the basic-level courts account for almost 5/6 of China's judges. Because China's courts at different levels are somewhat all courts of first instances, we cannot pinpoint the exact proportion of cases tried, mediated, and closed at the basic-level courts in regard to the number at the whole court system. Nevertheless, judging from the civil cases of the first instance with the most direct relations to the lives of ordinary people, this proportion is not below 90 %. No matter the total number of judges or number of cases tried, basic-level courts are the main part of the Chinese justice.

However, we do not know much about the courts and judges that have real impacts on the lives of ordinary people. Apart from the number of reported cases tried, mediated, and closed, as well as cases concerning judicial corruption and unfairness exposed by newspapers and magazines, basic-level courts and judges draw very little attention of jurists. Do we know about their living conditions? Do we know about their well-being? Do we know how they deal with cases of divorce, alimony, and inheritance? Do we know what kind of judicial skills and techniques they have? Do we know about their views, opinions, and judgment of China's judicial system? They have been ignored and become the "silent majority" and "unaccounted" numbers in the current judicial system, especially in regard

[20] *Law Yearbook of China (1987)*, Law Press, 1988.

[21] "Court management is a big subject" in *China Court*, Issue 12, 1994, p. 7, claiming that there are 18,000 people's courts in urban and rural areas in China. *Law Year Book of China* of 1998 (p. 138) says that there are 15,000 people's courts in urban and rural areas in China.

[22] Ibid. This number excludes court doctors and court police.

to legal knowledge. They are not only required to have their views, opinions, and suggestions in line with the courts of the higher level (which is reasonable to some extent), but also often regarded as needing education and improvement by jurists. It seems as if judicial knowledge and skills have nothing to do with judicial practice, but is only related to official titles, professional titles, educational background, diplomas and certificates, or articles full of all kinds of authoritative sayings (politically and externally). Judicial knowledge seems not to come from judicial practice, but from the minds and pens of jurists.

The complexity between laws and social practices is reflected and shown in the basic-level courts in the most direct, living, and distinctive way. Due to the labor divisions of systems, the basic-level courts have dealings with the majority of first-instance cases, and they therefore have to directly face a large number of factual disputes and related legal disputes. Courts above the intermediate level (especially the high and the highest) seldom deal with specific factual disputes directly. Even if they do so, due to the efforts made by basic-level courts, factual disputes have often reached a certain format by the time they reach courts above the intermediate level (the result of this kind of format is usually efforts made by lawyers in the US, while in China, the efforts are made by judges of first instance due to the limited number of basic-level social lawyers).[23] The encounter between life of original state and laws happens mainly in the basic-level courts.

During this kind of encounter, laws are tested by life all the time and applied to the choices made by the ordinary of people by their behaviors. Even though major cases mainly occur in the city, if we give up the perspective of traditional moralism and idealism, the problems that are of the most theoretical significance and difficulty to the development of China's modern rule of law are actually most prominent and outstanding in rural areas. These problems cannot be solved by textbooks we have on hand, nor can they be covered or contained by existing legal theories. We can talk about them with a set of existing concepts or principles; we can even sacrifice the rights of ordinary people accompanying these problems to hold a memorial ceremony for the sacred "ideal" of rule of law. However, we cannot get rid of these problems with this set of concepts or principles. On the contrary, the long existence of these problems will take off the New Emperor's Coat worn by us jurists again and again. As a matter of fact, if we look at the basic-level justice demonstrated by the movie *The Story of Qiu Ju*, we see many problems put forward for us jurists in this movie which are not covered by any books![24] If we do

[23]Please refer to Chap. 6 of this book: Inbetween Facts and Laws.

[24]Please refer to Suli: "The Confusion of Qiu Ju and the Tragedy of Grandpa Shangang," *Rule of Law and Native Resources*, China's university of Politics and Law Press, 1996; Feng Xiang: "Qiu Ju's Confusion and Civilization of Vega," *Wooden-Legged Justice*, Zhongshan University Press, 1999. Issues raised hereby are, at least, law as a local knowledge, universality of law, and the demand of rural society on legal types; systematic conflicts of law concepts; comparison of legal remedy types, the social construction and complementary of rule of law narrative and anti-narrative, definition and formation of legal illiterates, definition of law, Qiu Ju's statement, law and literature, and etc. All these issues are only put forward in China at the moment and have not been studied systematically.

not take this seriously and study specific problems in an earnest manner, we can never expect rule of law to take shape. The rule of law is an undertaking for practice, not for speculation.

Why China?

This is not expected to be a problem. It is only because law transplantation from and connection to the outside world have been emphasized in recent years that this has become a problem. However, I believe that we must study China regardless.

We must make it clear that the problems of modern China have their legitimacy beyond all questions. I have mentioned this view, but I need to repeat this point here. In recent years, we have been looking at foreign countries in terms of judicial systems while nearly forgetting about the fact that the law is to be practiced and solve problems. It is meant to solve our imminent problems. No matter what the future of China's rule of law will be, what we need to solve first is China's real problems. Even it is necessary to transplant laws, we still need to understand what is actually needed. Copying also requires a vision. As a factual problem, China cannot simply transplant everything. Transplantation has its cost, and therefore, we must choose. Different countries have different circumstances, and we cannot possibly transplant anything from abroad. We need to have a choice. What to choose and what not to choose involve the standard of choice. As far as I'm concerned, the standard is not what a law used to be in other countries, but how it meets the demands of development in modern China as well as demands of Chinese people. If I were fat, I certainly wouldn't choose the costumes of Lin Daiyu (a very thin girl in *Red Chamber Dream*)—the precondition is my knowledge of me being fat. The mistake made by Dong Shi was not that she tried to pursue beauty and imitate Xi Shi, but that she did not understand herself and find the beauty that suited her.

This does not mean that we have to give up our pursuits, ideals, rational design of institution, or the ideal pursuit of jurists. We certainly can have our ideals and designs. However, it is priority for every generation to pay attention to problems they face and get to know the limit of their reason. It is true as the old saying goes: "sons and grandsons have their own blessings." The ideal "for the eternal peace" implies a will of power;[25] it pursues the hegemony of knowledge at least, and it implies deprivation of the right of choice from our descendents. Secondly, how can we imagine that our descendents or the fellows of the same generation will do according to someone's will? How can we assume that there won't be any new "accidents" to distort the preconditions that we have set in advance? We can't unless we presume that history has somehow reached its end!

[25]Please refer to Friedrich Nietzsche, *Beyond Good and Evil*, trans. Walter Kaufmann, Vintage Books, 1966. Please also refer to Michel Foucault, *Power/Knowledge: Selected Interviews and Other Writings, 1972–1977*, ed. C. Gorden, Pantheon, 1980.

Will our research on China's issues make the knowledge we have acquired lose its universal meaning? I don't think so. Whether this knowledge has its universal meaning is not decided by the objective intention or pursuit of knowledge producers, but decided by whether it is effective, and whether it can be borrowed and used by different people effectively. The producing areas of knowledge or knowledge resources themselves do not decide the market of knowledge (although I don't deny that other factors do influence the market of knowledge). It is dependent on the quality and effects of products. In this sense, knowledge products are the same as other products; televisions produced by Japan are sold around the world. It is true that China's problems are local compared to the general pattern of knowledge development, as well as experiences accumulated by developed countries in the Western world. However, if we do not see modernization as a process of linear evolution or see rule of law as a singular pattern, then experiences and knowledge of any country are or were local (don't forget that the basic systems of Anglo-American law of today originated from the customary verdicts on disputes made by circuit judges sent out by British Royalty, according to customs of the local ordinary people, and it was a very local practice). There has never been and will never be a sharp boundary between locality and universality.

We should not see China's modernization as a heresy to global modernization or that only the development of Western society is the orthodox. We should not see the process of China's modernization and rule of law as a continuous accommodation to the orthodox theory, due to which there is no practical or theoretical value in China's practical problems. China's population has taken up 1/5 of the world population, the problems it has do have legitimacy themselves. For at least, even if China's problems are heresy, this is the environment we are living in and our problems must be recognized, answered, and solved. We cannot forever borrow the name of the novel written by Milan Kundera—*Life is Elsewhere*, can we?

Academic Significance

China is now in a stage of unprecedented development with its legal system in a very important period of development as well. China's law science field should prosper. However, the development of law science does not necessarily go with the development of rule of law. The establishment of rule of law is a social formation and establishment of a kind of order. This is mainly the product of public choice and the process of trial and error. I reject the idealistic view that the development of law science is the reason or the main reason for the development of China's rule of law.[26] But I don't support the opposite determinism either. The relationship between these two may be interactive, dialectical, or mutually reinforcing. If the

[26] I have had some analysis and discussions on this point in some other places. Please refer to Suli: "Post-modern trend of thought and China's jurisprudence," *Rule of Law and Native Resources*, China's University of Politics and Law Press, 1996, especially section 4.

relationship is really the case, then research on China's legal construction is not all meaningless. Even if we presume that the development of law science cannot have decisive impact on the formation and establishment of China's legal system, I still believe that it might be indirectly effective, that is to say to promote a legal community through the formation of legal language and to construct a consensus needed by the legal system and social life, and to promote the establishment of rule of law. At last, if we presume that the research of law science does have independent academic significance not relying on legal construction, then we still must try our best to promote the development of law science as an embodiment of China's academism and the significance of the existence of Chinese jurists.

The question is how to develop China's law science. As far as I'm concerned, the current situation of China's law science is very unsatisfactory. Big and empty research and legalistic research from article to article are almost everywhere. Higher quality research relies on the writings of foreign scholars or scholars from Taiwan, as well as foreign and Taiwanese practices. Even though the explanation of legal texts enriches the content and explains how foreign countries or Taiwan region do things, why they do this hasn't been answered. Some scholars resort to a number of impractical and abstract values that cannot reach a practical consensus. Or they try to find an eternal truth of a priori in the eyes of researchers and make a practice or legitimate method that is effective in a certain time and within a certain area as the universally effective truth. As long as the legal practice of China's society does not match this theory, those scholars will usually replace the analysis of what it really is by judgment of what it should be. Although we are facing a dramatic change of modern society in China, China's circle of law science has not until now and seems not to be able to give strong response to the rapid development of the modern legal system in China. Our law science is basically dishing up same work of Western scholars without Chinese visions, insights, or findings. Even other disciplines ridicule our field as "childish" law science. This kind of situation is a shame to China's jurists. And it is the responsibility of China's jurists to change this situation.

As the old saying goes, "it is brave to be aware of one's shame," but it is not enough to be brave. We need to find breakthroughs in the development of law science. Generally speaking, this issue needs to be solved by studying China's problems. Specifically, I feel that judicial research does have huge potential for theoretical creation.

I have included a rather detailed analysis in Chap. 4 of this book. In order to ensure the smooth flow of my writing, I will make a brief summary here. My basic analysis is that continental law science takes legislation as its center, while judicial knowledge becomes blurred or even disappears in that knowledge system (just think about it, can you think of any academic writing by European scholars on judges and their role in justice?). Anglo-American law science takes justice as its center, and judicial knowledge is prominent in this knowledge system. However, this judicial theory develops mainly around the judicial opinions of judges in appeal courts, and its judicial systems as well as education system of law science have created conditions for this knowledge (just think about judicial review, Socratic Method, legal reasoning, legal explanation, constitution originalism, and due process). This leaves a big theoretical blank in this pattern, that is the research summary on practices and experience of first-instance judges. It is in this vast international academic vision that we are able to see virgin land that might be cultivated by China's law science.

China's scholars can get close to this resource easily. In terms of the blood relationship, China's contemporary and modern legal systems belong to a continental law system. Under this system, at least before the judicial reform in the early 1990s, the majority of cases were dealt with by judges, no matter whether they were factual disputes or legal disputes due to many reasons.[27] After the reform, judges still make decisions on factual and legal disputes. It is therefore fair to say that judges of China's basic-level courts are more similar to their continental colleagues while different from their American colleagues. Due to these features, judges of China's basic-level courts have accumulated large amounts of experience on how to deal with facts and have formed a series of systems, knowledge, and skills dealing with factual issues. One example of the system is that most of the factual disputes adopt decisions of collegiate panel hearings, which limits the possibly overextended discretion of judges presiding over the court on the facts. As a matter of fact, we have no detailed analysis even for this simple and common system practice, not to mention rational analysis, discussion, and criticism in system comparison. Knowledge and skills accumulated in this system have not received enough research or even elementary research.

The systems that China's judges of first instance rely on and form, as well as the knowledge and skills they have accumulated, do not come exclusively from the tradition of a continental law system. They are more connected to China's special characteristics and are indeed determined by it. The first factor is that China has a vast landmass and many ethnic groups. Even within the Han ethnic group, due to different geographic and cultural environments and a lack of economic exchanges, it is a common phenomenon that places are quite different from each other regardless of proximity. This forms a sharp contrast with European countries where there is a relatively small landmass with a high degree of social homogeneity brought about by industrialization and commercialization. In China's social environment, it is essential to have uniform laws and rules as guidance, but in order to ensure the effective enforcement and implementation of laws, it is not possible to implement uniform laws and rules in too rigid of a way. China's justice emphasizes being lawful, while judges often speak about "reasonable." Doing things according to laws methodically is often regarded as dogmatism. Research on these

[27]Those reasons are criminal procedure does not allow plea bargaining; in the civil procedure, the lawsuit fee for "interrogation system" (hyper-official principle as a matter of fact) is lower than the fee for the adversary system for parties concerned; precedents do not have a binding effect and thus lack detailed rule guidance; there is a lack of negotiations and reconciliation with lawyers intervening; today's courts lack funds and thus are more willing to encourage collecting more procedural fees; and a certain kind of superstition of judiciary caused by the campaign of promoting knowledge of laws in recent years.

issues (attention: research does not mean simple approval, but careful analysis and balance with doubts) might develop theories of law science and promote legal practice.

In addition, we must recognize that many of our impressions of judges come from textbooks, but seldom from empirical understanding. Many have been accepted by people as "facts," but they are actually not real. For example, many studies say that because China's judiciary does not have independent judges and there are systems like judicial committees, China's judges have little power. This impression or concept is only induced from many other concepts and propositions. If we add empirical research, it is easy to find out that the power of Chinese judges is not as small or as limited as people think, although it indeed has some limitations.[28] First of all, since judges have to decide on not only legal issues, but factual issues as well, they have a large degree of discretion. My empirical research in later chapters will also show that the situation in which judicial rights are too big does exist, and some judges have sought all kinds of systems to shift responsibility on some cases instead of asking for more power. This kind of discretion is also represented in the fact that so long as the results of a trial accord with the basic consensus of society on "actual justice," those offside judgments are usually accepted, recognized, and welcomed by colleagues or even the whole society. In March, 1997, under the precondition that China did not have any legal text or judicial practice concerning compensation for mental loss, Haidian District Court ruled to give the victim compensation on mental loss in an infringement case by making an interpretation on "disability compensation" of Article 41 of Law on Protection of Consumers' Rights and Interests.[29] Although this rule violated the de juris rule-of-law principle that laws are not retroactive, it was recognized widely by courts of the higher level and public opinions in society. There have not been any scholars raising objection or having discussions on this rule. Here is another example: While I was writing this book, the Haidian Court conducted judicial review on the internal rules of an academic institution.[30] I don't generally think that there is no reason for this expansion of judicial rights, but we must recognize that it possibly violates democracy (when justice overthrows legislation) and rule of law principle (laws are not retroactive), which brings about unexpected results. For those possibly negative results, society and the circle of law science must prepare instead of being predators unable to have foresight. However, due to certain political convenience seemingly profound but actually quite innocent, the practice

[28]As far as the discretion of American judges of first instance is concerned, especially on factual disputes, please refer to Jerome Frank, *Court on Trial, Myth and Reality in American Justice*, Princeton University Press, 1973 (original edition, 1949).

[29]"Jiang Guoyu files a lawsuit of personal injury compensation against Beijing International Aerosol Co. Ltd., Kitchen Equipment Factory of Longkou City, and Chunhai Restaurant of Haidian District, Beijing," *Communique of the Supreme Court of the People's Republic of China*, Issue 2, 1997, pp. 68–70.

[30]"Doctorate of Peking University filed a lawsuit against his university. Who's fault is it? What is the focus?" *Newspaper of People's Courts*, January 18th, 2000.

of the expansion of judicial rights has been recognized and even acclaimed by some scholars plainly, without discussing its potential danger or limit. Only these two examples are enough to demonstrate that the actual situation of courts and judges of modern China are not identical to the general description or feelings of courts and judges by jurists. Those all kinds of concepts and ideology we are accustomed to use are prone to prevent us from seeing the reality which is far more complex than the concept. We must have systematic research and analysis on the actual situation of China's basic-level justice. This requires efforts by at least an entire generation of Chinese scholars.

Is it possible in this modern environment of China that we can make a contribution to global society by conducting a serious research on China's judges—especially the knowledge and wisdom that basic-level judges show in dealing with disputes, while still making accurate generalizations in an academic language and exchange effectively with scholars from different countries?

It is necessary to point out that in terms of actual flexibility, the majority of Chinese scholars are unable to make major contributions to studying judicial systems of other countries. It is not only because that justice is practical or because of the demands of cultural background, limitations of language expression, or the inevitable limitation of studying foreign judicial systems though texts.[31] The most important thing is that generally speaking, the comparative advantage of Chinese research lies in the research of Chinese laws and justice. If we want to study foreign laws, we should not compete with other Chinese, but with foreign scholars (connected to the international world). Do Chinese scholars think that we have this kind of comparative advantage generally speaking? If we accept the precondition of the locality of legal knowledge, our research on foreign judicial systems cannot necessarily have higher knowledge, compared with research of another scholar on the judicial system of his own country. China's circle of law science shall be more practical in its theoretical pursuits and get more nutrition from the practice of social reform and construction of rule of law in modern China. This is our root and the closest, most attainable, abundant, and special native resource. Yes, we should learn from the advanced experiences of foreign justice, but normally speaking, China's scholars cannot ignore the theoretical significance that legal practice might have in China's society or forget about the valuable academic resources at hand. At least we have these resources and aim to explore these resources. What await us might be more actions of digging through resources.

[31]Although there are some exceptions, for example, Tocqueville (*Democracy in America*, translated by Dong Guoliang, 1988), whose insights of the American judicial system were not noticed by American scholars at that time, is often quoted by American scholars today. But this special case just proves (not overthrows) the ordinary. In addition, Tocqueville himself visited the USA and had conducted long-term, detailed field research. The opposite example was Montesquieu. His description and summary of the so-called English judicial system based on rumors in his book *The Spirit of Law* was regarded as a creative joke by scholars of later generations—Voltaire believed that Montesquieu's style of writing saved this book full of mistakes, although those mistakes did not reduce the ideological value of this book at all. Please refer to M.J. C. Vile: *Constitution and Separation of Powers*, translated by Suli, Sanlian Bookstore, 1997, p. 71 and 78.

Structure and Arrangement of This Book

Although this book is meant to study China's basic-level (especially in rural areas) judicial system, the focus is not introduction, but issues of practical and theoretical significance. It tries to dig into problems of justice in modern China that only Chinese scholars (due to their comparative advantages of living environment and cultural cultivation) can possibly feel sensitively and put forward, to make appropriate descriptions, and best attempt to make a detailed theoretical analysis. I hope this can challenge the wisdom of readers as well as give them pleasure.

Due to this pursuit, the book is rather loose in structure. It does not take normative or specific basic-level judicial systems as standard, or pursues the complete structure in related expression or covers every aspect of the matter, although that is the common practice of judicial books in modern China. If you read it carefully, you will notice that my theoretical principle line is explicit and consistent. It tries to set the basic-level judicial system of modern China to the background of China in the twentieth century, as well as in specific social conditions. The basic theoretical framework is historical materialism of Marxism—that is to say law is not to be understood from just law or justice itself, and the judicial system is not to be understood from the common development of human beings, but the relationship of material lives originated from the society is emphasized.[32] Based on this theoretical theme, I mainly absorb research results of sociology, especially the thoughts of Mr. Fei Xiaotong, Foucault, and Pierre Bourdieu of France, who were all influenced by and compatible with historical materialism of Marxism. They emphasize the mutual support and influence between laws and different aspects of life. I also absorb some thoughts of institutional economics and legal economics. From my perspective, these thoughts are communicable with the basic theory of Marxism and have enriched the theoretical framework of historical materialism based on analysis of social and legal issues, which have given historical materialism power of explanation, which is stronger and more delicate. I oppose historical idealism, which sees law and justice as products of knowledge and perception. I also oppose to the analytical access of historical idealism or moralism of China's tradition in the research of rule of law.

In terms of method, I absorb the analytical access of empiricism, functionalism, and pragmatism (there are consistent parts in the above-mentioned three); they emphasize that practice is the only standard for theoretical verification, and they stress the practical function of systems and laws and oppose to a priori metaphysics. I emphasize the observable effect and comparable utility and avoid empty talk as well as language games like concept analysis. I try my best to adopt an attitude of "calm and warm"[33] "sympathetic understanding"

[32]Please refer to Karl Marx: "Preface and Introduction to *Political Economy*," People's Publishing House, 1971, p. 2.

[33]About this kind of attitude, please refer to Richard A. Posner, *The Problems of Jurisprudence*, Harvard University Press, 1990, especially the Introduction.

(including criticism)[34], and put myself in their condition when observing the object of my research. I try to be "fair" in terms of review and criticism of myself and my career. I try to implement this theoretical pursuit throughout this whole book. In this sense, this is a theoretical work. However, what I pursue is not the abstract theoretical principle separated from our lives and our world completely, but the force of theory demonstrated in our lives. I pursue the unity of history and logic.

I divide this book into four parts according to systems, knowledge, law personnel, and research methods.

The first part discusses three representative systems in the basic-level justice systems of modern China. In articles related to "sending law to the countryside," I observe the political and historical background of China's basic-level judicial system from the macroscopic view of history. My analysis shows that the basic-level judicial system and justice of "sending law to the countryside" and "circuit riding" are actually an important component of construction of China's modern nation. That is why justice has a political function from the beginning, which is independent from functions of solving disputes and rule governance emphasized by normal justice. This research has put China's basic-level courts onto a new and vaster theoretical and political level of practice and has changed the basic access of Chinese intellectuals' understanding and research of this issue at present. At meso-level, I research on conflicts between court trail system with the administration system and analyze how the former is absorbed by the latter with the courts in modern China which has caused the weakening of the courts' trial function. Although this chapter is based on research of basic-level courts, I believe its inspiration to people is not limited to basic-level courts. At the micro-level, my analysis focuses on the system of judicial committees actually practiced by basic-level courts and tries to demonstrate in a fair manner (though critics may beg to differ) the complicated function this system has in the basic-level society of China and confirms it in a gentle language.

I do have many considerations to tend to while analyzing this system. Many judicial systems in China have Chinese characteristics. Few people make detailed empirical and theoretical analysis on those characteristics. Most people only have simple comparisons based on existing theories borrowed from foreign countries or propositions induced from concepts. The result is usually an ideological discussion, whether supportive or approving. In the judicial reform of today, many jurists have focused their attention on the judicial committee. They feel that it is not "connected to the world" and intend to do something to fix this problem. In this age, where my efforts are destined to be a failure at the very beginning, I hope that I can use my abilities to do some theoretical and functional analysis for this system that my predecessors have never done before. Even if this system will be

[34]This kind of attitude originates from philosophical hermeneutics of Gadamer. In China's research of modern jurisprudence, Liang Zhiping is the first person to introduce and apply this method. Please refer to Liang Zhiping: *Legal Arguments, Postscript*, Guizhou People's Publishing House, 1992, p. 180.

eliminated in the "turbulent" wave of reform, and I will have to testify for my own failure, I do not fear of this kind of testimony. It may occur that I will testify for "childish law science," to say the least. The success of a theory will not necessarily cause the success of its social practice. Identically, the failure of a practice does not necessarily imply the failure of its theory. In this sense, choosing a specific system has already had enough significance in terms of theories and methods.

In the second part, I will have an even harder and braver academic effort. I try to describe and analyze a number of traits and skills of the basic-level judges of China that cannot be despised or misunderstood after being seen in the current system of judicial knowledge. I try to find the systematic conditions in which this kind of knowledge and skills are produced. Taking evolutionary epistemology (which considers all adaptation as knowledge) as the basis, I first of all analyze the system location (first-instance courts) and its social location (China's basic-level society) of China's basic-level courts, then briefly analyze the knowledge genealogy of Western law science, and thus demonstrate some special knowledge produced by special location of China's basic-level courts. Then, in Chap. 5, I discuss the explicit characteristics of justice in China's basic-level judges, which pay special attention to the solution of disputes while not much to the rule governance. The analysis shows that this kind of characteristic does not come from a certain abstract culture, but a kind of adaption to the living environment of the society. I especially emphasize that the judicial practice attaching importance to dispute solutions lacks rules only when being viewed from the perspective of modern social rules. As a matter of fact, this kind of dispute solution often accords to rules with local features. In addition, I make analysis on some essential social conditions from dispute solutions to modern rule governance.

Chapter 6 discusses the format feature of modern justice, the problems it has brought to China's basic-level justice, and judges' handling of the so-called factual disputes. The analysis shows that in China's modern society, a large number of the so-called disputes are actually caused by the mandatory "format" of modern justice and law. The precondition of the modern formatted justice is a format of social events beforehand, which requires the process of social modernization to bring up. Chapter 7 discusses the interaction between statute law and customs and focuses on the analysis of the strength and universality of practical rules, as well as how judges deal with cases in which statute law rules have conflicts with customs and how they go between statute laws and customs. What is especially important is that why they go between them. I criticize the explanation of cultural theory and give an explanation of historical materialism as well as institutional economics on judges' behaviors. In Chap. 8, I try to generalize the knowledge and skills of basic-level judges when they deal with factual and legal issues demonstrated by this part and other articles of this book. The effort toward originality is very difficult.

In the third part, I discuss judges and other legal personnel in rural society. In Chap. 9, I introduce and briefly analyze the legal personnel of rural society. I especially introduce the situations of legal workers, people serving legal papers, and judges taking on the responsibilities of lawyers in certain contexts and ultimately make some tentative but non-superficial analysis. This chapter mainly puts forward questions, including some theoretical and social questions and tries to set a stage for analysis of the following two chapters. In those two chapters, I focus on the discussion of judges. Chapter 10 puts judges of the basic-level courts in China's social structure and context and makes a nearly comprehensive observation of social ecology. My conclusion is that although the cultural and professional training and quality is not high enough, such a situation cannot be changed under the conditions of a market economy, and it is therefore essential to reconsider the access of professionalism of judges. My suggestion is that the people's courts and certain courts of the basic-level shall have "quasi-judicialization" based on the current situations. This not only corresponds to the actual works of those judges, but is also conducive to the realization of the professionalism of judges. This article also analyzes in a detailed manner the role of Chinese armies in China's society as a talent selection institution and training system, as well as the congenital weakness of law-school education compared with judicial trial practice, and the types of legal knowledge needed in rural areas. I personally think that all these kinds of analysis are pioneering to a certain extent.

There is only one article in the fourth part, which mainly makes some reflections on problems in my field research. It is not a systematic introduction to the research method of this subject or a reflection of system theory, but only part among them, a comparatively complete reflection with academic innovation and common theoretical significance. Some other theoretical thoughts on methods related have been either mentioned specifically in other articles (like about the system of judicial committees), or require further classification. From my perspective, adding this article to this book has not reduced the theoretical property, innovation, and empirical property pursued by this book, but it serves as a kind of supplement and promotion. It may help readers to read this book from other angles (like the angle of research method) and focus on the analytical demonstration, instead of only caring about some results in the book. This article actually represents another pursuit that I have always devoted myself to when doing research and writing, that is thinking on methods, training of the way of thinking as well as self-inspection and counterquestioning the researcher themself during the process of research.

By Dawn of December 31, 1999
At Cambridge

Part I
Judicial System

Chapter 1
Why Send Law to the Countryside?

Divide our forces to arouse the masses, and concentrate our forces to deal with the enemy.

—Mao Zedong ("A Single Spark Can Start a Prairie Fire," *Collected Works of Mao Zedong*, vol. 1, the 2nd Edition, People's Publishing House, 1991, p. 104.)

War is politics carried out with bloodshed, while politics is war carried out without bloodshed.

—Mao Zedong ("On Protracted War," *Collected Works of Mao Zedong* (bound volume), People's Publishing House, 1966, p. 447.)

1.1 Question and Materials

This chapter aims to study the phenomenon that commonly exists when we are doing basic judicial investigation in the countryside, that is, "Justice to the Countryside" To the countryside or "Sending Law to People's Door." Sending law to people's door is not limited to the countryside, while the analysis in this chapter is. The case study for specific analysis is a case involving a court going to the countryside to use the law to recover loans. It was joined by Jiang Shigong, Zhao Xiaoli, and He Xin in 1996, when they were doing field research in rural areas in North China's Shaanxi Province. Mr. Jiang Shigong and Mr. Zhao Xiaoli used part of the materials to do relatively in-depth and creative research on this loan collection case and came up with many novel views.[1] However, what drew my attention

[1]Jiang Shigong: "Legal Knowledge, Legal Practice and Legal Appearance." The abridged edition of this article was published on Strategy and Management under the title of "Judicial Practice of Rural Society: Knowledge, Technology and Power," Issue 4, 1997, pp. 103–112. Zhao Xiaoli: "Relationship/Events, Action Strategy and Narrate of Law." Both these articles are collected in Wang Mingming (edited): Authority of China's Civil Society, Chinese University of Politics and Law Press, 1997.

© Foreign Language Teaching and Research Publishing Co., Ltd and Springer Science+Business Media Singapore 2016

S. Zhu, *Sending Law to the Countryside*, China Academic Library,
DOI 10.1007/978-981-10-1142-9_1

was not the case itself, but such a normal phenomenon "going to the countryside" which people take for granted and seldom ask about. This case is used here to make the analysis of this book based on facts instead of being vague or general. It is also a reflection on the function of basic-level judicial system in modern China. This book used some background materials which Mr. Jiang and Mr. Zhao's articles failed to cover or did not make public. At the same time, in order to avoid the doubtful situation that the specific case for analysis may not be typical or representative enough, I also make use of some interviews that I have done with some basic-level judges in Hubei Province as well as some social sense.[2]

In order to make this book easy to read, and so that readers do not have to look for original materials, I will provide a briefing on this case. The briefing needs to be simple and general; therefore, I am unable to demonstrate all background materials or delicate connections and meanings among the above-mentioned materials. Even if they are demonstrated, the readers may not necessarily pay enough attention to them. Many subtle parts will therefore be pointed out, supplemented, and unfolded in detailed analysis later. The general situation of the case is as follows:

A farmer, who lived in a village in the north of Shaanxi Province near the Mu Us Desert in Inner Mongolia, had borrowed from the county credit union RMB 200 ten years before, covering a loan period of 3 months. He failed to pay the money back. The credit union had made repeated efforts but failed to collect the loan, either by asking people to send a message, demanding payment face-to-face, or even going to the door to recover the loan. In 1996, encouraged by a campaign to "Use the Law to Recover Loans" emphasized by the related department of the local county government, the credit union filed suit in the local branch of county people's court. The president of the court headed to the village to collect the loan, together with people from the credit union. They not only borrowed a van from the county's Department of Agriculture and Industry, but also gathered a policeman. The above-mentioned researchers Mr. Jiang, Mr. Zhao, and Mr. He were lucky enough to accompany them. On arrival, the judge and his entourage first of all found a village cadre, and with the village head in tow, went to the borrower's home. The borrower had taken his sheep to pasture. The village head therefore volunteered to find him and bring him back. One of the researchers, Mr. Jiang, was from North Shaanxi Province; he was fearful that the village head would let the borrower hide from them. This was not the case. Upon his return, the borrower invited the group in for tea on the kang (the brick platform used for sitting and sleeping in traditional homes in northern China) without taking their shoes off (which showed great respect for guests). He then boiled water, served tea, and offered cigarettes. Being told about the identities of the researchers present, the borrower regarded himself as "losing face." After that, the judge opened the proceedings on the kang. First of all, the credit union and the court declared that the borrower had failed to pay another loan before this case, while the borrower stated that he had already paid the money back and he would be able to find someone to

[2]The training class of Zhongnan University of Politics and Law in Wuhan, Hubei, in May of 1997.

testify for him. (Supplementary investigation did find out that the former loan had been paid back.) The court then let pass the former "case" and turned to the inquiry into borrower's failure to pay the second loan. The borrower replied that he had no money and, in any case, that he had heard that the government (which actually is the bank) was forgiving all loans made to farmers. The judge scolded the borrower for relying on such rumors and referred repeatedly to the "Use the Law to Recover Loans" movement. The judge then told the borrower what he owed precisely, which amounted to over RMB 1,100. Among them, there was the principal of RMB 200 plus ten years' interest, which amounted to RMB700, legal costs, and transportation expenses covering the judge, which equaled to RMB 200, respectively. The borrower declared that he was unable to pay back such a large amount of money. At this point, the village head abruptly intervened, criticized the borrower for not paying his debts, and proposed, without consulting either the court judge or the plaintiff from the credit union, a compromise, whereby the borrower would repay the principal and interest if the other legal costs and transportation expenses were forgiven as the village head "let the borrower owe himself this favor." The judge acquiesced but said that this was the solution based on mediation and there would not be a penalty of 15 % added. He then warned that if the borrower would not accept the solution, the case would have to be transferred to the county court for trial and the penalties would be redetermined according to national laws and regulations. He also suggested that this solution was designed for the borrower's good. The borrower therefore went out and borrowed enough money to pay on the spot. It had not been clear whether this "court hearing" was a "trial" or "mediation" beforehand. But according to the following supplementary investigation, it was found out that this case file was produced totally based on mediation. There was no mentioning of the scene in the record. Nor was there any description of the bargaining during the hearing. It seemed as if everything in this case complied strictly with the statutory requirements.[3]

My attention to this case focuses on "sending law to the countryside" or "opening procedures on the kang." There are no modern countries in the world, especially among those developed countries drawing attentions of Chinese jurists, sharing this phenomenon. This might be a unique and typical Chinese phenomenon. It is so normal and commonly seen in China that it seems quite natural and no one ever questions or researches this phenomenon and its effects. There are occasionally some analyses, but they tend to serve the purpose of publicity or relate to ideology, regarding this as an example of justice going among the masses for their convenience, serving the people, or helping to navigate through the challenges of reform and opening-up. This chapter attempts to have some fresh analysis on this issue from the angle that the state power goes deep into the society and it is necessary to build a modern nation. Some other scholars have also been contacted for advice.

[3]The same with the previous note 1.

My explanation is that due to many natural, cultural, and historical reasons, China's modern state power still has a very weak control over at least certain agricultural societies in rural areas. By "sending law to the countryside," the state power tries to establish or strengthen its authority by means of justice in the periphery of its effective power, so that the order pursued by the state power can be implemented and put into force. Considering that the phenomenon of "going to the countryside" has been fairly common in China's modern history, the significance of this research is not only limited to justice. The analysis of this chapter therefore goes beyond justice going to the countryside and covers normal cadres that go to the countryside. It will even include the campaigns of "Science and Technology, Culture and Medical Treatment Going to the Countryside" launched only in recent years.

1.2 Why Send Law to the Countryside?

This is the basic question of this chapter, as well as the entry point of the research. When we do research on basic-level judicial systems, judges often talk about going to the countryside to handle a case. The "case-handling" mentioned here is not limited to the field investigation of the case, and it has little to do with case investigation (as in the above-mentioned case). There are court proceedings in the village from time to time as well as the phenomenon of "opening proceedings on the kang" as above-mentioned. Thus, my question is: Why does judicial power operate in this manner?

This kind of operation of judicial power does not occur only because there is a need to handle a case. A person, who gets used to judicial theories and systems on the book, or understands judicial procedures of developed countries in the West, will first ask such questions as why the court, supported by a national compulsory force, would not summon the "defendant." In addition, people do often say that China's national or governmental power gets too big in relative to civilian powers.

Secondly, it cannot be simply held that as long as the country establishes people's court in the village, it is bound to send law to the countryside in this manner. As a matter of fact, the Chinese Code of Civil Procedure only stipulates that the court can "go on circuit to hold trials on the spot whenever necessary."[4] Even this being the case, this law still stipulates the summon system.[5] Whether to go to the countryside is not a mandatory provision, but a decision based on careful consideration; it is a delicate trade-off of flexibility and adaptability. Since the reform and opening-up, specialization and professionalism have always been emphasized in

[4]Please refer to Article 121 of Civil Procedure Law of People's Republic of China (1991).

[5]Article 144 of Civil Procedure Law of People's Republic of China (1991) stipulates that "In trying a simple civil case, the basic people's court or the tribunal dispatched by it may at any time use simplified methods to summon the parties and witnesses."

the judicial field. This includes the dress code of the judicial officers, the way the court hearing is conducted, the education background, and professional training they have received; they have become increasingly institutionalized and standardized. But why is it necessary to leave such an obviously irregular "gap" (yet not the only gap[6]) on the basic-level judiciary? We cannot take "necessary" as a general answer. What we need to inquire closely is what exactly this need refers to. What is it composed of? In judicial practice, how on earth the judge and the court understand and deal with this "need" in their actual practice? (This is actually a perfect title for a dissertation which would also be considered very creative.)

Thirdly, we can neither say that courts and local governments have close relations in China or that the judiciary is in fact not totally independent, and therefore, in this case, in order to coordinate with and support the local government's central work, the judge is required to go to the countryside. I do recognize the fact that rural cadres often go to the countryside, and quite a few judges at the basic-level court come from the village, or live in such an environment for a long time. They are therefore affected by the customs of rural cadres going to the countryside to deal with cases. But this does not answer my question—on the contrary, it constitutes a question itself. We have to ask: Why this work style is so common in China's countryside?

Moreover, this phenomenon cannot be explained by the complexity and heavy load of county works. As a matter of fact, many local county governments have very relaxed work styles. Our researchers have discovered that county government officials often go to work no earlier than 9 in the morning and may leave the office as early as half past ten. This demonstrates that the local governments do not always have many affairs to deal with. Whether they are busy or not is often "seasonal" (this is not only related to natural seasons, but also affected by such factors related to political seasons, such as special tasks assigned by authorities of a higher level for things such as drought resistance and disaster relief). In addition, even if counties have too many affairs out of order, their complexity and variety cannot possibly exceed those of the State Council or many of the organizations in urban areas. The State Council and related organizations of urban areas are run according to Max Weber's bureaucracy principle.

An important, traditional explanation is that this is a style of work that goes to the grassroots, serving the people and solving their problems. I don't deny this factor—I'm even willing to recognize this as one of the factors. However, I can't simply accept this kind of explanation. It is true that Chinese government and Chinese Communist Party have for many years advocated for this kind of style of work and related ideology. But advocacy does not mean that judges will certainly obey automatically. There are some other practices proposed and advocated by Chinese government and Communist Party which are often not carried out earnestly and

[6]Section 2 of Article 64 of Civil Procedure Law of People's Republic of China (1991) stipulates that "With respect to the evidence that the party and its agent ad litem are unable to obtain themselves because of objective reasons or that the people's court considers necessary for the trial of the case, the people's court shall investigate and collect it on its own initiative."

practically at the grassroot level, such as the policy to reduce the burden of farmers. Another example is that at the end of 1980s and into the early 1990s, the Province of Shandong used to send circuit courts and executives to administrative organizations, enterprises, and public institutions around the province. This was in order to "send law to the countryside," bring on-the-spot trials, and "provide service to the reform." This kind of practice has been reported by *People's Daily* and promoted around the country. However, by April, 1995, the High Court of Shandong Province decided to withdraw all kinds of organizations such as circuit courts and executive rooms (around 647 altogether) by the end of June of the same year.[7] The third example is more relevant and interesting: at the beginning of the Founding of the People's Republic of China, although Mao Zedong appreciated the method in the trial of Ma Xiwu which was regarded as going deep into the people,[8] and the law circle also tried to implement it[9] and published specific academic writings[10] to support this. However, in urban areas, even before the Cultural Revolution, Ma Xiwu's trial method had been replaced by bureaucratic trial method of Weber.[11] These show that though the existence and elimination of a certain system is affected by preferences of leaders and popular ideologists, the system and method of social and economic production, as well as organizational structure of the society, have possibly more profound relations and do not submit to the logic of ideology completely.

---

[7]*Shandong Legal News*, April 21st, 1995.

[8]Please refer to Zhou Wangsheng: "Three policies of China's legislative reform: rule of law, institution and decision-making," *Xinhua Digest*, Issue 2 of 1996, page 10. Ma Xiwu was a senior leader in the Chinese Communist Party. When he worked as a commissioner in the Longdong Area, he also worked part time as the President of the Longdong Chamber in the High Court of Shaan-Gan-Ning Border Region. He often visited rural areas from time to time and conducted thorough investigation and research, as well as circuit trials, where he corrected some misjudged cases timely, and resolved some difficult cases which had been wrangled with for many years. He was thus very popular among local people, who regarded such kinds of case-handling as implementing mass routes and combining trials with mediation, as in"Ma Xiwu-styled Trials." It has three key points: thorough investigation and research; on-the-spot trial in different forms; and problem settlement with the help of local people (Zhang Xipo: *Ma Xiwu-styled Trial*, Law Press China, 1983, p. 41). This kind of trial method is very much similar to China's traditional Baogong-styled trial (local people did call Ma Xiwu as "Ma Qingtian"): It consists of senior officials with both administrative authority and judicial power; emphasizing personal moral quality, charisma and capabilities, caring about people's troubles and praising virtue and punishing vice. This is a very typical type of rule by man, which does not have any derogatory sense.

[9]In 1954, Ma Xiwu was appointed the Vice President of the Supreme People's Court. The President Dong Biwu requested for many times that he should summarize his judicial experience and make theoretical improvements. In 1955, When Chairman Mao Zedong met with representatives of the National Judicial Conference, he used to speak to Ma Xiwu, "Everything will be fine when you are here." Please refer to Zhang Xipo: *Ma Xiwu-styled Trial*, same as above, pp. 64 and 68.

[10]Zhang Xipo: *Ma Xiwu-styled Trial*, same as above.

[11]As for the bureaucracy of Max Weber, please refer to *Economy and Society*, translated by Lin Rongyuan, the Commercial Press, 1997 (this translated version is hard to read).

Naturally, it cannot be explained by traditions, customs, or habits. If traditions, customs, or habits can last for a long time, they might have some kind of effectiveness. Normally speaking, people will not stick to a certain specific tradition blindly in the long term without considering its effects. Otherwise, there will be no traditions that have changed. For those people or even creatures who stick to the principle that "laws of ancestors cannot be changed," regardless of their effectiveness, they will definitely be eliminated gradually during the process of evolution.[12] It is true that Chinese Communist Party has created the work tradition of going down to the grassroots level and countryside during the long period of revolutionary struggle. However, this tradition has developed with the trend of the times. The second and third examples mentioned above are cases in point. In addition, cadres working in rural areas have been substituted for many generations all these years, and it is then impossible to have the so-called problem of individual "habits" raised by Pierre Bourdieu. As a matter of fact, today's cadres going to the countryside and justice going to the countryside are not the continuation of the phenomena, in which "cadres of revolutionary areas work well by bringing their own food to office" any more. There are even some cadres going to the countryside asking for things to eat and drink. But we cannot draw hastily the extreme conclusion that justice and basic-level cadres going to the countryside only bring excessive burdens on the people. There are actually many hardworking cadres such as Jiao Yulu, and more importantly, many cadres not willing to work in the countryside even there are "benefits" of something to drink and eat or subsidies, and they believe it to be a hard job.[13] From the perspective of effectiveness and to the extent of convenience, sending the law to the door is actually not convenient for the work of trial and does not have good effectiveness in urban areas.[14] Last but not least, even if we presume that sending justice to the countryside is a tradition, custom, and habit, those words themselves cannot answer questions. On the contrary, questions need to be answered are: What kind of social structure or society needs to create this kind of tradition, custom, or habit? And why has the Chinese government and Communist Party consistently advocated the style of work of going deep into the grassroots?

Although ideology and sound traditions are not enough to explain "sending justice to the countryside" and "opening procedures on the kang," the observation of how ideology and traditions happen might help our understanding of today's similar phenomena. By then, the Chinese Communist Party chose the strategy of using rural areas to encircle cities during the process of building the political power of

[12]As for elimination and development of knowledge in organic evolution, please refer to Henry Plotkin, *Darwin Machines and the Nature of Knowledge*, Harvard University Press, 1993. Friedrich Hayek also touched upon this point in his many books. You may refer to the *Constitution of Liberty*, translated by Deng Zhenglai, SDX Joint Publishing Company, 1997.

[13]"It is indeed an ordeal for many officials to work in the court. Some wouldn't work in the court even given more allowances." Dai Jianzhi: "Singing the song of Nanniwan again," *People's Judicature*, Issue 11, 1994, p. 44.

[14]Please refer to previous note 7 and related text.

the nation. Mao Zedong attached great importance to China's rural areas and built bases in rural areas for the Chinese Communist Party to develop and achieve national victory. During the revolutionary wars, Mao Zedong also put forward the military strategy of "divide our forces to arouse the masses, concentrate our forces to deal with the enemy." It was during this revolutionary process that this ideology and tradition of going deep into the masses, and going to the countryside, and mountainous areas was put to work. Attaching importance to the countryside and going deep into the countryside is to ensure the Communist Party has a strong and powerful social basis as well as the Party's leadership over the revolution. "Going to the countryside" was actually a strategy of power operation from the very beginning.[15]

Fundamental changes have taken place in history today, and China in the end of the twentieth century is completely different from that of 1920s to 1930s. The Chinese Communist Party has become the national governing power which established the country 50 years ago from a local and weak power resisting the rule of the Kuomintang. Today, we cannot simply copy the analysis of Mao Zedong, but it is true that on the level of ensuring that power go deep into the countryside and function effectively, the problems needed to be solved by the Chinese Communist Party going deep into the countryside and building base areas by then are coherent to sending cadres and laws to the countryside. It is because of this that the key proposition of this article is that today's sending justice to the countryside is to ensure and promote national power, including the power of law to penetrate into and control rural areas effectively. From the angle of grand history, sending law to the countryside is the continuation and development of China's basic strategy of building a modern national country in the twentieth century.

We still have to ask, why must a country do this? The country itself means rule over the whole nation. Theoretically speaking, it has supreme power (i.e., Sovereign power), and legitimately monopolizes the use of violence. Why can't China do like the modern bureaucratic rule as Weber has described or conceived, which is to implement the country's will in the form of formal laws and procedures of formal nationality?

This relates to the characteristics of China's society as well as the feature of power function.

1.3 Operation and Space of Power

Advocacy for sending justice and law to the countryside is related to the weakness of national power in China's agricultural society. China is already a modern national country and has absolute power in the eyes of ordinary people, especially

[15]About the formation of this strategy, it is necessary to read constructively *Selected Works of Mao Zedong*, vol. 1.

for modern China, which has experienced a long period of planned economy. The analysis of this theory is probably not compatible with facts, however. As far as Foucault is concerned, observation of any power shall be at the micro-level, at the end of power function, and in the place where one power intersects with another.[16] Only in this area can we truly understand how to realize power. When observing the national power of modern China, we should not stop at the regulations of legal texts, or induce from the concept of a "communist country." Neither should we see whether those people exercising power have the title of a "national cadre" nor have relations with the country in this or that manner. We should see how ordinary people deal with people representing the country, and in what way people representing the country deal with objects that the national power intend to rule over. This is one of the possible areas of access for observing basic-level justice in China's rural areas.

If we analyze this case, we will see the weakening of the national power in the place where the case of loan collection happened. The case happened in a rural area in the north of Shaanxi Province, a place close to the desert. Theoretically speaking, the feature of locality and the vastness of geographic space might influence the functional methods of power.[17] The old saying that "the heaven is high and the Emperor is far away" speaks of this same truth. Survey materials from Jiang, Zhao, and He also proved this point. The office hours of local government were not regular, and "you might not find any person after half past 10 in the morning." A rumor became popular among villagers that the country might cancel all debts from loans. The borrower of this case failed to return his money for 10 years. The business office of the town had claimed to attempt to collect many times in vain. There were many "cases" where people had failed to pay back loans, so on and so forth. All these have shown that at least in this place, the dominance of national power is not strong enough, or at least not as strong as we normally imagine.

Thus, it is fair to say that this area is a marginal area of national power. This so-called marginal power does not mean the margin of capabilities of national power only. From another perspective, the marginal area is the margin of another power (such as the individual power and community power) to resist against national power, since power can only be seen in the collision between powers. Theoretically, this kind of margin means there is no consistent or dominant power relationship and it is quite possible to have flowing deformation of the power relationship of dominance. The country that is generally stronger may be relatively weaker at a certain point, but certain individual forces that are generally weaker may become relatively stronger at a certain point. We must therefore attach importance to the influence that might be caused by locality to the practical function of power. Due to the vast space of rural areas, borrowers may become the person

[16]Please refer to Michel Foucault, *Power/Knowledge: Selected Interviews and Other Writings, 1972–1977*, ed. by C. Gordon, Pantheon, 1980.

[17]Please refer to Michel Foucault, *Discipline and Punish, the Birth of the Prison*, trans. by Alan Sheridan, Vintage Books, 1978.

with power in another sense, while the lenders (even the country) can become the weak party all the same. The change of the strong–weak relationship between borrowers and lenders has its expression in the folk saying: "I don't have any money and only one life." If the situation reaches such an extent, and if the purpose of the lender is to "want money" but not "life" or the official or unofficial system does not allow you to want "life," then the strong–weak relationship between the borrower and the lender has experienced some subtle change. This kind of situation has become more and more common in China in recent years. The "debt chain" among enterprises is one example. Banks do not want enterprises to file for bankruptcy due to the revenue they receive is another example. The black humor among the people that "the borrower Yang Bailao threatens the lender Huang Shiren" certainly goes too far, but has a kind of meaningful summary on the change of relationship of dominance between the borrower and the lender.

It is not only possible in the natural space, but also possible in the people's space that the strong–weak relationship has changed. By the so-called people's space, I refer to the society of acquaintance in rural China. Compared with the community in which the borrower lives, the country is only a kind of concept that exists for him. Although the court chief and representative from the credit cooperative from the town collecting loans on behalf of the country or "according to law" do have undoubted political legitimacy, and have support of state force, they are more or less strangers from outside and the rights they represent do not have much of a strong basis in this area. The belief in the modern national state in China only came into being 100 years prior at most, but before a fundamental change takes place in the production method and relevant social and organizational structures in rural society, borrowers are prone to regard national power as an external force. It is easy and almost certain for the borrowers living in a society of acquaintance to form a relationship of mutual benefit and "legal protection between relatives" with people in the same community. The first draft of Jiang's article has shown this. Jiang, who was born and grew up in the north and Shaanxi Province, used to doubt whether village cadres would inform the borrower and let him run away. Although in this case, the fact afterward eliminated his doubt, this did not eliminate the possibility. On the contrary, the reason that Jiang had this kind of doubt at that time in that place is itself a support but not strong evidence. Our research in the basic-level courts in Hubei Province discovered that villagers usually refused to appear in court to testify for the criminal behaviors of their fellow villagers, even when there was irrefutable evidence. This situation became so common that the regulations on witnesses going to court and testifying made by the Criminal Procedure Law newly promulgated in 1998 could not be implemented.[18] This can be another

[18]But this is not the only reason, let alone the main reason. This kind of situation still exists in urban areas and is even worse. According to a report, in the trial of criminal cases, the court attendance of witnesses in Huangpu District of Shanghai is only 5 % and the attendance in certain city of Jiangsu Province is less than 10 %, while the attendance in court of a certain county reaches 25 % (but no witnesses appear before the court in bribery cases). Please refer to Wu Dingzhi: "Where can we find the right solution when witnesses refuse to testify," *People's Procuratorial Monthly*, Issue 3 of 1999, p. 6.

strong piece of collateral evidence. It is a common phenomenon in China's society that people tend to help people they know.

It is just in this natural and cultural space that we can possibly understand why the borrower can refuse to pay his loan back for 10 years even when the business office of the cooperative came to the door to collect the loan. All this shows that the actual control of the national power is quite weak in the village. From this point, there is another meaning for sending the cadre and court to the countryside, sending law to the door, and opening procedures on the kang. We cannot easily accept a theoretical presupposition that we are already used to. It is that the country is bound to be strong while poverty-driven and poor farmers are destined to be the weak party. In this geographic and cultural space, the national power sent out by the central government has become the final kick of the crossbow in this "desert margin," with a strong sense of metaphor.

We must also see that although modern countries have almost completely monopolized the legitimate utilization of force, this kind of utilization must still be legitimate. Countries cannot resort to violence only. It is true that people implementing rights on behalf of the country will sometimes abuse power and victimize the people, and even treat human life as not worth a straw in certain extreme cases. But these are not justifiable. No matter it is the official state ideology,[19] traditional Confucian ideology,[20] or the relationship of coexistence to some certain extent between village cadres and villagers,[21] it must limit the violent behaviors or behaviors threatening to use violence by loan collectors. We can see in the above case that the loan collectors did not threaten to catch the person failing to pay back the loan, they just threatened to summon him to the people's court in town for public trial in order to make him "lose face" in the village. This may not be counted as a threat in the legal sense, but "doing business according to law" and "collecting loans according to law," but in the local social context, it did constitute an actual and quite strong threat for the borrower or ordinary villager. This once again confirms what I put forward in another analysis that what constitutes harm, threat, and embargo is quite different in rural areas from that in urban cities.[22] As a matter of fact, the head of the court also used this kind of folk method of threatening here as a local and traditional resource (we will have more detailed analysis on this point later). But even this being the case, if the borrower really did not have the ability to return the loan, or even was not intending to return the money at all, while willing to lose face, this kind of threat did not work (as the saying goes that

[19]Such as, people's government, people's court, and the "rule of law" itself which supports and limits the country's use of force.

[20]Such as the traditional wording of parent-like magistrates.

[21]Among officials (including judges of people's court) working in rural areas, many are official deputies of the state—that is to say, taking salaries from the state. But their interests are not equal to the interests of the state. Many of them were born here, grown up here, and will die here. Most of them do not have any expectation of promotion. They also have all kinds of relations with the local areas. Those kinds of relations enable them to coexist with local villagers.

[22]Suli: "Rationality and feasibility of modern rule of law", *The East*, Issue 4, 1996.

weak people are afraid of strong people, strong people are afraid of people who are willing to risk their lives, and people who are willing to risk their lives are afraid of people who are willing to lose face). This once again shows that the national power which is supreme in name is actually not omnipotent.

Based on this, we could say that in terms of right implementation, natural space and cultural space are both important. And the locality of right function is also important. In the above case and other similar cases, it is because of locality that the specific relationship of rights between the country represented by courts and credit cooperatives and the borrower has changed beyond the imagination of me before the writing of this book.

1.4 Going to the Countryside—the Reconstruction of the Relationship of Local Dominant Power

The above analysis could approximately help us to understand why cadres of different levels from the basic level of authority in rural China have to go to the countryside, and why "going to the countryside" needs to continue after 50 years of modern nationhood. Generally speaking, "going to the countryside" can be regarded as a strategic choice made and realized by the state power which tries to build authority in the rural society. As far as this case of debt collection according to law is concerned, opening procedures on the kang can be seen as a reconstruction of state's dominant power toward a certain individual in a certain locality in rural China. It is also an expression of power operation of "concentrating our superior forces to destroy our enemies one by one."[23] In particular considering both the debt collector and the court is trying to use this case to create a precedent of demonstration as a good beginning for future's debt collection according to the law. It is therefore exceptionally important to build this kind of local power dominance in places where state power is rather weak.

Going to the countryside is one of the flexible methods to build power dominance in certain localities, and it is probably the only flexible method under the current restrictions. It is not, however, necessarily the method to ensure success. We need to reiterate the possible change of power relationships. From another perspective, going to the countryside may constitute a new threat to power operation and may even completely lose the hold that is already weak. First of all, as mentioned above, going to the countryside is one demonstration of weak power. Secondly, but more importantly, once the power leaves its own base or central area

[23]It is essential to point out that this tactic is not only limited in rural areas but also common in cities. When a court hears a case, there are a series of ceremonies and procedures which are actually intended to strengthen this kind of dominant power relationship. During our daily life, people will use this tactic subconsciously. For example, the teacher will ask a naughty student to "come to my office after class" and visit his home. Then even the naughtiest child will feel scared and respect this power authority.

and enters into a certain relatively strange community as an external force, it will be risky. There are folk sayings such as "even a strong dragon is not match for a local worm" and "close the door and claim oneself to be king," as well as military strategies such as "lure the snake from its lair" and "destroy the enemy while in movement." All these sayings show that power is usually more effective and less risky in its stronghold and familiar environment. During our interviews, judges often complained about the "difficult enforcement" of court orders. It is really difficult to enforce court judgment in some other places, since governments and courts of those places usually refuse to cooperate.[24] There was one judge claiming that when saving abducted and trafficked women and children together with the policemen, they behaved like Japanese troops entering the village since they "had to enter into the village silently," "avoid shooting guns" (these words were spoken by Japanese soldiers in the movie *The Guerrilla on the Plains*), due to resistance from locals. Once they found the person to be saved, they left "as hastily as they could." These cases show that even when there is support from the state power and external forces for just cause, it is still risky to enter into strange communities or regions. Going to the door to collect debts and sending the law to the countryside are similar cases. Thirdly, sending law to the countryside and opening procedures on the kang are bound to reduce the distance between law executors and clients. Due to the social philosophy that "if you are close to them, they become unruly; if you keep them at a distance, they are discontented" and "there are no great men in the eyes of relatives," apart from the special charm of judges themselves, this close distance association will certainly reduce the authority of judges and courts generally speaking and ultimately reduce the effectiveness of law enforcement.[25]

Although there are risks, courts have to implement decisions made by their superiors, as well as their own duties. In order to ensure the success of power going to the countryside, we must reconstruct a local, temporary power dominance relationship in this risky natural and cultural space. We must send more people as it is always true that "there is safety in numbers"; but we do not have that many people to send out in the people's court.[26] We therefore may be able to understand why the court in the above-mentioned case had to borrow a policeman to "swell the numbers." They had to take into full use all other factors that could be of used, and that is why the head of the court had to make it clear to the borrower that the researchers "were from Beijing," which was intended to let the borrower feel his "bad reputation" extend all the way to other places. This is actually one strategy of power operation. From this sense, I even believed that the small van was not for the convenience of traveling, but more likely this vehicle represented a power

[24]Judges say that there are three difficult areas to enforce court judgment, namely Henan, Hainan, and Hunan. Although it is kind of joke mentioning these three places, it is intended to bring out the difficulty in law enforcement in other provinces.

[25]Please refer to my more detailed analysis in "Thoughts on Legal Sociology of Legal Professionalism" (*China Social Sciences*, Issue 6, 1994).

[26]Based on our researches in the north of Shaanxi Province and in Hubei, we discover that there are normal 2–4 official staff in the people's courts in rural areas.

signal and it was a component to ensure the realization of power dominance in this locality. We can also further understand a series of specific tactics, strategies, and knowledge[27] used by the head of the court during the trial. This was like a battle during which the head of the court "concentrated his superior forces" with the purpose of ensuring the success of sending justice to the countryside.

Thus, we can understand some features of the basic-level justice system and even of the basic-level works. For example, the reason that mediation is more popular in rural areas and can be seen as a useful and effective technique and strategy, not because it was "welcomed" by people as some scholars usually think (there are many other things that farmers welcome! For example, gambling as a kind of entertainment is not allowed and even restricted by the government). Since villagers are not willing to go to court, mediation can be taken as a replacement as long as it can reach the purpose of debt collection. It is not that clear whether "opening procedures on the kang" is "trial" or "mediation." The tactic and strategy of striking and stroking, as well as striking before stroking against the borrower by the judge during the trial, may be related to this point, which will make bargaining easier. It is because of this that strict legal proceedings are not that important—if strict proceedings can make this "debt collection according to law" fail. We can even draw the conclusion that the "case making" (to determine the nature of "procedures" as trial or mediation and to handle the documents accordingly) by the court discovered by the follow-up study is almost inevitable.[28] The reason that mediation can come into the official justice system of China and become a legal procedure is not accidental, and because it is "welcomed" by the people. The more important thing is that it is an effective tool for power operation.

1.5 Village Cadres—Carriers of Local Knowledge

I have mentioned the issue of "local knowledge" in the above text. For example, mediation is necessary because the Chinese are afraid to go to court as they will lose face. Other examples are the uncertainty and the variability of "opening procedures" on the kang. This kind of knowledge was directly comprehended by the power executor, the judge in this case. It was more or less a kind of normalized knowledge (notions such as Chinese farmers being sensitive about their reputation, in favor of mediation, and prone to bargain), or knowledge that could be controlled freely by the judge (such as the final definition of the nature of the procedure, as well as "case making"). All these are pieces of local knowledge and skills that are certainly important, but still rather normalized "local knowledge." This can be knowledge in the textbooks to some extent—some are already included there.

---

[27]Please refer to articles of Jiang Shigong and Zhao Xiaoli, as previous note 1.

[28]As a matter of fact, during the research in Hubei and many other places, we have discovered that this file "making" phenomenon is quite common.

However, if we study this case carefully, we will notice that for a specific procedure and judge in a trial, these kinds of knowledge, skills, and strategies are not enough to ensure the effective enforcement of its power. The power operation must be based on a more detailed understanding of the object under the influence of the power,[29] and it is the so-called knowing the enemy and yourself can enable one to fight a hundred battles and win them all. Much specific knowledge on the borrower, the object under the influence of power, has become important: his or her personality, conduct, temper, family background, possible response to the judge, actual financial resources, the possibility of him/her borrowing other people's money to pay back debt, and how much he or she attaches important to his/her face. All these factors must be considered by the judge of the case to ensure the effective enforcement of power. All this kind of information is very useful local knowledge to the judge at this moment.[30]

This kind of knowledge is not up in the air and you cannot have it on hand and use it at your own wish. This kind of knowledge is not printed in textbooks. At least not every piece of it is there. But this knowledge is not only local, but also very personal. It is knowledge that not economic when in exchange, and therefore not worth mass production and being printed in the textbooks. This knowledge is, to a large extent, not able to be used by an official legal system and is therefore normally denied and refused by official systems.[31] When the rather weak external power enters into the village for a short period of time[32] to ensure the success of debt collection, this kind of knowledge must be used to concentrate one's superior forces. Thus, one of the problems is to find out the carrier of this kind of knowledge.

The knowledge carrier in these kinds of cases is normally but not necessarily the village cadre. As a member of a local acquaintance society, the village cadre lives in this community for a long period of time. Although he or she does not

---

[29]Foucault, as the previous note 17.

[30]Please note that the local knowledge I have used has been inspired by Clifford Geertz (*Local Knowledge*, Basic Press, 1983), but has major differences from his. Although the local knowledge of Geertz is local, the sequence of thought in his analysis has given this kind of local knowledge homogeneity at the same time. However, the local knowledge I refer is specific knowledge and knowledge which is meaningful only when connected with locality. It is a kind of knowledge exchange that is not economic and thus is not worth mass production, transmission, or textuality.

[31]For example, the principle that all people are equal before the law is, in another sense, denying the many differences people actually have. It does not mean that these differences are meaningless in law, since they are recognized by varying degrees in different manners as a matter of fact, and judges have discretion on these kinds of factual problems (accept or not accept, or accept ambiguously). But principally, if we recognize to many differences, the "law" cannot function as a law and becomes a "rule without model.".

[32]Please note that what I emphasize is the short term. If it enters for a long period of time, it can use some other methods to get this kind of knowledge, like extensive conversation and personal experiences. This is the phenomenon where other cadres are required to go to the countryside to "know situations deeply." As for a judge going to the countryside to hear cases, it does not belong to this situation. He or she just makes short visits and enters temporarily without the above possibility.

have much knowledge that is widely recognized by society and can sell out, his/her special living environment has enabled him/her to attain specific knowledge that many external law enforcers must pay attention to. They hold a deep understanding of the local environment and personality of each person in the community. Because he/she has this kind of knowledge, he/she is determined to play a special role and an important part when state power goes to the countryside. In rural society, it is not that only village cadres exclusively enjoy this kind of knowledge. Every villager has this kind of knowledge, but since the village cadre has been "labeled" by the national authority, he/she enjoys a certain kind of authority in the village. Moreover, due to their connection with the state power system, village cadres are usually the most traceable and convenient local knowledge storehouse when state powers go to the countryside. This determines that in the specific scenario when different types of cadres go to the countryside to do business (investigation of village cadres is certainly an exception), village cadres are indispensable. When we get to know the working styles of the people's court going to the countryside, all judges told us that the first job when entering the village is to find village cadres, get their cooperation, and then start work.[33] Village cadres are a base point for basic-level judges to acquire this kind of local knowledge.

The frequent and common appearance of village cadres in such circumstances cannot be seen only as convenience or a custom. Convenience or custom alone is not enough to constitute institutional practice.[34] Apart from convenience, there must be effective factors. Because village cadres have and represent some knowledge that is indispensible for power operations under such circumstances, when building a power dominance relationship in a relatively strange local area, village cadres are not temporary or indispensible, but they represent an indispensible part of this knowledge/power structure. Their appearances on the spot represents another kind of structural power/knowledge that is different from the official legal power of the state, which supports the operation of state power and law in rural

[33]When interviewing basic-level judges in Hubei, almost all judges of the people's courts emphasized that the first thing for going to the countryside to handle cases was to find village cadres like village head or accountant, and asks them to go together to find the client. A judge even told us the following story. A "judge" newly graduated from the college went to find the client himself. But because his words were so dogmatic and simple, he was beaten and driven out by the client with his glasses broken.

[34]Whether it is an institutional practice can be argued. This practice is not seen in a state's official laws or documents, and people can regard it as unofficial. However, if this practice has been widely accepted and given legitimate recognition by the state power as a standard, then this practice is undoubtedly institutional. As a matter of fact, this practice has been formally recognized as a working procedure and method during the power operations in our country, like the saying of "transmitting orders from above" and the request of being "closely connected to the masses." In addition, institutional legitimacy is different from literal legitimacy, and the institutional practices are sometimes not legitimate literally. "The first secretary is the boss" is obviously not in line with the democratic centralism system stipulated by the party constitution, and therefore does not have literal legitimacy. However, due to many reasons, this kind of situation is stable, long-term, and common and is therefore institutional. To judge whether a practice is institutional or not cannot be decided by whether there is a literal regulation.

China. People familiar with the rule of rural social practices understand this point well, although they may not be aware of this explicitly.

But why are village cadres willing to play this role? It can be explained only by interest exchange. Now that the village cadres have provided judges with this kind of knowledge/power and strengthened the state power represented by judges, judges are expected to save their faces. During the proceedings of this debt collection case, the village head dared to decide for himself to "remit" the 400 yuan traveling fee and (especially) the litigation fee without consultation with the head of the court. The head of the court not only did not refute it, but even gave his acquiescence. If a Western law scientist or judge who doesn't know much about China saw this situation, he would be stunned and speechless, if not faint on the spot.

The village cadre did not provide local knowledge for free. He used his knowledge to gain some symbolic profit. He "won his reputation" in front of this villager. Even cadres from the town (villagers do not distinguish judges from rural governmental officials since this kind of distinction is not of much sense to them at the moment) have to save face. As a result, he will now have a bigger authority among his villagers. Moreover, no matter what the real thoughts were inside the mind of the village head by then, he appeared to be thinking on behalf of the debt collector and help him to solve a difficult problem. The villagers would thank him more or less. This would be more conducive for the village head in his future power operation. In this case, the village head was actually in the position of an advantageous middleman. On the one hand, he used the power enforced against the villagers by the state power to strengthen his own position in the village; on the other hand, due to his/her local knowledge, he/she could influence the enforcement of state power and use the power of the villagers to enhance his own position with the state.

1.6 Another Possibility of Knowledge and Another Role of the Village Cadres

The analysis of power is not finished yet. Just as all knowledge has its two-sidedness, and there is possibility of power change, from the point of the state, there is a kind of danger for the village cadres to have knowledge, that is, to weaken the operation of the state power in rural society.

First of all, it has been mentioned above that village cadres were prestigious persons, and the head of the court had to care for them no matter whether he/she believed it or was willing to do it. Otherwise, if similar cases happen in the future, village cadres could simply construct a small trick or even behave inactively or uncooperatively, then the court power would be unable to enter into the village effectively. That is why during this case, the village cadre could decide for himself to remit the 400 yuan which in principle belonged to the state, though part of the money (traveling fee) was not necessary to be collected, which serves more as a chip for the judge to bargain with and win the client's compliance.

Secondly, the precondition for modern law or its effective function is a stranger society or individualistic society. But in this case, the village cadre was a member of this rural acquaintance society, which to some extent constituted another type of "acquaintance society" with town cadres. That is why once the village cadre was present, the game rules were destined to change and the seriousness proposed by the legal scientists was bound to be reduced. This is because there is usually no need or little need to have laws among acquaintances.[35] In this sense, we can understand why it is difficult for external observers to define the nature of this "proceeding" as "trial"or "mediation." We can also understand why "mediation" is a more common and effective way to settle disputes than judgment in China's rural areas up till now, although there has been consistent emphasis on the normalization of justice in recent years.[36] The reason may not really be the disqualification of judges, but the knowledge/power structure depended on by the operation of the social structure and state judicial power in the village. It determines that the ideal wish of judicial professionalism is difficult to be realized.

Thirdly, although the village cadre is the end of the state power in a certain sense, the real root of the village cadre is the village. They do not have any salary, nor do they have any hope of promotion. However, they have countless ties with their village. Village cadres belong more to rural society, but not the state power system. That is why under certain circumstances, village cadres are completely able to and often tend to use their knowledge/power to deal with the state. In the above case, the village cadre could have informed the borrower to hide out and cause the court to return without accomplishing anything, like the observer Jiang once voiced doubt about. To open our mind, we must be able to see that the phenomenon of hiding the truth of real produce in order to distribute more food among villagers did happen in China's rural areas during the time of the Cultural Revolution. In particular in the mountainous areas, the government was never aware of the actual land area of the village. The cultivated lands during the campaign of "learning from Dazhai" were often held back by village cadres. Because it was good for the whole village and welcomed by all villagers, it became a kind of local knowledge exclusive to the village. Since the village cadres know the rules of function of state power, they are more able to deal with the state and protect themselves. The worst case is that there might arise a serious case, in which laws and disciplines are violated. Partly due to the last point at least, we can also understand the other meaning to emphasize sending basic-level cadres to the countryside to know the situation. This point has gone beyond what the debt collection case has demonstrated, but the analysis has been established.

---

[35]Please refer to Fei Xiaotong: *Rural China and Rural Reconstruction*, Storm and Stress Publishing, 1993; Robert. R. Blake, *Behavior of Law*, Tang Yue, Suli (translated), Chinese University of Politics and Law Press, 1944; And Robert C. Ellickson, *Order without Law: How Neighbors Settle Disputes*, Harvard University Press, 1991.

[36]Please refer to *Law Yearbook of China*, China's Law Yearbook Press, 1998, for data of court mediation and judgment of civil cases.

When analyzing this point and looking back at the debt collection case, we will find that from the point of mediation structure in the sense of sociology,[37] this "court mediation" made by the judge after the trial, the court, and the business unit were more like a common "plaintiff,"[38] while the villager who borrowed money was the defendant, and the village head was more like a mediator. During the whole "procedure," the head of the court and the business unit exaggerated principals and interests owed by the borrower as well as the litigation and traveling fees, and then did the village head a special favor. The borrower resisted by all kinds of methods (including entertaining the guest). The village cadre made arrangements for "being considerate of the borrower." The whole process was more like a bargaining match presided over by the village cadre. The state power was disparaged to such a condition. This has proved a prerequisite judgment made by this article: The state power of China is relatively weak in rural society, at least rural society in remote areas. In the fringes of state power, as far as function is concerned, the village cadre plays a role similar to that of rural gentry described by Mr. Fei Xiaotong in his book *Imperial Power and Gentry's Power* 50 years ago, although we cannot simply equate the former with the latter.[39]

1.7 Conclusion

It was a surprise to me that I could go as far as this. But my analysis does not imply any judgment of "what we should do" regarding standardization, for example the state shall strengthen its administrative and legal control over rural society. I'm currently trying to understand China's "national conditions" by analyzing individual cases, but not drawing simple value judgments or inducing a certain political choice. Before I provide further systematic analysis on the pros and cons of this situation, I'm unable and unwilling to propose a simple political

---

[37]Mediation in the sense of sociology is an open texture of analysis. During this evaluation, who is the mediator and who are the parties concerned have been decided by the role and function in the actual case. Mediation in justice is a normative structure in which the law stipulates that the judge is the mediator.

[38]This point is tenable not only in form, but in terms of interests of different parties. (1) It appeared to be a private law case, but because the business unit belonged to the country, the court represented the country and the debt collection according to law by the court which happened after the regional and county government gave emphasis to the debt collection, this made the business unit share the same interests with the people's court; (2) due to the financial difficulties of the court, it is hoped that helping to collect debts could increase the "revenue" of the court (many judges introduced during the interview that in areas where local fiscal situation was in bad shape, the courts often took the initiative to ask the banks whether there were any cases of "non-payment of debt"), the court and the business unit therefore had common economic interest. That is why in a certain sense at least, they were the same. Based on this, this debt collection case to me was more like a "public law" relationship (the relationship between the state and its citizens) concealed by "private law" relationship (relationship among citizens).

[39]Wu Han, Fei Xiaotong, etc. : *Imperial Power and Gentry's Power*, Tianjin People's Press, 1988.

suggestion. If it is essential to propose something, then my preliminary view is that although the establishment of a national state has been completed as a whole, it has not been finished in many local areas. This is at least a fundamental restriction for whether the rule of law can be truly established in China's rural areas.

This conclusion is not based on the analysis of this individual case only, but has some circumstantial evidence. As a Chinese scholar pointed out in the early years of this century, the "state" before modern times was not the nation-state in the modern western sense, but a cultural community.[40] An important task of China in modern times is state-building.[41] As far as Mr. Huang Renyu sees, the biggest achievement of the revolution led by China's Communist Party on establishing a modern state was establishing successfully basic-level organizations of a modern state in China's rural areas.[42] Mao Zedong analyzed in detail in his early works such as Why is it that Red Political Power can Exist in China? The Struggle in the Chingkang Mountains, A Single Spark Can Start a Prairie Fire, and others. He addressed why China's state power could not go deep into the village and through that proposed the road to seize power by using the rural areas to encircle the cities, which has been proven by history to be correct. This shows that China's rural society is actually in a situation that reflects the saying "the heaven is high and the emperor is far away" in a certain sense. It is this situation that has led China's Communist Party to emphasize going to the countryside to mobilize the masses and to establish rural bases. Due to the strategy of China's Communist Party, the political situation of China's rural areas has indeed changed as a whole, and the state authority network began to enter into the villages from counties in the Qing Dynasty.

But this process cannot be completed with the establishment of a new regime. Due to the economic difference between the urban and the rural areas in China (which to me is the fundamental social condition for the previous situation to take place), the modernized and industrialized mode of production has not entered deep into the rural areas yet and this kind of situation cannot be completely changed for a period of time. During Mao Zedong's time, under the planned economic system, the administrative power of the state and the Party's organizational network closely intertwined with the state power and were very powerful and thorough. Despite this, Mao Zedong still realized clearly that he himself had not changed China but only a few places close to Beijing.[43] We should not think that it is only because this great man who "counted the mighty as no more than muck" and "was brave enough to ask the world who would be in charge" was just modest enough to realize this. There is indeed some truth in it.

[40]Please refer to Liang Shuming: *Highlights of Chinese Cultrue*, Xuelin Publishing House, 1987, pp. 18–20.

[41]Please refer to Prasenjit Duara: *Culture, Power and State*, translated by Wang Fuming, 1994, Jiangsu People's Publishing House; please also refer to Jiang Shigong: *Legal Transplant, Public Domain and Legitimacy*, School of Law of Peking University, master thesis, 1996.

[42]Huang Renyu: *China: A Macro History*, SDX Joint Publishing Company, 1997.

[43]When Mao Zedong met with Nixon at his old age, Nixon appraised Mao that "he had changed China." Mao answered by saying those words.

Since the reform and opening-up, due to the development of market economic factors, rural China has been remodeled in a certain sense. But due to the elimination of the people's community system and the withdrawal of the state power in rural areas to some extent, the actual influence of state's official power on rural society in certain areas has been weakened. It is even difficult for state power to enter into rural society in the name or method of "rule of law." This may be an important or even fundamental reason for "sending justice to the countryside" and "sending law to the countryside." Justice in modern China has inevitably become strongly political, since its function cannot be limited to the definition of western classic judicial theory on the court function as a dispute settlement and rule identification institution. It is nonetheless one of the components for establishing a modern nation-state. It is just at this background we may be able to understand the strategic meaning on another level of "sending science and technology to the countryside," "sending culture to the countryside," and "sending medical treatment to the countryside" proposed in recent years as well as the "Hope Project" and building the "Hope School," which has taken place all over the country. Viewing from the analysis framework of this chapter, we can say that they have inherited the basic strategy of Mao Zedong, which emphasized going deep into the countryside in a certain sense, however, in another manner which may be more effective for building a modern country.

However, going deep into the countryside in the past was very different from that of today. If the purpose of going deep into the countryside in the past was to mobilize the masses and to use the countryside to encircle the cities and thus the strategy of power operation was from bottom up, then the purpose of going deep into the countryside today is more about transforming and conquering the countryside with the strategy of power operation more from top to bottom and penetrating into the countryside from cities. After all, great changes have taken place in China even though the problems of rural China caused by modernization have not been solved yet.

The problems may be the most important inspiration to the analysis of "sending law to the door" and "sending justice to the countryside" and is also the essential and social structural reason for them to come into being and continue for a long time.

First draft on August 10th, 1997

Second draft on September 21st, 1997

Appendix: Experience the Modernity of Chinese Law

—A note to "Why Send Law to the Countryside?"

I

My friend Zhao Tingyang plans to write a book on issues of China's modernity specifically and asked me to write a chapter. I used one of my old writings to fulfill the task. It is not accurate to say that I only want to fulfill the task. I can deceive neither the readers nor my own academic conscience. "What is your contribution?" has always been one of the questions I ask myself for the purpose of my "Everyday examinations in three approaches" as proposed by Confucius. In the final analysis, I think this article is related to China's modernity. The only caveat is that I'm not willing to use the modernized vocabulary or propositions which are relatively popular at the moment to discuss this issue.

Why is that? Because I hate discussing issues such as "modernity" at the concept level. My hatred is due to my following doubts. How could you have meaningful exchanges without misunderstandings at such a highly conceptual level? How could you prove that you are not only talking to yourself and therefore beating around the bush? There is even the possibility that it is difficult to find out where misunderstanding arises, just like if you have gotten lost in the woods. The more important thing is that this kind of destined construction of "grand narrative" is very dangerous, since many trivial but not necessarily unimportant things may be ignored, suppressed, or distorted (intentionally or unintentionally) due to their incompatibility with the grand narrative.

It is because of this reason that I have chosen my article Why "Send Law to the Countryside"? to first of all feel and then understand some problems concerning the modernity of Chinese laws. I hope that due to this specific and lively individual case, we can connect certain daily practices of Chinese people with the issue of modernity, in order to enable those who are not good at or are not used to conceptual language to observe the modernity of Chinese laws (from my point of view, even if they do not understand this modernity, as long as they are able to find issues from their lives sensitively and to give theoretical analysis, it is certainly enough for them). At the same time, I hope this article can help those scholars or intellectuals who are used to grandly narrating at the level of concepts and propositions created by the Western countries to understand this kind of, or another level of, legal modernity.

I wish readers could read the main text first and then take a look at this note. If you think it is interesting and are willing to, you may read "Sending Law to the Countryside" once more, including that seemingly strange postscript which was deleted by the editor. Ultimately, I hope that the readers will use their own daily-life experience to question, challenge, or verify this article.

II

At the moment, many people are accustomed to connecting modernity of laws with "justice" or "social justice" or "rights"; or with specific legal principles (such as the right to silence of criminal defendant) or practices (such as the Simpson trial) of certain Western countries. However, justice is the word that is simply too abstract and big. It can cover almost everything and therefore becomes the pursuit of human society for thousands of years although some people may have never used or even heard of this word. Justice is a concept without time or life. In Holmes' words which are even more vivid, it cannot "wave its tail." It is only a tool used to express one's own feelings and to justify their desires. There is a story popular among lawyers: A new lawyer won his case and telephoned a senior lawyer, claiming that "justice has won." However, the senior lawyer ordered him to "appeal immediately." This shows the opinion of certain lawyers on the relationship between justice and laws. Posner's pedigree analysis demonstrates that "right" is actually a kind of instinct of human beings. Without this instinct, the human being cannot survive as a species. Whether you call it "right" or not, we were born with these instinctive feelings, and we did not simply acquire them in modern times. The legal principles or practices of Western countries certainly influence the modernity of Western society, but it does not equate to the modernity of Chinese laws. On the contrary, at least to the majority of Chinese jurists, these principles or practices more possibly have become the counter evidence of the "premodernity" of our legal practices at the moment, which have thus proved that we are not able to discuss about the modernity of modern Chinese laws, or we are at most able to discuss the modernity of Chinese laws through our wish to "be connected to the international world" and at the level of pure imagination. However, is this the modernity of laws as practice? As a matter of fact, it can only reflect the modernity in ways of thinking and feeling, as well as the psychology of modern Chinese people involved in the legal field.

What is more important is that in this kind of language, "modernity" has become a kind of ideology standard or concept of intentionality to judge whether something is right or wrong, desirable or not, but not a descriptive concept. It seems to be a priori inevitability, but not a possibility to feel the reality. Thus, "Life is Elsewhere" has become the basic feature of this kind of language. As related to that "God's perspective" is another basic feature of this kind of language.

III

We must observe modernity from contemporary Chinese law practice, but not from our feelings or intentions. The case which I "robbed" (robbery without plan or specific object) from contemporary Chinese law practice may help us to feel this kind of modernity.

First of all, this individual case demonstrates in what natural, geographical, and cultural environment China's laws function. China is a big country with vast territory and varied landforms, which causes the imbalanced development of political and economic culture in different parts of China. Contemporary Chinese laws function in and only in this kind of environment and thus present the "Mosaic" Phenomenon of legal practice to certain degrees. The venue where the loan collection case discussed in this article took place is a village "on the rim of the desert" and is therefore not a purely natural environment. It is expected to have certain implication or revelation to sensitive readers. Natural and geographic environments have left marks deeply on the function of contemporary Chinese laws. The law here is neither "formal rationality" of Weber, nor "materialization of law" by Jurgen Habermas. It is not justice in form or in essence. You may feel more or less incompetent when trying to analyze and feel Chinese society by Western concepts. There is not much deduction of legal concepts or legal reasoning here. No judicial robes or lawyers. There are neither direct policemen nor prisons. It represents a battle between judges on behalf of the state and its citizens by definition of political relations. But you may feel more specific person-to-person contact. It is mobilization of various resources (not only resources of political power), conscious, or unconscious utilization of strategies, and in pursuit of specific and trivial purposes of each individual in the process of the function.

But this is not like what some people may think—that it only shows "premodern" laws. This kind of evaluation may have some reasoning backing it. China's judicial system, especially judicial practices in rural areas, does indeed have rather strong imprinting of change from a traditional society of acquaintances to a society of strangers. This change has been described or analyzed by many Western legal sociologists in their writings. If we only pay attention to this point, my description here will be only a repetition of traditional academic propositions.

However, my analysis has been paying attention to and, to some extent, given expression to the fact that "sending law to the countryside" is related to the founding of China as a nation in modern times. As a result, sending law to the countryside, sending law to the door as well as the strategy from "Encircling the Cities from the Rural Areas" in the old days to sending culture, science and technology, and medical services to the countryside in recent years, which has been included in the analysis as a background, are coherent and interconnected with each other in a certain sense. They are also one battle after another during the process of forming and founding of a modern nation. They can even be regarded as the process of forming and founding a modern nation itself, since there does not exist a result outside this process.

It is just at this level that we are able to see the profound difference between this story and the "law" story of primitive societies in jungle wilderness witnessed and recorded by anthropologists in the nineteenth twentieth centuries, as well as the theoretical model of unofficially legal or non-legal solutions of disputes in the eyes of legal sociologists of academism. Seeing from this perspective, we can say that this story is indeed infiltrated by modernity. Its modernity does not mean that it happens in modern times. What gives it its modernity is not time, but a complete set of framework of political practices and political institutions. It is even difficult for us to say that it is totally modernity of another kind of law. It is closely related to modernity of the world.

History has therefore entered into this picture. "Sending law to the countryside" has been connected to the efforts and achievements made by the Chinese Communist Party to establish a modern nation-state during the time when revolutionary bases were being built. With this, we may be able to understand the strong political pursuit possessed by "rule by law" itself. However, this kind of historical connection is not only of political intentionality and political logic. This article shows their connection in knowledge pedigrees to a certain degree. My note which may make readers puzzled is that those metaphors of wars appearing from time to time in the article as well as strategy application of different parties in the "lawsuit" all have given the following: How strategies and technologies in the age of revolutionary wars are continued and transformed by different people in different manners or names in today's China. This exploration of pedigrees of contemporary Chinese legal knowledge and skills may not be deep enough, but can still demonstrate the modernity of contemporary Chinese law in another aspect.

Please do not misunderstand me as trying to use this individual case as a representation or miniature of Chinese law. I see it only as an individual case (it is up to readers themselves to understand it). There are many individual cases of this kind. It is just because there are many of them which are ordinary cases, people often forget or ignore them. They are not expected to inspire attention to their existence. I'm just trying to make it stand out in a possibly careful manner, but I'm destined to do so in an awkward language and to let people see what Chinese law is! As a result, it is true that this individual case under analysis happens in a rural area in Northwest China. Even if it happened in an urban area in a Southeast coastal region, as long as you are not too controlled by modern judicial academic language in Western countries or by which you shape your observation of the reality, sticking to what Wittgenstein insisted as "don't think, just look," then we can still see the fact that the classic legal language in Western countries cannot cover the generalized legal practices of China. After all, law is not provisions. Nor is it institution. In this sense, I believe that this individual case itself possesses enough power to deconstruct all kinds of new and old legal ideological languages.

IV

I don't and can't possibly ask the readers to accept that this is Chinese law. I don't even ask them to accept the conclusions of this article. There are multiple real forms of Chinese law. Any descriptions or analysis are destined to face all kinds of challenges, especially criticisms of popular legal languages. This article can still make people feel that the laws in our daily life are so subtle, delicate, and clever, and that our lives do have the possibility of argument and modern flavor. It can thus inspire us to pay attention to ourselves, to pursue our own languages, to focus on the reality, and to feel confident about our academic research.

This article is not creative enough but it attempts to be creative. It uses various Western resources of academic theories, but it does not copy mechanically any kind of Western social or legal theory, nor does it seek to promote certain Western academic theories. It therefore reveals a kind of indifference (either to copying Western theories to demonstrate the academic aspect of this research, or to criticizing or responding to Western theories to prove its own uniqueness). It uses writings of Mao Zedong, experiences of the Agrarian Revolutionary War, as well as colloquialisms among the Chinese people which can be felt more or less by everyone, but cannot traditionally enter academic anecdotes or pieces of gossip. It is complex, but these kinds of uses are not ideological, nor do they intend to prove the truth of the article or conclusion. It neither demonstrates feelings of foreign countries or foreign lands easily to be discovered by sociologists in the manner of hunting for novelty, nor puts on airs as a jurist who feels eager toward making standard evaluations as a judge for the society. It even does not show enough of the so-called conscience of intellectuals toward the poor or weak person in the case (but instead analyzes how he could become stronger in this specific dispute and thus rids him of the cheap sympathy he might get from other academic legal texts). He is cold, but not without stance.

At least, China's legal academics is itself part of China's legal practice. If there is reason in this, even when the above reasons could not convince you to believe in the modernity of Chinese law, then the importance, understanding, and introspective pursuits by this article to its (Chinese) experience, emotions, cases, language and even readers, the reasonable confidence of its research, and the seemingly indifference and mischievousness (meaning same as the word mischievous in the poem verse "the mischievous little boy picking seedpods of lotus by the brook") given to traditional academic boundaries and moral principles of traditional intellectuals, it can be seen as a proof of the modernity of Chinese law (academics).

In Weixiu Garden, Peking University
May 2nd, 1999

Chapter 2
Court Trial and Its Administration

Historical tradition gave rise to the French peasants' belief in the miracle that a man named Napoleon would bring all glory back to them. And there turned up an individual who claims to be that man because he bears the name Napoleon, in consequence of the Code Napoleon, which decrees "Inquiry into paternity is forbidden."

—Karl Marx ("The 18th Brumaire of Louis Napoleon," *Marx and Engles Collected Works*, vol. 1, People's Publishing House, 1994, p. 678.)

2.1 The Definition of Problem

The responsibility of the court[1] system in a country is to fulfill its judicial function as established by the country, which has become common sense. However, this is usually the standard analysis and stipulation of court functions from the perspective of politics and constitutions, as well as the tautology of "court's" definition. In our real lives, courts of different countries are composed of by many people (judges and other auxiliary personnel). They have their own fiscal budgets and expenditures, as well as other administrative and auxiliary works. It is therefore fair to say that every court has its internal administrative affairs. In all countries, at least part of this kind of non-judicial and administrative work can only be borne by courts themselves. Even though due to different systems, the total amount of

[1]These are called "judicial" departments in the USA, i.e., government institutions with judicial power. In China, "judiciary" often refers to a administrative organization subordinate to the government, and the national judicial power is shared by the court and the procuratorate. That's why in this article, the "court" will be used in areas when there might be confusions when talking about China's cases.

© Foreign Language Teaching and Research Publishing Co., Ltd and Springer Science+Business Media Singapore 2016

S. Zhu, *Sending Law to the Countryside*, China Academic Library,
DOI 10.1007/978-981-10-1142-9_2

this kind of work borne by courts of different countries is varied. For example, compared to the Supreme People's Court in China, the Supreme Court of the USA bears much less administrative work with federal judges having unsophisticated jobs.[2] Even so, the U.S. Chief Justice and Associate Justices of the Supreme Court, who are seen as symbols of pure justice, have to run many "errands" and perform administrative duties as well. Take the U.S. Chief Justice as an example, he (there hasn't been a *she* yet) has to take care of the appeal list of the Supreme Court, preside over meetings and case discussions of the Supreme Court and be conscious of time. As far as specific cases are concerned, when he belongs to the majority, he will designate a federal judge to write judicial opinion. All these are obviously administrative affairs related to judiciary falling into the category of court administration. In addition, more than 50 articles of federal laws stipulate other administrative work that the Chief Justice is responsible for.[3] All this administrative work is reflected by salaries. As a reward for more work, the annual pay of the Chief Justice is higher than those of other federal judges. Every federal judge has his own administrative work. Each of them has at least four law clerks and two secretaries. Law clerks are usually interviewed and selected by the federal judges themselves. They obey the assignments given by the federal judges and write judicial opinions according to the case judgments by the federal judges. If the former Associate Justice of the Supreme Court Lewis Powell was right in saying that each of the nine Associate Justices, with their law clerks and secretaries, constitute "nine small independent law firms,"[4] then every Associate Justice is the director of each law firm.

Courts in reality always have to implement administrative functions related to trials. It is because of this that administration in the courts necessarily overlaps and

---

[2]For instance, the U.S. federal courts have their administrative offices to "execute the basic administrative functions of the federal courts. It also collects and deals with materials of federal courts. … In addition, administrative offices are the connecting bond for federal [court systems], conference, legislative, and administrative institutions. The representative conference of administrative offices put budgetary requirements toward Congress, propose for the increase of judges, put forward suggestions of changing court activity rules or with major influence to the federation." In the U.S. federal court system, there are also Judicial Conferences for the USA, Circuit Judicial Council, and Federal Judicial Center. Since contemporary times, each court has had a non-judicial "court administrator," engaged specially in non-judicial works of court administration, such as drafting budgets, recruiting court staff, and managing court files. These institutions and people undertake certain decision-making tasks and daily works of administration similar to that of Chinese courts. Please see Peter Renstrom, *The American Law Dictionary*, translated and proofread by He Weifang, China University of Political Science and Law Press, 1998, pp. 45–47, 51–52, 60–61, 57, 84–85; Please also see Henry J. Abraham, *The Judicial Process*, 4th ed. Oxford University Press, 1980, pp. 175–178. In addition, about the administration of German courts, there is a very simple introduction to case distribution. Please see Fu De: "Judicial profession and independence of Germany," *Procedural, Justice and Modernization*, edited by Song Bing, China University of Political Science and Law Press, 1999, especially pp. 28–30.

[3]David M. O'Brien, *Storm Center: The Supreme Court in American Politics*, 2nd ed., W. W. Norton & Company, p. 178.

[4]O'Brien, *Storm Center*, the same as the previous note, p. 157.

mingles with trials, and even interferes with the execution of judicial power, and thus to a certain extent influences the implementation of judicial power. There is a well-known fact that the U.S. Chief Justice usually uses their own administrative power to seek and in fact gain certain special influences to judicial decisions. In the individual case of each justice, they usually try to be with the majority and designate themselves or judge with most similar opinions the job of writing the judicial opinion and thus influence the judgment and the future development of related laws.[5]

Although court administration has some major influences on court decisions, in the traditional research of normative jurisprudence, this issue hasn't been given enough importance, especially in China.[6] Since contemporary times, the judicial systems in China have been transplanted from Western countries. After the transplant, due to frequent social reforms, judicial systems haven't been able to establish independent traditions of practice but have halted in philosophy. China's law circle has for a long time placed extra emphasis on and illustrated the abstract judicial philosophy and principle of "judicial independence" or "independent adjudication." It does not know much, or strictly speaking, is not conscious of, reflect on or care about the real operation of courts. Many scholars try to avoid or ignore this issue intentionally or unintentionally due to the feeling that the recognition of the conflict between administration and trial will inevitably destroy the image of rule of law in one heart. The world of concepts is always more innocent and comforting than the real world.

In the limited systematic discussion of Chinese scholars I have seen, *Two Problems* in the *Chinese System* of *Judicial Management* published by He Weifang is an exception.[7] This article has, for the first time, put forward the problem of

---

[5]As for techniques and considering factors of the Chief Justice on distributing the job of writing court opinions, please see David J. Danelski, "The Influence of the Chief Justice in the Decisional Process of the Supreme Court," in Sheldon Goldman and Austin Sarat eds., *American Court System: Readings in Judicial Process and Behavior*, 2nd ed., Longman, 1989, pp. 486–499; Please also see Abraham, *Judicial Process*, pp. 218–215; O'Brien, *Storm Center*, pp. 159ff.

[6]In the USA, this issue belongs to the research of behaviorist politics traditionally. In the field of legal science, although lawyers dealing with law practices know this fact, and often use this established fact in their judicial practices, this issue is often ignored in legal writings. This is because on one hand, the law that lawyers care about is the decision that judges might make; the lawyers are not able to change the institutional framework of court function and thus generally not considering this issue. On the other hand, the focus of the law faculty is more about the normative legal research, and this unclean "judicial politics" is just what traditional law professors try to get rid of.

[7]It was originally published on *Social Sciences in China*, Issue 6, 1997, and then included in He Weifang: *Judicial philosophies and Systems*, China University of Politics and Law Press, 1998. The name of the article was changed to *On Non-administration and Non-Bureaucratization of Justice*. You may also see related analysis in Hu Jianhua and Li Hancheng: "On Self-management of Court Judicial Administration," *People's Judicature*, Issue 12, 1992, pp. 33–34. Hu and Li's article basically emphasizes that the internal administrative works of the courts shall be managed by courts themselves, but not by judicial administrative organizations. The article also mentions examples in foreign countries, but the authors have obviously not realized that judicial functioning inevitably clashes with judicial administration.

administrative systems in the contemporary Chinese courts (i.e., Justice in He's article) rather systematically and sharply. His article pointed out that the court system in our country has serious administrative and bureaucratic colorings, such as the hierarchy of judges, judicial committee systems, relationships between courts of different levels and others. He believes that this has seriously influenced the trial function implemented by China's courts.

I share He's view on many issues he has put forward. However, I believe that He's analysis could go deeper and make some adjustments to its framework of analysis. To a certain extent, He's article stops at normative research. It compares the Western (mainly American) or the so-called international standard formal judicial system with the formal system expressly stipulated by Chinese law. This approach forbids him from having deeper understanding of and giving more relevant criticism to problems related to China's judicial system. If my previous analysis of court administration is somewhat to the point, then factors influencing the trial function of China's courts include not only "Organic Law of the People's Court," all kinds of procedural laws, and formal trial systems expressly stipulated by other relevant laws, but also administrative systems and customs in the courts related to the trial. If we only pay attention or pay too much attention to formal systems and confuse trial systems with administrative systems in the analysis, then we are prone to attribute problems caused by internal administrative systems or customs of courts to the setup of the trial systems, or to exaggerate drawbacks of certain trial systems in the courts.[8] It can certainly serve the purpose of a wake-up call when using an "international standard" as a comparison since we can help people to have a new understanding of the problem by changing the frame of reference and thus pushing the problem to be solved. However, this comparison of principle itself will not help people solve their problems. It is always easy to emphasize principle. And the principle can be and always be rather simple. The principle of judicial independence or independent adjudication can totally "clean up" or "segregate" administrative works of courts in terms of concept or principle. But in real life, this kind of cleaning-up or segregation can't eliminate internal administration which is indispensible to the operation of courts.

This chapter focuses on the level of actual operation and how the administrative system of China's courts influences or may influence the trial function of courts. It mainly observes from the conventional system setup inside the court system. My basic view is that due to unavoidable internal administrative affairs, administration inside the courts is legitimate and necessary. However, this kind of administrative system might erode and distort the trial system. Many of the problems faced by

[8]A typical example is that He Weifang and I have different views on trial committee system. Apart from the above mentioned, you may see He's view from "A Few Comments on Trial Committee System," *Peking University Law Review*, vol. 2, Law Press, 1999. This article has also been included in He's collected works *Judicial Philosophies and Systems*, which is the review of my paper "Observation and Thoughts on Trial Committee System of Basic-level Courts" (*Peking University Law Review*, vol. 2, Law Press, 1999; the article is the third chapter of this book). However, my discussion only focuses on the trial committee of the basic-level courts.

China's court system, like judicial independence or independence of adjudication, are connected to mishandling of or insufficient attention to this problem. My conclusion is that what is important is not to reject administrative affairs, but to gradually and systematically separate the courts' administrative function from their judicial function with the development of the social division of labor.

2.2 Two Institutions and the Structure of Courts

I will first of all mention two intertwined formal institutions in China's courts. These two institutions in principle are directed at, respectively, the trial work which is the court's constitutional function, and the internal administrative work of courts.

First of all, I will address the trial system. From the level of a formal system, China's courts at different levels are all composed of by one president and several deputy presidents, tribunal directors, deputy tribunal directors, and judges.[9] There is no difference in trial duties of presidents, deputy presidents, tribunal directors, and deputy tribunal directors as stipulated by law. On the contrary, according to Article 6 of Judges Law, those presidents and directors are the same as the other judges during the trial. They are judges first of all and thus must execute their duties. Inside the courts, according to the Organic Law of the People's Court, specific tribunals are established with tribunal directors designated, but the law doesn't stipulate the specific functions of those tribunals or special responsibilities of tribunal directors. There is only one express stipulation for responsibilities of tribunal directors, that is, the chief judge of the collegiate panel should be appointed by the president of the court or by the tribunal director.[10] Strictly speaking, this is neither a stipulation of judicial responsibilities nor a distribution of judicial power and its limits. It is just an unavoidable and auxiliary distribution of administrative responsibilities. According to the Organic Law of the People's Court, it is up to the collegiate panel or a single judge to hear specific cases.[11] In practice, only cases of the first instance in basic-level courts can be tried by a single judge. Cases at the higher courts and above, as well as cases of the basic-level courts which are not simple, shall be tried by a collegiate panel of at least 3 judges.[12]

---

[9]Article 19, 24, 26 and 30 of the Organic Law of the People's Courts.

[10]Please see Article 10 of the Organic Law of the People's Courts; Article 94 of Detailed Provisions of the Supreme People's Courts on the Court Trial Procedures of Criminal Cases (1994); Article 42 of Civil Procedure Law. But in the basic-level courts during our research, chief judges are actually designated by tribunal directors.

[11]Article 10 of the Organic Law of the People's Courts.

[12]Article 147 of the Criminal Procedure Law; Article 11 of the Organic Law of the People's Courts.

According to the Organic Law of the People's Courts, there is also a specific organization for collective judicial work—a judicial committee, whose purpose is to discuss and decide on important, complicated, and difficult cases.[13] This is another institution related to the trial system. It is not clear by which procedure that cases tried by a collegiate panel or single judges can enter judicial committee for discussion and decision. There is no detailed stipulation in the Organic Law of the People's Court, Civil Procedure Law, or Administrative Procedure Laws. It is only stipulated that if a president of a people's court of any level finds a court decision or ruling which is already legally binding that has errors of fact or law and thus needs review, he or she shall submit it to the judicial committee for discussion and decision. It is then up to the judicial committee to decide whether it is necessary for review.[14] The Criminal Procedure Law and the Supreme Court's interpretation of it generally stipulates the procedure for cases tried by a single judge or a collegiate panel to enter a judicial committee for discussion and decision; that is, they shall be submitted by the collegiate panel or the single judge undertaking the cases.[15]

This is a formal institutional arrangement of China's current laws on the judicial system of courts at different levels. Only seen from the words, as far as implementing judicial functions is concerned, this kind of institutional arrangement is different from the court system of Western countries in many aspects. Because the judicial organizations of courts in Western countries are different from one another, from the conceptual and logical point of view, it is difficult to say that the internal judicial organization and system of China's courts have problems. Even the judicial committee system much criticized by the circle of jurists is not unreasonable if considering the series of restraining factors of Chinese society.[16]

[13]Article 11 of the Organic Law of the People's Courts.

[14]Article 14 of the Organic Law of the People's Courts, Article 177 of the Civil Procedure Law, Article 63 of the Administrative Procedure Law. If this regulation is followed strictly, during the trial procedure of civil, economic, and administrative cases, decisions made by collegiate panel or single judges are supposed to be effective rulings unless errors occur and be put forward by court presidents. The judicial committee has no right to interfere. However, it is discovered through investigation of basic-level courts that it is not usually the case. On this point, you may refer to Chap. 3 of this book: "The Judicial Committee System in Basic-level Courts."

[15]Article 149 of the Civil Procedure Law. Please also see the Interpretation of the Supreme People's Court on Several Issues Concerning the Implementation of the Criminal Procedure Law of the People's Republic of China (for trial implementation) (1996) Article 115 stipulates that for difficult, complicated, and major cases, if the collegiate panel thinks it necessary, it can ask the president of the court for his decision to submit those cases to the judicial committee for discussion and decision. Cases stipulated by this Article include cases of the death penalty, on which judges of collegiate panels have major disputes, which are protested by people's procurators, or have a major impact on the society, and other cases which need the judicial committee to discuss and decide. This article also stipulates that cases tried by single judges can also be suggested by the court president to be submitted to the judicial committee whenever single judges think necessary.

[16]Please see Chap. 3 of this book "The Judicial Committee System in Basic-level Courts" for related analysis and discussion.

If following this system strictly, we can't say for sure that a president, vice president, tribunal director, and deputy tribunal director have more legitimate judicial authority than normal judges either in terms of correctness or determination of judgment. As far as judicial trial is concerned, they are only judges and share equal judicial rights.[17] According to this institutional arrangement, president, vice president, tribunal director, and deputy tribunal director definitely have a kind of capability of influencing other normal judges and even decisions within the existing court judicial system. For example, they may influence decisions by designating chief judges or collegiate panels. However, since this kind of administrative authority affiliated with trials does exist in a court with many judges, it is impossible to expect neutralizing this kind of influence under the condition that no extra transaction fees or institutional disadvantages are added. There is no experienced research up till now to demonstrate that other institutional settings will have any less transaction fees or disadvantages. Even if we presume that the operational mode of American courts is desirable, this kind of influence unnecessarily exceeds the influence of Chief Judges of American courts on other judges.

There is also a necessity to discuss settings of various divisions inside the courts. According to the Organic Law of the People's Court, courts of all levels have to or may set up (of basic people's court) different divisions: a civil division, criminal division, administrative division, and an economic division (later changed into civil division 2), as well as appoint a division director and deputy director.[18] Although the American courts do not have this setting, as I have mentioned before, relevant laws haven't stipulated the specific functions of those divisions in the trial. Judging from the division of labor based on specialization inside the courts, especially considering current Chinese judge's relative lack of adequate cultural and legal professional studies, this division of labor based on specialization may be able to make up for the disadvantages of the lack of professionalism (this still needs real evidence to prove that it can be of that effect) and be conducive to judicial specialization (although from another point of view, this kind of division of labor also has its disadvantages which I will discuss later). As a matter of fact, courts of continental countries also have this kind of division of labor or set up

[17]This is also demonstrated in legal regulations of judicial committee system. According to Article 11 of the Organic Law of the People's Court, judicial committees "practise democratic centralism," but not "executive accountability" as prosecutorial committees practice. Please also refer to Article 87 of the Detailed Provisions of the Supreme People's Court on the Court Trial Procedures for Criminal Cases (1994), "decisions made by judicial committee can pass only when more than half number of the committee members approve." Our research has discovered that this has been widely implemented in the basic-level courts. Those attending judicial committees, regardless if they are president, vice president, or tribunal director, will have one vote for each. It is also true that this common conclusion does not eliminate the possibility that the real life that president or certain committee member exerts influence on other committee members intentionally.

[18]Article 19, 24, 26 and 30 of the Organic Law of the People's Courts.

various kinds of special courts.[19] There is also a trend of special courts emerging in the USA.[20] Due to the division inside courts, there certainly will be some administrative affairs and the necessity to set up division directors.

If this is China's judicial system, there is nothing to be said against it even though it is not perfect. However, this set of institutions is not only for China's courts to execute their judicial trial functions, or even to execute administrative functions affiliated to trial, but also undertake some other functions. Because even some administrative chores affiliated with trial need to be dealt with, it still can't explain why almost every court and every division have so many deputies. The institutional settings inside China's courts must have some other functions which have not yet been included in the academic views of researchers on standard constitutions, judicial systems, or politics.[21] What matters most to the issues discussed here is the internal administration of courts.

The administrative affairs of the Chinese court system are much more complicated and onerous than those of American courts. According to the law, presidents and vice presidents have to undertake not only many administrative works related to trial,[22] but also administrative works that are not directly related to trial such as

[19]For example, the Supreme Court of France has 6 trial divisions, separately dealing with cases of private laws, economic and trade, industrial relations, social insurance, and criminal cases. Please see You Rong (chief editor): *History of Foreign Legal Systems*, Peking University Press, 1992, p. 436. There are also civil division and criminal division in German and Japanese court systems. Please see Zeng Guangzai (writer and compiler): *Constitutions and Governments of Western Countries*, Hubei Education Press, 1989, pp. 548, 625. In addition, there are also Federal Patent Court, Administrative Court, Labor Court, Social Court and Fiscal and Tax Court in Germany. Please see "Court System in Germany," in *Judicial Systems and Procedures of the United States and Germany*," Song Bing (editor), China Political and Law University Press, 1999, pp. 128–131.

[20]Richard A. Posner, *Federal Courts, Challenge and Reform*, Harvard University Press, 1996, ch. 8.

[21]For example, setting a large number of deputies has created many symbolic resources for the convenience of appointments. There is also distribution of other political powers and material wealth and resources to go with it. This kind of institutional setting therefore serves the purpose of resource distribution. But these very important aspects are not that related to issues discussed in this chapter, so there is not much to say about it. Other scholars may well analyze Chinese and foreign court system further from this point if interested.

[22]For example, Article 11 of the Organic Law of the People's Court stipulates that "Members of judicial committees of local people's courts at various levels are appointed and removed by the standing committees of the people's congresses at the corresponding levels, upon the recommendation of the presidents of these courts"; Article 11 of the Judges Law stipulates that "The assistant judges of the People's Courts shall be appointed or removed by the presidents of the courts where they work"; Article 47 stipulates that The number of persons on a commission for examination and assessment of judges shall be five to nine. "The chairman of a commission for examination and assessment of judges shall be assumed by the president of the court it belongs to."

disciplinary inspection, supervision, and even statistics.[23] In addition, there are also a large number of administrative affairs which, although not explicitly stipulated, need to be or are, in fact, undertaken by presidents and vice presidents, such as the appointment, removal and deployment of directors and vice directors of each division, chief judges, and deputy chief judges of people's court at the basic levels, as well as principals of non-operating departments in the courts, evaluation and promotion of judges, and other factors. With courts of all levels getting increasingly complicated, works related to appointment, removal, and deployment of officials in related institutions have increased. There are even more unofficial but administrative and transactional duties. According to our research on basic-level courts, this kind of work includes all kinds of part-time education provided by the court system to improve the cultural and professional qualities of judges, judicial reform, various works to improve working conditions of courts, and to increase benefit packages of people working for the courts (such as "development cases" like building dormitories and office buildings). This also includes all kinds of evaluations through comparison and inspection, taking part in large number of works not related to the judiciary such as poverty reduction, disaster resistance, donation, development of social culture and ethics, as well as attending various kinds of meetings called up by local party and political leaders. Every court is therefore given many administrative affairs. Like many factories, enterprises, institutions, and schools, the courts in China are themselves a unit, and sometimes even a small "community."

The large number of administrative works goes to not only the court level, but to each division as well. Some of those works, such as allocation of cases, composition of collegiate panels, and designation of chief judges, are legitimately undertaken and implemented by directors and deputy directors, but not by presidents of the courts, at least in the basic-level courts of our research. Those administrative affairs as mentioned in the above paragraph have given divisions to many administrative works due to the requirement that "each task must be pinned down to a specific person."

It is because China's courts are a unit and a community in which there are many administrative affairs that China's court system itself has a relatively strong institutional demand for administration. It is necessary to set up so many presidents, vice presidents, directors, and deputy directors to deal with administrative affairs, manage the community, safeguard, and increase community welfare.

Here is one thing that we need to be careful with. The court and its divisions have their institutional demands of administration and have established a corresponding administrative system to fulfill this demand, but this does not necessarily

---

[23]Article 8 of Notice of the Supreme People's Court on Issuing "the Temporary Measures of Supervisory Departments in the People's Courts to Investigate and Deal With Cases of Disciplinary Violation" stipulates that "the Supreme People's Court establishes Supervisory Department, which is responsible for leading and managing supervisory works of national court system under the leadership of the President of the Supreme People's Court. It also supervises the Supreme Court, its working staff, president, and vice presidents." Article 4 of Several Regulations of the Supreme People's Court on the Judicial Statistic Work of the People's Court stipulates that the statistic work shall be regarded as "an important job of the court of which the president or a vice president of the court is in charge."

result in the strong administration of the court system. As for what has been mentioned before, the court system of every country, such as the American court system, all have administrative works as well, no matter how few they are. However, the American courts don't have a strong feature of administration. Even in theory, the increase of administrative affairs does not necessarily add to the administrative features of the institution. The constitutional separation of powers in Western countries only appears under the historical background of dramatic increases of state administrative affairs in contemporary times. The increase of affairs and the division of labor gave rise to departments of specific functions to deal with different types of problems. This kind of division of labor not only improves efficiency, but also encourages different functional departments to form their own operational logistics.

The problem in the administration of China's courts is caused by the interaction and combination of functions of two sets of institutions aiming at separately dealing with two different kinds of problems inside the court system. There are no divisions of functions when installed by the system or desired by us. Both of these two sets of institutional settings have their rationale. Since the basic social function of the court is trial, its internal administration should be used to support the trial function of the court from the perspective of institutional logic, and thus should be auxiliary. However, these two sets of institutions are attached to the same institution and function in an institutional space where institutions are intertwined with each other. Then, the logistics of these two institutions may mix up and mingle with each other. My research at the basic-level courts has found that these two sets of institutions are not only often mixed up, but the progression of positions is often put upside down by building the trial system into an administrative system with the court as one of its parts. The administrative system plays a big role in the court's implementation of its trial function. Some are positive but more often negative, although the specific evaluation depends on the angle and position of the observers and readers. In addition, when these two institutions interact with each other, there is a series of informal but in fact quite influential trial institutions formed, which differs enormously from the formal trial institution from legal texts.

2.3 Administrative Judicial Institution in the Judicial Process

The above contents are only demonstrations of my logic and ideas.[24] We must observe in detail the actual process of a court to decide its judgment if we want to find out the informal judicial institution that actually works.

---

[24]As for formal systems mentioned in this chapter, they are court's organizational structures and operational procedures stipulated by written law; informal systems refer to systems that are not explicitly stipulated by the above law, but are customs and conventions which people working in the court usually observe voluntarily or involuntarily and even must observe, as well as ideas to go with these customs and conventions. The reason that we call these customs and conventions "systems" is that they, like formal legal regulations, restrict people's behaviors and have become

When a case enters into the court and is, for example, determined to be a civil case, it will be transferred to the civil division of the court for trial. Commonly speaking, the division director will determine whether the case will be tried by a single judge or a collegiate panel. If a collegiate panel is chosen, then the division director will be entitled to appoint a chief judge. The authorities of the division director have been explicitly stipulated by law and have a feature of administration, but they are also collateral administrative activities that can't be avoided. This is exactly where the administrative institution of the court interferes with the trial and drags or includes the judgment into the administrative institution.

For a long period of time, judges without administrative posts have been accustomed to regard themselves under the leadership of the president, vice president of the court, director, and deputy director of divisions inside the court. They are used to asking their leaders for instructions and reporting to them on rather important issues, no matter whether they are or are not regarding a trial. It has become a tradition of courts of all levels although there is no explicit legal stipulation. Even a simple case tried by an independent judge, or a case on which a collegiate panel has reached an agreement and made decisions, the decision will normally be reported to the division director and later the vice president in charge for approval. If the case is difficult or controversial and cannot be solved by the division director and vice president in charge, it will be reported to the president and then to the judicial

Footnote 24 (continued)

social norms which people have to obey. The definition of system here is different from the system we usually refer to (as a formal organizational institution or rule). However, more and more people nowadays accept that "the institutions are, in substance, prevalent habits of thought with respect to particular relations and particular functions of the individual and of the community, … the institutions of today—the present accepted scheme of life." (Thorstein B Veblen: *Theory of the Leisure Class*, Cai Shoubai (translated), the Commercial Press, 1964, pp. 138–144.) It is necessary to point out that some institutions are formal, but are restricted by all kinds of informal institutions and thus ineffective. They are just institutions on paper. The informal institutions are regarded by institutions only because they are effective in the real life. It is fair to say that informal systems are, generally speaking, institutions that are actually influential. An important example is the Bankruptcy Law stipulated in 1980s. We should also point out that when we study courts in modern China, it is not that clear what is formal institution and what is not. It also depends on the perspective and definition of researchers. For example, it is a reality in China that party committees or the Communist Party are in charge of cadres and that it is a basic principle stipulated in the constitution that the leadership of China's communist Party should be upheld. From this perspective, the influence and function of the Party inside the court should be a formal institution. But if we only look at the Organic Law of People's Courts and other texts of procedural law, the actual influence and function of the Party inside the court is not explicitly stipulated by law, but is established by the development of China's modern history. As far as the court institution is concerned, the party committee of the court is therefore an informal institution of court function. However, it is not important to distinguish whether the party committee of the court is a formal or an informal institution. What is important is what I will discuss later: that when we observe the court institutions, we should pay attention to not only institutions explicitly stipulated by law, but also those informal institutions that are actually influential.

committee for discussion. The president can directly intervene in the case trial according to certain laws or his administrative duties under certain circumstances.[25]

The collegiate panel or independent judges are not really what the jurisprudential circle or legal circle criticize as "those who try don't decide" or "try cases without giving decisions." As a matter of fact, before handing the case to a division director or vice president in charge, the collegiate panel will, and actually must, put forward a conclusive decision, generally speaking.[26] The division director will examine the opinions of the collegiate panel on the case. If he or she agrees with the collegiate panel, he will submit the case to the vice president of the court for approval. If he or she does not agree with the collegiate panel, he or she will briefly write down or speak out his or her opinion and ask the collegiate panel to re-evaluate. When the case reaches the president or the vice president of the court, it will meet the following three situations: First, the president agrees with the opinion of the collegiate panel and issues a court decision; second, he or she does not agree with the opinion of the collegiate panel and, like the division director, he or she will ask the panel to reconsider the decision; third, if he or she thinks that case is important and/or complicated, he or she will transfer the case to the judicial committee for discussion.

Generally speaking, either the division director or vice president in charge has complete and final power to decide the case. The collegiate panel's opinions are only an important reference. The collegiate panel may well insist on their initial opinion and once again ask the division director and the president to approve and issue the decision. This is because the signature of the case decision is from the members on the collegiate panel, not of the division director or the president.[27] The main body taking the responsibility of the consequence of the case decision is still the collegiate panel. It is true that the collegiate panel may also receive the "instructions" from the division director and the president to rediscuss the case, but normally speaking, those instructions from the director or the president are not always clear and definite, and sometimes obscure regarding purpose. This is, on the one hand, for the convenience of avoiding the responsibility. If the case is wrongly tried in the second instance, those giving instructions can explain their instructions in one way or another. On the other hand, the formal judicial institution has some restrictions after all, and the director or the vice president themselves are not

---

[25]As for related legal regulations, please refer to Article 10, 11, 14, 16, and 37 of the Organic Law of People's Courts; Article 6 of the Judges Law; Article 42, 47 and 177 of the Civil Procedure Law; Article 47 and 63 of the Administrative Procedure Law; Article 30, 147, and 205 of the Criminal Procedure Law; and Article 26, 112, 115, 120, and 283 of Detailed Provisions of the Supreme People's Court on the Court Trial Procedure for the Criminal Cases.

[26]Please refer to Article 149 of the Criminal Procedure Law. Our research has found out that it has become a convention in civil and administrative procedure.

[27]Article 138 of the Civil Procedure Law stipulates that "the judgment shall be signed by the judicial officers and the court clerk, with the seal of the people's court affixed to it." Article 164 of the Criminal Procedure Law (1996) stipulates that "the written judgment shall be signed by the members of the collegial panel and by the court clerk, and the time limit for appeal and the name of the appellate court shall be clearly indicated therein."

legitimate parties or organizations to try the case.[28] The judicial committee is the judicial organ of the highest level established inside the court. It does not hear the case nor give judgment directly though. But once the case enters into the judicial committee, the committee is entitled to give decisions to settle the case which the collegiate panel needs to implement,[29] and issue judgment on behalf of the collegiate panel.

We can see that the judicial institution stipulated by law has been transformed during the actual process of trial and has become the actual but informal institution of court trials in China.

First of all, there is confusion between judicial institutions and administrative institutions. The division director has become a superior to the independent judge or the collegiate panel to a certain extent; there are not only division directors but vice presidents in charge of the division and the president between the legitimate judicial organizations like collegiate panels or independent judges and judicial committee. A case trial is therefore not finally decided by the judge nor the collegiate panel undertaking the case, but needs to be reported to the division director, vice president in charge, and even the president consecutively for "approval." Once this practice has become a convention and been given a flavor of institution, then those administrative leaders can sometimes intervene in the case directly, which gives them major influence on the case trial. If not from the legal text, but from the point of power to decide the case, we will find out that the judicial institution of the court is not the institution of an independent judge or a collegiate panel, but a collegiate system of four, five, or even more people.

Secondly, it is not only the trial function mixed up with the administrative functions, but more importantly, the judicial institution has become the auxiliary to the administrative institution of the court. The independent judge, collegiate panel, and judicial committee are only organizational forms of the court to carry out judicial functions. They are not independent organizations or individuals that carry out judicial powers. The independent judge and collegial panel are in fact and also in principle must carry out judicial activities under the guidance of the division director and the president.

[28]We not only feel about this point through the interviews with judges, but also read from some official documents that judges undertaking cases try to resist the erosion of judicial power by administrative power of the court through certain legal regulations. Article 14 of the Reply of the Supreme People's Court on Several Questions related to Detailed Application of Laws in Serious Criminal Cases Tried by the People's Courts (September 20, 1983) has left traces for this kind of resistance. A question from the Province of Zhejiang is that "for the serious criminal cases that are currently severely punished and given speedy trial, is it possible that on the legal documents issued by the courts, there will be no signatures of judicial officer and the court clerk, but only a seal of the people's court affixed to it?" The reply of the Supreme People's Court to this is that "Article 122 of the Criminal Procedure Law stipulates that 'the written judgment shall be signed by members of the collegial panel and by the court clerk'. It still needs to be carried out currently."

[29]Article 87 of the Detailed Provisions of the Supreme People's Court on the Court Trial Procedure for the Criminal Cases stipulates that "decision of the judicial committee shall be implemented by the collegial panel. If there is a disagreement, the decision can be submitted to the judicial committee for review by the president."

Thirdly, there is also some kind of "trial grade system" inside the court, especially on some difficult, complicated, and major cases. A judgment of courts at a certain level is actually the product of progressive approval process inside the court. Not only has the judicial power of the presiding judge been divided, but the judicial power designated to the court of this level by law has been highly decentralized.

There are many other factors reinforcing the influence of the administrative system on judicial institutions. One of them is the appointment and removal of judges. According to the Organic Law of the People's Court, the president, vice president, division director, deputy director, and judges all have equal judicial functions; the court can only appoint and remove assistant judges of the court, while the judges can only be appointed by the standing committee of the same level.[30] Up until now, the appointment by the standing committee has only been procedural and a necessary formality. The majority of judges are nominated by leaders of different courts. Leaders of the division and the court first recommend certain judges and then the personnel department will examine those candidates. Then the Party Committee of the court, composed by the president, vice president, director of political department, and the leader of the disciplinary inspection group, will make their final decisions. However, once whether a judge can get his position is, to a large degree, decided by some other "judges" who are working in the same court as he or she, then his or her case trial will definitely be influenced by them and he or she will tend to figure out "what those leaders think." And the division director and court president will also use this power pattern to influence the case dealings. During this power structure, judges with administrative functions have different decision powers from those without administrative functions. Thus, judges inside the court have various ranks.

2.4 Collective Decisions of Administration

Be sure not to think that this kind of institutional arrangement of China's courts only gives actual judicial activities a strong feature of administration or that the decision of cases of China's courts are all administrative bureaucracy. The administration of judicial decisions of courts is only one of the features demonstrated because of the mix-up of two sets of institutional functions. It is not fair to generalize the judicial features of China's courts only because of this. The mix-up of these two sets of institutional functions also demonstrates other features, one of which is the mode of "democratic" collective decision. The "democratic" or collective decision mentioned here does not necessarily have the positive meaning given by the current popular ideology. It only refers to the decentralization of decision powers, and that every person involved in the process may exert a certain

[30] Article 35 of the Organic Law of the People's Court.

influence on the final decision. In principle, this feature seems to go against the feature of judicial administration as above mentioned. This kind of paradox does exist in reality. If the court was purely administrative, then the trial would have the strict system of the chief executive taking full responsibility. But the judicial institution in China's court is not like this. It has the features of administrative instructions and decentralized decisions. It is the combination of two, with one reinforcing and supporting the other.

The judicial committee is a democratic organization with group decision making of the administrative trial of the court. I have discussed it in some other papers and will not give unnecessary details here. The general process of trial discussed before demonstrates this from another angle. In this informal institution, trial decision power has been divided in the process from prosecution to court decision. The hearing and the adjudication are not concentrated in any specified organization or individual.[31] Any individual related to this process can speak and intervene and his opinions will be accepted to some extent as long as they are sensible. Of course, the result of this democratic group decision making normally is that nobody will take the final responsibility for the result of this case—and it becomes difficult to ask someone to take full responsibility.

It is therefore not difficult for us to understand another informal institution which is never stipulated by law, but commonly exists and functions in every court's affairs meetings. Our research has discovered that sometimes division directors would take the cases still under trial by the collegiate panel to the court affairs meeting for discussion and require that all judges of the division should participate in the discussion. Cases under discussion are sometimes those in which director and collegiate panel have strong differences. More judges are asked to participate in the discussion so that their opinions would be heard and collective wisdom would be adopted. It can also be the case that there are differences in the collegiate panel itself and it can not put forward a convincing and complete opinion, and thus wants to hear about views of other judges. Judges are working in the same office without separate space for research and case consideration; thus, it is very easy for them to feel accustomed to exchanging ideas with other judges on cases they are "not sure about," and to ask for and listen to suggestions and recommendations of other judges.[32] This kind of practice of judicial democracy is in sharp contrast with the above-mentioned administration of courts. Although this kind of democratic way of collective decision may not get approval from the jurist circle.

This democratic way of collective decision is even shown inside the collegiate panel sometimes. The collegiate panel is usually composed of three judges, one of

---

[31]The collegiate panel can even suggest submitting the decision of judicial committee to the committee for review. Please see Article 87 of Detailed Provisions of the Supreme People's Court on the Court Trial Procedures for the Criminal Cases, which stipulates that "the decision of the judicial committee, … if [the collegial panel] still has different opinions, it can suggest the president to submit the decision to the judicial committee for review."

[32]Mr. Ling Bin, a student of Law Faculty of the Peking University discovered this relevance during his internship. I would like to thank him for his contribution here.

which is the specific undertaker of the case who is taking main responsibility for the factual and legal issues of the case. The preparation of the case before the trial, examination of evidence, writing the initial settlement suggestions are basically all done by the judge himself. Other members of the collegiate panel only glance over the files and participate in the trial. According to their impressions from the files and the trial, plus reports of the judge undertaking the case, members of the collegiate panel will put forward their own opinions. Due to the normal situation that the composition of the collegiate panel is relatively stable with the same members cooperating with each other, judges of the collegiate panel will try their best to maintain a relationship pattern of collaboration. The principle of majority rules is practiced in the collegiate panel,[33] and the judge undertaking the case would normally want his opinions to be accepted and supported by the other two judges. If the opinion of the judge undertaking the case is always the minority during the panel discussion, it means that he or she is not competent. As reciprocity, whenever there is no substantial dispute, the judge who wishes the result of cases he or she undertakes be recognized by other judges would tend to recognize the results of cases undertaken by other judges.[34] This reciprocity does not mean that there is always an agreement on the collegiate panel. We can only say that within the discretion scope allowed by law, judges of the collegiate panel will try their best to reach an agreement.

We can still notice even from here that the decision manner of collegial panel is influenced by the court administrative system of current times. Compared with micro-group analysis[35] related to foreign court decisions, an important factor in the collegial panel of China's court to facilitate more co-operations among judges is the administrative system of China's court, which has never appeared in relevant foreign researches. If there is no agreement in the collegiate panel, the case will enter into the administrative judicial system in the court when the division director and vice president in charge will be asked for instructions. This will add to the work load of the division director, vice president, president, and even the judicial committee. But generally speaking, these people or organizations do not welcome

[33]Article 148 of the Criminal Procedure Law.

[34]As for this point, if judging from the concept, it does not correspond with "independence of judge" or the so-called internal independence of judges. We must point out that this kind of viewpoint actually forgets about the fact that a judicial decision always comes from a court which is an organization but not from an individual judge. Group cooperation is necessary and essential since none of us know which judge has a correct view or whether he or she is always right. Cooperation and compromise among judges to a certain extent is actually effective, and at least can prevent going to extreme. As a matter of fact, the important judicial opinions (i.e., majority opinions) produced by the decision mode of the Supreme Court of the USA admired by many Chinese scholars are mostly product of comprise by a majority of judges and even all judges.

[35]For example, American judicial research has discovered that the probability for the three-judge judicial tribunal to have disputes is sharply lower than the tribunal composed by 7 or 9 judges. The smaller the trial group, the lower the ratio of opposition. Please see Richard J. Richardson and Kenneth N. Vines, *The Politics of Federal Courts*, Little, Brown and Company, 1970, pp. 122ff; and please refer to Sheldon Goldman and Thomas P. Jahnige, *The Federal Courts as a Political System*, Harper and Row, 1971, p. 178 for related explanation.

such an added work load. If the dispute of the collegiate panel on the case trial emerges, it will do no good to any judge. If a collegiate panel cannot solve its own disputes, it will possibly make leaders in the court think that judges on the collegiate panel are not competent in their professional work and not capable enough to deal with cases, which may affect their future interests. This factor will force every judge on the collegiate panel work hard to reach an agreement. This shows that even in the democratic group decisions of the collegiate panel, there is also a trace of the administrative systems of the court. After all, the collegiate panel is only a judicial system built in the court.

2.5 The Final Review

Based on the abstract, this chapter "describes" the decision process of judgment inside China's courts, as well as its complex features. This is a description of "ideal type." In reality, the decision process of every court and even every case is different. But this chapter has roughly generalized the basic features of the process of China's courts, especially the courts at the basic level in trial cases. This kind of generalization is different not only from the former trial system of court regulated by law, but from the court administrative system as well. It is actually the combination of the actual function of these two systems in reality.

This chapter neither intends to go deep into discussion of the rationality or limitations of this system[36] nor tries to trace back to their historical origins or transitions. It does not want to investigate other external systems or social factors which create the administration of the court's judicial system, although these external factors may be preconditions for the court to demand and have a powerful administrative system. I would like to excavate certain implied meaning of research on countermeasures and jurisprudence based on the above-mentioned description and analysis.

As far as countermeasures are concerned, although this chapter has pointed out that the judicial system of China's court is dominated by the internal administrative system of the court and to a certain extent has become the subsidiary to the internal administration of the court, and I have implied criticism on this, I still don't try to avoid or reject court administrative issues by using ostrich tactics. I do

[36]Although this chapter has made criticisms on the internal administrative system and the judicial system of China's court, I still don't deny that they have played certain positive roles in China's social environment today. For example, because the average professional qualities of judges in our country are not high, reporting for approval level by level makes more people take part in the case trial. This can, to a certain extent, bring the collective wisdom into play and avoid a wrong judgment; also, it may, to some extent, limit malpractice and corruption of certain judges. From a long-term perspective, whether to implement trial function by this system is reasonable or economic is still doubtful. To support such trial, system demands huge costs and approval at different levels will surely increase litigation costs of clients and delay the litigation. The major reason for the current judicial reform is to increase the efficiency of litigation.

not aim to replace the logistics of life by a logistical life. On the contrary, this chapter has pointed out that the purpose to establish court is to implement its judicial function, but as long as the court is established, administration can't be avoided. So the issue that has been ignored for a long time or forgotten intentionally by China's jurists should be treated seriously. At least from the experience of the Supreme Court of the USA, for a court to effectively implement its judicial functions, the administrative ability of the chief justice is one of the very important factors, apart from his experience of judicial trials or legal knowledge.[37] When China discusses its court reform or judicial reform nowadays, it cannot restrict itself only to reforms in the mode of trials. The reform of the administrative system should not be excluded. This is even more important in modern China, since the administrative affairs faced by China's courts are more in terms of quantity, more complicated, and more onerous. The goal for making efforts should be possible reduction of administrative affairs brought to courts of all levels by institutional defects such as problems of "receiving subsidies from the government" within the general framework of reform in the state political system. However, this goal can't be reached in the short term, as the number of administrative affairs cannot be reduced dramatically within a short time, not to mention be eliminated completely. The internal administration of the court is a practical issue that China's court has to face over the long term. Jurists can eliminate these issues in the jurisprudence framework of separation of powers or judicial independence. But those issues cannot be eliminated from our lives.

---

[37]In the nearly 200 years since John Marshall took the post in the Supreme Court of the USA and the institutional importance of the Supreme Court was truly established, there were altogether 12 Chief Justice (excluding Chief Justice ahead of John Marshall since by then the Supreme Court hadn't established its authority) in the Supreme Court, among which 5 of them did not have any experience in trial courts before taking the post, 3 of them did not have any experience of court trial before taking the post of Chief Justice of Supreme Court, 1 of them had 1 and a half years of experience in the federal court, and John Marshall himself had only 3 years of experience in courts similar to the basic-level people's court in China. The four most capable Chief Justice widely recognized by the US law circle are John Marshall, William Howard Taft, Charles Evans Hughes, and Earl Warren. They were all good at administration. Before taking post of Chief Justice, they all served as very important administrative leaders or exhibited excellent administrative talent: John Marshall used to be Secretary of State, William Howard Taft used to be President, Charles Evans Hughes used to be Vice President and Republican presidential candidate, and Earl Warren used to be the Governor of California. Please refer to Abraham, *Judicial Process*, pp. 56–58, table II. If there had been no Chief Justice Marshall and his excellent talent as a politician not as a lawyer, the Supreme Court of the USA and even the US Constitution would be unimaginable. Benjamin Nathan Cardozo used to point out that "Chief Justice gave to the constitution of the USA the impress of his own mind; and the form of our constitutional law is what it is, because he molded it while it was still plastic and malleable in the fire of his own intense convictions." Please see *The Nature of Judicial Process*, translated by Suli, Commercial Press, 1998, p. 107. Benjamin Nathan Cardozo's comment was objective, but was regarded as inconceivable to legalists: the first regulatory responsibility of a judge to observe constitution and law has gone so far as to mold the so-called most rigid constitution of the USA. However, this is a history which does not necessarily follow standards and logic, and often seems to be like this.

The other key point hidden in this chapter is that the problem of China's courts may not be the large number of administrative affairs (although this is certainly one factor), but may lie in the mixing up of functions of administrative institutions and trial institutions. There is no division of different court functions which is based on its basic function or constitutional function. If we need to increase the level of specialization and professionalism of the court, then this division of functions deserves more attention. I can't agree with some scholars who believe that the problem of China's judicial reform is to eliminate those systems inside the court which fail to integrate into the world, like the system of a judicial committee. As far as I see, a judicial committee is one of the few formal judicial institutions inside the courts of our country. As a trial institution, its function is quite reasonable in China's basic-level courts. If it is eliminated, under the current court administrative institution, the current administrative feature of the court will be further intensified to my prediction (dominated by current court administrative institutions, how the single judge or judges of a collegiate panel can possibly "hold up the court directly" under the pressures of a misjudged case investigation system, supervision of justice by the people's congress, and supervision by public opinion). I don't deny that the operation of the judicial committee of courts at all levels have problems, but those problems exactly reflect that because the judicial committee system is built in the current court administrative institution, the logic of administration limits the composition of its members, restricts its role in the Chinese court, and weakens its judicial function. If the judicial function of this system is earnestly strengthened, separated from the current administrative institution of the court, and made the legitimate and last judicial decision organization inside the court, it may not be in line with the idea of the independence of judges, but rather the strong administrative feature of "leading cadres assuming responsibilities" of court can be weakened dramatically, at least.

If this analysis can hold water, then the reform of judicial methods or systems of court can start with the separation of system functions. Even from my own perspective, the transformation of functions of the Chinese court can be realized and the system logic of the court as a trial organ be cleared only be getting hold of this point. That's why the approach of my research overlaps with the popular approach taken by the current court system, but there are still some differences. The popular viewpoint of the current court system and jurist circle is that there are two ways to consolidate China's judicial or trial independence. One way is to reform trial methods, and the other way is to settle the power over finances and personnel, that is to say to "receive subsidies from the government" financially while enjoying the power of choosing appropriate persons for jobs. These two aspects are very important indeed. But my analysis has demonstrated that this kind of reform is not good enough and even misses the point. As a matter of fact, the current reform of trial methods can also be seen and even should be seen as reform of the administrative institutions of the court. It actually intends to separate the procedures which mingle with the trial and have the feature of administration from the trial process (such as the so-called holding the court directly). But my analysis that members of the collegiate panel are trying to seek common grounds in the last paragraph of the previous section have demonstrated that even the current jurist circle is optimistic about the system of trial by collegiate panel, despite in fact being influenced by court administrative institutions through some other channels. We must realize that if we don't separate and adjust the functions of these two institutions inside the court, even when we have "government subsidies" and power to use appropriate personnel, it will be difficult to weaken the current administrative features of China's courts. On the contrary, the administrative features of the court system will be even stronger. The result may be that the court is more independent of administrative departments, but there won't necessarily be any improvement in the issue of trial independence, since in terms of judicial professionalism, a judge in the highly administrative court which is independent of administrative departments does not necessarily enjoy more power of judicial decision than judges under current situation. There is even the possibility that they have fewer powers of judicial decision.

In addition, this chapter has demonstrated that it is not to the point to simply discuss judicial democracy, democratic participation, and the fact of democratic supervision, which is to give a prescription with popular ideology and cure disease with panacea. The administrative trial process of China's court also has its decision democracy, although this kind of democratic product is not the desired end product.

We must emphasize that China's court has gradually formed its own system of logic and professional tradition of justice based on its separation of functions.[38] In Chinese history, there was no distinction between judges and administrative officials. The court of contemporary times was approximately separated from "Yamen" (government office) based on the philosophy of the separation of powers, and it was easily seen by political leaders and ordinary people as an administrative organ to settle disputes, but not a typical judicial institution. Without separation of powers, it was naturally very difficult to foster professional judges. Without professional judges, the execution of court trial functions could only be ensured by logic and an administrative system, which has in turn changed the due system and logic of the court. From this, we can see that the formation of judicial independence of trial independence is not only and even mainly not based on how it is stipulated by law and whether it has transplanted or believed in certain philosophy or principle, but a product of a series of comprehensive social conditions.

For the purpose of legal research, this chapter has, first of all, demonstrated how different institutions auxiliary to the same organ but targeting different problems erode each other and deform institutions. The administrative institutions seriously erode and assimilate other institutions of certain organs. This phenomenon is often seen in modern China. There are examples everywhere. The administrative logic of the university outweighs the logic of university as an organ of education and scientific research. The administrative logic of enterprise outweighs the logic of an enterprise as a market business. The analysis of this essay may therefore somewhat enlighten the research in the institutional problems of many social

[38]Please refer to Suli: "On the specialization of legal activities," in *Rule of Law and its Native Resources*, China University f Politics and Law Press, 1996.

organizations in modern China. As a by-product, it also challenges the popular and strict philosophy of the separation of powers, which has to some extent become a new ideology. No organization in reality can implement a single and pure function. The histories of constitutional development in many Western countries have actually proved this point.[39] In addition, this research can also help us to understand how the institutional functions (i.e., responsibilities) of a certain organ have changed or transformed.

Secondly, in terms of research on the judicial system, the empirical approach of this chapter helps to eliminate the research blind spot brought about by the traditional approach of jurisprudence to discuss court functions. It also brings the internal administration which is requisite to the court into the vision of research jurists. It may help us to have a fairer and more comprehensive understanding of the system by which the Chinese court actually functions. It may also provide a new but more practical understanding on issues currently existing in the Chinese court system, as well as the possibility and approach of the reform of the court system. It is not a kind of criticism of ideology simply based on judicial principle or international standards.

Thirdly, for a long period of time, China's jurisprudence and jurisprudential circle paid attention only to research on legal texts, but not to those informal systems. They ignore informal systems, especially those taking shape in the formal systems, although people are generally restricted by those informal systems. This chapter starts from analyzing two formal systems inside the Chinese court and points out the obvious but often neglected informal systems that have been formed by the mix-up of these two formal systems. These informal systems, no matter whether they are regarded as custom or habit, are large in number and play practical roles in many aspects of modern China. This research not only proves that we must have empirical research and analysis of a large number of specific systems in order to discover (but not approves since discovering may only aims to transform) all kinds of informal systems that actually influence social lives. It also demonstrates that unlike what many jurists have imagined that the informal systems only exist in Chinese rural areas that wait to be modernized. They are just living with us, within the fields which to our belief are under the complete control of formal systems and in which the formal systems play their roles.

First draft on Feb 26th, 1999

Modified and finalized on March 6th in Weixiu Garden, Peking University

[39]Please refer to M.J.C. Vile: Constitutionalism and the Separation of Power, translated by Suli, SDX Joint Publishing Company, 1997.

Chapter 3
The Judicial Committee System in Basic-level Courts

To acquire knowledge, we need to study the phenomena of nature. We study the phenomena of nature in order to acquire knowledge.

—The Great Leaning.

3.1 The Definition of a Problem

The judicial committee mentioned in the last chapter is a specific system with Chinese characteristics in the courts of modern China. In recent years, with the slogan of "integration into the world" getting more and more popular, and with the development in reforms of the judicial system and amendment of litigation procedural laws under way, the jurist circle has more thoughts on this system. In general, some views are already published[1] and discussed in academic circles that tend to call for the abolishment (although most of them do not say it

[1]Several related articles are, for example, Wang Qiguo, Zhang Diqiu: "On Due Attributes of Judicial Independence," *Science of Law*, Issue 3, 1989; Lü Yazhong: "Thoughts on Improving the Working System of Judicial Committee," *Legal Science Monthly*, Issue 5, 1996; Kong Xiancui: "Legal Guarantee Mechanism Need to be Established to Ensure the Independent Trial of People's Courts," *Modern Law Science*, Issue 5, 1995; Tan Shigui: "On Judicial Independence," *Tribune of Political Science and Law*, Issue 1, 1997. The essay of He Weifang: "Two Problems of China's Judicial Management System" (*Social Sciences in China*, Issue 6, 1997) mainly criticizes the setup and function of judicial committee from the point of judicial bureaucracy. In addition, there are some articles focusing on international standard to review China's judicial procedures. The judicial committee has been criticized as well. For example Chen Ruihua: "China's Code of Criminal Procedure After Amendment—Analysis From The Point of International Standard of Criminal Justice," *Modern Law Science*, Issue 5, 1996; Yue Liling, Chen Ruihua: "International Standard of Criminal Procedural Justice and Criminal Procedure Law After Amendment (I)," T*ribune of Political Science and Law*, Issue 3, 1997.

© Foreign Language Teaching and Research Publishing Co., Ltd and Springer Science+Business Media Singapore 2016

S. Zhu, *Sending Law to the Countryside*, China Academic Library,
DOI 10.1007/978-981-10-1142-9_3

publicly) of judicial committees. We have not seen any argument with different views. However, this situation does not mean that this view predominates in the jurist or legal circles. On the contrary, it may be because the people supporting the judicial committee are in fact in the majority. With approval by the Organic Law of the People's Court and other laws, they tend to take it for granted psychologically.

From the practical and long-term point of view, to truly prove the rationality and justification of a system, we must make sure that it functions normally under many specific restrictive conditions of the society and that people actually accept and approve this system. But at a time when reform is needed and "reform" itself has been regarded as an ideology, a system which is in fact feasible still needs to prove the justification and rationality of its existence intellectually. When "integration into the world" and "Chinese characteristics" can be used as trump cards in discussion, a system which only claims that it is localized is not convincing enough. If we launch our discussion only from the above two propositions, no matter what our intentions or final conclusions are, the discussion is in fact just a new ideological language. The more sufficient our discussion is, the poorer our thoughts are reflected. The superficial vitality is only a kind of "aphasia" caused by a lack of empirical research and theoretical reflection. It is also true that arguments lacking in thoughts and theoretical powers sometimes are not necessarily short of strong action powers. Once social trends including "Chinese characteristic" and "integration with the world" emerge, people sometimes have to compromise and make concessions. China's jurist circle should not give up its independent empirical research and theoretical thoughts regarding all events, nor should it give simple approval only because certain systems have "local characteristics," just as it should not give simple approval only due to "integration into the world." For this reason, the research and thoughts on judicial committee systems are meaningful. Its meaning is not only limited to whether it should be abolished or not.

In summary, there are approximately two points of argument for those who stand for the abolishment of judicial committees. First, there is no judicial committee in the courts of developed countries, whether they are of an Anglo-American legal system or of a Continental legal system. Second, by discussing important, complicated, and difficult cases put forward by judges,[2] the judicial committee infringes on independent trials of justice, especially for the judge. Consequently (this logic relation actually does not necessarily hold water), it is not conducive to the just execution of social functions by justice. In fact, these two arguments and their grounds are very different. We should first of all focus on what I think are the most important issues.

[2]Article 11 of the Organic Law of the People's Court.

The first argument that the judicial committee is not in line with global practices is in fact an inductive reference. Let us suppose that this induction is complete, and it is truly a "world" practice.[3] We naturally should attach importance even if it is only practiced by Western developed countries. Whether from the point of functionalism or from the point of sociology of evolutionary rational knowledge of Popper and Hayek, we normally assume that a system must have its own reason of existence, i.e., its contextual rationality, if it is established, and it should be respected and understood by latecomers and outsiders. In this sense, the practice that courts of all developed countries in the world function without a judicial committee deserves attention.

But this is exactly the reason that weakens the persuasion of this proposition as an argument. First of all, we can very well point out, based on the same reason, that there is rationality for the judicial committee to persist for a long time in modern China. Secondly, the persuasion of the proposition from inductive reasoning has been widely recognized as limited since the time of David Hume.[4] The existing inductive reasoning must be incomplete induction, which is always based on what it used to be and what it is now. This kind of induction may construct expectations for the future, but it cannot stipulate that the future process should be or must be as it is. Particularly speaking, systems are all formed to deal with normal problems in formal ways. Their true meaning is practical and points toward the future, which is forever open-ended. Hence, the truly persuasive argument must go deeper into detailed theoretical analysis and argumentation than simple enumeration. Thirdly, this argumentation implies the end of knowledge, viewing the systems created by Chinese and foreign ancestors in a specific social and historical space and time as the end of knowledge and the embodiment of the truth. This actually denies the necessity and possibility for people creating new systems and knowledge by practice and also implies that the specific time and space in which the systems and knowledge are born and function is forgotten completely.[5] It is doubtless that this kind of view may remind us to be cautious instead of pompous, but on the other hand, it may also cause us to lose confidence in and attention to our long-time experience. If our task is only to pursue the words of our ancestors and foreigners, then being a scholar would not mean anything any longer. Suppose

[3]As far as I have recently seen, this is actually an empirical proposition based on China's current endeavors to cope with the practices of developed countries, since I have never noticed anyone citing "laws" of the Maldives or Eskimo to criticize judicial committee. I am saying this not to "make a fuss," but to try to demonstrate that the so-called practice and the fact that people think this argument is convincing have implied the pursuit of "modernization" of modern Chinese. If we say that there is a certain cause–effect relationship between the existence of judicial committees and the modernization of a country, I am afraid it will be far-fetched and unconvincing.

[4]David Hume, *Treaties of Human Nature*, translated by Guan Wenyun, proofread by Zheng Zhixiang, the Commercial Press, 1980.

[5]About the reliance of knowledge on time and space, please refer Chap. 6 of this book "Inbetween Facts and Laws" and Chap. 8 "Delivery of Judicial Knowledge of Basic-level Judges."

the truth were already there and established, then by what significance could our research be regarded as academic or scientific? Certainly, the true situation is that "there is nothing new under the sun," but we cannot accept it as a fact before this assumption is confirmed. In a sense, the life of a scholar is to go beyond those boundaries that are already known.

The reason that the first argument is not persuasive is because this argument does not constitute a reason alone. As a matter of fact, a "practice" cannot become a standard for reference and an objective to strive for naturally. "Practice" can become persuasive and be regarded as a frame of reference and deserving of pursuit only when it has been built with a "natural connection," with certain accepted desirable targets in people's minds. Even if the global practice is to eat bread, it does not prove that you should give up having rice, unless you could prove that bread is more nutritious and thus more desirable than rice. But once it has been proved that rice is more nutritious than bread, it is not necessary to discuss whether eating rice is a common practice or a special case.

Thus, in comparison, the second argument is more practical and more powerful and deserves more attention. What people really care about is the impartial and effective execution of social functions by courts and judges to the promise of judicial independence, as well as the social prosperity and modernization induced from the above. The paradoxical persuasiveness of global practices actually lies here. Thus, to observe in detail the actual influence of judicial committees on judicial independence, especially the actual influence on the judicial impartiality which places more importance in the back and is assumed to have a direct cause–effect relationship with judicial independence, will be of more strategic significance in argumentation. In addition, because this argument underscores the role played by a judicial committee in real life and is an empirical proposition, it is possible for us to observe, test, and verify through empirical study and avoid definitions of scholasticism and a war of propositions. This article tends to observe whether this objection is true and reliable.

3.2 Approaches, Methods, and Materials

The above two arguments of objection are supported by some empirical evidence. There are many scholars who have pointed out lots of real examples to prove that the judicial committee does have disadvantages, like "trial without decision and decision without trial," "court decisions after hearing," "collective irresponsibility," and others.[6] This is somewhat persuasive beyond any doubt. However, there are still not enough reasons to abolish a judicial committee system based on this. History has told us that there are no systems that are perfect enough to have no

---

[6]As in note 1.

disadvantages. If we abolished systems because they have disadvantages, then I'm afraid there would be no systems left to implement, at present or in the future. It is right to have a mentality of pursuing perfection, but the mentality exists only because every real system is not perfect. Perfection means no room for improvement, an end of history, and system solidification with no development or changes in the future and no relations between systems and specific space, time, and environments. Thus, it is not specific, but universal.

Empirical research does not equate to wishes supported by experience (though there is a relationship here). It seeks to understand as comprehensively as possible the advantages and disadvantages of a system, make a judgment based on the comparison of advantages and disadvantages, and then make a choice. It does not discover from real life something to support, intensify its experience, expressions, or even certain doctrine. The latter "research," even supported by some experience, still makes people take a part for a whole and stick to their own argument without mutual understanding, communication, and meaningful discussion. The research conclusions obtained from this mentality and stubbornness, whether supporting or opposing a system or view, are in the same category, since they have identical argumentation.

To really verify or develop a proposition which may have, or be viewed as having, universality, one important point is to pay attention to or make effort to find out examples which are opposite to universal propositions or one's own knowledge from empirical research. Karl Popper regarded it as "falsification," which is regarded by Chinese as "fuss making." Certainly, it is very difficult to strictly copy Popper's "falsification" in humanities and social science research. In social life, "fuss making" is not liked in any country, and this kind of human nature often finds itself in the academic circle. But nevertheless, the basic requirement for empirical research is to put as many facts as possible opposed to the judgment we have made before. More specifically, if we oppose to a judicial committee, it is necessary for us to pay attention to those facts and evidence which at least seem to be in favor of a judicial committee and vice versa. This is neither without principle, nor personality split, or the so-called "tolerance". This is the only way for us to increase our knowledge. Hunger for knowledge, if it still has any real meaning, does not simply mean to solidify what we already understand, but to try to understand what we have not understood.

Facts do not naturally support or oppose a certain view. Their evidential weight and persuasion constitute theories. Different people have different value-related judgments on the same facts and have their own views on the significance of the facts. Considering this factor, this chapter will not discuss in a general way whether the judicial committee is in line with the concept of judicial independence. Nor will it explain the advantages and/or disadvantages of judicial committees. It will only try to demonstrate how the judicial committee system is connected to certain realities and characteristics of Chinese society and to reveal "the logic of things." Of course this may only be a kind of ambition. As a matter of fact, nobody could display to the readers all characteristics of Chinese society. Different people will have different views on whether these characteristics do exist and whether they are reasonable or not; thus, it is up to the readers themselves to understand the judicial committee system based on their own experience and feelings of their social lives in China. But this will not prevent me from putting forward some conclusions and views based on these materials. It must be noted that although I put forward those realities and characteristics, and emphasize and admit their influence on the function of the system, it does not mean that I approve or agree with those realities. It only implies that I see them as a social environment or a restrictive condition that will not change much for a short period of time and in which courts and judges will have to function.

There is still a need to choose an appropriate starting point. I do not care about texts. Nor do I attach importance to the intention of people who have created this system. Related authoritative historical documents have talked about the original purpose for setting up the judicial committee, which is to "mainly sum up the trial experience, and study major and difficult cases."[7] Due to the historical conditions at the beginning of the establishment of New China, it can be said that this system was in connection with how to ensure the Chinese Communist Party which had just obtained political power to establish and take the charge of the unified justice, as well as reform the "outdated justice" from the very beginning. It was in fact one of the system measures to ensure the centralized and unified leadership of the Chinese Communist Party and the state power, as well as stable political power which functions effectively.[8] As far as this system designed by the Chinese communists is concerned, people with different positions certainly have different judgments and comments. Thus, it will be difficult to conduct effective discussion-based materials presented by this chapter.

There is another important reason to ignore the texts and the intention of system design; that is, I don't think that the intention could determine the operation of this system after its birth or its institutional functions actually gained during the operation. The initial design of the judicial committee system when China was newly built and its actual functional change are typical examples. From this point of view, the initial purpose of the system designer is not important.[9] Nor is it

[7]Dong Biwu: "To earnestly implement and execute the Organic Law of the People's Courts and the Organic Law of the People's Procurators," and "Speech made at the conference attended by procurators of PLA military procurators and presidents of PLA military courts," selected from *Dong Biwu Collection*, People's Publishing House, 1985.

[8]Please refer to Dong Biwu: "On the ideological work of the Party on political and legal aspects" and "Issues related to the reform of people working for the outdated justice," as the previous note.

[9]"But 'purpose of law' is the last thing we should apply to the history of emergence of law. … the origin of the emergence of a thing and its ultimate usefulness, its practical application, and incorporation into a system of ends, are *toto coelo* separate; … and overpowering and dominating consist of re-interpretation, adjustment, in the process of which their former 'meaning' and 'purpose' must necessarily be obscured or completely obliterated." Nietzsche: "On the Genealogy of Morality," translated by Zhou Hong, SDX Joint Publishing Company, 1992, pp. 55–56. Please refer to Suli: "How are systems formed?" *Journal of Comparative Law*, Issue 1, 1998.

original,[10] although they cannot be ignored completely. It is a common phenomenon in the transition of human social systems to put new wine into old bottles. It is also frequently seen in the evolution of legal systems.[11] Thus, when we observe this system today, we should pay more attention to how this system operates today and what its institutional functions actually are.

The other point that makes me confused is how to operate with judicial independence as an abstract concept and explicit ideal at the empirical level. Judicial independence at the level of general understanding is roughly that the judge will make just rulings freely based on his or her review of the case facts and understanding of law, without any direct or indirect restriction, influence, temptation, pressure, threat, or interference from any aspect or from any reason.[12] As empirical phenomena, however, the power execution of every judge is bound to be affected by all kinds of influences, restrictions, temptations, and even pressures which are desirable or undesirable in his or her society,[13] unless this judge has no power or is of no significance. Take the most "independent" US justice as an example: In every lawsuit, lawyers of both sides usually make arguments by all means and try to use their testimony and confrontation to influence and induce judges to make decisions in their favor.[14] In all criminal cases and the majority of civil cases, the jury enjoys ultimate authority on factual disputes. This does not only restrict but also fundamentally eliminate the role of judge's review on the case facts in regard to justice (it is the same even when the judge agrees with

---

[10]The Foucault Reader: Nietzsche, Genealogy, History, translated by Suli, *Review of Academic Thoughts*, Issue 4, Niaoning University Press, 1998.

[11]For example, the transition of the jury system in the Anglo-American Law, the consideration system of the contract law, and action in ream of the maritime law. History has changed both the appearance and function of those systems.

[12]Please refer to Article 2 of World Declaration of Judicial Independence.

[13]In the analysis model of Posner, even judicial independence itself can be understood as a design of former members in the legislative organ to ensure their stable transaction with social interest groups. In other words, the so-called judicial independence is to make sure that the justice be influenced more by former members of the legislative organ instead of their successors. Posner even concluded further that the shorter the expected valid period, the weaker the judicial independence on this legislation. Posner even quoted some empirical research results to support this point. Please see Richard A. Posner, *Economic Analysis of Law*, 4th ed., Little, Brown and Company, 1994, p. 533 and its note 4.

[14]Alan Dershowitz wrote in one of his books that one of the rules for judicial struggle is "not one person is really in need of justice," but "what is sarcastically is that the result actually arrived at is probably a kind of approximately fair justice." *The Best Defense*, translated by Tang Jiaodong, Law Press China, 1994, pp. 5–12.

jury's decision).[15] Apart from judges of the Supreme Court, almost every judge has to, to some extent, consider whether his or her judgment will be repealed or changed by courts at a higher level, and thus, they will adjust decisions accordingly.[16] Even the judges of the Supreme Court of the USA who enjoy the strongest independence will ask for support in judgments of certain cases and vote for each other to make sure that their own votes have decisive power. The Chief Justice or certain judges with more charisma will try to influence the decisions of other judges, and they most certainly do have some influences.[17] A most famous example is the Brown V. Board of Education case. Newly appointed Chief Justice Warren made "tremendous efforts in persuasion" in order to make judgment more authoritative. He even spoke about the unity that the Supreme Court needed to obtain at the time. The opposition judges were finally persuaded into reaching an

---

[15]There are many general descriptions and empirical research of this kind. For example, a famous American judge Jerome Frank, based on his judicial experience of many years, said that "the jury is the worst possible enemy of this ideal of the supremacy of law." He thought it would be better if the judge himself hears the case. Generally speaking, those supporting the jury are trial lawyers, since they "have immediate interests that can influence the jury." Please see Henry J. Abraham, *Judicial Process*, 4th ed., Oxford University Press, 1980, pp. 138–139. Posner thinks that one of the actual roles of the jury is to let people of different experiences and views review the case in order to counterbalance the specialty of the professional judge. Please see *Economic Analysis of Law*, as the previous note 13, p. 583. Kalven and Zeisel discovered in their famous research in 1960s that in criminal cases, about 25 % of juries had different views on the case disputes from the judge's judgment. Please see Kalven, Jr. And Hans Zeisel, "The American Jury: Some General Observation," *American Jury*, Little, Brown and Company, 1966. According to many scholars, the American society in the 1960s had a higher social homogeneity. But in 1970s, the social homogeneity was lower and thus disputes between the jury and the judge should have grown, which meant that juries had much stronger restrictions on the substantial judgments of the judges.

[16]When analyzing and reviewing the opinion of Oliver Wendell Holmes that "law is the forecast of case outcomes, Posner pointed out that most of the judges would be very sensitive about the overruling of their judgment by higher courts. They therefore would forecast decisions of higher courts and adjust their judgments accordingly. Although Posner thought this kind of practice undesirable. Please see *The Problem of Jurisprudence*, translated by Suli, China University of Politics and Law, 1994, p. 285. Please also see, Alan Dershowitz believes that the most important is that the judge "doesn't want higher court to overrule their judgment, … they see overruling of original judgment by higher court as personal humiliation and career failure…" as previous note 14, p. 6. In modern China, at least a large number of basic-level courts have such regulation as if judgment is overruled or changed by higher court, the judge of original judgment will lose some bonus or other visible or invisible interests. This has made Chinese judges of basic level whose incomes are not that high are more sensitive and careful about the overruling of their judgment at least in theory.

[17]There are so many empirical researches of this kind with different perspectives. Please refer to, for example, Herbert Jacob's empirical research and theoretical model based on organization theory, "Courts as Organizations" in *Empirical Theories about Courts* (Keith O. Boyum and Lynn Mather (eds.), 1983), pp. 291ff. David J. Danelski, "The Influence of the Chief Justice in the Decisional Process of the Supreme Court," and David J. Danelski and Jeanne C. Danelski, "Leadership in the Warren Court," both articles are collected in Sheldon Goldman and Austin Sarat (eds.), *American Court Systems*, Longman, 1989, pp. 486–499, 500–510.

agreement on the ruling.[18] There is another famous example: In 1936, under the threat of Roosevelt to "repackage the Supreme Court," the Supreme Court of the USA changed its judicial judgment on the legislation of President Roosevelt's "New Deal."[19]

Many of those easily available examples and case studies[20] do not deny the concept of judicial independence and its desirability. Nor do they try to disclose the hypocrisy of judicial independence in the West. I'm just trying to point out that from the empirical level, and judicial independence does not mean that judges are not influenced by, restricted, or interfered with. As a matter of fact, in practice, one of the key issues of judicial independence is to use a set of mechanisms to prevent a judge from using his or her power to pursue personal interests, or to prevent them from imposing on the society their individual and even lofty ideals, which are beyond the social standards.[21] However, it is difficult for us to distinguish what is just, desirable for the society, and/or at least tolerable limitation, restriction, and influence supporting judicial independence and ensuring justice, from what is not influence of this kind.

The fact that it is difficult to distinguish does not mean that we are unable to distinguish them at all. In theory, for example, I can design a set of questionnaires which include a series of questions which did really happen and which I myself design. I can even include many social backgrounds and conditions which I will discuss later into the questionnaire to make it a public survey. There also some other methods, but those methods are not only expensive, and, as far as I'm concerned, are not possibly accurate or realistic. For example, the public may have a high demand for judges' morality (to enforce laws impartially), but they do not understand that many legal issues actually cannot be solved by moral traits of judges. As another example, not many ordinary people in China now think that a judge can and should ignore his or her "superior" (president, country magistrate, and chairman of people's congress), or ignore volatile public opinions. We can certainly add many restrictions, but I'm afraid those tricky questionnaire surveys cannot be well understood by ordinary people who will not have the time or energy to cooperate with us.

My starting point is judges' own reviews of judicial committees. I have solid reasons to choose this as a starting point. First of all, although judicial independence

---

[18]Please refer to Bernard Schwartz, *Super Chief*, New York University Press, 1983.

[19]Many writings about US Constitution have recorded this incident. Please refer to David M. O'Brien, *Storm Center: The Supreme Court in American Politics*, 2nd ed., Norton, 1990, pp. 87ff.

[20]This may be least imported by China's jurisprudence when learning from the West. Up till now, what have been "imported" most are still those propositions and categories of political philosophy in the eighteenth and nineteenth century published in the twentieth century, but not results or methods of empirical research which attach importance to experience that has been greatly developed since the twentieth century.

[21]Please see Posner's analysis of this issue: "but independence means only that judges decide cases as they like without pressure from other officials, it is not obvious that independent judiciary is in the public interest..." *The Problem of Jurisprudence*, same as the above, p. 8.

is initially a political topic (on which every citizen can make his voice heard), this issue was actually raised by judges in modern times[22] and was realized with the emergence of judges as an occupation group.[23] For this reason, generally speaking, judges not only should be more sensitive toward this issue, but due to the rule that "only toes will know whether the shoes fit," their feelings should be most distinct. Secondly, we have a basic assumption from common knowledge; that is, nobody wants to be "looked after" forever, even when this looking-after is not excessive. Thus, if the judicial committee often inappropriately interferes with, restricts, or influences the independent judgment of judges, then those judges would certainly feel more strongly than outsiders. They also have a better understanding of advantages and disadvantages of judicial committees, and their analysis is more to the point. This approach has highlighted the objective feelings and perspectives of judges and avoided to impose certain views on others, which must be implied and brought about by the action of using systematic "general rules" or idealized logic as the standard for judgment.

If we divide judges into judges of first instance and judges of appeals (second instances and retrials), we choose to study the judges of first instance in the people's courts of the basic level. We have reasons for this choice.

First of all, it is about the attainability of materials. Promoted by the Zhongnan University of Politics and Law situated in Wuhan, as well as the Hubei High People's Court, and founded by the Ford Foundation, Zhongnan University of Politics and Law has organized trainings for judges of basic-level courts and intermediate courts in the Province of Hubei since 1995. I was lucky enough to become one of the lecturers for this class twice a year. At the time of writing this article, I have been lecturer for this training class seven times. This kind of situation has provided possibility and convenience for my project research and concentrated interviews. If interviewing judges of courts above the intermediate level, I would face inconveniences related to time, access, and costs.

Secondly, work in courts of first instance is more complicated, and knowledge and experience of judges of first instance cases may be of more significance to our research. I have two reasons for saying this: First instance is expected to resolve

---

[22]The earliest example about judicial independence that be quoted most frequently by people today is the famous anecdote about British Chief Justice Sir Edward Coke's boycott of interference of justice by King of England James I. Please refer to George Holland Sabine: *A History of Political Theory*, translated by Liu Shan, Commercial Press, 1990, pp. 509ff.

[23]About general demonstration, please see Suli: "On Specialization of Legal Activities," R*ule of Law and Its Native Resource*, China's University of Politics and Law Press, 1996, especially paragraph 2. In fact, the most important and central argument about Sir Edward Coke's boycott of interference of Justice by James is that judges have special skills of justice, that is the so-called the artificial reason, not the political philosophy and ethic philosophy popular in the textbooks of jurisprudence. The judicial censorship actually showing judicial independence of the USA is also creation of US Chief Justice Marshall. Please see Suli: "How Do Systems Take Shape?"*Journal of Comparative Law*, Issue 1, 1998.

factual disputes and legal disputes. But normally speaking, instances of appeals pay more attention to legal disputes (the second instance in China cares more about legal disputes but pays attention to factual disputes as well) and is therefore relatively simple. Their different positions make their demands for systems dissimilar and even quite different.[24] Second, judges of first instances build every case from scratch, but judges of appeal (second instances) not only have advantages in regard to legal information and professional training, but also have judicial opinions of judges of first instance as reference for their own decisions. Even if judges of first instance make an incorrect judgment, the reference cannot be denied. In addition, in China, the majority of first-instance cases are undertaken by basic-level courts and intermediate courts (intermediate courts also undertake a large number of cases of second instance), and thus, our research focus will be naturally on judges of basic-level courts.

The materials for analysis and discussion in this chapter are mainly our interviews of judges in the spring and autumn of 1997 and the spring of 1998, as well as our field research of some basic-level courts in the spring of 1998. We have interviewed in detail about 100 judges of basic-level courts and a few judges of intermediate courts. Their degrees of education are mostly high school or higher.[25] Although there are a few university graduate or junior college graduates among them, a large number of them have obtained their legal training, diplomacy training, and even a bachelor's degree in law through correspondence college, TV university, and especially part-time college in the legal system, among which none is a graduate with a bachelor's degree in law or legal training before working in the courts. According to our field research, this kind of situation can approximately

[24]Please refer to analysis by Posner in *The Problem of Jurisprudence*, the same as previous note 16, pp. 261ff. It must be noted that as far as the system level is concerned, China's second instance is even simpler than the instance of appeal in the USA. It is because first of all, China adopts statutes system and its applied laws are relatively simple, but the USA adopts case law system in which judge-made laws and legal interpretation are very important and complicated. Secondly, China has a higher social homogeneity than the USA, and thus, the application of law and legal interpretation in China have less disputes than those in the USA. Then, the challenge to the professional knowledge of judges of appeal is much lower in China. But under special circumstances (e.g., when there are conflicts between laws and public feelings or local interests), this kind of high homogeneity has obviously higher pressure on judges directly hearing the case or judges of first instance than judges of second-instance courts. Also please refer to related analysis of the following section of "analysis of two examples."

[25]Due to the phenomenon of education devaluation in China in recent years, the actual education level of judges may be lower than that in their files. Please refer to He Weifang: "Realizing Social Justice Through Judiciary: A Perspective On Current Situations of Chinese Judges," *The Age Heading Toward Power*, edited by Xia Yong and etc., China University of Politics and Law Press, 1995, pp. 225ff.

reflect the education degree of judges of basic-level courts in this province.[26] This is of special significance to my analysis. Judges interviewed are aged 25–45, with average time working in the court between 8 and 10 years. About half of the interviewees are presidents of courts or of higher positions. Some judges themselves are members of judicial committees and "management personnel," and they are therefore somewhat different from judges "being managed." I will give appropriate attention to this point in my analysis.

During the interview, most judges showed that they were very well aware of their courts. They were not only familiar and sensitive with related legal texts, but also understood issues in the workings of courts in today's China and were socially sophisticated. Generally speaking, they felt proud of working in the courts as professionals and even had moral superiority compared to those working in other governmental organizations or departments,[27] but they also did not avoid many problems existing in the works of the court system, or even serious problems that required immediate solutions. They did not lack self-criticism or self-reflection. There was one judge that was most typical and moved us most. This judge took the lead in conducting judicial reform 10 years ago, made remarkable achievements, and was therefore established as a model judge for many years. During the interview, he had profound reflections and criticisms on his own reform measures, which have been widely promoted as model experiences in those years and in principle overturned his reform approaches in those years.

We are quite confident that the materials we have obtained through interview are reliable and credible. First of all, these interviews were conducted one by one. Since the interviews were conducted far from where judges worked, and their colleges and departments were not involved, these judges were less inhibited during the interview than normally speaking. Secondly, the focus of our interview was court operation. We did not pay direct attention to whether a specific case was dealt with correctly or incorrectly, and started from their normal experiences and feelings (but we also did not refuse to understand and even sometimes made detailed inquiries of specific cases or case details mentioned by the interviewees); thus, it did not constitute threats posed by the superior when checking over the work. Thirdly, from our observation, most judges interviewed were quite honest. They did not avoid questions and even criticized issues related to court personnel and financial systems, as well as issues related to the working style of the party

[26]In principle, it cannot explain the basic situations of professional training for judges in the basic-level courts in China. Our research is targeted at judicial training classes. Judges obtaining formal law bachelor degree normally do not receive this kind of training. But our field research and interviews have enabled us to notice that most of the basic-level courts seldom have and even do not have graduates of bachelor's degree from formal law schools. Even in the basic-level courts in certain counties in the suburbs of Shanghai Municipality, university graduates account for only 10 %, not to mention graduates with a bachelor's degree in law. Please seeWang Yuan: "Court Independence and Its Dilemma" (not published).

[27]Almost all interviewed judges claimed that among public security organs, courts and procurators, courts are the most honest and are complained about the least by ordinary people, although this claim is not reliable enough.

and the general mood of society. They even had true and credible self-criticism or self-mockery. Fourthly, there was a special relationship between the research and the interviewees. I was a lecturer for short-term training classes from another place without any potential, public, current, or future interest conflicts with the judges I interviewed. Nor could I bring them any special interests. This kind of special relationship and my special identity enabled us to enjoy mutual trust of a certain degree: They could prefer not to say something, but they at least did not feel compelled to tell lies. We also enjoyed mutual respect of certain degree: It was worthwhile to tell the truth to interviewers from Peking University. Some judges even brought us some difficult cases for analysis. Also, since there were a large number of judges interviewed, and we used to conduct similar research and studies in provinces like Shaanxi and later went to some basic-level courts and people's courts in Hubei Province for field research, we had different interview materials and field research materials on hand which could complement each other. Although in theory, complementary materials do not necessarily help identify truthful and deceptive answers, my social experience and intuitive judgment are enough to inspire confidence: The materials we have obtained are guaranteed.

3.3 Composition and Operation of Judicial Committees

The judicial committees of basic-level courts under our research all have similar composition. They are normally composed of 9–11 people, namely the president of the court, vice president, and directors of main tribunals.

There are principles regulating the scope of cases under discussion. If the case is tried by a single judge, the judge himself or herself is not certain of the nature of the case or application of law, and he or she has to report to tribunal directors in advance. If the director has the same tentative opinion as the judge undertaking the case, then a conclusion can be reached on the case. If not, the director will report to the vice president in charge. If the vice president is not certain, he or she can report to the president and deliver the case to the judicial committee for discussion.

If the case is heard by a collegiate panel which has a different view from the tribunal director, then the director will report to the vice president in charge who will give suggestions and ask the collegiate panel to rehear the case. If there is still no agreement after retrial, then the vice president will report to the president and submit the case to the judicial committee for discussion.

Why on earth are these cases submitted to the judicial committee for discussion? Only very few cases are submitted to the judicial committee for discussion nowadays.[28] According to our knowledge, in the court of a county which hears

[28]According to the Civil Procedure Law, if judgment or decisions which are already legally effective in the court are found to be wrong factually or legally, and the president of court finds it necessary to rehear the case, then the case will be submitted to the judicial committee for discussion. But as an informal system, the judicial committee will still discuss and decide civil and economic cases with difficulties, although there are only a few of them.

more than 4000 civil and economic cases annually, there are only 20 cases submitted to the judicial committee for discussion. It is said that since 1995, in order to implement a "system of being held accountable for misjudgements," plus be in line with the newly appointed vice president in charge transferred from another unit with rather weak professional abilities, the number of cases submitted to the judicial committee for discussion was on the rise. In 1996 alone, more than 30 cases were submitted to the judicial committee. Another basic-level court also claims that in recent years, there are few civil cases, 3–5 at most, submitted annually to the judicial committee for discussion.

For those civil and economic cases for discussion, they are basically cases with an uncertain nature and are interfered with by related local organs or leaders (especially when local or department interests are involved). Judging from some specific cases discussed, some cases actually do not have any factual or legal issues of difficulty. However, if they are decided according to law, the incapability of implementing the judgment or implementing itself will bring serious results.[29] The reason to submit these cases to the judicial committee for discussion is mainly because it is necessary for the court to decide whether it will come forward as a "unit" to coordinate, implement, and carry out judgment.

There are about 10–15 % criminal cases annually, among which about 20 cases are submitted to the judicial committee for discussion.[30] It is said that cases of detention, probation, or without treatment should be submitted to the judicial committee. Apart from this, those discussed in the judicial committee are difficult criminal cases. The so-called difficult cases can be divided into three categories. First are cases with major social influence and strong social reaction. Second are cases interfered with by the People's Congress or other government organizations, and cases in which there remain legal doubts and uncertainties. As a matter of fact, those three categories of cases might overlap with each other and even coincide, such as the case of a policeman shooting someone according to law, which I will discuss later.

It is said that mostly administrative cases will be submitted to the judicial committee.[31] The fundamental reason is that administrative cases always involve local government or its subordinate organizations. Generally speaking, however, the number of this kind of case in basic-level courts is relatively small.

According to introductions, the specific working procedures of the judicial committee are as follows. First of all, the judge undertaking the case introduces

[29]Please refer to the section of "analysis of two examples" later in this chapter.

[30]According to Wang Yuan's research, there were 31 criminal cases discussed by judicial committee in a court in certain county of Shanghai Municipality in 1997, amounted to about 8.2 % of all criminal cases dealt by this court in the same year. But the average percentage each year is about 10 %. Please see Wang Yuan: "Court Independence and Its Difficult Situation" as previously mentioned.

[31]This point is quite different from legal regulations. According to Article 63 of Administrative Procedure Law, the president of people's court is responsible for submitting cases to the judicial committee for review only when the decisions and rulings that are already legally effective are found to be against law and need to be retried according to regulations.

the case, especially introducing the points of disputes, and puts forward the reasoning of the different parties. When the case itself does not have any problems, he or she will then put forward the difficulties faced by the court. In theory, the judicial committee will review the case files. It is said that the committee actually cannot read all the files since there are so many cases and it is impossible that every committee member reads files carefully enough. It is also difficult to make judgments due to these reasons. On the other hand, it is not necessary to read all the files, because in many cases, it is not the facts or laws that are not clear, but rather the dispute in its nature or the difficulty in resolution due to all kinds of reasons.

When discussing the case, the first in command (the president) normally does not speak and lets other members talk, especially committee members with rich experience in dealing with this kind of case, which may include the present or former director of the tribunal participating in the judicial committee, the vice president in charge of or formerly in charge of this kind of case. The president will always give his or her opinion last, allegedly to maintain the image of "being correct all the time."

Legally speaking, all committee members are equal. But this does not rule out the situation that in a few cases, "the first in command" or other members of a judicial committee will try to influence others and they do have certain influence on other members. Even so, nobody will have the final say, and there are different opinions and arguments. It is said that some arguments are for the sake of work and not targeted at individuals, and thus, this kind of dispute itself will not cause personal conflicts, excluding those members that already have conflicts or misunderstandings. The judges interviewed believe that this kind of discussion is for the public interest. (A member in our research team used to use his acquaintance relationship to attend meetings of a judicial committee in the court of certain county in Shaanxi Province as an observer. According to his report, during the discussion, those members did argue honestly for the sake of work. However, this example is not that common and thus not persuasive enough.)

In most situations, the judicial committee will respect suggestions put forward by the judge undertaking the case after discussion, or make a choice from several analytical suggestions, but will often reach an agreement. The judicial committee will also have rather big disputes in a few cases. At these times, it will not decide the case by vote, but require necessary materials to be supplemented and ask the superior court to make the law clear while leaving the case decision to the next meeting. There are only very few cases brought to the meeting for discussion at many times. If there is still no agreement after many discussions, then the judicial committee will have to decide by a vote.

The decision mechanism of the judicial committee is majority rule. Everyone has only one vote, including the president. The minority is subordinate to the majority, but the voting situation and suggestions of everyone will be recorded. Externally, the judicial committee and the collegiate panel will be jointly responsible for cases decided by the judicial committee. In particular, due to the "system of being held accountable for misjudgement" and the related economic benefits (year-end bonuses), this situation is getting stricter. If a certain case is remanded for retrial by the superior court (which is regarded by many courts as "misjudgement"), the members holding the majority view will have to take the responsibility for the "misjudgement." The specific methods of taking responsibility are different from place to place. It is said that in a court of certain county, every member has to have 50 yuan of bonus cut because of "misjudgements" recorded in their files.

3.4 Views and Reasoning of Judges

During the interview, although many judges put forward some critical opinions or suggestions for possible improvement on the operation of judicial committees, no judge ever questioned the function and necessity of this system. Having built enough mutual understanding and confidence, with talks being rather candid, we would question the function of the judicial committee positively and point out the "disadvantages" of judicial committees that had been raised by many scholars. To be in line with previous analysis, our question was not whether the judicial committee would affect the free handling of cases by judges, but was roughly whether the judicial committee would influence the case handling or impartial decision of judges (inappropriately), or the question of "how you think of abolishing judicial committee." All—without exception—judges thought that generally speaking, there was no issue of the judicial committee affecting case handling and judicial justice. They did not deny that in a few situations, there were disputes between their personal views and decisions of the judicial committee, but they obviously saw these disputes as normal disputes in work and could accept them as long as the final result turned out to be fine. This shows a very practical attitude.

They did not deny that some members in the judicial committee (especially the president or certain non-professional vice president) were not professionally competent, or that in some cases, certain members would have bigger influence on the decision of the judicial committee. Nor did they deny that sometimes due to interference of local party or political departments, or social pressure, the practical role of the judicial committee was damaged and even there were decisions against their convictions (such as the above-mentioned case of a police shooting). But generally speaking, they held that the judicial committee did more good than harm to their courts at least at this stage and that it should be maintained. In fact, if we analyze carefully, all these "non-denials" have demonstrated an attitude that "the role of the judicial committee should be strengthened," but not the other way round. However, in today's world, where every taxi driver in Beijing might be a political reviewer, it is not something to hear people supporting or against something. It was still quite surprising to encounter such identical answers!

We are not going to accept their comments and judgments only because of this. Theoretically speaking, their identical answers may be completely because they have been living in this system for so long a time and there is not another system as a frame of reference. They therefore accept the natural rationality of this system and completely lack the ability to doubt and challenge the rationality of this system. It is just like the situation that people always accepted that "the earth was the center of the universe" before Copernicus. There is another possibility that because these judges live in this system, they have some kind of vested interest which is seen as inappropriate to scholars or the ordinary people.[32] In order to safeguard this inappropriate vested interest, judges have formed a professional ideology on the judicial committee.[33] These two possibilities are both there. But this reasonable guess alone cannot prove their existence and is not convincing enough, because people can put forward all kinds of countless illustrative guesses which might be established logically. They raise guesses which are completely adverse. I will discriminate these two possibilities from two levels.

I will first of all analyze these two possibilities from a theoretical level in general. We admit that according to the fundamental principle of Marxism that social consciousness is based on social being. The institutional environment will definitely constitute a composing role to people's opinions and ideology. However, we cannot use the principally correct and basic viewpoint of philosophy and deduce every tiny problem. Otherwise, we cannot explain why, after such a long span of planned economy, people would still automatically pursue market transactions, farmers automatically contract production quotas to individual households, and the work passion which was absent in the system of people's communes suddenly vanishes. We cannot explain why many senior cadres and even those senior leaders of the Chinese Communist Party and the People's Republic of China who in those years participated themselves in the design, establishment and operation of the planned economy—Deng Xiaoping included—would finally actively advocate or not oppose the introduction of market factors, and even the establishment of the socialist market economy system. There are plenty of examples in history telling us that just those people who have lived in a system that inappropriately restricts personal freedom and creativity would be the earliest to feel the malpractices of this system most profoundly and then would be the earliest to demand for change and always use their daily actions to change this system in practice.[34] We cannot say for sure that so many judges have lost their ability of reflection and criticism of this system due to system internalization.

This kind of logic analysis needs the support of empirical evidence to be more powerful and convincing. As a matter of fact, judges we interviewed, especially those being in certain position or who used to be in certain position,

---

[32]The reason that I previously emphasized "inappropriate" is because that if not harming the political and social functions of the court, then some vested interests are appropriate and should be protected. Such as the stability of the system which benefits works of people who live and work in this system and is a kind of vested benefit. And in a certain sense, it can be said that the legal system is to protect an expected and vested benefit.

[33]As for the ideology formed due to professionalism, especially the formation of ideology of legal professional, please see analysis of related foreign scholars, Richard A. Posner, "The Material Basis of Jurisprudence," in *Overcoming Law*, Harvard University Press, 1995, p. 33.

[34]The majority of the main leaders of the communist movements were not from family of workers or poor peasants. The reformer of the Church in those years, such as Martin Luther, was a priest himself. Those are some typical examples.

all held reflections and criticisms of certain levels and sometimes even to a profound degree on the current judicial system of China. Some of their mentalities are exactly the same or generally consistent with opinions of scholars who study judicial systems today on issues related to the reform of personnel systems, jurisdiction, and the financial systems of courts. In general, they hope and strongly demand for judicial independence and less inappropriate interference from local government or other departments. They have even put forward a series of rather detailed proposals. If we accept the proposition that judges lack the abilities for criticism and reflection on the current systems, this is against common sense and dangerous; this equates to the claim that judges do not understand the importance of judicial independence, that they do not know what they need, and that only scholars and other people can design systems for them. This kind of claim has created a very dangerous theory premise for the interference of judges or justice by us or others either now or in the future. This also cannot explain why they have raised sharp criticisms on the current court system at all. We face a paradox that cannot justify itself.

Secondly, do judges have vested benefits from the system of judicial committees? And more importantly, what kind of vested benefits do they have? In order to answer these questions, I still have to start from the common proposition that we cannot presume that all judges interviewed have a sense of social justice. I don't deny that there are corrupt elements among judges. But generally speaking, compared with legislators, scholars, and even common people, judges cannot possibly lack sense of social justice and conscience. That being said, "good men" and "bad guys" are distributed normally in society, with no relation to career. We have no reason to say that judges completely disregard social interests and stick to a legal system only for their own benefits. The more important thing is that, once accepting this assumption, the current demand about social justice or judicial independence will lose its legitimacy—can we let those people who lack a sense of social justice exercise judicial power independently? When we analyze issues, we must always pay attention to whether our proposition can maintain its logical consistency. Those rigid and dogmatic opinions which separate legislators or scholars or ordinary people from judges, and believe that the former is more reliable, are not only unconvincing, but bound to fall into a seemingly radical position that is unable to maintain self-consistency. Judges are professional characters. They are people who live in this world and are definitely share the common morality, values, and judgments of ordinary people.

Logic is a weapon to refute, but is not enough to establish a proposition positively. I still have to return to the empirical level to observe. The so-called empirical level here is to analyze whether those judges' reasons to support the judicial committee are reasonable and convincing in the Chinese social environment of today.

Reasons for judges to support the judicial committee are as follows. First, they believe that under the current situation, if the decision of a single judge or of the majority of judges in the collegiate panel (i.e., an agreement between two judges only) is implemented uniformly, it is very likely to bring about judicial corruption or injustice. In the basic-level court, we can see from the previous section that apart from administrative cases (I will discuss this exception briefly later), the majority of cases do not enter into the judicial committee nowadays due to the increase of the number of cases or other reasons of feasibility. Normally speaking, cases submitted to the judicial committee are relatively major civil, economic, and criminal cases, or cases that are not only major, but also difficult and on which the collegiate panel cannot reach an agreement. Since the cases are relatively important, there are influences from all parties, including messages passed on by leaders of the local party or political organs or departments, pleadings, and gifts from acquaintances and even some public but rarely seen bribery. The judges interviewed all believe that in this situation, if there is only trial by a single judge or by a collegiate panel, then there will not be enough restrictions and supervision over the abuse of power. Certainly, there are some cases whose judgments are so wrong that people can see at a single glance that judges have cheated. These cases will be investigated later, the decisions will be corrected, and judges having done malpractice will be dealt with (but this can still not make up for the court's reputation that has been seriously damaged). However, the problem is that normally judges will behave so wrongly, since most judges will not give up their professional credentials, prospects, freedoms, and reputations due to some immediate or even huge benefits. Even if there is malpractice, they will normally use some reasoning and basis that can hold water, such as facts found, evidence adoption, calculation methods of costs or damage compensation, measurement of penalties, and others. As far as these issues are concerned, people with a little judicial experience can tell that different judges will often have different judgments and there is no such repeated certainty as in sciences.[35] This also means that even people may feel some cases are dealt with unjustly, they can hardly find out from experience whether judges have done anything wrong.[36]

Thus, as far as I see, the practice that courts submit all cases of detention, probation, or with holding of treatment to the judicial committee for discussion is fairly reasonable. It is easy to make mistakes on those changeable cases and therefore arouse people's doubts and leave society with a bad impression. For a case that can be sentenced to 3–7 years of imprisonment, if a judge gives only 3 years, some people may think that the sentence is lenient, but it is not that unfair. However, if a case that should be sentenced to 2 years of imprisonment is sentenced to 2 years of probation, people may feel that this is obviously unfair. To ordinary people in today's China, probation equates to no punishment (please note the "local standard" of punishment that is shown here). Here is another example: In some major and complicated civil and economic cases (with large amounts of money involved), if a judge plays a strategically corrupt trick in some place, there may well come the situation that who wins the lawsuit does not actually win, and the loser of the lawsuit does not actually lose, but earns big, and there seems

[35]Please refer to Richard A. Posner, *The Problems of Jurisprudence*, as previous note 16, Chap. 6.

[36]American judge Posner used to analyze this issue and related system installation like challenge system. Please refer to *The Problems of Jurisprudence*, as previous note 16, especially Chap. 1.

to be nothing to complain about (stipulations such as one side supposedly being compensated 1 million yuan, but the compensation of the court decision was only 700,000 yuan. It may seem one side wins the lawsuit, but only the parties concerned can tell who really wins and who really loses). It is in those complicated cases with large amounts of money involved that parties of lawsuits are more willing to influence the presiding judge through irregular and even illegal methods. Submitting those cases to the judicial committee for discussion may not necessarily prevent miscarriage of justice brought about by corruption, and in extreme cases, there is the possibility that the whole court has been bought off, but this kind of possibility will be reduced greatly. Several judges interviewed said that "you can buy off one, two, or even more judges, but you can hardly buy off nine people (the total number of members of the judicial committee, although in principle, the judicial committee does not have to agree unanimously)." Judges also believe that once the case is submitted to the judicial committee, you cannot just tell people what to do next, but have to put forward reasons. If you have no reason, and the decision you put forward is not correct, people will be suspicious and thus form a kind of restriction.

Secondly, the judicial committee may have played a role or will play a better role of standardizing law enforcement within a jurisdiction and raising the professional qualities of judges. In every basic-level court, there are normally nearly 20 courts and detached people's tribunals. Because the legal texts definitely have generalities, it is impossible for them to include all situations that actually happen. Due to the rapid development and changes of Chinese society, many traditional legal practices or laws formulated many years ago cannot meet the needs of the present. Due to the vast territory and different local customs and conditions in China, during the actual hearing and case handling, judges of courts will often have some new specific practices with regard to cases on hand. Those specific practices may meet legal requirements in principle, but some of them may not meet legal requirements in principle (although they may meet or basically meet the needs of daily life in the place and are demanded by the situation by then). Without coordination, there will be a situation that judges, collegiate panels, and people's courts in the same jurisdiction have different standards of law enforcement. Although this disunity or the situation in which law enforcement can be dealt with flexibly is not necessarily bad, either for a province (and even the whole China) where there is unbalanced development in politics, economy, and culture in different places, or for a transforming Chinese society. It has some rationality in practice—but this kind of practice will not give the same cases the same or even similar treatment and will cause unequal protection of law, which will leave the impression of judicial injustice, even the judges themselves have no such intention. On the other hand, Chinese justice is not the common law system and has no tradition of stare decisis or directly quoting the precedents of other courts. Apart from exchanging views in private, judges cannot and are not allowed to directly quote or borrow legal precedents of other judges. This has prevented China's basic-level courts from forming a common view on handling similar cases and forming a kind of institutional or habitual practice. It has also prevented judges from sharing their experiences with others as well as the accumulation of judges' knowledge and the formation of judicial tradition.

The works of judicial committee in this regard can help to make up for this flaw. During the interviews, judges did not talk about case law system, but many judges mentioned that the judicial committee would guarantee that the judicial practices within the jurisdiction of the court are uniform and help to form some regular and specific practices and restrict the discretion of individual judges. In particular, under the situation that there is the absence of explicit legal texts, the collective consultation of the judicial committee can help to form some rules and resolve problems that are not regulated by law but must be and issues that are entitled to immediate resolution. Certainly, this kind of activity, similar to judges "making laws to fill in the gaps," is not appropriate in the academic circles—even if the issue of legislative authority is not considered temporarily. However, the daily work of judges often requires them to do this and they even have to do this while carrying out obligations of judges. I think that this practice is even beneficial to the rule of law of China in transformation for which some specific detailed experiences can be accumulated. It can also help to change the features which legislation in our country commonly has, but are normally thought by judges to be too formalized and lack operability based on judicial experience.

Last but not least, apart from the issue of uniform rules, the issue of abilities of judges must also be raised. If according to the ideal standard of judges or requirements from the law of judges, which has been passed recently, there are quite a number of judges of basic-level courts who are not up to the standard either in their cultural quality or in legal professional quality. Many judges of basic-level courts are officials transferred from other governmental departments. Some are middle school or primary school teachers who passed the examination to be enrolled in the courts. Quite many of them are demobilized military men. There are certainly judges who have received systematic and formal legal education, being engaged in judicial trial for a long time and thus have rather high judicial ability in the basic-level courts, but there are only a few of them.[37] Although China's court system has provided legal education at spare-time universities for many years in order to change this situation,[38] honestly speaking, the field research has made us believe that due to reasons I have discussed in detail in other chapters, and it is hard for the cultural and professional qualities of Chinese judges to be improved substantially within a short period of time, especially in the basic-level courts.[39] A practical problem that the basic-level courts are facing today is that the large number of and most common legal disputes of the grassroot society

[37]Please refer Chap. 10 of this book: Professionalism of Judges in Basic-level Courts.

[38]Please refer to He Weifang: "Realizing Social Justice Through Judiciary," as previous note 25.

[39]One of the most important points is that the income of judges is too low today, especially compared with the pay of lawyers or businessmen which law school graduates may choose to be. Secondly, basic-level courts are located in small cities (towns), which are obviously not attractive to the majority of young graduates of law school (around 22 years of age). Please refer Chap. 10 of this book: Professionalism of Judges in Basic-level Courts.

in modern China must be dealt with and solved mainly by judges whose cultural and business qualities are somewhat below those of the ideal judge. Apart from improving professional training and providing further education and training, the judicial committee is obviously a possible system setting inside the court to improve judges' qualities and standards of judicial trial. Many judges have pointed out explicitly that the judicial committee has played the role of making specific judicial practices uniform within the jurisdiction of the court, helped to solve difficult and new cases, and played an active role in guiding judges to handle the case and improve the professional standards of judges.

3.5 Are the Reasons of Judges Trustworthy?

We are not that quick to believe readily the reasons of judges to support the judicial committee system. We have two doubts: First, the logic of organization of China's court system has always been greatly influenced (e.g., the court management is similar to that of a government organization. The court is a unit in which the president has a decisive role on the personnel arrangement of the court to a certain degree) by administrative bureaucracy (in academic sense).[40] Persons in charge of the basic-level courts are rarely produced from the court system, but mostly transferred from other party or governmental departments. They will intentionally or unintentionally bring their habits they have developed through the work of party and government offices into the court system. With the addition of influence of China's traditional views on official ranks, many scholars, and I myself, suspect that the reasons given by judges do not work well in practice. We have put forward the following question: To what extent can the president decide or influence the decision of the judicial committee?

Those judges do not deny that there is this kind of influence, but they also think that due to all kinds of reasons, this kind of situation is not as serious or common as imagined. Firstly, the judicial committee adopts the system of one person, one vote, and their votes and reasons are each recorded. So the president will not speak casually but be the last to speak, in order to maintain his or her image of "being always correct." Even if the president voices his or her opinion, which has some influence, it cannot necessarily control other people's votes. Secondly, the system of the court of second instance being the court of last instance has played a certain role of restriction on the president or other members of the judicial committee who intend to exercise authority improperly, since no one wants his or her case decision to be sent back or be corrected, not to mention to have one's "wrongness" recorded. Thirdly, because most of the presidents are not "born" in the court

[40]On issues of administration and bureaucracy of management system of China's courts, please see He Weifang: "Two Problems of China's Judicial Management System," as previous note 1. Please also refer Chap. 2 of this book: Court Trial and its Administration.

system, they have relatively less direct influence on the court and the court system. On the contrary, just because that they are not familiar with the business, they have to rely heavily on the judicial committee, especially those professionals who understand business. Fourthly, members of the judicial committee are not necessarily ready to be controlled by others and follow their mistakes.

During the interview, we also noticed that at least some judicial committee members are clearly conscious of the requirements of this system. For example, when we question the influence of the president over the judicial committee, one vice president of a court in a certain county quoted clearly related legal texts without thinking and points out that the principles of organization and decision of the procurators are different from those of the courts. He says that the procurators implement a system of chief executive accountability, in which whenever there are disputes, it is up to the chief procurator to make the final decision. However, the courts implement a system of democratic centralism in the judicial committee, where the president has only one vote.[41]

This example does not have decisive persuasion. Many of my friends in the academic circle have provided me with many counter examples. I cannot seemingly obtain more convincing and common empirical evidence by taking part in discussions of many judicial committees in the courts of other places.[42] I therefore do not dare to say that this principle has been implemented in the judicial committees of different courts to a certain degree. But there is at least one thing that is clear: That is, in terms of systems and principles, the current regulations on the judicial committee have been given rather cautious and careful consideration, and what is more important is to implement them and put them into practice. This has at least demonstrated that some judges in the basic-level courts are more familiar with relevant legal systems than we imagine. They do not fail to understand their responsibilities and powers. However, due to the current social morality in China, I will not claim innocently that all of them are brave enough to use these principles to safeguard their own power and authority, but the legitimate resources of this

[41]Please see Article 11 of the Organic Law of the People's Court of the People's Republic of China: People's courts at all levels set up judicial committees which practice democratic centralism. The task of the judicial committees is to sum up judicial experience and to discuss important or difficult cases and other issues relating to the judicial work. The presidents of the people's courts preside over meetings of judicial committees of the people's courts at all levels; the chief procurators of the people's procurators at the corresponding levels may attend such meetings without voting rights. Please also refer to Article 3 of the Organic Law of the People's Procurators of the People's Republic of China: The chief procurator exercises unified leadership over the work of the procurators. People's procurators at all levels shall each set up a procuratorial committee. The procuratorial committee shall apply the system of democratic centralism and, under the direction of the chief procurator, hold discussions and make decisions on important cases and other major issues. In the case of the chief procurator disagreeing with the majority's opinion over a decision on an important issue, the matter may be reported to the standing committee of the people's congress at the corresponding level for final decision.

[42]Even if there is a possibility for us to attend and observe, there may occur the problem of "uncertainty principle" due to our presence. To this reason, the materials we might use can only be provided by people attending the judicial committee.

system are already there. Moreover, what is more important to me is that this system resource has already come into or is beginning to come into the view of judges. As long as the condition allows, they will "use the policy to the full" like reformers in many other places and finally form stable, ethical conventions.

Our second doubt, which is also a doubt of many other academics, is whether the judicial committee will be greatly influenced by a member with stronger professional abilities (such as director of a tribunal or the vice president in charge) and thus make the case discussion a kind of formality. Some judges admit that during their practical works in the judicial committee, opinions of a member who is familiar with the trial of similar cases certainly influences other members a lot; but normally speaking, other members also respect their opinions. In theory, this will always enable a certain member to manipulate the other members. Let us assume that inside the court, some members may not be necessarily familiar with cases with little relation to their business due to the division of labor. Under this situation, it is especially easy to have this kind of manipulation. Thus, some opinions of judges mentioned above to support the judicial committee may not count that much. Due to formalities, the practical function and legitimacy of the judicial committee as a system is naturally challenged.

Judges interviewed believe that the possibility that individual members are more influential cannot be ruled out really, but this does not mean that he or she can manipulate other members or that other members are ready to be manipulated. Other members do not speak out with their opinions, but show agreement after "going over" the case only once. This does not mean that they have given up their ability to think or that they lack the ability to analyze issues. The above three reasons for the limited influence of the president also apply to individual members who are influential in the judicial committee for other reasons. We certainly hope that every judge can think independently, but in fact, there are always some people that are relatively more influential in any organization, including courts, in which independence is emphasized.[43] We cannot presume that all people have the same analytical abilities on the same problem. Nor can we presume that people have their own mind only when they have different views and are engaged in fierce debate. Different opinions or heated debates are only one, but not the only, way to show independent thinking. Respecting dominant opinions of an individual or a few people does not demonstrate that people are led away by the individual and thus lose themselves. The supervision and restriction of a system are often shown

[43]This has been shown in American courts as well. For example, Judge Bennan who worked in the Supreme Court for a long time from 1956 to the end of 1980s was thought to be the soul of liberal judges. Judge Marshall who held the office at almost the same time was thought to be lack of his own opinions. In 1990s, Chief Justice Scalia was believed to be the brain of conservatives in the Supreme Court, and Chief Justice Thomas always followed the former in viewing his opinions. Certainly, those were because of ideology reasons. In addition, judges in the US Supreme Court always respect opinions of some "experts" more on some problems of specialty. For example, some judges are better at issues of antitrust, and other judges will respect their opinions more on antitrust cases. This kind of respect on specialties of individual judges does not mean that judges give up their own thinking.

by conflict and dispute, but the truly institutionalized restrictions are more often shown as a convention.[44] When a member must put forward his or her reasons to make others accept his or her opinions, even though people seem to accept his or her reasons, he or she is in fact already under restrictions. This seemingly superficial "formality" is actually not "formality" at all; it is actually the significance of procedures we have emphasized.

Apart from this, judges also put forward an important reason for why it is hard for individual members to manipulate the judicial committee. That is, in the basic-level courts, there is no strict division of labor. The situation that a person stays working for one division from day one until his retirement is extremely rare, if there are any examples at all. The majority of judges used to work for the people's courts where they would deal with all kinds of cases. County courts are not big, and there are only a few positions for division directors. Some capable judges, especially directors of divisions, do not have many opportunities to be promoted. They are usually transferred from one division to another (the administrative and non-professional feature of courts is demonstrated once again; the criminal court is certainly an exception). For this reason, judges in basic-level courts are not like judges of intermediate or high courts. The latter are relatively more professional, and the difference in professions is more distinct. Because the judges of basic-level courts are transferred from different divisions, after a long period of time and in such a small "community," as long as a judge is smart enough, even if they have not dealt with certain kind of case, they certainly have analytical abilities. One judge used to remark that "even if I haven't tasted the pork, I have at least seen the pigs running."

The key issue here is that cases submitted to the judicial committee for discussion are often cases whose natures are difficult to determine. Judges are not always certain about cases, or there are no appropriate laws, or the cases cannot be solved merely by applying laws, and judges do not always have much deep and detailed knowledge about related laws. Being familiar with applicable legal texts is not necessarily the most important quality for members of judicial committees. What is more important is the ability to analyze problems and get hold of the crucial points of the problem. In the judicial circle, this ability is a kind of common ability, but not a kind of knowledge that can be obtained or exclusively enjoyed only by dealing with criminal or civil cases. Cases submitted to the judicial committee of the basic-level courts are all relatively major and difficult cases in the locality. Generally speaking, cases in the basic-level courts are rather simple. There are cases related to financial bonds, intellectual property rights, stock futures, and other very specialized and highly technical cases. Based on all these conditions, members of judicial committees in the basic-level courts will not go so far as to be confused or manipulated by individual "experts," as long as they have certain practical experiences in court.

---

[44]Foucault has exactly the same opinion. Those who are interested can see Michel Foucault, *Discipline and Punish: the Birth of the Prison*, trans. by Alan Sheridan, Vintage Books, 1978.

We also seriously made a detailed inquiry, which we later admitted as being rather stupid, that if the president is rather arbitrary or if the local party and government organs and officials press the president, will the judicial committee members still not be influenced or manipulated by the president? The judges admitted that under such circumstances, the judicial committee normally cannot withstand the pressure. They believed that this question actually exceeds the scope of questions targeted at the establishment of the judicial committee. Just as what one judge said when answering our question, "one system can only solve one problem." If one encounters such an arbitrary president, even if the judge is a single judge—as long as the judge is working under him or her—it will not solve any problem. On the contrary, if county leaders press the president, the president can, to some extent, withstand by using opinions of the judicial committee. Some judges have even raised examples in this regard.

3.6 Observation from Another Perspective

The above statements on functions of the judicial committee are mainly from the perspective of the judicial committee (although our interviewees are not necessarily members of judicial committee). After all, the judicial committee (or its members) are different from common judges: The former governs people, while the latter are governed. This kind of difference in position may cause differences in perspective and judgment. Even though most of the members of the judicial committee have earned their positions by working through one level after another and have been governed by others once, the circumstances have changed with the passage of time. For this reason, perspectives and reasons for the judicial committee, such as to prevent corruption of judges, to standardize judicial criteria, to make sure that the laws are uniform, and to improve the professional abilities of judges, may better reflect the considerations of the pros and cons of the judicial committee.

The interview also shows that no ordinary judges think that the judicial committee as a system inappropriately intervenes into their power. As said previously, in many times, it is the presiding judges themselves who demand submitting the cases to the judicial committee for discussion (when the single judge is not sure about case handling, the collegiate panel cannot reach an agreement). Why don't the judges think that their powers are intervened upon inappropriately? Why do they even take the initiative to give up the power which they can completely exercise by themselves and give up their "judicial independence" and freedom (especially in the case of single judge trials)? We do not simply think that as long as judges approve, this system has adequate legitimacy. It is absolutely possible that judges giving up this power just reflect certain kinds of drawbacks (e.g., we may well say and we will discover later that the judicial committee has sometimes become one of the tools for judges to shift their own blames inappropriately). If we analyze and observe the phenomenon of giving up power in a more detailed manner, we may be able to find other deeper functions of the judicial committee, as well its secondary functions on ordinary judges.

There are indeed deeper functions. For ordinary judges, the first and foremost may be to resist favors and protect themselves. All basic-level courts are set up in a county town (or county-level city) where there are often several tens of thousands of people. Everyone living in this kind of town knows there are acquaintances or acquaintances of acquaintances everywhere. People can always manage to talk to people they want to know. Judges in most basic-level courts are locals who are locally born and bred. There are countless networks here, such as networks of fellow villagers, working colleagues, classmates or schoolmates, friends, and the relationship between different departments and between superiors and subordinates. What is more important is that the political ideology in our country has always emphasized that the courts shall be integrated with the populace. The central and local governments also demand that all courts shall play the role of "protecting reform and opening up." There is no isolation between courts and society to prevent justice from being disturbed.[45] Under such circumstances, once a case, especially one that is relatively important, enters the court, the home of the presiding judge will often be "packed by all kinds of lobbyists" (the name of a political novel by Wang Meng). The lobbyists are from both the sides of the plaintiffs and defendants, which overburdens judges. However, it is difficult to expect any judge, as long as he or she is not too otherworldly or living in the world of textbooks, to "enforce laws impartially and strictly" and shut the door upon all his or her relatives and friends as required by textbooks or campaign materials. If we put ourselves in their positions, we can understand that judges do need a system to help them to resist or get rid of those complicated relationships. The judicial committee actually plays this kind of role to a certain extent. When talking about this point, almost all judges say that they often tell the lobbyists or gift-senders who they do not want to offend that "this case will be submitted to the judicial committee and I myself can't decide" and in other words refuse them politely. Even to those people (including some leaders at the county-level) they cannot afford to offend, they have to give some promise first and then offer some lip service, but will still add at last sentences like "it is up to the judicial committee after all." In fact, in a few cases, when there are enough adequate reasons and local interests are not involved, the judges even resist inappropriate interference from leaders of the county party and government organs and prevent unjust and misjudged cases.

In order to demonstrate the implied meaning of this feature, I will compare the system of China's basic-level courts with that of American courts of first instance here. The customary view is that due to all kinds of reasons, Chinese judges have too much restriction and less power of discretion compared to American judges (many Chinese scholars have emphasized that there is not enough judicial independence in China, which also has reflected this judgment). If we observe carefully, however, this may not necessarily be the case. In China, judges of first

[45]Please refer to Suli: "On Specialization of Legal Activities," as previously mentioned; He Weifang: "Realizing Social Justice Though Judiciary," as previously mentioned.

instance have monopolized judgment of factual disputes and legal disputes. In this sense, Chinese judges have bigger decisive powers on cases than American judges of first instance. However, this bigger power has brought them bigger risks on another level, and China's judiciary and other systems are unable to provide them with enough system protection to avoid those risks. For this reason, China's judges at the basic level are more vulnerable than American judges. They are more prone to become the target of attacks from society and even volatile public sentiment. The so-called targets of attack consist of two aspects. One is the object of lobbying, entertaining, gift-sending, and even bribery; the other is the object of all kinds of revenge.[46] In American justice, civil cases entering court trials usually have juries and criminal cases must have juries. The jury will decide whether there is enough evidence to prove whether somebody is guilty or at fault and whether there should be compensation as well as the amount of compensation. The judge will only make decisions on the legal disputes. Juries therefore share the deciding power of the case. It seems as if they have deprived judges of some powers, but at the same time, they have also spread the decisive risks that American judges have to undertake. Judges do not have to and normally will not take too much risk for even major cases.[47]

In China, the reason that the judicial committee can exist and receive approval and support from judges to a considerable extent is implied in the reason that the judge has put forward: They hope that there will be a system that can share their responsibilities and risks in the specific social environment of China. In fact, they have depended on this system positively (such as resisting lobbying) or negatively (such as passing on problems to a higher level after the system of being held accountable for misjudgement is implemented). If we put ourselves in the position of the basic-level judges in China, most of whom are destined to live in this small county town for a lifetime without the kind of income, job security, and even personal security enjoyed by the American judges, but not compare Chinese judges with judges of foreign developed countries abstractly, we can then understand, though not necessarily agree, why these basic-level judges would sometimes give

[46]At least before early 1990s, when a Chinese newspaper or magazine praised a judge, it would mention that he or she "is not afraid of threat, and not lured by promise of gain," etc. These frequently used words may be truly related to the factor that Chinese people are accustomed to moralize legal issues, but they, on the other hand, truly demonstrate that these two "attacks" are outstanding threats to Chinese judges.

[47]For example, as far as the criminal case of O.J. Simpson is concerned, although the judge of first instance declared that Simpson was acquitted of a charge, nobody made irresponsible remarks on the judge. This was largely due to the fact that the fact-finding was done by the jury. However, if there is a similar case in China, what will be the destiny of this judge? Just think about the case that "fake goods producers in Jiajiang accused fraud-busters" which made the sensation throughout China in 1996. The court in Jiajiang County was questioned by the People's Congress only because it allowed the fake goods producers to file a lawsuit. It was also blamed by media reports from Oriental Horizon, etc., aggressively and without legal foundation. The difference can be seen here.
However, it does not mean that American judges are free of risks. There are also all kinds of threats targeted at American judges, such as on the cases of artificial abortion.

up the power said to be given to them by the law. We should not start from some seemingly good, big principles only, but we must find some practical but also feasible "Chinese" system to protect judges under the situation that the principles are adhered to. The system of judicial committee is Chinese, but it is not due to the influence of "Chinese traditional culture" at all. It is a must to solve China's specific practical problems. In this sense, the system of judicial committees does have vested interests in common judges (not only members of judicial committee); but those vested interests are not improper.

3.7 The Problem with Judicial Committees

We still have to discuss some specific problems and possible improvements for judicial committees. During the interview, normally speaking, judges support the system of judicial committee, but when they discuss the judicial committee of their own courts, they still put forward or demonstrate some problems that need to be improved. This has given support to my hypothesis previously mentioned that people inside the system do not lack judgment entirely. Although the judges cannot say much about the theory, it still reflects that they do not accept the system blindly. They not only have the ability to reflect, but have indeed made some reflections, even though the direction of their conclusion may not necessarily be definite, or not in line with the classic presentation of judicial independence which we are familiar with.

One of the issues they have pointed out is that the judicial committee is not professional enough. This has been shown by the fact that normally speaking, the president and the vice president, whether they have any judicial experience or not and no matter how much judicial experience they have, are members of judicial committees in every court for sure. However, in at least some courts, the president and certain vice presidents are transferred from other departments many times. They do not have a particularly long period of and abundant experience of judicial practice. Some of them even do not have any experience related to justice or law. The reason for this problem is that although the judicial committee is established as a professional institution, members of the judicial committee are actually deployed as an administrative or semi-administrative position and usually related to the administrative level of officials taking position in the court. This has reduced the function of the judicial committee as a professional institution at least in theory.[48] But the deeper reason is related to the "implementation problem" discussed in the next chapter.

I don't want to talk about the issue that the lack of professional knowledge may cause individual problems of his or her personal decisions here, but only two aspects this has brought to the collective decision-making abilities of the judicial

[48]Please refer to Xie Renzhu: "The Judicial Committee Will be the Authority in Trial Profession," *People's Judicature*, Issue 2 of 1994, p. 23.

committee. First, a member that lacks professional knowledge is more prone to be tempted by others. If he or she happens to be the president, we also need to consider whether he or she is aggressive or not and whether the "democratic style of work" we used to talk about is good or not. If he or she is aggressive and not that "democratic," when accepting somebody's opinion, he or she will not reflect upon it and have careful consideration, since no matter how independent a person is, it is impossible for him or her to be free of the influence of external information. However, if he or she is not that aggressive and is "democratic," then he or she will often be manipulated by others. On the other hand, in order to stay consistent or win over the majority as necessary, or just to allow the president or other colleagues a way out of an embarrassing situation, members with better professional knowledge are bound to accommodate some members with inadequate professional knowledge. Although in theory, to be too professional is not necessarily an advantage at all times. It can be a disadvantage sometimes, like a lack of common sense. But as far as we see, the problem of China's judiciary at the moment is inadequate professional knowledge, not too much. For this reason, how to make the judicial committee a committee emphasizing professional judicial knowledge is a question worth thinking about.

Based on our research, the main improvement measures may not be appointing more judges with professional and technical titles such as presidents or vice presidents (in comparison, tribunal directors entering the judicial committee often have rather rich judicial experience). It is certainly good to appoint presidents and vice presidents from experienced tribunal directors from the court. But I think what is more important is to change the organizational method of the court to that of similar administrative organs. Currently, in one court, there are often two to three vice presidents in charge of civil and economic trials, criminal trials, administrative trials, and execution separately. They have to, from time to time, share works of staffing, organization, logistics, judge training, discipline inspection, reception, welfare, trade union, and some other temporary jobs with the president and other vice presidents. In the current system, even if knowledgeable judges are appointed as vice presidents, as long as they are in charge of other works for a long time, they will also drift apart from their judicial profession and have no time or energy to pay attention to trial. If the function of the judicial committee is to be strengthened, the more important thing is to do some research on the features of the organization of the court and pay attention to promoting professionalism against the background of social transition in China against the backdrop of market economic reform and institutional reform. Among them, the most important feature may be to disconnect the judicial committee from their administrative titles and strengthen its function as a business institution of court.

The second issue is that in some courts today, there are still relatively more cases decided by the judicial committee ultimately. In principle, only cases considered difficult by single judges, cases on which trial tribunals cannot reach agreement, and major cases are demanded to be submitted to the judicial committee for discussion. But in practice, due to the limitation of professional quality judges, judges have to submit cases which are not that difficult to the judicial committee for discussion, especially those new cases emerging during the social transition of China, or some cases involving local interests and local government organizations, or cases involving execution issues mentioned above.

What I want to particularly point out is that in recent years, encouraged by the system of being held accountable for misjudgement, and due to the different standards of courts at all levels on misjudging as well as the tendency of getting more severe, judges are under a large amount of pressure, which has reversed the trend that fewer cases are submitted to the judicial committee for discussion to some degree. Once some judges find cases with questions or new types of cases, in order to avoid responsibilities and protect interests from being harmed, they will ask the vice president in charge for instructions and even submit the cases to the judicial committee for discussion and decision.[49] This kind of situation not only overburdens the judicial committee (during the interview, when asked about this problem, almost all members of the judicial committee did not want the number of cases submitted to the judicial committee for discussion to be increased, but wanted them reduced. This certainly demonstrates that the judicial committee does not always want to largely maintain and control the final decision power of cases as some academics have imagined). Some judges have pointed out that if the judicial committee cannot concentrate on studying and deciding those cases with general meaning and guiding significance, it will not be good to the development of the judicial committee as a professional organization.

If we only want to solve this specific issue, apart from improving the professional qualities of judges and strictly restricting the scope of application of the system of being held accountable for misjudging, there is another possible way: to refer to the standard of choosing appellate cases by the US Supreme Court. According to US Constitution and related judiciary acts, the Supreme Court must make decisions on all appellate cases, which is its legal duty. But in practice, since modern times, the US Supreme Court has gained more and more discretionary power on whether to accept those appellate cases. It only accepts and hears cases that must be investigated and actually upholds the verdicts of courts at the lower level on the majority of appellate cases (above 95 %).[50] In another word, it is entitled to accept appellate cases selectively. China's judicial committee is not a judicial level and has a different nature, but it still can borrow this practice. Roughly speaking, it means to keep the power of single judges or the collegiate panel to ask

[49]The reason for launching the system of being held accountable for misjudgement is to enhance the sense of responsibility of judges as well as judicial independence. However, as a matter of fact, if the result is not against people's wishes, it can still be regarded as totally unsatisfactory. This has even made judges more afraid of taking responsibilities and lack of judicial independence. This has been totally out of expectations of system designers. It has also further supported my analysis on research approach, i.e., why we shouldn't attach too much importance to the intentions of system designers, but should focus on possible and actual effects.

[50]This is very similar to *certiorari* (the original Latin meaning of this word is "to make it more certain" or "to know more about the situation"). *certiorari* means that the US Supreme Court decides to review the case due to its major legal issue. It is decided by the Chief Justice, but not a legal duty.

the judicial committee to discuss cases, but at the same time, to require judges or the collegiate panel undertaking the case to put forward judicial opinions for reference. In the end, it is up to the judicial committee to decide whether the case is major enough to be decided by the judicial committee. Many judicial committees in the basic-level courts are functioning in this way, but they usually do not ask judges or collegiate panels to put forward written opinions, and it has not become a stable system yet. The advantage of this practice is that, on the one hand, it encourages judges and collegiate panels to make decisions as independently as possible, and on the other hand, the judicial committee can realize their own supporting function.[51]

3.8 Analysis of Two Examples

The second section of this chapter has demonstrated the legitimacy of the judicial committee from the stake of an ordinary judge, but this demonstration is not yet complete. Though the judges' comments on the judicial committee are reasonable and accord with economic rationality, we still need to realize that this kind of reason and rationality is based on that of individual judges under restricted conditions. If we need to discuss the systematic rationality of a judicial committee, we must observe beyond the perspective of individual judges. Normally speaking, it is difficult for judges themselves to have broader observation and understanding of the system, and their social characters are not allowing them to do so. This task is in need of more scholars' attention and should be undertaken by legal and sociology researchers.

Legal and sociology researchers must realize their own limitations first of all, and this kind of self-awareness cannot be of lip service only, but should be put into practice. They must make their best efforts to define the limitation of their rational pursuit and thinking, even though it may not be possible to define absolutely clearly. During this research, I have two basic limitations. First, there is a limitation on questioning the restrictive conditions. Limitless questioning is bound to fall into the vicious indefinite in philosophy, that is, the observation on the so-called causa finalis or restriction. Even though this causa finalis can be discovered, it will be far away from or have nothing to do with specific issues at hand, and this kind of inquiry will certainly involve observation on a broader scale and require more abundant knowledge, which cannot be done alone by any single scholar or even one subject. For this reason, I think that the inquiry on the essential and direct social reason for the judicial committee to exist should be limited. The second limitation is supplementary to the first; that is, it should be based on materials provided by the interviewed judges and related to the function of the judicial committee instead of based on any other materials that can be used. This is a necessary limitation to ensure that this chapter will not deviate from the core theme.

[51]Please refer to Abraham, *Judicial Process*, for relatively more detailed introduction, as previous note 15, pp. 183ff.

I want to briefly discuss two simple cases obtained during the interview and research. One is civil, and the other is criminal. The reason I chose them is because not only do they have representativeness, but they also support or oppose reasons given by judges. What is more important is that they allow us to see specific problems faced by China's basic-level courts and judges from a broader angle, as well as the rationality of contextualization of the judicial committee because of this. Those two examples were not put forward when interviewing about the problems of the judicial committee but when discussing other problems. They drew my attention. These specific examples obtained unintentionally may inspire us more than common demonstration and illustration.

The details of the first case, as previously mentioned, are roughly as follows: The defendant Mr. Wang (a policeman) and other policemen in the local police station set up checkpoint on the road at midnight to check the situations of moving traffic according to the unified plan of "taking severe measures against criminal activities" assigned by the higher authorities. The decedent and other two persons (all were university students about to graduate) rode a motorcycle after drinking alcohol and refused to stop the motorcycle for inspection. They pushed through the first two inspection lines, still refused to stop after the police inspector fired two warning shots up in the air, and pushed through the third inspection line which the defendant was guarding. The defendant Mr. Wang shot to the ground from behind and injured the calf of a person on the motorcycle (not the driver). However, the motorcycle continued to speed, and when it reached the crossing about 690 m away from where the shot was fired, it crashed into a trailer truck, killing one rider (neither the wounded, nor the driver) and injuring the other two. It was later found out that those three persons had indeed done nothing else illegal except that they refused legal inspections from the police, which constituted an unlawful act.

This case is rather simple. It is true that it is unfortunate. However, Policeman Wang's firing was an action to perform his duty according to laws and disciplines. It is hard to say that the shooting itself has a direct or close cause–effect relationship requested by law with the death. The problem is that the family of the victim originally had two sons. The victim's brother drowned while swimming shortly after graduating from the university one year prior. To his parents, both sons died an unnatural death. The victim's mother asked the police station to arrest policeman Wang and required heavy punishment by law. The local police station made some concession, agreed, and actually gave economic compensation to the victim's family (judging from a legal perspective, this was a compromise of principle), but refused to deal with policeman Wang according to the law and punish him heavily. The victim's mother was so angry that she wrote down a suicide note asking to redress the injustice for her son and then hanged herself. There is an old saying in the locale that "if you want to win a lawsuit, someone has to die." As long as someone is dead, those without reason will become reasonable. In addition, there were a few policemen in this area behaving badly and bullying people, causing great anger among local people. The family of the victim mobilized more than 200 people to encircle the local government, which shut down the government. Both the county government and party committee ordered the political and legal department to deal with this issue rapidly and seriously in order to "maintain stability and unity." If it was necessary, the police station would arrest the defendant on the charge of mayhem, and the procurator would institute a public prosecution according to Sect. 3.1 of Article 134 of the Criminal Law.

This case had no difficult points. Anyone with certain trial experience, common sense, and careful consideration would feel difficult to say that the behaviors of officer Wang constituted an illegal action, let alone a crime. However, if the court made this kind of decision, it could not satisfy the local people. Neither could it meet the requirements of the local party and political leaders who did not want to be criticized by superiors because an accident occurred. An originally common case then turned out to be a difficult and major case (with strong social responses/government interference/difficulties). It was a case that had to be sentenced, but the sentence would be clearly very unfair to officer Wang. The case was given attention by the judicial committee from the very beginning and was then submitted to the judicial committee in the end.

Some people would think that the interference from the county committee and the county government was an important factor in the difficulty of the case; it was certainly so. However, this kind of blame was not that fair. If we temporarily suspended the factor of party and political interference, we can see that it would still be a difficult case for the presiding judge, because the judge was living in such a community and it would be impossible for the court decision to be free from public opinion. This has reflected a deep and major contradiction of Chinese society in its transitional period. We cannot offer detailed analysis here, but simply speaking, the logic of rule of law in modern society and its demand on the court roughly are, to a large extent, to maintain procedural justice strictly. But the logic formed in traditional agricultural society and the expectations of the court is to maintain "substantive justice." When natural and man-made disasters occur, ordinary people are accustomed to moralize the problem and view the issue simply from the perspective of a good man or a bad guy, demanding the law to make a corresponding response. Against such a background, a judge or a collegiate panel cannot resist strong social pressure or scrupulously abide by the logic demanded by law even when they want to act according to law. In this small community, in order to protect themselves or the safety of their family, or even just to protect their own conscience, judges are naturally prone to give up rights or powers that belong to them theoretically and pass on problems to the higher level, that is, to resort to the judicial committee for self-protection.[52] The problem here, superficially, can be dis-

[52]According to our follow-up survey, the judicial committee of that county could not resist the strong pressure. At the initial discussion, the judicial committee had several opinions, which all believed that defendant's behaviors had not constituted crime. But constrained by pressure of the society and local government, they admitted that the behaviors of the defendant were suspicious of wrongdoing (which strictly speaking was already a progress). However, in the end, the judicial committee made concessions by 5–4 and sentenced the defendant a year of imprisonment with one year of suspension. The judge interviewed said that "during the trial, the defendant's face was covered with tears… the local policemen refused to go out on patrol for several days." Many years later, when I once again came into contact with the parties concerned of this case, I was told that in order to make the defendant Wang accept the judgment, the leaders of the local police station in the county promised to help Wang's son get employed as an exchange. And they actually kept their promise!

cussed by borrowing a concept or proposition of the system of judicial independence; but such borrowing is useless. What is involved here is a social precondition for a modern judicial independence system to occur and develop, as well as a structural change of a society. For this reason, it is a process that takes time and is not a problem that can be solved instantly by a concept, a proposition, an ideological education, an attitude rectification of court, or a judge devoted to his or her duty and protecting of the law.

The case has reflected some other problems of Chinese society, which will be shown clearly in the second case.

A farm secretary in a county hired a tractor to bring his dead relative back home and asked two fellow villagers to help him. They crossed the Han River by ferry and then went ashore. The river bank was so steep that the tractor glided backward. The three men tried to stop the tractor by using their shoulders, but it was in vain. The secretary asked the ferry to help. However, because of a submerged anchor, the steel plate that helped the ferry ashore cut off a leg of one fellow villager. The villager filed a lawsuit against the secretary, asking for a compensation of 150,000 yuan. The secretary would not compensate any money and claimed that "If you want money, I have none. If you want a life, I've got one." The villager "rolled the court" (rolled on the ground of the court room) to illustrate his condition. Both sides threatened to kill themselves if the court could not make judgment.

The reason for the court's indecision was not because the facts or laws were not clear, but that the sentence could not be implemented since the secretary had no money for compensation. The case was submitted to the judicial committee. The president of the court himself called together 6 departments and units of the county related to this case (!) in order to first of all distinguish right from wrong and then "to solve the problem by using all kinds of social forces." The specific measures included the following: (1) There was a middle school on the farm where an entrance guard was needed. The court asked the education commission of the county to arrange for the disabled villager to become the entrance guard with monthly salary of 250 yuan. His livelihood would then be ensured with his salary adjusted year by year. (2) The court asked the township government of the disabled villager to reduce and remit all taxes, retentions, and workloads of his responsibility fields, until his children reached 18 years of age. (3) The court asked local agricultural bank to loan 20,000 yuan to the secretary so that he could compensate the disabled villager, among which, 6000 yuan would be assigned to make an artificial limb (to ensure that the villager could move around, make a living, and work in the school), and the rest 14,000 yuan would be compensation. (4) The court asked the farm where the secretary was working to pay the villager 10,000 yuan as a kind of welfare. (5) The ferry that caused the trouble was contracted by a farm worker, who had to pay up to 10,000 yuan to the farm every year, and thus, he was asked to pay another 5000 yuan to the villager. The case was settled in this manner. Both sides were very satisfied. The secretary apologized to the villager with his eyes filled with tears, saying that what he had said before had gone too far.

This case was not complicated either. There were neither unclear responsibilities, nor unclear rules. However, if the case was sentenced in a normal way to emphasize the judicial function only, it would not help solve the problem. Some serious social results may have been caused (some suicide would be committed), and because the sentence could not be implemented, the court would have totally lost its authority. The court must "pay attention to whether its judgment would be implemented and would be recognized by society" (remarks by the president of the court). The presiding judge had to submit this case to the judicial committee for discussion and decision only because of the distinctiveness and complexity of the case. Even if the presiding judge had made the same decision as the above measures, the judge or the collegiate panel would have found it impossible to implement the decision since so many units and departments were involved and their coordination and cooperation would be needed. The only way to solve the problem was to submit the case to the judicial committee for discussion and decision and to let the court coordinate among different departments.

Both these cases demonstrated one issue, that is, in China's modern society, especially at the basic level in rural areas, they lack risk-sharing mechanisms and social insurance mechanisms that help to defuse natural and man-made disasters. For this reason, having related laws and rules only does not work. In addition, even when there is such risk-sharing mechanisms, the people are not accustomed to seeing problems by the principle of the following mechanism (like in the previous case, they tended to moralize the natural and man-made disasters and publish a person). Not to mention using this mechanism to solve problems and accept the decision of mechanism. Once a problem arises, the party will normally ask the government to solve the problem. Even if a lawsuit is involved, the court will be asked to solve it in the manner of an administrative department.

This has thus put forward the second problem: In today's China, courts and judges have to pay more attention to practically solving disputes. This kind of preference forces them to consider the actual implementation result of a court's judgment. It is also prone to cause the issue of "administrative bureaucracy,"[53] since the problem cannot be solved by giving a judgment only. It is true that when a court makes judgments, it will consider whether its decision can be implemented. This phenomenon does not belong to China alone.[54] However, the Chinese court has to consider whether it can implement its decision by itself. In the USA, the

[53]He Weifang: "Two Problems of China's Judicial Management System," as in previous note 1.

[54]This issue is also a factor to be considered when court makes decision in the USA. For example, the two most well-known cases in the USA—Marbury v. Madison and Brown v Board of Education—are, to a large extent, took into consideration whether the court judgments could be implemented effectively. In the former case, such consideration had made Chief Justice Marshall deny that the court had jurisdiction over this case after he had attacked the government. But in the latter case, after having declared that racial segregation was against the constitution, the Supreme Court did not require the government to make correction immediately, but allowed the government to gradually eliminate racial segregation it thought as deliberate. As for Chief Justice Marshall's consideration in the case of Marbury v. Madison, please refer to Chinese materials provided by Suli: "How are systems formed?" as in the previous note. But please note that in these two American cases, the implementation issues considered by judges are actually whether other organizations can implement the decision. However, in China, the implementation of judicial decisions is one of the jobs of court.

implementation of judgment is not the judge's business. In order to solve the problem in a perfect way, China's court has to come out and coordinate all parties involved in the case settlement. This is especially true in the second case.

There is one issue that I have mentioned before but has not been discussed yet. That is why almost all administrative cases or economic cases involving large amounts of money will be submitted to the judicial committee. The crucial reason for this also lies here. Dispute settlements of this kind involve interest coordination of many departments. The problem here is not at all about how a judge with strong professional abilities or high moral standards will decide on it to make the case fairer, but how to actually implement and carry out a seemingly reasonable decision. This task exceeds far beyond the ability of any single judge or collegiate panel. They have to submit to the judicial committee the problem which is not that complicated in terms of legal rules, but extremely complex when being handled, and ask the court to coordinate and settle. During the process of solving problems in this manner (successfully and satisfactorily), the court will unconsciously or consciously intensify its features of an administrative organ to require the position of subcounty-level organization and to continuously seek support from the local party, political government, and people's committee.

This has thus put forward the third question, which is even deeper. Whether the basic function of basic-level court is implementing and forming rules (to solve problems generally) or solving disputes (to solve problems specifically)?[55] If neither can be neglected, which one is more important and which direction should be taken? It is obvious that Chinese courts or scholars today rarely elaborate on this problem or realize it in practice.[56] People are still accustomed to see court as another channel or department to settle disputes. The high expectation of

[55]Many writings of foreign scholars have pointed out the two functions of court, and they have especially emphasized the expectation function of rules. As far as I see, these two functions cannot be separated completely in the activities of court. Moreover, functions of modern court have gradually changed from dispute settlement in the past to "establish a set of rules to influence the future behaviors of parties of the current case and other people" (by Posner) through resolving detailed disputes. Please refer to Posner, *Economic Analysis of Law*, as previous note 13, p. 521. As far as dispute settlement is concerned only, it is not necessary for the parties concerned to turn to court for help. There are many disputes settled by some other means among people—administration, mediation, arbitration, and self rescue. As long as there are no favorable relations between the deciding organization or people and the parties concerned, the settlement is not necessarily more unfair than that of the court. And the courts are not necessarily more impartial or have a special channel towards the truth of the matter than other organizations or people settling the dispute (we may therefore judge that the currently popular saying that bring all disputes to the court is a ideological fairy tale, behind which there is a huge interest drive from some special interests groups like judges, lawyers, law school professors and students). In today's society, the more important function of the court is to ensure that rules are formed in daily life through its special activities. The formation and confirmation of rules has huge positive externalities than settlement of disputes, since it can provide guidance or reference for settlement of other disputes. It is just in this sense that it is more suitable to regard the court as a organization to provide "public goods" instead of private goods.

[56]I used to discuss this issue particularly in "the lawsuit of the *Story of Qiu Ju*, Qiu Shi's rat poison case, and freedom of speech." *Rule of Law and Native Resources*, as previous mentioned. I emphasized the significance of freedom of speech as a rule and praised highly the attention paid to rules demonstrated by court judgment of these two cases.

"substantive justice" or even "strict liability"[57] and the emphasis on a "satisfactory settlement" of cases[58] will force judges, especially basic-level judges facing most first-instance cases, to be unable to act only according to rules (which is totally different from judges intentionally disregarding rules due to corruption).[59] They have to put the dispute settlement in the center, and this naturally requires a more powerful person or organization (judicial committee and even court president) to ensure the settlement of dispute. This is no longer a simple issue of judicial independence, but the development of a social division of labor which realizes modern justice and judicial independence, a historic issue in the transformation of court functions, as well as issues of rule of law in the modern sense, or rule-based governance.[60]

I can go on analyzing, but this will exceed the research subject of judicial committees and would require a broader vision, which is not the task of this chapter. The analysis here is just to point out that there are reasons of deeper social structure and function for the judicial committee to exist and obtain some factual legitimacy. And these reasons cannot be avoided by ostrich tactics when considering whether to keep or abolish the judicial committee.

3.9 Conclusion

I can approximately make the following conclusions based on the above analysis.

[57]The high expectation of "strict liability" by people in the basic-level society in China has been demonstrated in these two cases. But from the perspective of legal system, "strict liability" is an effective rule formed in the social condition in which the science and technology so lags behind that it is impossible to distinguish negligence from on purpose, and the society lacks effective risk-sharing mechanism. Only under this vision can we understand that "liability for fault" is a product of progress in social life conditions, but not a product of pure intellectual development. As for analysis of "strict liability," please refer to Oliver Wendell Holmes, Jr., *The Common Law*, Little, Brown, and Company, 1948, and Richard A. Posner, *The Economics of Justice*, Harvard University Press, 1981, especially Chap. 6. For this reason, due to some changes in social conditions nowadays, "strict liability" has somewhat revived in justice. However, China's jurist circle and legal circle should have a clearer thinking of its practical logics and should not think that "strict liability" must be more "just" than "liability for fault.."

[58]This factor has also penetrated into the language about judicial justice which is currently quite popular. Please think about the Jiajiang anti-counterfeit case mentioned in previous note 80 and two cases analyzed briefly in this chapter (especially the first case); you will see that when there is a strong public sentiment, acting according to rules will be regarded as judicially "unjust." This may be a tricky problem of rule of law in China's changing society.

[59]This is an important reason for why I started from basic-level judges, but not from judges from intermediate courts and above. In comparison, courts above the intermediate level mainly deal with second-instance cases (in jure). Thus, in terms of dealing specific dispute, judges of the intermediate courts are and need not to be as sensitive as the judges of the basic-level courts, and they feel less social pressure.

[60]Lon L. Fuller therefore regarded law as "an undertaking to make people's behavior submit to governance of rules," and please see *The Morality of Law*, rev. ed., Yale University Press, 1969, p. 106; the Chief Justice of U.S. Supreme Court Antonin Scalia had one important essay named as "The Rule of Law as a Law of Rules." Please see, Antonin Scalia, "The Rule of Law as a Law of Rules," *University of Chicago Law Review*, 1989, vol. 56, p. 1175.

First, we cannot make the general conclusion that China's judicial committee system in the basic-level courts is good for judicial independence or judicial justice, especially currently. As previous analysis has pointed out, at the theoretical level, judicial independence is an abstract concept, but at the practical level, judicial independence is a set of systems, a set of complex social practices, and an institutional practice supported by all kinds of social conditions. If we study judicial independence only at the conceptual level, or use systems, regulations, or practices from this or that Western developed country as standards, then it would be difficult for us to really understand China's issues, problems faced by judges at China's basic-level courts, as well as China's issue of judicial independence. We must borrow empirical studies of Western scholars to inform our empirical study and make new systematic analysis and demonstration of judicial independence—a traditional political and philosophical concept.

As for the execution of power, judicial independence involves at least three interwoven dimensions. First of all, there must be a set of systems which support the execution of ultimate authority by the judge and does not bring too big a burden of liability to him (such as lifetime appointment and high-salary system for judges, even the jury, etc.[61]). Secondly, there must be a set of effective restriction mechanism to prevent judges from pursuing their own interests or even running after moral ideals far beyond social standards which they themselves believe should be pursued by the whole society. Finally, judges should have a set of corresponding special skills to make decisions on disputes.[62] Apart from these, there must also be certain social conditions. If we want to solve the problem pragmatically, we should not simply focus on one aspect of independent trial and decision by judges, or see this aspect as the fundamental approach and only insurance to realize judicial justice. Nor should we see this aspect as a panacea that can kill every disease and have immediate effect.

We also obviously realize that judicial independence does not mean that judges are free from any restriction. It only requires that judges should have restrictions

[61]Here, I am only giving analysis to the supporting point of judicial independence, not imply that China should or should not adopt those systems. The system of jury certainly has its advantages, but it has disadvantages as well. As for overview of these kinds of disputes in America, please refer to Abraham, *Judicial Process*, as previous note 15, pp. 136–140. What is more important is that European Continental countries do not have jury systems. US federal judges are all appointed (for a lifetime), but in some states, the election system is adopted and judges are not appointed for lifetime. All these foreign systems need to be studied in detail in their own systems and contexts.

[62]Judge Posner thinks that the latter two problems are actually the key issues in judiciary. His summary is "how to prevent law specialists from becoming a professional privilege level, and prevent that their purposes are too much different from purposes demanded by the society and understood by the public" and "how can a judge, under the situation that he himself hasn't experienced any event causing disputes, make a thorough investigation on the factual truth of the cases which he is asked to try." Please see *The Problem of Jurisprudence*, translated by Suli, China's University of Politics and Law Press, 1994, pp. 7–8 (with some changes in the translation).

on actions which the society thinks improper and prevent the judiciary from realizing social justice systematically. We have no reason to assume that a judge will surely attach importance to social justice and equity and try his or her best to realize social justice only because they are a judge. We have no reason and should not assume that people taking the post of judge are generally speaking more honest than people holding other public posts on purely a priori grounds (we certainly cannot assume as well that only because someone is a judge, they must have worse moral standard than ordinary people generally; but these two assumptions often take turns appearing in articles criticizing the judicial committee system and even appear in the same article). Restriction is always necessary, with no exception to judges. It is because of this that judicial independence cannot be understood from personal qualities. This is the issue of systems, as well as sets of systems.

If we give emphasis to systems, we must get rid of the approach which gives too much attention to judges' personal moral qualities and forms judicial independence based on this. We often hear reports on a certain judge who is not afraid of threats or cannot be lured in by promise of gain.[63] Superficially, it aims to praise good qualities of the judge and seems to demonstrate the possibility of "judicial independence" or "judge independence." As far as I'm concerned, this has shown that we—no matter the country or the society—actually do not care to use systems to resolve problems which can only be solved by people's high moral qualities in China's traditional society. It even requires the judge make tremendous personal sacrifice (personal security and their family's safety) or resist huge temptations to ensure the impartial operation of justice. In this sense, this kind of propaganda and praise, as well as using these to put the judicial system in order, precisely demonstrates that our mentality of system building has major defects. The mentality remains traditional, which links judicial independence and justice to the personal moral standards of judges. This is actually an approach of rule of law emphasizing rule of man. In modern society, a relatively good system does not necessarily require (but would be better to have) people with outstanding moral standards and intelligence (talents) to function. It can function normally with people of intermediate moral standard, intelligence levels, and knowledge.

We can neither assume that a person who is willing to realize social justice and whose moral character is impeccable is surely able to realize judicial justice if implementing power independently. Judiciary certainly requires a certain level of moral qualities. However, since legal practice has become comprised of knowledge and skills that can be obtained only by special studies in modern society, the modern judiciary's responsibilities are far from problems that can be judged correctly

[63]For example, "He's house was burned down only because he tried to punish local villains and protect social security. He was falsely accused and framed up twice only because he wanted to enforce law impartially and didn't bow to the powerful and the rich." Please see Liang Gonghua, Guo Minzhen: "I can't leave the village people alone!" *People's Judicature*, 1991, Issue 1, page 4. You may find more vivid and terrifying report from Xiong Yi: "The Critical Moment," *People's Judicature*, 1991, Issue 8, pp. 45–46. Three judges in this article were attacked by the defendant with a knife, and the tribunal director "even had his intestines exposed."

with just a high level of moral qualities; it requires specialized knowledge and skills. If a person with impeccable moral character but no special judicial knowledge or skills takes the post of a judge, not only will the independent implementation of his decision power be seriously harmed as a matter of fact (e.g., the judge has fair subjective intention, but is actually prone to be led by others in one way or another. Or perhaps if a judge has too strong of a moral sense but lacks proper understanding of functions of legal systems or of his or her own role, he or she may give a severe sentence to a person who refuses to help someone who is dying and thus constitute "a misjudged case"), but the legitimacy of the independent or even monopolistic implementation of decision power will also be questioned (why do people always ask an organization or a person who always makes wrong decisions and whose judgment is not as good as normal people's to resolve disputes? Is it simply because it is called a court and he or she is called a judge?). Up until now, Chinese jurisprudence and Western jurisprudence have been basically concentrating on demonstration of political and moral philosophy when discussing judicial independence. If we really look back, we will find out that judicial independence has always been related to the development of special skills of the judiciary, although they are not solely related.[64] For this reason, as far as modern judicial independence that can be practiced is concerned, we should not be satisfied with this narrow understanding of justice: an upright judge who is brave enough to "decide on behalf of the ordinary people" decides the case at his own will according to law (or according to customs and his own beliefs when there is no legal regulations). This ideal is too far away, not only because the fair result pursued by the judiciary depends not simply on individual morality of judges; but what is more important is that even when there are judges with good morality, there is no recognized and reliable mechanism in the world to pick them out.

I believe that this chapter has already demonstrated that the judicial committee has complicated multiple functions in China's judiciary and is far more complicated than modern Western developed countries' systems. It is also entangled with the social reality of modern China that cannot be fully demonstrated by words. For most Chinese people and jurists who have lived here for a long time, this kind of reality can be felt. They sometimes admire, dislike, or even detest the circumstance, but it is hard for them to link it by internal logic or grasp it rationally. When describing their institutional experience, Western scholars always consciously or unconsciously construct it by selecting and accumulating important details of their living environments. For this reason, those already popular in the West may not be able to take roots in China's reality. It has nothing to do with whether Chinese people like it or not. It is not an issue of whether China makes

[64]Please refer to Suli: "On Specialization of Legal Activities," *Rule of Law and Native Resources*, China University of Politics and Law Press, 1996, especially Sect. 3.2. In fact, among examples of judicial independence which most frequently quoted by people, British Lord Chancellor Sir Edward Coke resisted interference of justice by King James. Its most important and key argument is that judges have special skills of justice, that is, the so-called artificial reason but not political and moral philosophy which is popular on textbooks of jurisprudence.

enough efforts to transform Chinese society either. For example, as for issues of how to prevent laws from transforming in China's acquaintance society,[65] it cannot be changed simply by criticizing feudal cultural tradition irrelevant to the subject. Neither can it be solved by simply encouraging or demanding judges to be impartial and incorruptible, do things according to law, and be strict in enforcing the law. In the long run, in order to change this situation, the market economy needs to be developed further, and society needs to be mobile. The structure of the acquaintance-based society at China's county and village level must be changed, no matter whether a society of strangers is desirable or not. As far as I see, it needs at least a few decades of time. Another instance is that judges of modern China are seldom graduates from law school, and the majority of them have not received regular or systematic university education. Although Judicial Laws require new regulations and qualifications of judges, but this is not enough to actually change cultural and professional qualities of Chinese judges within a short period of time (this has more probably provided justified reasons for certain "career training organizations" to exist and "sell diplomas" publicly). In recent years, the law education favored by the society has not been able to make many law graduates enter into the courts, not to mention basic-level courts relatively removed from the city center.[66] Even though some of the graduates are entering the court system, they are not necessarily playing roles they expected due to many reasons.[67] The issue

[65]On this issue, some people may propose the judge rotation system. If we do not consider practical restrictions, this system is feasible in terms of logics. However, once put into the specific society, its limitation is exposed. First of all, only a few judges can be rotated, and most judges cannot be rotated. And rotation is certainly restricted by financial resources. Secondly, effective rotation must be cross-domain. If only rotation within the county, it is only a change in the form but not in the content. However, the number of judges that can be rotated may be smaller if cross-domain functions are involved. Thirdly, both rotation and non-rotation have their advantages and disadvantages. It is sometimes good for judges to implement functions if they are familiar with a region and local customs (languages included) and not necessarily always on the contrary. Even if we do not consider these pros and cons, the rotation of a judge is not the job transfer of a person, but involves relocation of a whole family, which requires special fees up to tens of thousands of yuan (including transportation and losses. People often say, "relocation three times equals to being burnt down once."). If the judge himself has to pay for part or whole of the fees, it will further reduce judge's relatively meager income. If the country pays for these fees, it will increase a large number of expenses annually and thus increase costs of the society and individuals. Due to financial limitations, rotation cannot be frequent or involve too many people. But if the rotation is not frequent and only a few people are involved, there will be no obvious effect on the rotation. If the rotation is ordered through administrative method, talents in court system will flow out further, and the actual expenses of judges will increase due to rotation. As far as I'm concerned, especially considering that courts nowadays are in severe short of funds, this seemingly good suggestion is basically a showy empty talk.

[66]The majority of graduates have entered the circle of lawyers, business, and politics. Among my classmates, only less than 10 % entering the judicial system (courts, procurators, public security), and the minimum level is the intermediate procurators. However, the number of full-time lawyers and part-time lawyers greatly exceeds the number of people working in the judicial system. Please refer to Chap. 10 of this book "Professionalism of Judges in the Basic-level Courts."

[67]The main point is that their knowledge is not appropriate for needs. Please refer to Chap. 10 of this book "Professionalism of Judges in Basic-level Courts."

of cultural and professional qualities of basic-level judges will continue to exist for a relatively long period of time. All these issues cannot be solved by "Great Leap Forward"-style methods in the short run. This means that some things which do not constitute problems in Western countries are actually unavoidable problems in China, and in this sense, modern China and Western developed countries face different problems.

To put forward, problems do not mean that we should give up our efforts, judicial independence, or judicial justice that is promised. I just say that if we want to make our efforts effective, we have to consider how to form China's judicial independence system and judicial justice under China's current changing social conditions. We need to find out which problems can be resolved by simply establishing or abolishing systems and which problems cannot be resolved by this method within a short period of time. Thus, we will define the limitation of our reasoning and efforts, and plan the direction for the "investment" of our limited resources. Although we need to consider that the proposition of China's national conditions is sometimes nearly dogmatic and even causes some resentment, we must make it clear that the proposition is not put forward to give into the present situation, but is oriented toward reform. It does not demand conservation, or require jurists and judges to give up their social responsibilities. It aims to understand our problems more comprehensively, foresee and understand all kinds of results that the prescriptions to solve problems might bring about as much as possible, and thus make a choice with more advantages and less disadvantages.

Judicial independence needs to accord with a set of systems in the society that can coordinate and supplement it. It cannot be done by one system alone. Its realization requires us not only to eliminate the interference of administrative power which we are usually aware of and give our attention to it, but also get rid of the improper influence of social conditions of people, the media, and other forces. We even have to reject interference from measures put forward by scholars or politicians in the name of reform which may have pretty good results on one or a few events. For this latter aspect, the improper correction system of misjudged cases, as well as the so-called people's congress's supervision over the judiciary, has actually caused some practices of supervision over trials of specific cases.[68] Although it may have good aspirations, and can prevent or actually does prevent some miscarriage of justice in some aspects, generally speaking, these two kinds of practices constitute a new threat to judges' judicial independence. And from the long-term perspective, they are not conducive to fostering judges' professional qualities or sense of honor and responsibility in the judiciary and thus go against judicial independence.

We can step back and ask, if we eliminate the system of judicial committee now and push China's judicial independence a step forward, can we make sure

[68]For a successful example which has been publicly reported only recently, please see "To Correctly Understand the Supervision of People's Congress over Judicial Work—A Research on Correction of a Court Misjudged Case by Xinyi Municipal People's Congress of Jiangsu Province," *People's Daily*, June 10, 1998, page 9.

that justice will be more fair and reasonable? It is certain that at the level of symbol and sign, it may be considered "progress" (but it also depends on whether you approve that symbol or sign). But ordinary Chinese people (it is actually the same to all Chinese people) are always good at finding ways to avoid the system reforms imposed on them if they find the system harms their interests. One example is the promotion of the system of being held accountable for misjudgement that has resulted in the increased number of cases submitted to the judicial committee for discussion. The old saying that "Whenever there is a rule, there is a way to get around it" is a secular but classic summary. Surely, if we have come this far, even I myself cannot necessarily accept that the judicial committee be eliminated at once—since "there is a way to get around it" anyway. However, the real reformation of the system requires buildup for a long time;[69] "Now we should take a step from the very beginning," but there is pride and enthusiasm in this difficult situation. If we put this into practice, those practitioners will become a modern Sisyphus that commits suicide. When we try to understand and learn Western systems, we should not just follow suit, or pay attention only to whether the appearance of the systems are "alike." We should make more efforts to discover the internal logic and practical functions of a set of systems. Research of this kind will not only enable us to understand advantages and disadvantages of a system deeper, but more importantly help us to find out the route that the system relies on for its growth and development.

In a certain sense, this article really defends both powerfully and mildly for a system of judicial committee. However, this kind of defense, first of all, does not mean that the judicial committee is a system that can solve all problems related to China's judicial independence and justice. It is also not the only system to solve these problems. It only emphasizes that under the current social situation in china, it has relative rationality, especially in basic-level courts. It addresses issues that I consider problems that the basic-level courts face but cannot be solved for a short while. Thus, the function and rationality of the judicial committee have been limited. I am not defending it from the position of foundationalism. For this reason, if someone is bound to say that the judicial committee cannot resolve the issue of government interference or arbitrary presidential appointment, or cannot guarantee judicial justice, I would have to admit it. I think this kind of debate is of no reason. Since the foundationalist view of the system is not possible in the reality of system building, it will definitely cause system nihilism. The death of Socrates is enough to refute the democracy and rule of law which people firmly believe today. My defense is that even if the social conditions are appropriate, one system can only resolve one problem or a few problems, while a set of systems can only solve a set of problems. I dare not believe that there is any so-called system (not system type) for "long-term peace and order" and "of universal application."

[69]Please refer to my analysis of the formation and establishment of American judicial review in the article of "How are systems formed?" (as previously mentioned).

However, in another sense, this article can be regarded as a more thorough self-criticism and self-examination of the judicial committee system. When I point out the relative rationality of this system, I believe that the advantages of judicial committee outweigh disadvantages in terms of judicial independence and judicial justice in China's basic-level courts and that it is a relatively beneficial, effective, and impartial judicial system and second best only based on the restrictive conditions of Chinese society today and in the foreseeable future. This conclusion does not mean that only because this system has Chinese characteristics, it is the universal truth that we should naturally adhere to forever. When there are changes to the preconditions, such as the cultural and professional qualities of judges improving, the loss of a society of acquaintance gradually fading away with the market economy, and the functions of courts changing, it may be possible that the judicial committee can be eliminated, or if not, its practical function will be gradually transformed.

This does not mean that courts of all levels in today's China should stick to a uniform system of judicial committee. As far as the courts above the intermediate level are concerned, their environment (in rather big cities with a higher degree of defamiliarization), problems (more instances of appeal), professional, and cultural qualities of judges (with more judges with bachelor's and master's degrees in law), and internal divisions of work (more detailed and specialized) are distinctively different from those courts at the basic level. We can and must conduct thorough research on problems like whether it is still necessary to maintain a judicial committee system and how we should strengthen its professional functions. We should also make it clear that even though there are such differences, it does not mean that courts above the intermediate level should eliminate the judicial committee system right now. The research conclusion of this chapter is based on research of basic-level courts; the significance of this research conclusion is naturally limited and cannot be extended automatically to courts above intermediate level. Specific conclusions must be drawn through special empirical survey and research. Certainly, the perspective and approach of thinking about and analyzing problems may be of some significance of reference for similar research in intermediate-level courts.

Naturally, the conclusion of this article does not say that the judicial committee system is superior to judge independence in the West (nor the opposite, either). This is not only because talking about Western systems in general itself is suspicious, but also because that if we do not see the social conditions and other systems matched in which judicial independence in the West happens, it will be difficult for us to discuss advantages and disadvantages at a meaningful level. To rephrase it in a way in which I may be considered by others as of no position and thus get the worst of both worlds (certainly it would not matter since I don't want to ingratiate myself with anyone), Western practices have Western reasons, while Chinese practices have Chinese reasons. No one can substitute for the other. As Zhuangzi once said, "from the perspective of Tao, there is no difference between being noble and being cheap," and "from the perspective of things themselves, they will regard themselves as noble while viewing others as cheap."[70] This may be useful, although today's common situation is usually the opposite!

First draft on March 18, 1998

Second draft on June 23, 1998

Modified again on July 2, 1998, in Weixiu Garden, Peking University.

[70]"Autumn Water," *Zhuangzi*.

Part II
Judicial Knowledge and Technology

Chapter 4
Courts of First Instance and Appellate Court

All adaptation is a specific form of knowledge.
—Henry Plotkin (Henry Plotkin, *Darwin Machines and the Nature of Knowledge*, Harvard University Press, 1993, p. 228).

4.1 Judicial Knowledge as a Kind of Local Knowledge

This section mainly studies some more detailed problems of judicial knowledge and available technology for judges in basic-level courts.

There is one question that readers are quick to put forward, that is, why should we study judicial knowledge and the technology judges have in basic-level courts? Moreover, the theme of this section has implied one proposition, that is, there may be judicial knowledge and technology in this world that more belongs to judges in basic-level courts. This is certainly the case. To many modern jurists and students of law faculties in China, this proposition is ridiculous. For them, knowledge must have universality and judicial knowledge is therefore universal as well, such as judicial independence, judicial justice, legal doctrine of non-retroactivity, judicial review, and stare decisis. It is in this kind of understanding of knowledge that the introduction of the concept of local knowledge" (which may also be translated as "specific knowledge") into China's jurisprudence is somewhat doubted or looked down upon. He Weifang is worried in one of his articles that "the exaggeration of 'locality' of knowledge about legal order is bound to close our minds, and we will unconsciously make the statement of some Western scholars that law is a kind of universal 'local knowledge.'"[1] When Liu Zuoxiang and Liu Pengfei look into the future of China's jurisprudence in the twenty-first century, they use the proposition

[1]He Weifang: "Two Problems of China's Judicial Management System," *Social Sciences in China*, Issue 5, 1997, p. 130.

© Foreign Language Teaching and Research Publishing Co., Ltd and Springer Science+Business Media Singapore 2016

S. Zhu, *Sending Law to the Countryside*, China Academic Library,
DOI 10.1007/978-981-10-1142-9_4

of Posner in *The Problems of Jurisprudence*—that many problems of jurisprudence are cross-cultural and cross-temporal—to support a universal legal theory, which also implies criticism against law as a local knowledge.[2] I think the above two arguments are both problematic.

If we only worry about the "exaggeration," then this kind of worry is reasonable, but of little significance. Any "exaggeration" is no good. Why shouldn't we worry about exaggerating the universality of knowledge? Could it be said that the latter exaggeration is surely correct? Not to mention, the main problem of jurisprudence in today's China is that people are not aware of the locality of jurisprudence at all. What He Weifang is worried about is actually that the proposition of "law as local knowledge" has the potential force to overturn all efforts made in recent years to have Chinese law and jurisprudence "integrated with the world." He is afraid that people will therefore not take a broader view into the world and isolate themselves, a practice by which China used to suffer great losses. This kind of worry is a kind of political consideration. However, the proposition itself is about the property of legal knowledge and has nothing to do with whether the person who accepts the proposition is open-minded or not. If we need to judge whether someone is open-minded or not, we never judge by seeing which theoretical proposition he or she accepts or supports, but by seeing whether he or she makes continuous efforts to study problems and conduct research on real problems. On the contrary, whatever propositions are accepted, local or universal, if I declare myself as sticking to this proposition without making efforts to study problems or investigate actual situations, and only repeat what predecessors and other people may have said, this is not an open-minded attitude as far as I see. Being open requires a curiosity and pursuit—and even "greed" of the unknown. Every unknown must be specific and be attached to a specific time and space (locality), and thus, any knowledge must be local first of all (though latter application may be universal).

Secondly, when studying any specific problem and thus seeking some kind of local knowledge, researchers are prone to refer to and compare other kinds of knowledge. This book aims to study China's judicial system at the basic level and emphasizes observing knowledge of basic-level judges. From the perspective of many well-known jurists, this is completely "out of fashion." However, if we do not have other kinds of legal knowledge, judicial knowledge of other countries, or judicial knowledge of courts of superior levels as a reference and for careful comparison, we will have no way to identify what is specifically judicial knowledge of basic-level judges, and it also would be impossible for us to do so. The locality of knowledge is inevitable and must have patterns and qualities demonstrating a universal connection with other local knowledge. On the contrary, if we only emphasize universality of knowledge without adhering to a specific time and space, it will be impossible for us to solve a large number of specific problems, or we can only add one sentence such as "analyze problems case by case." However, it would still be a kind of prevarication by adding this principle, since it does not identify specific problems nor how to analyze cases.

[2] Liu Zuoxiang, Liu Pengfei: "Outlook of Problems in China's Jurisprudence at the Turn of the Century," *Chinese Journal of Law*, Issue 4, 1999, p. 5.

Thirdly, since there are some people emphasizing universal knowledge and believe that due to universal knowledge (which can be applicable everywhere), it is more likely to stand still and refuse to make progress and even impose their so-called universal knowledge on others in the name of truth. Even this kind of opinion still cannot answer the question that where this knowledge comes from (even if it exists in my mind, then it must be local first of all—in my mind!). As a matter of fact, any kind of universal knowledge must and can only be evolved, developed, or abstracted from local knowledge. The concept of transaction cost is local in terms of place of origin (What Ronald Harry Coase studies is "modern enterprise"), but this concept has been extended widely to research in other fields. The system of judicial review is an American system first of all and was later promoted gradually in certain countries. Attaching importance to the research of local knowledge will not result in the closed-mindedness of researchers. Neither will it make local knowledge lose the common significance that it may have. On the contrary, to realize the locality of knowledge means that we begin to realize that our knowledge, our ability to know, and even our life have a limit. Then, we are willing to understand the conditions and preconditions of producing and using certain knowledge, which thereby strengthens our ability of reflection, sensitivity, and self-criticism and encourages us to further existing knowledge. It would be right if He Weifang changed his sentence from "... is bound to close our minds" to "... it won't close our minds."

Liu Zuoxiang's query is more problematic. As far as I see, the author may be in such a rush that he does not understand Posner's original words well. Even if we presume that Posner is right (I personally believe he is), what he has said is simply that many problems of jurisprudence are cross-cultural and cross-temporal. Posner does not say that methods and knowledge to solve these problems are definitely cross-cultural and cross-temporal. As a matter of fact, Posner's following long argument is just about methods to solve problems that are not cross-cultural or cross-temporal.[3] We can give an example: If a married couple wants to break up because the wife and the husband are not on good terms, then this problem is undoubtedly cross-temporal and cross-cultural (if we include animals, then the problem is even cross-human nature). However, the solutions of this problem are different in different societies (or species). Even in developed countries in the West, there is a variety of solutions, and theoretical bases of marriage laws are different. Permission to divorce and non-permission to divorce are two solutions; strict control of divorce and freedom of divorce are two solutions; and divorce with and without fault are

[3]There are many examples. For example, regarding the debate on legal definitions caused by Nuremburg Trial between Hart and Fuller"fuller", Posner has pointed out explicitly that this debate is, to a large extent, a debate of two different judicial cultures. Take Posner's analysis of the problem of origin of law as another example. The same problem is there to find out qualified and competent agencies. But in Posner's point of view, the solution of European countries is to emphasize legislation, while justice is emphasized in Anglo-Saxon countries. For another example, regarding the problem of fact-finding in judiciary, the jury is relied on in Anglo-Saxon countries while it is up to the police, the prosecutor, and the judge together to identify in European countries. These kinds of examples can be found everywhere in Judge Posner's book. Please see Richard A. Posner, *The Problems of Jurisprudence*, Harvard University Press, 1990.

also two solutions. The first two solutions are complete opposites of each other, but each can still hold water. It is difficult to argue which one is better, even if you have preference. Different solutions can be compatible with the same problems. Both yellow cats and black cats can catch a mouse. It is the same when discussing rule of law, different people have different arguments while none is exclusively correct.

As a matter of fact, judicial knowledge is a kind of local knowledge.[4] This kind of knowledge has been gradually produced and reproduced during the process of judicial professionalism in modern times.[5] As I have mentioned in a previous section, in order to ensure the effective function of law and judiciary, more detailed local knowledge is always needed (for example, about the characters of litigants).[6] In this next section, I further demonstrate that the problem of this kind of local knowledge exists in courts of different levels. This chapter can be the introduction of this part which discusses the "locality" of China's basic-level courts to pave the way for discussing the locality of knowledge that basic-level courts produce later. However, before discussing this problem, I will briefly track down and observe the genealogy of legal and judicial knowledge in Western developed countries and the social and institutional conditions in which it has been produced.

4.2 Outline of Judicial Knowledge Genealogy

At present, the lessons about judiciary in legal textbooks are always seen as a product separate from specific social and institutional environments; it is thought to have empirical and universal truth and has exhausted the true essence of the judiciary. This kind of lesson may be somewhat necessary as training for career ideology, but from the standpoint of legal sociology, this lesson is not convincing. As far as I see, judicial knowledge cannot be a clear discovery of eternal truth by human reason (rationalism). It can only be the product of judicial practice (empiricism), and a kind of institutionalized knowledge gradually accumulated by judges when meeting factual disputes which require their judgment under specific constraint conditions. Because any judiciary must be attached to a certain time and space, and time and space are changing continuously, knowledge produced is at least provincial in terms of its origin, although its applicable scope or reference meaning is not necessarily limited to a place of origin. I don't want a philosophical discussion of common epistemology here. I just want to understand the problem

[4]If we can remember the story of Chief Justice Edward Coke and King James I of England, then we can understand this point. Chief Justice Coke says that law is reason, but not a kind of common reason. It is a kind of "man-made" reason which only judges and lawyers know about. Chief Justice Coke has supported its demand of judicial independence by emphasizing the locality of knowledge.

[5]Cf. Richard A. Posner, "The Material Basis of Jurisprudence," in *Overcoming Law*, Harvard University Press, 1995; and "Professionalism" in *The Problematics of Moral and Legal Theory*, Harvard University Press, 1999.

[6]Chap. 1 of this book "Why Send Law to the Countryside?".

by analyzing Anglo-American legal knowledge genealogy accumulated by taking judiciary as a central element.

European jurisprudence is quite different from American jurisprudence.[7] Many researchers in the past, including myself, tend to attribute this kind of difference to philosophical traditions of European rationalism and Anglo-American empiricism.[8] But as Foucault has pointed out, this kind of method, uncovering origin, tradition, and unity is actually a kind of man-made fabrication.[9] As a matter of fact, a kind of discursive practice is always produced together with a certain non-discursive practice. In Foucault's words, which are probably easier to understand but also possibly partially misunderstand, a kind of knowledge always goes with a series of constraint conditions and corresponding systems in which this kind of knowledge is produced.

In European countries, the key issue that jurisprudence focuses on has always been legislation and code compiling. What the jurists care about is how to compile a code that can be universally applicable around the country and which can be promulgated and implemented through parliament. This kind of legislation or code centralism enables the "formal rationality" of jurisprudents to be brought into full play. This kind of tradition has a series of other social conditions apart from humanity's longtime superstition of words and assumptions that words correspond to the things that they "represent."[10] For example, comparatively speaking, the territories of European countries are not that vast, and their ethnic groups are relatively unitary, and thus, national industrialization and social standardization are comparatively easy. Additionally, the revival of stipulate laws ensures that to unify national order by legislation and code compiling is relatively easy. Under such a legal system and social condition, the problems faced by a judiciary are comparatively simple, and the role played by judges in the judiciary is much smaller compared with that of judges in Anglo-Saxon law.[11] For this reason, although China's modern legal system has adopted a continental law system, and at least before 1980s, there have been more translated legal writings regarding the continental legal system than the Anglo-American legal system, and we seldom have seen or have never seen any knowledge summary or theoretical generalization on trial practice from continental scholars. This happens not because continental judges do not have trial knowledge, but because the continental legal system centers on

[7]Suli: "What is Jurisprudence?" *China Book Review*, Issue 5, 1995.

[8]Hayek deals with this problem in this way to a large extent, please see, Hayek: *The Constitution of Liberty*, translated by Deng Zhenglai, SDX Joint Publishing Company, 1997.

[9]Foucault: "Nietzsche, Genealogy, History," *Social Theory Review*, translated by Suli, 1998. Please also see Foucault: *The Archaeology of Knowledge*, translated by Xie Qiang and Ma Yue, SDX Joint Publishing Company, 1998, especially the first section of Chap. 2 "unit of discourse."

[10]Michel Foucault, *The Order of Things, An Archaeology of the Human Sciences*, Random House, 1970.

[11]About judges and judiciary of continental European countries, please see Henry A. Abraham, *The Judicial Process: An Introductory Analysis of the Courts of the United States, England, and France*, 6th ed. Oxford University Press, 1993.

legislation and code compiling and has made knowledge of judges silent or unseen and thus naturally not able to enter into the vision of jurists as a kind of knowledge.

American jurisprudence centers on the judiciary,[12] and the tradition has been created by American judges under restrictions of special social, political, and legal systems. Different from continental European countries, America has vast territory and a strong tradition of local autonomy (federation). It has also adopted the common-law system of the UK. Because of these factors, plus strict separation of powers and a judicial review system that was been formed later, American judges have played an enormous role in the production of social order compared with judges of any European countries (including the United Kingdom[13]). Judges making laws (especially in the name of common law) have been a common and widely recognized fact in the USA. At the same time, in order to safeguard their decision and legitimacy of their positions, judges must also restrict and protect themselves by stare decisis (common law) and "legal interpretation" (statute law). For this reason, the USA has formed jurisprudence centered on judges and court activities. The most disputable issues in American jurisprudence are all judicial problems.

Although we can say in general that American jurisprudence is the product of American judges and lawyers, if we observe more deeply, we will discover that American jurisprudence, which centers on a judiciary that mainly brings together experience of American judges of appeal and the most fundamental legal dispute that it has to answer, is how judges of appeals discover and apply laws in all kinds of manners and names.[14] In this judicial system, there are only a few summaries of judicial experience of judges to deal with factual disputes, and this set of systems in America does not demand judges or lawyers to attach importance to knowledge and technology in this respect.

First of all, the USA has always used an adversary system and adherence to the jury system in the trials of criminal and (part of) civil cases. The biggest limit (and also the biggest contributor at the same time) to knowledge invention in this system is to basically exclude factual disputes of cases from the thoughts of judges and jurisprudence. The adversary system has exempted judges from the responsibility of evidence investigation and collection. All evidence is investigated, put forward, and verified by lawyers (including local prosecutors in criminal cases, whose title is literally translated as "regional lawyers") by cross-examination. The jury will at last make judgment on evidence in terms of fact. It can be said that in this system, judges basically do not have to deal with factual disputes and even do not have to

[12]Posner, *The Problems of Jurisprudence*, as mentioned in previous note 3.

[13]As for roles played by American judges and British judges in their own judicial systems, please refer to P. S. Atiyah and Robert S. Summers, *Form and Substance in Anglo-American Law: A Comparative Study of Legal Reasoning, Legal Theory, and Legal Institutions*, Oxford University Press, 1987.

[14]"What in the minds of ordinary legal theorists are some legal theories. They only pay attention to appellate courts, and those theories are all from those appellate courts."Posner, *The Problematics of Moral and Legal Theory*, as previous note 5, p. 213, note 40. Please also see Anthony T. Kronman, *The Lost Lawyer, Failing Ideals of the Legal Profession*, Harvard University Press, 1993, pp.110ff.

care about factual disputes.[15] It is only in a small number of cases in which facts are extremely clear that judges are needed to make decision on factual disputes.

Secondly, the USA has adopted a system of stare decisis, which requires that judges should strictly follow judicial precedents of the courts they work in and courts of higher levels. This makes judges and lawyers (including jurists) focus their attention on related precedents and interpretations of courts at higher levels. Even where statute law and constitutional cases are concerned, since the application of written laws must also be subject to interpretation of judges, what subordinate judges and lawyers care most about is still interpretation of related statute laws of appellate courts on specific cases. Thus, here comes the well-known legal definition of Holmes that law is the prediction of a judge's judgment, which can only be understood in this tradition.[16] At the same time, a large number of justices of peace who deal with ordinary factual and legal disputes cannot get approval from other judges at all,[17] and their legal knowledge has been completely neglected in this knowledge system from the very beginning.[18]

Thirdly, due to high adversary fees, in the USA, a large number of judicial cases with relatively simple and explicit factual and/or legal problems are solved outside the court through all kinds of agreements. Among criminal cases, about 90 % do not have court hearings and are closed by means of plea bargaining or plea agreements between lawyers of both sides.[19] Among civil cases, 95 % of them reach an accommodation before trial through all kinds of means (including through lawyers).[20] Only those rather major and ambiguous legal disputes, which are referred to by Holmes as "hard cases," can really initiate real litigation.

---

[15]Holmes therefore said in a letter to Pollock that "I hate facts"; "I always say the chief end of man is to form general propositions, adding that no general proposition is worth a damn." Please see *The Mind and Faith of Justice Holmes, His Speeches, Essays, Letters and Judicial Opinions*, ed. by Max Lerner, The Modern Library, 1943, p. 444.

[16]Oliver Wendell Holmes, Jr., "The Path of the Law," in *Collected Legal Papers,* Harcourt, Brace and Hows, Inc., 1952; Holmes reiterated this definition in a letter to Pollock and explicitly referred it as the legal definition in the lawyer's sense. Please see *The Mind and Faith of Justice Holmes*, as previous note 15, p. 449.

[17]The English abbreviation of justice of peace is J.P., and it is often confused to be"justice of plaintiff," which means that judges only listen to plaintiffs and there is neither adversary nor proper procedures.

[18]Frank used to suggest that trial judges should have special education and training. But his suggestion was not given importance to in American jurist and judicial circle. As for Frank's suggestions and reasons, please see Jerome Frank, *Court on Trial: Myth and Reality in American Justice*, Princeton University Press, 1973 (1949), pp. 247ff.

[19]Robert A. Carp and Ronald Stidham, *Judicial Process in America*, 4th ed., Congressional Quarterly Inc., 1998, p. 151.

[20]"Beyond Litigation—an Interview with Robert Mnookin," *Stanford Lawyer*, Spring-Summer 1989, p. 5; quoted from Mary Ann Glendon, *A Nation Under Lawyers: How the Crisis in the Legal Profession is Transforming American Society*, Harvard University Press, 1994, p. 224. Please also see Kenneth M. Holland, "The Federal Rules of Civil Procedure," *Law and Policy Quarterly*, 1981, p. 212, quoted from Robe A. Carp and Ronald Stidham, *Judicial Process in America*, as previous note 19, p. 197.

For this reason, if we only have an extremely simple and rough analysis of genealogy regarding judicial knowledge, which is often seen as universal, we can find that this judicial knowledge is mainly the product of judges in Anglo-American law, especially the American legal system. It is those judges who accumulate knowledge about judges of appeals in order to solve problems they face. The legitimacy and effectiveness of their knowledge are related to systems and associated problems of the knowledge. It mainly focuses on the selection, interpretation, and creation of legal rules by judges of appeals. All American jurisprudence is developed around key issues such as the legitimacy and constitutionality for courts to make laws, stare decisis, fact distinction, legal interpretation methods, and investigation of legal origins of constitution. This has formed a sharp contract with continental European law.

This conclusion does not deny that Anglo-American jurisprudence has some kind of transcendence. It probably has relatively big referential meaning and inspiration for judges of appeals in many countries outside the USA and has broken the superstition of European judicial modes and the mode of rule of law and jurisprudence which believes in legislative supremacy. After having seen this point, we should not forget the institutional conditions of Anglo-American legal knowledge production, and neither should we forget that its knowledge has the inevitable character of locality (instance of appeal) as well, or that American legal education is centered on instances of appeal or legal trial.[21] Although the American jurisprudence centered on this is enough to support an Anglo-American judicial system, as legal knowledge and even as judicial knowledge, it is still very incomplete. It is not only local (Anglo-American), but also is only part of this locality (instances of appeal).

When we turn to analyze the characteristics of China's basic-level courts, we can see this kind of judicial knowledge is insufficient.

4.3 China's Basic-level Courts as Courts of First Instance

According to all kinds of procedural laws in China, there is no difference between courts of first instance and appellate courts, in very strict sense. Apart from a few maritime, railway, or military courts which try cases according to exclusive jurisdictions, the original jurisdiction of any other kind of case is divided by courts of

[21]"It would be possible, of course, to teach the law by studying its operation at the trial and pretrial levels rather than concentrating as exclusively as American law teachers do on the decisions of appellate courts. But appellate opinions have the great advantages of bringing out the legal issues in a case with an economy and precision that trial transcripts, for example, rarely do." Anthony T. Kronman, *The Lost Lawyer*, as previous note 14, p. 110.

all levels under the name of "subject matter jurisdiction"[22] Although there is no clear division of courts of first instance and appellate courts, China's basic-level courts are undoubtedly courts of first instance for the majority of civil and criminal cases. Intermediate-level courts, high courts, and even the Supreme Court have the right of first trial on a number of cases, but their main task is instances of appeals (the second instance or retrial). It must be noted that those appellate courts (second instances) are not only engaged in purely jure. According to related procedural laws, when they hear cases of second instance, they have to examine both laws and facts, and even sometimes hear the cases over again in courts.[23] It seems to be similar with basic-level courts, but there are still major differences.

First of all, when those "appellate" courts hear appellate cases, they can choose to open a court session or not open a court session. When there is no court session, the judge will hear the case mainly according to the case files, that is, the written records of the judge from the basic-level court and testimonies presented by both sides in court.

In addition, the so-called trial Trial in the court of second instances is actually mainly concerned with "determining the nature" (I will demonstrate in Chap. 6 of this book that the so-called process of determining the nature is not a factual dispute in the strict sense, but more a legal dispute under the guise of a factual dispute) and makes judgment according to official documents. If the facts are really unclear, the court of second instance will send the case back to the original court for retrial. This kind of investigation of cases is substantially different from the trial system in which the judge of first-instance courts faces both litigation parties and cases in their original state. This kind of difference can be described in Laotze's words: "Tao that can be described is not the universal and eternal Tao." When a life incident has been transformed into words or language, it is difficult to say that the case details constructed by those words equate to the life incident itself. It is necessary for judicial first instances to "distort" life incidents, and it is essential for the function of judiciaries. I shouldn't and wouldn't make excessive demands, however. What I want to point out is that it is due to this difference that, even in China, courts of second instance seldom determine questions of factuality. We count "determining the nature" as part of the purpose, but it will still be different from the nature of the court of first instance.

[22]Please see Article 18, 19, 20, and 21 in Chapter Two of Civil Procedure Law of the People's Republic of China (1991) and article 19, 20, 21, 22, 23 in Chapter Two of Criminal Procedure Law of the Peoples Republic of China. This kind of jurisdiction system has its reason. Particularly in the later period of 1970s when China's court system was beginning to be rebuilt, there lacked judges of good professional qualities, and it could be fully understood to set out this kind of subject matter jurisdiction. However, with the professional quality of people working in court system being improved, in order to prevent judicial injustice and ensure that all people are equal before the law, to promote the further professionalization of judiciary, and encourage law-school graduates to enter into courts of lower levels, this kind of system of subject matter jurisdiction must be under reform.

[23]Article 151, 152, 153 of Civil Procedure Law. Article 187, 189 of Criminal Procedure Law. Article 59 and 61 of Administrative Procedure Law.

Moreover, even if the trial results of first instance and second instance are of the same accuracy, due to judicial hierarchy, judges of different levels take different factors into consideration. Trial judges must consider judgments of judges of second instance, but the latter can refer to but not necessarily consider judgments of the former. Appellate court judges do consider the opinions of judges of higher levels normally, since the second instance is the final judgment and there are, after all, typically only a few cases applying for retrial. US Supreme Court Justice Jackson famously said that "Our words count not because we never make mistakes. We never make mistakes only because our words count." If there were higher level of court above US Supreme Court, then quite a number of judgments made by the Supreme Court would likely be overruled.[24] This kind of system actually makes appellate courts "always have reasons" to work, no matter what.

Other factors affecting judges of basic-level courts are different from those affecting judges of second instance. There is different composition of judicial personnel, and China's system of trial by a single judge happens typically only in courts of first instance. The professional qualities of judges are different. Judges of second instance normally have stricter training and a more careful division of labor. The time pressure is different with cases of second instance; typically, they have much less time pressure. In some cases that might cause social disputes, the social pressure undertaken is different. Due to the delay of trial times and changes in trial location, or because there is already judgment from the first instance (no matter what the judgment is), judges of second instance will have less influence from local people. In addition, in many cases, parties concerned in the first instance in basic-level courts normally do not hire lawyers or legal staff workers. However, in cases of second instance, there must be lawyers or people with legal knowledge to participate.

Last, when the majority of cases are given a court decision at the first instance, parties concerned will not lodge an appeal due to all kinds of reasons even if they have the right to appeal. For this reason, most appellate cases are, generally speaking, more difficult and either have no proper laws or disputes on the treatment of laws. In a word, cases that lodge an appeal are greatly different from cases that do not lodge an appeal (as for the specific difference, this could be a topic for a doctoral dissertation).

Due to those differences, we can see that judicial knowledge and knowledge based on judicial experience and techniques of US appellate judges are probably not applicable in trial practices of judges in China's basic-level courts. How could we imagine that judges in China's basic-level courts are able to freely write judicial opinion similar to that of Holmes or Cardozo or Posner?[25]As a matter of fact, the majority of judges in courts of first instance in the USA cannot write outstanding judicial opinions either; American trial judges do not write judicial opinions

[24]Brown v. Allen, 244 U.S. 443, 540 (1953), Justice Jackson, concurring opinion.

[25]Judge Posner, who was proficient in economics, used to make the following announcement in a judicial opinion in 1986: "if P X H [p] > (1-P) x H [d],we should issue a ban." Quoted from Dahlia Lithwich, "Richard Posner, A Human Pentium Processor has been Assigned to Settle the Microsoft Case," in http://www.slate.com/assessment/99-11-23/assessment.asp.

which we often see today, but we are prone to supposing that it is a common practice for American judges to write judicial opinions. Many American jurists even think that trial judges should not write judicial opinions at all.[26]

China's current legal education system and even legal education systems of a number of other countries have not provided any knowledge for judges in basic-level courts to deal with factual disputes. Even those courts that value judicial practice most, such as moot courts, are still far from genuine judicial practice. I once interviewed a judge who graduated from a famous law school in the 1990s; she presided over a court in a county-level city. She lashed out at the moot court produced by law schools, which she thought was useless. If we give careful analysis, we will find out that this judgment is quite reasonable. The purpose of a moot court is to help students to get familiar with court procedures and deal with legal disputes from the very beginning of their training. It is designed only for this kind of training, and it is constructed more in the mode of instance of appeal as a matter of fact. However, when courts hear cases of first instance, they never lodge debate from the very beginning. They always present evidence first and then determine evidence. Only when both parties basically reach agreement on case facts, the judicial game can go on, and the debate can be lodged on the nature of the case and application of law. The precondition for court debate must be and can only be clear facts. If the basic facts of a case are not clear, then the case cannot be "a case," not to mention to lodge a debate on the nature of the case and application of law. However, the verification and determination of facts can never be solved though debate. On the contrary, the debate must be based on verified and found facts. Either the facts are clear of they do not exist; there is no such thing as an unclear fact. Debate cannot change certain facts, but can only change or correct people's understanding of facts by putting forward a new fact or point of view. It can also put forward a set of theories to have a new understanding of a series of facts. This kind of knowledge related to fact-finding is not truly taught by any law school in the world. Moreover, it cannot be taught (thus we may have new and true understanding of why there is "law" school, not "fact" school). In the judicial practice of different countries, when there come factual disputes or problems related to facts, "free evaluation of evidence though inner conviction" by the judge is always emphasized, or in cases in the USA, a jury system is adopted to decide. As for the reasoning, Posner believes that it is to avoid the embarrassment of judges for not being able to give out reasons on fact-finding.[27] It is true that fact-finding cannot be explained. Wittgenstein used to say somewhere, roughly: "I just think it is red, but cannot explain or demonstrate why it is red; if you don't think it is red, then it is you who doesn't accept our game and I can't persuade you into believing it is red through debate."

---

[26]"I don't think those great judges of local courts will have to make great efforts and spend several months of time to write a legal opinion that have a new idea. And on this issue, opinions of those judges almost certainly do not count."Henry J. Friendly, "The 'Law of the Circuit' and All That," 46 *St. John's Law Review* 406, 407 n. 6 (1979), quoted from Posner, *Federal Court*, pp. 336-337. Posner agreed to this opinion.

[27]Richard A. Posner, *The Problems of Jurisprudence*, Harvard University Press, 1990, pp. 208–209.

If the majority of current judicial knowledge and techniques are developed around instances of appeal (second instances), then because the institutional spaces and problems of basic-level courts and courts of second instance are different, some knowledge of appeals will be difficult for judges in basic-level courts to use.

4.4 The Basic-level Courts as China's Courts of First Instance

Then, can experience of judges in courts of first instance in the USA and other countries be helpful to judges of China's basic-level courts?

First of all, as I have mentioned above, because continental European jurisprudence is centered on legislation, I haven't seen up till now any judicial experience summarized by continental European jurists after detailed research. In the USA, the instance of appeal is central, and there is not much research on trial judges either. Such research has not been given enough academic respect. When writing this chapter, I was a visiting scholar at Harvard University. I tried to find research materials on trial judges, but it turned out that there were not many materials of this kind. I wanted to find some materials of American magistrate courts and judges but could not find anything.[28] This not only demonstrates the current situation of American jurisprudence, but also shows that the American legal academic circle and publishing circle are very subservient of those that are in power and who fund them Knowledge is always influenced by power at anytime and in any place.

There is little judicial research or documentation related to courts of first instance. For example, some scholars that hold the post of appellate judge have mentioned in their writings about the distinctiveness of trial judges and have put forward their opinions on some specific problems in first instance courts.[29] There are few letters, memoirs, or academic research that directly or indirectly put

[28]I have found two books which mainly discuss magistrate judges. One is an extremely thin brochure written by an Australian, which introduces the development history of magistrate judges in the UK. The other is a politics study on the appointment of magistrate judges in the UK in the seventeenth century and eighteenth century.

[29]Such as Jerome Frank, *Court on Trial: Myth and Reality in American Justice*, Princeton University Press, 1973 (1949); also Richard A. Posner, *The Problems of Jurisprudence*, Harvard University Press, 1990; *Federal Courts: Challenge and Reform*, Harvard University Press, 1995. Frank put forward an important problem of trial judges, such as the problem of uncertainty of facts, as well as the influence of judge's personal physiological reaction on judgment which is easier to happen in the trial of first instance. The latter point has been widely ridiculed at, but this kind of ridicule is unfair. As far as I see, what Frank has put forward is problems of trial judges (dealing with a large number of cases rapidly, trial by a single judge), but critics are making criticism from the judicial philosophy of instance of appeal (hear legal disputes freely and selectively, trial by judicial tribunal). The different perspective makes many scholars unable to give enough comments to Frank's real insight. Please see Oliver Wendell Holmes, Jr., "Law in Science and Science in Law," in *Collected Legal Papers*, Harcourt, Brace & Howe, 1952 (1920), p. 237.

forward the distinctiveness of trial judges.[30] There are a handful of scholars who have conducted rather detailed research on some specific problems of courts of first instance.[31] These materials are useful to Chinese trial judges, but they are insufficient.

Secondly, although there are a large number of records of all kinds from courts of first instance, it is not really possible for me to study trial judges in the USA and other countries in any kind of significant way. This not only demands a large amount of money and lots of scholars, but more importantly, it may not be worth the efforts. We have a large number of trial judges right here in China, so I beg the question: Why do Chinese scholars regard what is abroad and neglect what lies close at hand? If not because of superstition or tradition, I can only say that it is a kind of subservience.

Even if the research is conducted, judges in our basic-level courts do not play such an important role in the court system. As I have mentioned, knowledge comes about not only as a fruit of pure intelligence, it always has some attachment to a set of power mechanisms.[32] The knowledge and techniques of American trial judges are related to the American judicial system. For example, in the USA, lawyers always participate in the first trial, and the jury attends the hearing of certain civil cases and all criminal cases. The juries solve factual disputes. For this reason, the experience of American trial judges still focus on legal disputes to a large degree. China is unlikely to introduce American-style juries. Even if it was introduced, it is just a kind of concept and will ultimately be a Chinese jury backed by the legitimacy of American judicial theories. Does China want to, and can it afford to, have such a discrepancy?

China's basic-level courts are not only courts of first instance, but serve as China's courts of all instances. Although many people may instinctively have an ideological dislike of this emphasis, I hope that the following analysis will prove that my emphasis is not out of ideology, but this kind of dislike is likely out of ideology.

---

[30]Such as, Judge Angela Bartell, *Judicial Decision Making in the Trial Court*, Disputes Processing Research Program Working Papers Series 8, Institute for Legal Studies, University of Wisconsin-Madison Law School, 1986; Judge Charles E. Wyzanski, Jr., "The Importance of the Trial Judge," January 12, 1959, in Walter F. Murphy and C. Herman Pritchett, *Courts, Judges, and Politics: An Introduction to the Judicial Process*, 4th ed., Random House, 1986, pp. 108–110; Judge Joseph A. Wapner, *A View From the Bench*, Simon and Schuster, 1987; Judge Robert Satter, *Doing Justice: A Trial Judge at Work*, Simon and Schuster, 1990; and Judge William G. Young, *Reflections of a Trial Judge*, Massachusetts Continuing Legal Education, Inc. 1998.

[31]As for research of juries, Richard O. Lempert, "Uncovering 'Nondiscernible' Differences: Empirical Research and the Jury-Size Cases," *Michigan Law Review*, vol. 73, No. 4, 1975.

[32]Michel Foucault, *Discipline and Punish: the Birth of the Prison*, trans. by Alan Sheridan, Vintage Books, 1978; please also see Chap. 11 of this book "Power Resources of Legal Sociology Surveys."

Although the word judiciary can erase the judicial differences of different countries of the world from a conceptual standpoint, China's basic-level courts do indeed have a kind of irreplaceable distinctiveness in this world. Otherwise, many kindhearted, sincere legal scholars and jurists would not be able to imagine how some judicial reform measures which seem to be completely necessary, reasonable, and sensible can bring huge functional difficulties to China's basic-level courts. How can China implement a judicial adversary system with almost no lawyers? In such an environment, the judge may indeed warn both parties: "You may argue, but not call names." If we ask both parties to testify, how do they testify in a place where many adults are illiterate? In a community with extremely small mobility where all people are fellow villagers, how could you ask a neighbor to appear in court and prove that the accused has cut off the state-run electric wires? In the county where I conducted the survey, in the first half of 1997, 31 witnesses were summoned to criminal trials, but none of them appeared in court to testify![33] Even if you could force them to appear, if they are still not willing to truly testify and only say that "I can't remember clearly," what can a judge do? How could we possibly prove he or she can remember and is deliberately refusinga testimonial? In a time when criminal defendants are given "the right to remain silent," on what reasoning can you deprive a witness of his or her right to silence?[34] If a client—a women facing divorce litigation—totally depends on the judge to make decisions for her, how can you be ruthless enough to declare that she has lost the lawsuit

[33]Chen Guangzhong admits in one of his speeches that in the current judicial trial, the rate of witness appearing in court is less than 1/3 and "even lower," "which makes the reform of today's [trial method] actually fail or half fail." Mr Chen suggests to improve the "summon by force" on witnesses (Chen Guangzhong: "A few questions about criminal procedure law," "Review of Jurisprudence in the 20th Century, Lecture V" organized by the Law School of Peking University, December 22, 1999).

I think that this is just trying to use new dreams to realize (or review) the old dream. Summoning by force cannot possibly change this situation fundamentally. If a person is not willing to testify, even the God cannot do anything with him/her, especially under the current condition that "the right to silence" is emphasized. If he or she says that he or she cannot remember clearly, how can you prove that he or she can remember clearly but refuse to testify on purpose? Can you punish he or her? Please remember that criminal procedure jurists think highly of the principles of presumption of innocence and not to be compelled to testify against oneself. At the present, many designs of China's procedure system are Utopian from the very beginning and do not take the operation issue into consideration. People always think that what America can do today not only should be done by us, but must be done well. This attitude is completely in line with the attitude of "how much the land can produce depends on how brave people are." The motivation is the same, and what changes are the time and the theme.

[34]If we adhere to the consistency of principle, I really do not know how Chinese jurists can answer this question. As far as many papers I have seen currently are concerned, they on the one hand advocate that criminal accused have "the right to silence" and on the other hand deprive witnesses of their "right to silence." The problem here is not about being unfair or intelligent as far as see, but is blinded by a lust for money.

only because she is illiterate, inexpressive, and thus cannot find the burden of proof?[35] Can today's noisy legal assistance reach those remote rural areas? All those questions are unimaginable in the lives of jurists, but must be tackled by China's basic-level judges in their real life by finding alternative means in accord with the Chinese way.

Are we jurists not Chinese? Why do we have a different feeling toward judiciaries? Some people may raise this kind of question. It is true that trial judges and jurists are of the same profession, but our professions are quite different. Just think about it: For jurists, there are legal or judicial problems that we cannot solve, but we can at least avoid discussing or writing about these problems. We can choose what we are good at to show our gifts and talents and sometimes "show off" such talents. Jurists are free in this regard. However, judges of basic-level courts are not able to do so. They cannot put the case aside and decide to deal with it once they figure it out only because the case is difficult—perhaps because they cannot find applicable laws or there is not enough evidence. They are not the Danish Prince Hamlet who indulges in endless reflection, but more like soldiers with officers behind them at every moment. They have to do it whether they want to or not. This is the destiny of trial judges. Do you remember Article 4 of Napoleonic Code? "Judges are prohibited from refusing justice on the ground that there is no regulation in law"; otherwise, they will be declared guilty! In China, indecisive judges will be, at the very least, regarded as incompetent. We professors of jurisprudence can at least cover ourselves up a little in our profession, and our words and behaviors about judiciary will not produce any direct legal result for which we have to undertake responsibility.

The other thing that we have to pay attention to is the penetration of bureaucratic and political culture guided by and dominated by administration in the court system in China. The courts of various levels in China can be said to be department subordinate to local governments in a certain sense. Although the courts of various levels today are normally a"half level higher" than the rank of other subordinate governmental departments of the same level, this "half level higher" just proves its administration, not the opposite. However, the actual power of an organization cannot be determined by levels. In the system of separation of powers in the USA, the Supreme Court has the same power as the president and the Congress in name. At the time the American Constitution was stipulated, Hamilton

---

[35]"In the outcry to reform trial method and to emphasize the burden of proof of client across the country, the head of [local people's court] is filled with difficulties. It is not that he doesn't want to try the reform, or let client to undertake the burden of proof in order to relief the burden of the court (sic--quoter), but under the condition that the majority of inhabitants are uneducated and lack basic and common legal knowledge, it is just unrealistic to emphasize testification by client. If it is fully aware that the client doesn't know how to testify and is not able to testify, but is waited until he or she testifies, it is no difference to throwing the case out of the court... As a result, the trial method of court should be mainly circuit trial system."Quoted from Meng Tian: "Traveling Around Mountains—Notes of Interview on Yong Ning People's Court in Yi Ethnic Group Autonomous County, Yonglang, Yunnan Province," *People's Court*, Issue 8, 1994, p. 39.

pointed out that the judicial branch was "the least dangerous branch."[36] This is only really a complimentary comment. To say it frankly, it is the department with the least power.[37] In China, the Political Consultative Conference is of the same level as the government and the People's Congress, but their real powers are different. I am not going to put forth more discussion about it here. What I want to point out is that when studying China's basic-level courts, we need to pay attention to the administrative system of China's courts, pointed out by He Weifang sharply,[38] as well as the administration of the internal management of court, as I have previously mentioned.[39]

Even in a relatively ideal situation, in the judicial system, the relationship between the court of first instance and court of appeal (second instance) is bound to have aspects of a bureaucratic tier system;[40] that is, it is up to the "superior level [court] to decide" (think about the famous saying of Chief Justice Jackson I quoted above). For the sake of unity, efficiency, and professionalism of law, there must be certain professional levels.[41] However, the difference between a court of first instance and a court of appeal (second instance)—at least in this professional community of judges, lawyers, and legal professors—should be understood as a difference in the division of labor. In the judicial system, they actually jointly facilitate the regularized settlement of disputes and the formation of systems though their competitive advantages. The knowledge of courts and trial judges are not interchangeable in this judicial system. At this level, the basic-level court is not the court "of a lower level," and is not a "subordinate" court. Judges of basic-level courts and courts of higher levels actually have equal contributions to the knowledge needed for judicial function, although their decision powers and scopes entrusted by the state political power system are different. Furthermore, people normally attach more importance to decisions of the court of appeal, which is normal, since people normally emphasize the results, which is not necessarily actual justice. Starting from the perspective of systems and the division of knowledge, many jurists and lawyers gradually realize that the superior court must highly respect the judgment of the lower court (courts of appeal in different countries normally adopt in jure or in jure as a matter of fact, which demonstrates that judges of appeal have institutional respect for knowledge and judgment of trial judges on factual disputes). They believe that even superior courts sometimes

---

[36]Please see *Federalist Papers*, Chapter 78, translated by Chen Fengru, the Commercial Press, 1980, p. 391.

[37]Montesquieu used to have this candid comment in his "The Spirit of the Laws," quoted from *Federalist Papers*, p. 391, note 1.

[38]"Two Problems of China's Judicial Management System," as previous note 1.

[39]Please see Chap. 2 of this book "Court Trial and its Administration."

[40]Please see Hu Jianhua and Li Hancheng: "To Understand Correctly the Relationship Between the Superior and Subordinate Courts," *People's Court*, Issue 11, 1992, pp. 35–36.

[41]Posner, *The Problematics of Moral and Legal Theory*, Harvard University Press, 1999, especially Chapter 3.

overrule the judgment of lower courts on legal disputes, it is not because such thinking, reasoning, or interpretation of the lower court is wrong, but only because it maintains some other forms of values in regard to the law (such as the stability or universality of law, or coordination of conflicts of legal rules in different jurisdictions). They also believe that even the thinking, interpretation, or reasoning is wrong, judges of a court of appeals can still be enlightened from this (at least prevent repeating these kinds of mistakes).[42] This is a kind of professional ethics and consensus produced in the legal professional community through long-term professional training.

However, in China's legal circle and law science community today, there is a severe lack of this kind of consensus; not only inside the court, but among jurists themselves, there is a kind of unpleasant "timeserving attitude." It is hard for China's judges in courts of first instance to get rid of the influence of bureaucracy. Due to many reasons (such as the goal of their ratio of cases being remanded for retrial to be lower), they try their best to "maintain personal good relations" with the higher court and its judges. The higher court or its judges may judge inappropriately from time to time and sometimes even take advantage of the influence of this kind of bureaucracy. Jurists always look down upon basic-level judges and their practical wisdom. In the judicial system, there is a trend to believe that "the higher authorities are always right." This kind of situation has formed a restriction on the development and accumulation of judicial knowledge and techniques of judges in China's basic-level courts.

4.5 The Ending as a Beginning

The above analysis has set the position of the institutional and social space of China's basic-level courts. For scholars, this kind of position itself may have not much significance. Its real meaning lies in helping us to see that it is just in this space, with people's (judges of basic-level courts) pursuit of their own benefits and their potential creativity that some specific judicial knowledge and technologies can be produced. Because any knowledge is linked to a certain time and space, both its genesis and utilization are a kind of response to specific restrictions in space. For this reason, it is not impossible to study Chinese judges with a broad vision and a serious attitude, especially the knowledge and wisdom demonstrated by basic-level judges when settling disputes; to dig into the theoretical and practical potential and to generalize it in academic language; to exchange views with scholars in different countries across the world; and to make an academic contribution of modern Chinese lawyers and jurists. This kind of knowledge not only highlights judicial knowledge that has been suppressed by the continental

[42] Posner, *The Problems of Jurisprudence*, as previous note 3, pp. 79–86; and *Federal Courts: Challenge and Reform*, as previous note 26, pp. 175ff.

European law system, but also the judicial knowledge of first-instance judges suppressed by the Anglo-american law system. In terms of expanding the knowledge system related to the judiciary, it also has its own meaning.

This chapter has only pointed out this kind of possibility theoretically, but it is far from enough. In the following chapters hereafter, I will discuss this issue in a more detailed manner. First of all, I will discuss how China's basic-level courts as courts of first instance will certainly pay more attention to dispute settlement, as well as related issues caused by this. The following two chapters will analyze and discuss how china's basic-level judiciary deals with factual disputes and legal disputes based on individual cases. I will discuss how the so-called determination on the nature is actually more related to legal disputes, but has nothing to do with factual disputes. I will also analyze how China's many current social conditions make factual disputes difficult and how the judiciary itself changes this situation. On the issue of legal disputes, I will discuss the interaction of statutes with customs, and how customs penetrate into and enter the judiciary, thus influencing social life as rules. In this process, we can also see the creative works of judges in China's basic-level courts. In the last chapter of this part, I will try to generalize how a court's specific institutional position and space-time location encourage Chinese judges to adopt and accumulate some specific knowledge and technologies not in line with regulations of classic judicial textbooks in their judicial practice. I will try to give some theoretical analysis, summary, and interpretation, so that it can enter into the jurists' vision and obtain legitimacy of academic research.

As an appendix of this chapter, I have translated a personal correspondence with a judge in an American district court. I hope this letter will help readers to understand the importance of trial judges. And, if you are sensitive and empathetic enough, you can find out from the poem quoted in the letter the candid desolation of a talented and emotional trial judge tramped by the current judicial system and judicial knowledge system in today's America.

Early hours in Cambridge, December 17, 1999

Appendix: The Importance of the Trial Judge

The following is a letter written by Charles E. Wyzanski, Jr., the judge of a District Court for the District of Massachusetts to Senator Leverett Saltonstall when he was informed that his name had been presented to the president as a nominated candidate for a position as a judge of the US Court of Appeals for the First Circuit. The letter can be found in Charles E. Wyzanski, Jr., "The Importance of the Trial Judge," January 12, 1959, in Walter F. Murphy and C. Herman Pritchett, *Courts, Judges, and Politics*: *An Introduction to the Judicial Process*, 4th ed., Random House, 1986, pp. 108–110.

Dear Lev,

I am deeply appreciative of your suggestion that my name be presented to the President and the Attorney General for their consideration whether to nominate me as a judge of the United States Court of Appeals for the First Circuit… that you regard me as worthy of that high office is a great compliment. And were I to be appointed to a judgeship in that court, I should regard it as both honor and an opportunity for public service.

Yet I am persuaded that it is in both the public interest and my interest for me to decline to allow my name to be considered for the United States Court of Appeals…

The District Court for the District of Massachusetts seems to me offer at least as wide as a field for judicial service as the Court of Appeals for the First Circuit. The District Court gives more scope to a judge's initiative and discretion. His width of choice sentencing defendants is the classic example. But there are many other instances. In civil litigation a District Judge has a chance to help the lawyers frame the issues and develop the facts so that there may be a meaningful and complete record. He may innovate procedures promoting fairness, simplification, economy, and expedition. By instructions to juries and, in appropriate cases, by comments on the evidence he may help the jurors better to understand their high civic function. He is a teacher of parties, witness, petitioners for naturalization, and even casual visitors to his court. His conduct of a trial may fashion and sustain the moral principles of the community. More even than the rules of constitutional, statutory, and common law he applies, his character and personal distinction, open to daily inspection in his courtroom, constitute the guarantees of due process.

Admittedly, the Court of Appeals stands higher than the District Courts in the judicial hierarchy, and Congress by attaching a larger compensation to the office of the Circuit Judge has expressed its view of the relative importance of the two courts. Yet, not all informed persons would concur in that evaluation. My revered former chief, Judge Augustus N. Hand, always spoke of his service in the District Court as being more interesting as well as more revealing of his qualities, and more enjoyable, than his service in the Court of Appeals…

Although less spectacular litigation may ordinarily be carried from the District Court to the Court of Appeals, statistics will show how small a percentage of a reasonably good trial judge's decrees are in fact appealed. The District Judge so often has the last word. Even where he does not, heed is given to his estimates of credibility, his determination of the facts, his discretion in framing or denying relief upon the facts he found…

The District Judge is in more direct relation than is the judge of the Court of Appeals to the bar and its problems. It is within the proper function of a District Court not merely by rules and decision, but by an informed, intelligent, and energetic handling of his calendar to effectuate prompt as well as unbiased justice. It is the vigor of the District Court more than the action of the Court of Appeals which governs the number of cases which are ripe for appeal, and the time between the beginning of an action and a final judgment in an appellate court. And, paradoxically, it is not infrequently the alertness of the District Judge and his willingness to help counsel develop uncertain points of law (even though the development of such points inevitably increase the risk of error by the trial judge and of reversal by the appellate court) which makes a case significant in the progress of the law when it reaches a court of last resort.

While it may well be true that the highest office for a judge is to sit in judgment on other judges' errors, it is perhaps a more challenging task to seek, from minute to minute, to avoid one's own errors. And the zest of that task is enhanced by the necessity of reacting orally, instead of after the reflection permitted under the appellate judge's uninterrupted schedule of reading and writing.

I realize that the trial judge lacks the opportunity to benefit from the collegiate discussion open to an appellate judge. His ties with his brethren are less intimate. Consequently, he runs the perils of excessive individualism. Few there are who can gently chide him on his foibles, remind him of the grace of manners, or warn against the nigh universal sin of pride.

Yet perhaps the trial judge's relative loneliness brings him closer to the tragic plight of man. Was not Wallace Stevens speaking for the trial judge when he wrote:

> Life consist
> Of propositions about life. The human
> Reverie is a solitude in which
> We compose these propositions, torn by dreams…?

Sincerely,
Charles E. Wyzanski, Jr.

Chapter 5
Dispute Settlement and Governance of Rules

The Rule of Law as a Law of Rules.
—Antonin Scalia (Antonin Scalia, "The Rule of Law as a Law of Rules", *University of Chicago Law Review*, 1989, vol. 56, p. 1175).

5.1 Pose a Question

In this chapter, I will analyze in detail a question I mentioned briefly in Chap. 3 that has not been given enough attention in the jurist circle: is the basic function of the court to implement and form rules (to solve problems universally), or to settle disputes (to solve problems specifically)? When neither can be neglected,[1] which one should we give more importance to, and which direction should we take?

Rule governance is important; this can be said to be the key of modern rule of law.[2] Although the approaches are different, the main countries in the two major legal systems of the world have pursued and realized, to a certain degree, governance of rules. In the continental European countries, in short, the governance of rules is centered around systemized statute rules or statute rules with "rationalized form," as described by Weber, and judges constantly return to and affirm rules of

[1]This kind of saying has already become a classic, but in modern China, the judiciary has another basic function, that is the establishment of a nation state. Please see my analysis in Chap. 1 of this book "Why Send Law to the Countryside?"

[2]About this point, please refer to note 4 of Suli: "China's Rule of Law in the Modern Vision" (*Knowledge of China*, Jiangxi Education Press, 1998).

© Foreign Language Teaching and Research Publishing Co., Ltd and Springer Science+Business Media Singapore 2016

S. Zhu, *Sending Law to the Countryside*, China Academic Library,
DOI 10.1007/978-981-10-1142-9_5

statutes.[3] In the Anglo-American legal system, it seems as if people do not take rules as seriously: judges (especially American judges) have a greater amount judicial discretion. Especially in common law cases, they can actually make laws, change rules in the name of interpretation in the trial of specific cases, and even withdraw original judgments—which actually has the effect of retroactivity. American federal judges can even conduct constitutional review on legislation and declare it a violation of the constitution. Despite all this, due to the system of stare decisis and the judicial hierarchy system that supports all of this, the governance of rules is thus formed. In another word, the governance of rules in Anglo-American law is formed as a by-product in the process when judges hear specific cases. For this reason, to many judges, the rule of law concept of "the rule of good law" by Aristotle has been replaced by the rule of law concept of "governance by rules" in modern times. The issue of good law and bad law is often undertaken by other political departments of government (legislation and administration). Judges take the position of "unwilling to take care of something which is not one's concern," which is of comparative institutional functionalism and adopt a self-restraining attitude as follows: "While beyond our world, we should takes everything as it is and engage in no discussion" (or less discussion).[4]

In this chapter, I will first of all demonstrate that in the trial (including mediation) of basic-level courts in China's rural areas today, dispute settlement is still at the center.[5] Why is this the case? My research will demonstrate that the attention paid by basic-level judges is reasonable. However, the purpose of my research or the conclusion implied is not to inflate dispute settlement or give up governance of rules. The research itself is to "find pleasure in it"; during the process, value judgment can be said as "nothing to me." My purpose is more to find out whether the

---

[3]The continental European legal system has some reflection on this point, rejects too much moral rationalization, and emphasizes the "materialization" of form rationalization and laws with rational forms; for example, Gunter Teubner, "Substantive and Reflexive Elements in Modern Law," *Law and Society Review*, 1983, vol. 2, pp. 239–285 and Jurgen Habermas, *Between Facts and Norms: Contributions to a Discourse Theory of Law and Democracy*, MIT Press, 1996.

[4]Some people may raise an objection, especially pointing out the judicial review system or constitutional court in some countries. But those systems are still based on the premise of complying with the constitution and the authority of the constitution is beyond the doubt of judges. Moreover, the judges cannot challenge law or constitution in the name of "goodness." There may also be some people proposing the so-called revival of "natural law," but this is only the academic debate in the jurist circle, and has basically nothing to do with judges or the judiciary. This attitude is most typically reflected in a letter of Chief Justice Holmes to his friend Laski: "as you may know, I always say that if my compatriot citizens want to go to hell, I will also help them. This is my job." Please see *Holmes-Laski Letters: The Correspondence of Mr. Justice Holmes and Harold J. Laski, 1916–1935*, vol. 1, pp. 248–249 (M. D. Howe ed., 1953). Please also see Richard A. Posner, *The Problematics of Moral and Legal Theory*, Harvard University Press, 1999, Chap. 4.

[5]As a matter of fact, courts of different levels in China pay more attention to dispute settlement at different degrees. But the reasons for this kind of trend are quite different. For courts of intermediate level and above, the reasons may be the system of level jurisdiction, social pressure, economic benefits of courts in the trial and, etc. This chapter is not going to discuss such problems which are more of an accident.

governance of rules is important, and should we care about the governance of rules? In China's modern judiciary, especially in the basic-level court, how possible is it to realize the governance of rules? Why do judges in basic-level courts pay more attention to dispute settlements? I also want to analyze when judges go against the rules of statutes, are there no rules to comply with? Is the reason for this judicial character of not paying attention to statute rules due to the insufficient quality of judges (as what the majority of scholars believe) or restrictions of other problems? What kind of trouble can this judicial character bring about? In addition, do courts of different levels possibly have a unified judicial purpose—such as affirming and implementing rules?

5.2 Two "Cases"

I believe it is best to begin with individual cases.

When I conducted my survey in the people's court, I went to the village judicial office/legal service office, which was located opposite to the court to get some information. While I was talking with a graduate student from the local political and legal college who was interning, a woman, about 50 years of age who lived where the village government was situated, came into the room accompanied by a young judge working in the people's court. She demanded a divorce from her husband who had left her more than 20 years ago and had not been heard from since. She asked the legal worker to write a written complaint for her. Before I had gone to the judicial office for interview, I had seen this woman in the people's court. At that time, she filed an oral complaint against her unworthy son who had beaten her many times for not giving him money. Her claim was to "break off mother–son relations." But why would this woman suddenly come to the judicial office to write a suit for divorce? I felt suspicious.[6]

[6]My suspicion was that whether the court was willing to deal with one more case and charge one more legal fee. My suspicion was not unreasonable, since my research of the basic-level judicial system for many years had shown that due to courts below the intermediate level would normally make efforts to increase the number of cases dealt with by the court and to increase legal fees. "Finding more case resources" and "generating more profits" have become the most important jobs of courts below the intermediate level and have also become the most commonly used phrases used by judges we interviewed. One of the reasons is that the increase of cases dealt with has actually become one of the main indicators to measure job performance of a court, from the cities to rural areas, although nobody knows since when this shift in objectives occured. Although it has not been stipulated expressly, courts in different places have already taken it as a perfectly justified standard. Even the Haidian District Court of Beijing Municipality which has been recently commended by the state and rated as a National Outstanding Court takes the growth rate of case numbers as one of the main indicators to prove its job performance in the court work reports published in early 1999. The Supreme People's court has this tendency as well. The logic of the courts is economic. It seems that products of factories and enterprises are dividends, but products of courts are cases dealt with. For this reason, to ensure the increase of cases dealt by the court has become an implicit direction pursued by courts of all levels and has

After I talked with the judge who accompanied the old woman, I put forward this question straightforwardly. The judge said that after several "police officers" informally heard the woman's narrative, they put forward the solution of divorce collectively, believing that it could solve the woman's problem in a more practical way. The logic of the judges was approximately as follows: although it was illegal for the son to beat up his mother, and he did it several times, it was very difficult to deal with this case. The woman's claim—to break off their mother–son relationship—had no legal basis, thus the court could not deal with this "case" "according to law." Although the judicial principle of "no trial without complaint" was not considered,[7] it was still difficult for the case to constitute the crime of abuse in regard to the punishment. Even if the son was guilty as charged, the woman was not necessarily willing to see her son in jail (this is likely why she only asked to break off mother–son relations and did not accuse her son of the "crime of abuse"). The court wanted to help "solve problems" for these common people; they took the initiative to interfere and declared that the crime of abuse was established. They were faced with a difficulty; detention of 10 days, or half a month, or even 2 years still could not prevent the accused from beating his mother again after release. Or if a tort was constituted in this case, how could the court deal with it—the son had no money to compensate the mother. Certainly, a ban could be issued according to Article 134 of General Principles of the Civil Court to prevent harm, but it still could not solve the problem since there was not corresponding police force to guarantee the implementation of the judgment. Such a ban would be just an empty promise. It was just after comparing the possible results of several dealing methods that the judges would try to encourage the women to abolish the marital relationship that did not exist anymore, and to find a new husband who

---

Footnote 6 (continued)

become a political institutional logic difficult to defy in China's modern courts in order to function. Even so, during our interview, many judges and even presidents of courts expressed that they could not understand and even bluntly disliked this indicator. They indicated explicitly that they did not know why the more social disputes and cases equated to more achievements in one's official career. In practice, they had to write reports in this format and report to the local people's congress. The other reason is that there is a severe lack of funds in the court. Since the second half of the 1980s, under the slogan of "for the service of reform and opening up to the outside world," the court tried to used all kinds of measures to generate profits in order to meet the funding needs of case handling and equipment, while at the same time trying to improve the living standard of people working in the court. This chapter is not going to discuss the pros and cons of this practice, but I mention it just as a background to demonstrate to the reader that my doubt is not without foundation.

[7]According to the stipulations of Article 260 of the Criminal Law of the People's Republic of China (1997): "A person who maltreats a member of his family shall be sentenced to fixed-term imprisonment of no more than two years, criminal detention or public surveillance if the circumstance is flagrant." It also regulates that the crime "shall be handled only upon complaint."

could protect her. This practice might be able to protect the rights and interests of the mother more effectively than laws and a judiciary could.[8]

Due to limits on time and other conditions, I was unable to see how this case was resolved in the end and what kind of legal remedy, or quasi-legal remedy, it got. But the readers do not have to pay too much attention to such a problem, since how this case was solved is actually not that important to the main theme of this chapter. What is more important is that, from this very simple case, we can see that a main focus of judges in basic-level courts in China when dealing with issues is how to settle disputes well, not just to abide by their duties and implement extant legal rules. Once we see this, we see the way of thinking and resolution of the judge is totally guided by pragmatism.[9] Under the restrictions or support of all kinds of local conditions, they have balanced all possible remedies (legal and otherwise), especially by comparing results of all kinds of remedies, and then making a choice which is believed by judges to be the best to the litigant—and can be basically accepted by the litigant and approved by local people. Here, the foundation for litigation, responsibilities of judges regulated by law, and relevant procedural or substantive regulations, are not that important. What is important is to

[8]Many people will raise doubt with this explanation. As a matter of fact, I used to be dubious of it as well. Many years of social and academic experiences have made me realize that behind many high-sounding words, there are always hidden motives and activities that are not as proper—such as the realities behind the slogan "judiciary gives reform and opening-up an easy ride." Another explanation from this judge has basically convinced me. The judge said that there was not much money involved in filing this complaint. The legal cost was 50 yuan at most, but judges had to do a lot of work. The court did not make money to try this kind of civil case. The judge told us that the more important thing was that because the husband of the women left home for many years and nobody knew his whereabouts, the women had to make an announcement through newspaper, which cost 200 yuan, and the court was ready to pay this money on behalf of the women. In addition, case number was not important to this court. The court was near a village of a county-level city with a rather developed economy and many disputes related to contracts. By putting those cases together to deal with them would increase legal fees. Thus, the court had no problem finding individual cases to increase the total number of cases. The judge said that to find out more case resources does not mean to finding more cases in general, but to find cases that are easily dealt with and with high legal fees. It is true that the problem of cost benefit have to be taken into consideration when finding out more case resources. The answer of this judge has convinced me.

[9]Pragmatism is a fascinating and charming concept. In judiciary, especially related to the above two cases introduced in this chapter, we are easy to relate it or equal it to substantive justice. The strict substantive justice often ignores cost-effect analysis. But the approach of pragmatism will take these factors into consideration and even stick to procedural justice because the cost of substantive justice is too high. Thus, the pragmatic concept I adopt is not the traditional presentation of "what is useful is truth," but a solution with a relatively reasonable result in specific time and space achieved by judges under the restrictive conditions of systems and environments and after comparing all possible solutions. Judges normally do not adhere to—especially in some difficult cases—the only correct way to solve problems. Pragmatism is "instrumentalism trying to use ideas as weapons to promote effective action and be guided by future." As for its legal implication, please see Richard A. Posner, *The Problems of Jurisprudence*, Harvard University Press, 1990, especially the introduction.

deal with the disputes well, to make sure that the result turns out well, and to "make one party rest assured." Relevant legal regulations are often a justified foundation, and a restrictive condition that must be considered or avoided under certain circumstances.

If we try to generalize the judicial characteristics of basic-level courts, we will have two troubles. First is the problem of universality, while the process of abstract generalization is, at the least, questionable. We can certainly give out a large number of cases as examples on this point, but it is not necessary, and any enumeration will inevitably fall into the question of Hume on the problem of induction. We may need to resort to our common sense to decide whether to accept this incomplete induction. What is more important is the second trouble; that is, it actually has not constituted a "case" in strict sense. It has not entered into the official process of judicial trial and is just wandering in front of the gate of the court. People may well say that in official trials, judges may pay more attention to rules, but not, or at least not only, to dispute settlements. In order to answer such questions, I must observe judicial practices more thoroughly.

A new observation confirmed my generalization. Having left this court, we went to another people's court in a village located in a mountainous area, where we witnessed a trial of alimony. An old couple sued their four sons. The case was finally settled by court mediation. What is related to this chapter and has left me strong impression is that at the final stage of court mediation, the judge not only put forward the problem of alimony in its narrow sense, but also considered problems such as with whom the old couple would live, their grain ratio, medical fees when they were ill, funeral fee and coffins after they died, and even considered the cooking oils that the old couple used, including animal fat and vegetable oil, the vegetables the old couple consumed, whether there were green beans and soybeans in the grains provided by the sons, and the necessary amounts. In the eyes of "we, the jurists" from the cities, such problems seemed too trivial to become legal disputes or be related to rules—more like "family business." Many problems were put forward by the judge himself. Although some of the problems, such as vegetable oil and animal fat and soybeans and green beans, were excluded by cash payment based on agreement (I will discuss later the theoretical and practical implications of this detail), the familiarity with and tireless attention to details of daily affairs by this judge demonstrated in the case were highly appraised by me and another researcher. Here, we once again saw a judge trying his best to settle disputes, not confirming legal rules (though he unconsciously abided by certain legal rules). Due to his attention to dispute settlement, the judge even forgot about certain basic rules. For example, the problem of legal remedy details should not be put forward by judges and in a broad sense, this violated the basic judicial principle of "no trial without complaint" and the inactive and neutral institutional role of judges.

5.3 The Difference in Concern

I can give some other examples mentioned in other articles.[10] In these cases, we researchers, after many years of training in law school, obviously have different concerns from judges at basic-level courts. We pay more attention to responsibilities of foreign courts and judges taught in the legal textbooks or those we understand. But this kind of ideal constitutes a sharp contrast to the actual role of China's basic-level judges in their judicial activities, in a broad sense. If we strictly follow ideals, then the court and the judge in the previous case should strictly follow the judicial principle of "no trial without complaint," and should not take the initiative to settle disputes actively in the manner of a law-enforcing department. If the litigator does not have appropriate cause of action, the court should simply dismiss the lawsuit. The judge should not take on the lawyer's role and provide legal consultation and services to the parties concerned. Although this complies with the political ideological goal "to serve the convenience of the people" and the judge "as servant of the people," the practice violates judicial professional ethics regarding "the neutrality of the judge," and is unfavorable to the other party. In the latter case, we noticed first of all that although according to Marriage Laws, sons and daughters have obligations to support their parents, but the defendant did not sue their two daughters who had been married for many years, and the judge held the hearing. From the perspective of legal regulations, it was not necessary for the judge to pay attention to, and especially to take the initiative, to propose remedies such as animal fat, vegetable oil, soybeans, and green beans. He should simply make decision or mediate according to law. We believe that the majority of Chinese people who have received formal training from law school, including many judges of second instance, will share our opinion.

Our concern is indeed different from that of basic-level judges. It does not mean that we do not care about dispute settlement at all, but that we pay attention to rules. As a matter of fact, every person will pay attention to how to settle disputes or debates. Even those judges of second instance who mainly focused on in jure topics that do not care about the actual settlement of disputes, but only the rules.[11] On the other hand, the basic-level judges included in our research are not careless regarding legal rules. In the former case, the judge refused the "claim" request of "breaking off mother–son relations" from the very beginning, and at the same time, suggested her divorce. In the hearing of the latter case, I saw with my

[10]Please refer to Chap. 3 of this book "The Judicial Committee System of Basic-level Courts."

[11]For example, the US Supreme Court often moderate judicial decisions due to dispute settlement and implementation issues. In the famous Plessy v. Ferguson in 1896 which recognized the principle of "ethnic segregation and equality," one of the basic reasons for the Supreme Court to accept this principle is that he law cannot eliminate racial prejudice among people. This reason may be wrong, but it is not dogmatic. In the Brown v. Board of Education in 1954 which overturned Plessy case, the government was requested to adopt moderate speed to eliminate ethnic segregation, which also demonstrated a judicial prudence.

own eyes the presiding judge took great pains to explain to the baffled parties concerned that they had the "right to demand withdrawal" and "debate" in order to strictly comply with regulations of civil procedure law,[12] and warned the parties about the discipline of the court—although the behaviors of the parties proved that his warning was in vain, and the judge did not employ his gavel and shout "order," as many American judges would do—he simply let it be.[13] It seems obvious that rules have constituted a strong restriction on judges of basic-level courts, who are trying their best to comply with legal rules.

Even when they have made such efforts, as in the above two cases, what has impressed me more is the efforts made by judges for "overcoming law."[14] At least in terms of the efforts of settling the above two disputes, it seems as if the related legal rules did not play a role in "saving transaction or litigation costs," as taught to us by textbooks of jurisprudence or law and economics. On the contrary, they increased the cost of judges in settling these two specific disputes. I don't want to discuss whether such rules are reasonable or not, or whether they have reduced transaction costs or information costs as a whole. What I have noticed is that related legal rules are actually disconnected from case handling. If the judge really wants to solve the problem properly, he or she has to mobilize and utilize his or her own wisdom (no special appraise or depreciation to this kind of wisdom here) to make efforts outside legal rules or in areas where there is no explicit regulation in law. Judges care about settling specific issues, the legitimacy of results, and the validity of forms. They care about the human relationships of this result with the local community, as well as the legitimacy of the results that are compatible with the formal legal power structure system. They have a strong tendency toward pragmatic reason. They are guided by the result, not the principle, by individual cases,

[12]In another civil court, during the stage of court debate, the judge said in the debate, "you could argue, but not call names" since he could not explain to the parties what a "debate" was.

[13]At least some of those disciplines have been violated publicly but unconsciously. What has impressed me most is that the presiding judge told both parties that they "should not leave the court on their will and their departure must be approved by the court." But during the court debate, one of the defendants stood up and left the court as he spoke. His natural attitude was just like the defense attorney or prosecution lawyer in American movies who made final statement to the jury. Before he left the room, he spat to the floor in front of the judge (which was only a habitual action, no less than the meaning that the Asian Football Confederation gave to Hao Haidong who also spat and was given one year of suspension), and went to the bathroom. Nobody—except we two researchers from outside—including judges, defendants, plaintiffs, and audience present thought it was strange, rude, or abrupt.
Certainly, the word bathroom was really not appropriate to be used here. It was only a toilet built by several wooden sticks and planks adjoin the backwall of the court. From the huge gap between the planks, you could see mountains and brooks in the distance. The toilet was unsophisticated, but it was not the "unsophisticated" (temporary) we people living in the cities understand. It was actually for the long-time use. Beside the toilet was a pigsty of the wife of the "chief judge" in this court. She raised 7 pigs there to cover expenses for the family.

[14]It is the name of a book published by Judge Posner in 1995. People will point out that the law that the judges of people's court tried to overcome are different from what Judge Posner tried to overcome. Well, if the reader can see this point, he may well feel serious supporting differences behind the nametags of "judge" and "court."

not the rules. In Weber's words, it is substantive rationality, not formal rationality. The knowledge they utilize, if seen from the existing orthodox legal knowledge system, is more non-regularized knowledge, a type of specific and local knowledge.

5.4 Why Care About Dispute Settlement?

In the current context, I don't have to make a legitimacy defense for the attention and knowledge of my colleagues nor myself. Although I have often been seen as a heterodoxy, which some jurists cannot get used to, and are even fed up with (I have been, therefore, labeled as conservative, or post-modernist, or significant of a dangerous ideological trend), from the perspective of genealogy of knowledge, I may more belong to mainstream jurisprudence, that is, I agree with modernization and the uniform rule of law, while revealing from time to time my affection toward jurist knowledge that I have been with for 20 years. However, when I see those phenomena in basic-level justice, I dare not deny the attention or knowledge of basic-level judges. What's more, if the readers know something about Chinese society and have a little sympathy to the life of Chinese people, and have read the detailed description in note 202 and truly understand my intention—it will be difficult for them to easily deny or refuse the attention and knowledge of those judges. However, what is more important is that I want to understand why China's basic-level judges pay more attention to the actual solution of problems, but pay unusual attention to those orthodox legal rules? According to Weber's view, this is mainly the product of legal cultural influence.[15] This view has been agreed to by many Chinese scholars, including me myself in recent years.[16] After several years of field research and interviews, I've noticed that this explanation is really problematic. On the contrary, Max's viewpoint of historical materialism and their explanatory framework provided by new institutional economics and laws and economics which actually have successive relationships (though some may deny this) with this tradition, and in some aspects have stronger explanatory power.

As long as we reobserve the above two examples, and at the same time think seriously about the social conditions of rural areas in China, we cannot have but one conclusion, only when we think carefully about trivial and detailed problems and ensure that those trivial problems can be solved, then a case or a dispute can be really solved. If we make judgments only according to the law without considering such specific problems, even though the judgment or the treatment is correct in terms of the law and has the legitimacy and justification of formal institutions, it would be difficult or even impossible to implement such a judgment; furthermore,

---

[15]Max Weber, *On Law in Economy and Society*, trans. and ed. by Max Rheinstein, Harvard University Press, 1954.

[16]Suli "What Kind of Law Does Market Economy Need?" *Rule of Law and Its Native Resource*, China University of Politics and Law Press, 1996.

the cost of implementation would be too high for the judgment to be implemented universally. Thus, the governance of rules is not realized in the end.

In the "case of breaking off mother–son relations," if the court had turned down the claim simply according to legal rules, the result would have been that we would have seen one case less from the institutional level. But in China's rural society, this dispute continues to exist and will exist for a long time. It will be repeatedly raised in this people's court, until one day, the son mistreats the mother so heavily that his behavior constitutes a crime. A criminal charge will be filed and the son will be imprisoned. Even if this happens, the case will remain unresolved. After two years, the son will be released, and the problem will happen again. In America, this kind of case is often dealt with by the police. But in China's rural areas, due to financial limitations, there are only a few police and other security people[17] whose main task is to help the village government to do "big jobs" (to fight against crime, gambling, to urge people to hand in grains or to pay money, family planning, poverty alleviation and, etc.); this kind of internal dispute inside a family is typically forgotten or ignored by the limited law enforcement force in the village. This has once again demonstrated that due to financial and personnel limitations, China's rule over basic-level rural areas is fairly weak, and state power is unable to practically and effectively implement and carry out the legal order or legal rules in the society at the foundational level.[18]

The conciliation before the court in the "alimony case" is also the same. Due to an inadequate enforcement force, one of the characters of China's court is that it "has to consider whether it can execute its decision by itself".[19] Therefore, in this kind of case at least, in the court, under the guidance of the judge and deterrence of the law, an agreement reached by both sides will be much easier executed as compared with a forced judgment of the court, and the execution cost will be much lower. But for the agreement to be executed practically without causing disputes, one important thing is to be careful enough to make clear the definition of "property rights," and this kind of definition must fit the local economic situation of China's rural area as well as the production means and living conditions of farmers. Otherwise, even if the literal agreement may have been executed, there will be new disputes as a result. The food problem is solved, while the problem of spending money emerges; the problem of having a meal is solved, while the problem of eating vegetables is still there; the problem of eating vegetables is solved, but the problem of having edible oils still remains. If any of those problems remain unresolved, the whole dispute will happen again, and will probably—although not necessarily—constitute a new litigation. For an ordinary person, this means a lot of inconvenience, and even certain pains. For a judge, he or she is

[17]In China's rural area, there is usually one local police station in a village. Some villages have three or four police areas. Each area often has one "police officer," and a public order joint defense officer. And one village has only one judicial assistant.

[18]Please refer to Chap. 1 of this book "Why Send Law to the Countryside?".

[19]Please refer to the section of "Analysis of Two Examples" from Chap. 3 of this book "The Judicial Committee System in Basic-level Court."

brought into the same case again, which will continue to be a challenge, but lack intrigue. What's more, China's basic-level courts, especially judges of the people's courts, often have deep connections with local community and share with the community the feelings and moral principles to some extent.[20] For this reason, from whatever angle, he or she will not want this to happen once again in his or her own court or somewhere else.

Hence, the problems faced by the judge in China's basic-level courts are not only to make fairer decisions which are more in line with rules, but also to consider how to implement and carry out such decisions. He or she has to solve these problems, which look neat from the perspective of stipulated rules, but are extremely complicated when actually handled in some manner which is not in line with legal rules or the institutional roles of judges but can actually "settle disputes." It is true that the basic-level court is, therefore, in a very awkward situation. In our research, many presidents and judges of basic-level courts have told us of one defining experience, that is, the court must "pay attention to whether its judgment can be implemented and can be recognized by the society." We should not simply regard this remark as a symbol of populism which lacks modern legal sense, but instead we should try our best to understand under what social restrictions they have this kind of experience.

There are many conditions that restrict judges in China's basic-level courts, but due to different situations in different places, there are also many different restrictive conditions. I could possibly list them all in this article. What is important is not to enumerate every possible or practical restrictive condition, but that we should have this sense when studying China's judicial systems and pay attention to all kinds of restrictive conditions. The attention and knowledge of judges is usually a product of responding to those restrictive conditions in the society. The functions of judges of different levels can be regulated in words, but their actual function and performance has to be limited by specific restrictive social conditions.

5.5 Rules Behind Particularism

By now, many readers may think that the purpose of this article was to raise and justify the tendency of "anti-intellectualism" or "particularism" of China's basic-level judges. This is actually not the case. The reason I choose to analyze these two cases which do not have strong moral features, and are neutral and truly "illegal" in terms of what judiciary is, is at one level to understand more sensibly some phenomena in China's current legal atmosphere, which may seem strange, but may not necessarily be strange when investigated, and are excessively moralized by

[20]This is a basic judgment from my research in China's central region. I will write another article to analyze this point which will not be discussed in detail here.

legal personnel or journalists who have become critical due to idealism and conceptual jurisprudence. This will help us to better understand some problems of China's courts, to find ways to solve problems, and thus understand the difficult task of assessing China's rule of law.

Superficially, the particularism demonstrated by a judge's orientation of dispute settlement is at the cost of sacrificing rules, but this conclusion can be drawn only when we assume that only stipulated rules are rules and their legitimacy is approved. If viewing this from another angle, at least in the above two cases, the thinking and handling of judges are not necessarily unguided by the rules. Take the details of the alimony case as an example. In this case, the judge took the initiative to put forward details of the settlement like green beans, soybeans, animal fat, and vegetable oils. From the perspective of people living in cities or other areas, or of commercial society, or from the angle of common payment methods all over the country, it is actually a very individualistic and special handling. In China's history, the general rules of payment to support the elderly support such a decision. For judges who have lived in this environment for a long time and are accustomed to solving problems in this manner, this practice is the rule. In this sense, the judge has complied with local rules. As with what we have seen in the court, the judge puts forward this kind of issue freely without any hesitation. Parties concerned responded to this issue naturally and exchanged their views without silence or objection caused by surprise. It showed that they shared this local public knowledge and rules.

For this reason, the problem may not be what it seems to us: That the judge has violated the rules of "no trial without complaint" and "remedy should be put forward by the plaintiff." The problem is that when a nationally stipulated rule and a national system of legal rules dominated by urban society are determined as a standard reference, dispute that emerges between local rules and national rules. It is because of this concept of law's orthodox status and its dominating power that any accommodation of the judge's decision to local rules is, to us researchers that mainly accept the orthodox status of national rules (I, therefore, still belong to mainstream jurisprudence), irregular, attaching importance to dispute settlements, and particularism at the cost of sacrificing rules. Here, we can see that the dichotomy and conflict of following principles and solving disputes are actually brought about by modernization and construction of a modern national state. The formation of a national state requires uniformity of rules and a monopoly of violence and force. Local rules have gradually lost their orthodoxy in this process.

For this reason, whether the judge strictly follows national rules is neither a moral issue nor an issue of a judge's quality. At least in the above two cases, the judges' intention, in the secular sense, was totally for good, although the stipulated law would not necessarily accept it. Here, I don't want to make a moral evaluation on the purpose or the intention of judges. What I have seen is only what kind of habits the judges will have, the knowledge they will accumulate, and the judicial tradition and style they will form under specific kinds of social and environmental restrictions. As long as this kind of character and knowledge is formed, it will be difficult for the judge to bring them into the trials of other cases, and even to the cases which the judge seeks to make personal gains. When we disclose the problems of violating the law and the discipline related to the personal moral quality of judges as in the latter category, we try to solve this kind of problem by simply strengthening administrative judicial supervision, as well as supervision of public opinion. However, because they have not really touched on the social reasons of these problems, these measures cannot be effective for a long time, and will be buried in oblivion the profound social conditions which give rise to this "violation of the law." Supervision by public opinion can possibly enhance this judicial style, which makes judges pay more attention to whether the individual cases obtain approval from society or the community. Basing decisions off this and forgetting about governance of rules completely can form a vicious circle, however.

I have many doubts regarding the effectiveness of improving a judge's quality—this includes emphasizing repeatedly the importance of rules, emphasizing following the law and being strict in enforcing it, making rule of law a new ideology, as well as the formal education of judges.[21] Knowledge that is really useful must be able to solve real problems, and the truth is always relative to problems that need to be solved. If you ask me how old I am, I could tell you that I live in the Weixiu Garden of Peking University where my house is indeed located. My answer is true, but this kind of "being true" does not answer your question, and thus is meaningless. My true answer and wrong answer are the same.[22] For this reason, to introduce general judicial principles and judicial knowledge with common truth is not the right remedy. Even universal truth will lose its "truth" in specific contexts. Since there are all kinds of disputes in China's basic-level and rural society which are not standardized, then those disputes need to be solved by irregular methods if not necessary. This is a problem that is often forgotten.

It is not a denial of the role of building society and unifying standards which is played by the law, especially by the legal activities supported by state power. But we must notice that this kind of role is often limited. The law in practice is only uses state power as its backup force as a last resort. When someone riding a bicycle runs a red light and is caught by a security guard who criticizes us or even gives us a fine, most of us will accept the criticism and fine obediently. The reason is not that our physical strength is not as good as theirs, nor that we are afraid of being caught after running away (if we did run away, most of us would not be caught. Nobody would even care to catch us due to the cost), we have accepted the legitimacy of the security guard as a symbol of state power. It is not because of the strong power of the old man or women or because they can immediately call the police to make us obey, but because our mind and behavior has been molded

[21]This kind of situation is almost universal. In American law schools, the professional ethics lessons are not only disliked by students and even complained much by professors who teach those lessons. Please see, such as, Thomas D. Eisele, "From 'Moral Stupidity' to Professional Responsibility," *Legal Studies Forum*, vol. 21, 1997, p. 193.

[22]This example comes from William James: The Meaning of Truth, A Sequel to "Pragmatism," *Collection of William James*, edited by Wan Junren and Chen Yajun, Shanghai Far East Press, 1997, p. 37.

by social life. Thus, the state power or legal rules can borrow this old man or women to have governance of rules over us.

For this reason, to realize regularized governance, one very important precondition is that the object of rule governance itself must have a certain degree of regularity. This regularity cannot be resolved by setting rules and bringing irregular phenomena into a regular clause. Just as Engels once spoke sarcastically on Mr. Duhring, you could include the shoe brush in the category of mammals, but this does not help it to get mammary glands. The unity of being, or rather, the question whether its conception of unity is justified, is, therefore, precisely what is to be proved, but not assumed nor imagined.[23]

5.6 Modernization and Rules

I myself seem to be trapped in a "vicious cycle": a precondition of governance of rules is that the social life itself has been regularized, and regularization of the society must be built according to the governance of rules. Thus, I'm at a dead end, logically. However, this is not the situation. It is exactly the place where I need to reemphasize the relationship between rule of law and modernization, and to observe the governance of rules in connection with the overall transition of modern society. This is an opinion I have emphasized in some other articles, that is, the modern rule of law is a component of modernization projects, but not a continuation of the rule of law concept or philosophy in history.[24] Modernization itself is a process to rebuild the world where we live, as well as us ourselves, as part of the world we live. It has made everyone of us standardized to a certain degree, and has standardized and regularized our living environment, behavior, and even sentiments to some degree. Only at this time can the law as a rule function effectively. During the process of modeling people, law, or legal philosophy as a factor does function, it is only one of the factors. Every aspect in social life is functioning, and some are playing bigger roles.

I can still feel this question in some of the details of alimony case. The judge mentioned payment specifically: mentioning green beans, soybeans, animal fat, and vegetable oil; however, both sides of the lawsuit agreed to reject the judge's proposal for a money payment, which is more common, standardized, and regularized. Why? As far as I see, this has shown that due to the development of the market economy, monetary circulation has greatly increased in China's rural society, and both sides of the dispute can and are willing to settle their disputes through more regularized methods of payment, which will have a lower cost. In China's rural areas, prior to reform and opening up, because the farmers lacked cash, a large number of alimony cases could not be settled through a cash-based,

[23]Engels: "Anti-Duhring," *Max and Engels Selections*, vol. 3, People's Publishing House, 1994, p. 381.

[24]Suli: "China's Rule of Law in Modern Vision," as previously mentioned.

regularized payment method,[25] but rather by payment in kind, such as soybeans, green beans, animal fat, and vegetable oil. Judges had to accommodate their reality and adopted payment in kind to settle disputes, which was special from a national or modern perspective, but regular in the locality. It is just from the large amount of practice of this kind that the judge has formed his or her attention, and accumulated his or her judicial knowledge. Such social conditions have constructed his or her knowledge genealogy and formed his or her judicial style.

Facilitate the change of payment and increasing the money available to farmers is only one factor. There are other factors as well. For example, there is a market where you can buy soybeans, green beans, animal fat, and vegetable oil with money. This is a condition which is similarly important. If there were no such relatively eternal and easily accessible markets, the old man would not want the other party to substitute payment in kind with a cash payment. In this case, the old man insisted that the coffin should be payment in kind, because in this mountainous area, coffins have become an increasingly scarce good due to government-advocated cremation, as well as some other factors. Without convenient market or at least a public market for coffins, if he has money, he still cannot purchase a coffin freely at any time. Even he himself surely doubts whether his son will take the effort to buy a coffin for him after his death.

Thus, this kind of more convenient and regularized governance for paying alimony in cash which, in the eyes of urban people, is simpler and perfectly justified, is actually not that closely related to whether there are rules and whether those rules are clear or not, as we have imagined. However, it is more closely related to the popularity of money, the emergence of markets for agricultural products, convenience, and other factors which I can't mention all.[26] The rules can only work when actually being attached to these minor, trivial systems and factors which are often believed by the legal people of academia to have nothing to do with laws.

What is equally important in this dispute settlement, at least, is that we also see that when social conditions change, and some new rules are made possible, the parties concerned do not stick to traditional local rules. In the alimony case, both parties of the lawsuit rejected the proposal put forward by the judge based on previously accumulated knowledge and thus rejected the judge's judicial style to take every detail into actual consideration. They "forced" this judge to adopt a more regularized method to deal with this issue. In this case, this kind of regularization did not prevent the dispute from being settled. As far as the payment was

[25]I could clearly remember a saying of farmers at that time: "The chicken's butt is a bank"—hens laying eggs is the only method for them to get circulated money. Although after the reform and opening up, the food problem of farmers were changed fundamentally, but the change of situation of lacking circulated money happened much later. The reason that the farmers did not accept IOU or green note was not only because it was compulsory, but more importantly, because they needed cash. For this reason, the "IOU" or "green note" as an official certificate for owing money has become the substitute of circulated money in many places.

[26]For example, in face of the plea of "breaking off mother–son relations," the important reason that the court did not issue a ban was that it lacked police force to ensure the actual execution of the ban.

concerned, dispute settlements and governance of rules obtained a new form of unification. To exaggerate a little bit, what I saw here was not the judge promoting law among ordinary people, but the people promoting laws to the judge.

With this, we can begin to understand more deeply that the governance of rules cannot be separated from the project of modernization. It can be said that all aspects of modernization (including activities of the law itself) are building a world that is relatively more regularized. During this process, the rule governance of laws is a matter of obtaining realistic possibilities. The analysis of this chapter is to remind us to reconsider whether "governance of rules" is the product of modern society more from the perspective of empirical analysis, but not from the ideological perspective. The acknowledgment of rules by modern society is not only a regulatory requirement, but a practical issue and process. The building of rule of law is, therefore, mainly not about how decision makers or people in power make decisions, but a process of remodeling and integration of the society, and a formation of a systematic institution, organization, and environment. In the words of Foucault, only when there is a set of non-discursive mechanisms can the discursive mechanism (of rule of law) be activated and function.

First draft on January 30, 1999

Second draft on March 18, in Weixiu Garden, the Peking University

Chapter 6
Inbetween Facts and Laws

The Tao that can be told is not the eternal Tao.
The name that can be given is not the usual name.
The nameless is the beginning of the heaven and the earth;
And the named is the mother of ten thousands things.
—Laozi, Chapter I.

6.1 Introduction: Weber and Qiu Ju

At the end of the last century or the beginning of this century, based on the deduction that the law will be continuously rationalized in its forms, Weber used to worry that the judiciary of the future might turn out to be a vending machine by which you could put in a written legal complaint and get your judgment automatically.[1] Weber's imagination was obviously limited to the time when he lived. First of all, his imagination was only targeted at the vending machine, but in this last winter of the twentieth century, as Windows 2000 is announced to be marketed, the vending machine is hardly anything. Second and more importantly is the judicial function imagination of the vending machine by Weber. Here, Weber might subconsciously give up the Cultural Relativism he had been adhering to in other times, and be consciously or unconsciously influenced by a high concept and form-rational philosophy of law and jurisprudence pursuit in Germany at that time, as well as by German judicial models of inquisitorial systems (especially in criminal

[1]Max Weber, *On Law in Economy and Society*, ed. by Max Rheinstein, trans. by Edward Shils and Max Rheinstein, Harvard University Press, 1954, p. 354; Weber's *On Law in Economy and Society* was written at the end of the nineteenth century and the beginning of the twentieth century.

© Foreign Language Teaching and Research Publishing Co., Ltd
and Springer Science+Business Media Singapore 2016
S. Zhu, *Sending Law to the Countryside*, China Academic Library,
DOI 10.1007/978-981-10-1142-9_6

law).[2] He might firmly believe that all facts of legal disputes entering into the judicial machine are "naturally" in order, clear, and complete, could be described by a set of clean, neat, and accurate legal language, and could form a system through a set of legal core concepts (key words); furthermore, those all complaints were in line with the format of the "vending machine," describing completely causes of action, facts, applicable laws, and remedies that the machine could recognize and deal with. Or he might also believe that the form rationalization of the society would finally sweep the world, annihilate any difference between individual feelings and social culture, and thus any cases would be already formatted before entering into the judiciary without the interference of any lawyer, prosecutor, or other legal agent. Otherwise, Weber would not have this kind of worry.

In order to make this point clear, we may be able to take Qiu Ju as an example once again. Think about it. If it was Qiu Ju who went to the court, what kind of cause of action would she put forward? What kind of rules would she resort to? What kind of remedies would she ask for? Would all this be in line with the requirements of the judicial vending machine? How would the vending machine style of judiciary imagined by Weber cope with it?

This judicial machine may be able to understand Qiu Ju's cause of action—the village head had beaten up Qiu Ju's husband and she asked for legal remedies, but it surely could not recognize the obviously local rules appealed to by Qiu Ju—stipulations such as "cannot kick the area of the his body which might kill him." Nor could it understand the remedies demanded by Qiu Ju—"to give an explanation." On the issue of Qiu Ju going to court, the function rule of the modern judiciary is that beating up someone has violated the personal right of the citizen, and the law will take action only when the behavior causes relatively serious results. The judiciary might not accept Qiu Ju's judgment and distinction of the importance of different body parts, or accept the specific cultural meaning given to that "area" by Qiu Ju or the community she belonged to. As for the village head beating up someone, the judiciary could not possibly give Qiu Ju the explanation she wanted, but only really cause confusion. Either the law would not attend to the case, or the village's head would be caught. As long as such kinds of "legal illiterates" who ask for "explanations" as in the Qiu Ju case, Weber's forecast of rationalized result of the judiciary will not come true.

But Qiu Ju's existence did not prove that Weber was wrong. As a matter of fact, Qiu Ju's existence, from another aspect, just proves that Weber was not someone who suffered from imaginary fears. More and more research has indeed demonstrated that the modern judiciary (even the judiciary in today's China, which is not that modern) is indeed like a machine that has been programmed in advance. It is like a Pentium III computer, although it has fast computing speeds, and vast application fields, it can only deal with documents compatible with preset programs that meet the program's requirements. In words that are familiar to people today,

[2]About the ideals and pursuits of jurisprudence in Germany at that time, please see Mary Ann Glendon, Michael W. Gordon, and Christopher Osakwe, *Comparative Legal Traditions*, 2nd ed., West Publishing Comp., 1994, pp. 56–57.

they must be formatted documents. The programmed function of judiciary must have a corresponding formatted world. Just as Mr. Feng Xiang has pointed out, the modern rule of law has created a lot of "counternarratives" like Qiu Ju's through its own narrative to confirm its legitimacy.[3]

Qiu Ju is only a fictional character, but this does not mean that her experience must be fictional. There are plenty of people who share a similar experience. The last chapter has mentioned a rural woman putting forward a claim of "breaking off mother–son relations" in the local people's court.[4] But there is no such cause of action in law and, at the same time, this woman does not want to accuse her son of the crime of abuse, sending him to prison. For this reason, the law-abiding judge has to, on one hand, reject her claim in law, and on the other hand, "go beyond the law" to play the role of a lawyer and suggest that she divorce her husband who left home more than 20 years. Does not this "un-recognition" and rejection of the claim by this legal machine reflect that the function of the legal machine requires that the case should have a specific kind of recognizable and treatable format?

These two examples are somewhat tragic, seem to deliberately make a mockery of the "the law," and thus are easily regarded as "anti-rule of law." In facing this kind of question, we cannot but think of the romantic knight summarized by Holmes: It is not enough to admit that his lover is great, and you have to admit that she is the best. Otherwise, you will have to accept a duel.[5] This kind of attitude, if not for pushing forward the group interests of legalists, must at least accept blindly the optimistic discourse of the mainstream ideology of rule of law and fail to face up to certain imitations that exist in social life and the law itself, and the inevitable embarrassment of the rule of law. As a matter of fact, every matter has its advantages and disadvantages, if we really realize the limitations of the law, it may well help us to understand and improve the pursuit of the rule of law in modern China, instead of making a choice between the rule of man and a utopia of rule of law.

This chapter tends to analyze the treatment of a judicial case which is not that irritating, based on this attitude. I try to display how China's basic-level judges are tangled between formatted judiciary and unformatted reality. Based on the analysis of individual cases, I will focus my discussion on two related, but not too closely related, issue of "factual disputes" in the judiciary. At the micro-level, I will analyze the issue of "nature determination" in China's basic-level courts in paragraphs 3 and 4 and try to demonstrate how judges in China's basic-level courts deal with unformatted social reality according to judicial formats, as well as the "facts" that cannot be covered through modern legal concepts. At the macrolevel, I will analyze why the question of unformatted social life exists and why the formatted judiciary has difficulty answering questions from the perspective of economic production.

[3]Feng Xiang: "Qiu Ju's confusion and Vega Culture," *Wooden-Legged Justice*, Zhongshan University Press, 1999, pp. 18ff.

[4]Please see Chap. 5 of this book, "Dispute Settlement and Governance of Rules."

[5]Oliver Wendell Holmes, Jr., "Natural Law," in *The Mind and Faith of Justice Holmes: His Speeches, Essays, Letters and Judicial Opinions*, ed. by Max Lerner, Modern Library, 1943, p. 394.

6.2 A Dispute on a Farm Cattle and Legal Disputes

First of all, let us see the whole story of a settlement of a dispute; but please remember that the history can never reoccur, and any description can only provide an outline.

In 1984, villager A borrowed 300 yuan of RMB from villager B, who was his relative living in another group[6] in the same village. He borrowed a head of farm cattle with this money plus his own capital of 300 yuan (without a proof). In 1987, villager B asked to share the cattle with the plaintiff, because the cattle which he and other people "together raised" died and he had no cattle to use. Villager A claimed that according to their oral consultation at that time, he did not have to pay back the borrowed money, the money would be the "joining fee" of villager B by which villager A would ensure that villager B have cattle to use every year, and the villager A had the ownership of the cattle (there was no sufficient evidence either; but villager B admitted at the court that he "he could not raise cattle well, and whenever he did, the cattle would die. He therefore asked villager A to raise it for him"). Villager B claimed that when they were in the partnership, the cattle was reduced to 600 yuan (there was a witness who turned out to be a relative of villager B and used to have economic disputes with villager A. The witness could only prove that both sides talked about the reduction of the cattle price, but did not know any other details). Villager A also claimed that when he resold the cattle for a profit the next year, the price was 1100 yuan.

Both parties admitted that in the 9 years after that, villager A had ensured that villager B had cattle to use and villager B did no't make any new investments on the cattle. The two had several minor conflicts in the time frame of the cattle dispute. During these 9 years, villager A resold cattle three times on his own (villager A claimed that the main purpose for resale was to ensure that the cattle "could be used well." Otherwise, after more than 10 years, the original cattle would be too old to be used). The accused knew of the resale only afterward and did not raise any objection to it. In June 1995, the female buffalo bought by villager A gave birth to a calf and the villager sold it after one year by which he earned 1000 yuan. As usual, villager A did not inform villager B in advance and did not share the profit with villager B (this is only a factual description and did not imply that villager A had an obligation to inform villager B or share the profit with villager B). After a month, villager B went to villager A's home and led the cattle away on the excuse of plowing fields. After a few days, villager A came to know that villager B had sold the cattle for 1400 yuan.

Villager A therefore went to the people's court to lodge a complaint. He claimed that he owned the cattle while villager B only had the right to use the cattle. This case was about a "partnership" on farm cattle and villager A asked for the

[6]Please note that this area was a mountainous area, with one administrative village covering many natural villages (of which there were only 2–3 families) which were miles of distance from each other.

return of the cattle as well as compensation for his economic loss. However, villager B claimed that according to their oral agreement in 1987, it was a "partnership" and he wanted to divide the property.

After investigation and evidence collection, the judge of the first instance believed that in this case, "the cattle did belong to a feeding partnership." It had been originally discussed that the investment should be divided. The profits produced during the partnership were to be shared, but villager B did not do his part in feeding the cattle and thus should profit less. According to this decision, villager B should obtain an extra 360 yuan apart from the original 300 yuan. (In the conclusion report, the judge of first instance gave reasons for this division, among which the main one was that the 1800 of profit should pay for the remuneration for villager A's service of feeding the cattle for 9 years (1080 yuan = 120 yuan/year × 9 years), and the rest of 720 yuan should be shared by the two parties, with each one getting 360 yuan).

Villager B was unsatisfied with this kind of distribution and lodged an appeal. The court at the intermediate level decided that this case had "unclear facts and insufficient evidence," repealed the judgment of first instance and demanded a retrial. In the letter to the court of first instance, the court of the intermediate level put forward 2 opinions about the facts: (1) "Had villager B obtained the right to use the cattle or the common ownership of the cattle by paying his money?" (2) When making the investment, did they appraise the cattle, and what would the market price of the cattle be at that time?

The court of first instance reorganized a collegiate panel to retry the case. Under the situation that neither party had given new evidence, the retrial judge believed that the head of cattle was a "joint procession." It had been originally discussed that the investment should be equally divided, and the profits earned during the joint procession should also be shared in a reasonable way. However, villager B did not do his duty of feeding the cattle during the period of joint procession and thus should share less properly. Based on this, apart from the investment of 300 yuan, villager B should be given 650 yuan. (The retrial judge did not stage the specific reason of this division in his concluding report). Villager A refused to accept the verdict, due to the benefit cost (Is it really worth spending another 100 yuan of appeal costs and corresponding sentiments of nervousness, anxiety, and even anger for just 200–300 yuan more?); he did not lodge an appeal.

This case was not particularly complicated. There were many "facts" in this case without evidence, and it was difficult to prove those facts, but it did not affect the settlement of the dispute (e.g., was it a partnership or a relationship originally? Was it a common procession or just getting the right to use?), although it was possible but not necessarily influential of the basic pattern of benefit distribution. In this sense, I think that as long as the dispute settlement is the only concern, this case actually has no problems of "unclear facts." The two key facts in the dispute settlement were recognized by both parties: (1) at the beginning of the partnership, both parties had a major investment on the cattle; (2) villager A had been feeding the cattle for 9 years while villager B had no input. Any ordinary person who is fair and reasonable, but not a legal person who tries to find out the "essence" of the cattle or of the legal relations between the plaintiff and the accused, would believe according to common sense, instinct, "justice," or "reasons" that the original investment of both parties should be respected; furthermore, villager A should share more of the property division; or that there is simply one way: villager A should appropriately share more. As a matter of fact, both the judge of the first instance and the collegiate panel of retrial had repeated these two points in judgment and had emphasized the second point. It was actually the real basis for the judicial decision and the pretext of the first trial and retrial.

Under the pretext that villager A should get more in an appropriate way, how to divide property specifically is only a judgment of discretion and practical reasoning (during the retrial, this also included certain compromise to requests of villager B, as well as face-saving for the court of higher levels, etc.); since the specific division neither has explicit legal regulation, nor could be deduced from the law or the definition of legal concept. In this sense, as far as the property division of these two judgments is concerned, I may "feel" the former decision is fairer, but I can't demonstrate that the property division of retrial decisions must be wrong—unless I am a follower of the "right answer" of Ronald Dworkin.[7]

If this kind of analysis is correct, we can see that the judgment of this case does not require any complicated legal analysis. It is even doubtful whether there is any legal inference different from common practical reason.[8] The judgment of this case has nothing to do with the legal knowledge of professors in law school; it is related to common sense. No matter how extravagantly and reasonably you analyze this case, whether you quote Holmes or Rawls, Lord Denning or Jhering, it seems that the only similar result turns out to be fair. However, is not justice supposed to solve problems fairly? The history of this case has indeed demonstrated a battle related to a factual dispute—the property nature of the cattle, and the essence of the relationship between the plaintiff and the accused. Why is this?

6.3 Factual Disputes in China's Justice System

A person who is used to China's jurisprudence will normally believe that this case involves a "factual dispute," that is, what is the nature of relationship between the plaintiff and the accused. The intermediate court repealed the judgment of the judge of first instance based on the reasoning of "unclear facts and insufficient evidence." However, the dispute of this case is actually not the kind of "factual

---

[7]Ronald Dworkin, *Taking Rights Seriously*, Harvard University Press, 1977, Chap. 7.

[8]Nowadays, scholars of all factions in America increasingly believe that the judicial rationality used by judges is not actually like what the Chief Justice Sir Edward Coke says that it is a special "artificial reason." The so-called legal interference is actually no different from other practical reason. Please see, for example, Roberto Unger, *The Critical Legal Studies Movement*, Harvard University Press, 1986, p. 11; and Richard A. Posner, *The Problems of Jurisprudence*, Harvard University Press, 1990, p. 459.

dispute" that we usually talk about. A traditional factual dispute in judiciary is normally in regard to the problem of how to reconstruct the whole story or the truth of the case based on various facts from second-hand reports.[9] But in this case, the whole story is anything but unclear—there are some unclear facts that are not very important to the judges and thus can be (and are actually) ignored. As far as judges are concerned, what is unclear in this case is an issue that only modern legal textbooks or certain legal scholars pay attention to—what is the relationship between the plaintiff and the accused on the cattle? What is the property attribute of the cattle? It looks like a factual dispute, and these answers appear to already be there before the case and we are only waiting to discover it. This is not actually the case. This dispute was constructed, and the answer to this dispute was also constructed. The more important thing to attend to is how to construct this dispute; the answer has nothing to do with solving this case, or with how to distribute benefits or whether the distribution result is fair or not (please see analysis of the previous chapter). It is only related to the legitimacy that is requested by the judiciary and the unity of judicial concepts and terms. In another word, it is related to the judicial format.

In order to explain this point, we must "contemplate" the judgments of the first instance and the retrial.

First, we must explore the concept of "partnership." This is not a concept recognized by General Principles of Civil Law, but this does not mean that judges hearing this case have no idea about the meaning of this folk concept. In this case, taking the context into consideration, it roughly means[10] that villager B has the right to use the cow, but does not have ownership. At least he does not enjoy the same rights as villager A. If only from the point of investment (assuming that both parties have the same investment), it seems unfair to villager B. If taking other factors into consideration and defining the relationship between the plaintiff and the accused regarding cattle, it is not that unreasonable. The reasons are as follows: First is the fact that the head of cattle was already been owned by villager A and villager B only joined later, as well as the arrangement that both parties made regarding feeding the cattle by the time villager B joined. Even while the initial expectation of villager B was "the partnership," we still could not imagine that villager B would accept this kind of property arrangement, which was obviously not good to him but only beneficial to villager B (to abandon half the property rights and to feed the cattle free of charge). Secondly, villager A resold the cattle for many times on his own, which villager B knew but never raised objection to.

[9]Please see, Jerome Frank, *Courts on Trial: Myth and Reality in American Justice*, Princeton University Press, 1973 (1949), especially Chaps. 3–6.

[10]This kind of definition on folk concept is actually dangerous, like "the woman with mysophobia" in Wang Shuo's *The Anima Is Fierce*, who "can't help polishing everything." The "mysophobia" that rejects realistic mess may help us analyze and handle certain facts with legalism, but it will alter the meaning of the facts described or referred to, as well as judically change the distribution of interests. In this sense, this partial accuracy usually results in an overall distortion.

This showed that both parties believed that villager A had a right to deal with the cattle on his own. Thirdly, according to our interview with the judge of the first instance, the local custom is as follows: on the joining feeding, if the head of cattle dies, the loss will be borne by the cattle owner alone, and those who join the feeding do not have to undertake the risks. The owner has to pay back the investment of joining feeding. But in the partnership, both parties have to share the risks of accidental death of cattle. The accused also said in the court hearing that the reason he did not want to feed the cattle was that he was unlucky and could not feed cattle well (he used to feed cattle together with others on several occasions, but the cattle died each time). Thus, villager A payed 300 yuan to obtain the long-term right to use the cattle with no risks, which was a good reason for villager B to accept. Fourthly, we must view this property arrangement in the possible perspective and expectation of villager B when this event happened, but not simply accept his explanation at the time of lawsuit. After 9 years, China's market economy provides more opportunities for development and profit. In particular, when seeing villager A has profited from selling calves, there would be enough benefits to drive villager B to make new explanation.

But in the first instance, the judge seemed to refuse a version of "joining feeding," almost from the very beginning. The following is a record of a dialogue between the judge of first instance and villager A in the inquiry before the court session.

Judge	When you joined the feeding (with villager B) in 1987, how much was the cattle you fed actually worth?
Villager A	It was worth 1000 yuan.
Judge	What evidence do you have?
Villager A	According to the market price at that time.
Judge	Who could prove that your cattle could be worth 1000 yuan?
Villager A	XX from village XX.
Judge	Could he convert the price of your cattle in 1987? in 1987, when you joined the feeding, (villager B) paid 300 yuan, did you ask anyone to convert the price?
Villager A	No. At that time, only the couple (of villager B) and I were present.
Judge	When (villager B) joined the feeding, you didn't convert the price. Now you said that your cattle was worth 1000 yuan, what is your evidence? Now you two have a dispute, and you can't present the evidence of 1000 yuan, what do you plan to deal with it?
Villager A	It is up to you to resolve.
Judge	If you can't put forward the evidence that your cattle was worth 1000 yuan, we can only deal with it at the price of 600 yuan, because you did not convert the price, nor present any evidence. Objectively speaking, money in a partnership should be shared equally. If you have any objection, you must give evidence within two days; otherwise, the court will give judgment according to law.

The judge started from the concept of "joining feeding" and then transferred to "joining a partnership" and finally determined the legitimacy of the "partnership." Why? Superficially, the main reason was the problem of putting to a proof, but this was not the most important reason. Because if you see in detail, you will notice that the judge has only inferred in regard to "paying equal money." However, it is stated in the law that in a "partnership," both parties should pay equal money, but that does not mean that all those involved pay equal money to be in a partnership. As the previous analysis has demonstrated that the partnership here can be said to only be conducive to villager B, but joining feeding will be beneficial to both parties. For this reason, even if they paid equal money, it is not the case that the judge cannot determine this was actually just "joining feeding." The trouble is that the concept of "joining feeding" cannot be connected with the General Principle of the Civil Law. There is only the concept of "partnership"[11] in the General Principle of the Civil Law, but not the concept of "joining feeding." Supported by mainstream ideology of rule of law in modern China, which emphasizes that everything must be done according to law, and in the corresponding judicial system where the court of appeal supervises the implementation of legal texts, it is difficult for the judge to define what "joining feeding" is in stipulate law, and he cannot find an appropriate basis for dealing with it in stipulate law. In order to make sure that his series of decisions afterward have legitimacy, the judge has to deal with this case according to this set of stipulated laws and the supporting conceptual system; they must make clear the facts being faced by the concept of stipulated law. He must eliminate the concept of "joining feeding." In another word, he abandons "joining feeding" not because the relationship between the plaintiff and the accused is not "joining feeding," but because "joining feeding" does not match the civil law theory that currently legitimate in effect and format. The judge is unable to establish an unquestionably stable connection between the judicial facts and the key words of civil law. Here, a set of legal concepts which has legitimacy has rejected another set of concepts that does not have this kind of legitimacy.

The judge of first instance enjoys some other conveniences, including choosing the concept of "partnership," because any concept not only has the ability to reject some facts, but also is able to construct other facts. When choosing "partnership," the judge could not only legitimately leave out those "facts" of the prior borrowing money in 1984, or whether they had converted the price when in partnership in 1997, or the price of cattle in 1988, which had been put forward by both parties themselves, and might have been contradictory to each other and hard to prove—those "facts" have become unimportant under the guidance of the concept of "partnership;" some other facts could be integrated into this kind of discourse, such as the fact that villager B had never fed the cattle. From the fact itself, it could not derive the conclusion appearing in the judgment that villager B "had not served his duty of feeding the cattle," since both parties might never think of feeding cattle by villager B initially, and what villager B had hoped was only that he

[11]Section 6.5 of General Principle of the Civil Law.

could have cattle to use every year and get rid of the bad luck of his raising of a cattle (at least according to what he himself thought). This duty might never exist. However, if the judge adopted the concept of "partnership" once, he could bring this originally unrelated fact under his command as perfectly justifiable and get ready for the rationality of his judgment (the sharing ratio) in the next step.

It was the same case in the retrial. The judges of the second instance felt that the dealing of this case was anything but substantially unreasonable. Due to assignment of responsibility (which more focuses on trial of law), as well as the comparative advantage in knowledge (which is more sensitive to legal texts and legal key words), they pay more attention to the issue of legal text than judges of first instance. They noticed that the fact determination (nature determination) by the judge of first instance on this case had some issues with legal text. According to the regulations of General Principles of Civil Law, "individual partnership refers to two or more citizens associated in a business and working together, with each providing funds, material objects, techniques, and so on according to an agreement"; "partners shall make a written agreement covering the funds each is to provide, the distribution of profits, the responsibility for debts, the entering into and withdrawal from partnership, the ending of partnership, and other such matters"; "the property provided by the partners shall be under their unified management and use. The property accumulated in a partnership operation shall belong to all the partners"; "the operational activities of an individual partnership shall be decided jointly by the partners, who each shall have the right to carry out and supervise those activities. The partners may elect a responsible person. All partners shall bear civil liability for the operational activities of the responsible person and other personnel."[12] This case did not have those elements necessary for "partnership." For this reason, no matter how reasonable the benefit distribution decided by the judge of the first instance was, the distribution had no basis of stipulate law, and in this sense, the fact determination of this case had some "mistakes." But this mistake was neither that this case was not handled properly or unjustifiably, nor that the case details were not clear, but that the "partnership" determined by the judge of first instance did not accord to the determination and features of "partnership" in stipulate law. In China's current judicial system, this mistake is big enough to overthrow the legitimacy of a decision.

The legitimacy of the judgment of this case must be reconstructed based on substantive law, which has been explicitly recognized by both the court of second instance and the retrial judge. To do this point, the judge must completely avoid

[12]Article 30, 31, 32, and 34. In addition, Article 50 of Opinions of the Supreme People's Court on Several Issues Concerning the Implementation of the General Principles of the Civil Law of the People's Republic of China (for trial implementation) stipulates that "if the parties have no written partnership agreement between them and have not been approved for registration by the administrative department for industry and commerce, but meet other conditions for partnership, and meanwhile have been proved by two or more persons without any relation of interests to have entered into an oral partnership agreement, the people's court may determine that they are in partnership relations.". However, as far as this article is concerned, this case could not meet the requirements since there is no witness.

determining the nature of the 10-year-long relationship between the plaintiff and the accused (no matter whether it is a partnership or joining feeding) and reduce the experience characteristics of concepts so as to bring facts about that are not in order with the concept of stipulated law. The court of second instance and retrial have returned back to the General Principles of the Civil Law, and discovered sections 6.1 and 6.2 of Article 78 in the General Principles of the Civil Law, "property may be owned jointly by two or more citizens or legal persons"; "there shall be two kinds of ownership, namely co-ownership by shares and common ownership. Each of the owners by shares shall enjoy the rights and assume the obligations respecting the joint property in proportion to his share. Each of the common owners shall enjoy the rights and assume the obligations respecting the joint property." With these two lines, the judge of the retrial can avoid the details experienced by the property in the real world that could not be fit neatly into the General Principles of Civil Law or other related texts simply by the fact of the property value of cattle and the amount of funds paid by both parties and through the definition of property. This has not only completely avoided the folk concept of "joining feeding" proposed by the parties concerned in this case, as well as the vague fact of "managing" cattle, but also completely avoided discussing the statutory requirement of "partnership." Although the redetermination of case facts may influence benefit division (which has changed the benefit division in this case), it is not necessarily the case.[13]

6.4 Facts, or Law

Chinese judges often regard handling factual disputes in an Anglo-American judiciary as "nature determination," which is indeed more accurate and precise, considering the above analysis. In today's China, especially in basic-level administration of justice, due to many factors that will be discussed in the next section, many social activities cannot be simply included in the current system of legal concepts. For this reason, one of the important tasks of China's judicial first instances is to try its best to pack irregular folk activities with transplanted legal concepts and conceptual systems and to enable them to find their own place in this legitimate conceptual system. This is most prominent case is in criminal law practice. One of the important theoretical pretexts of crime set by law is that all actions that should be punished by criminal law in the world can be included be a set of preestablished conceptual

[13]It must be pointed out that the implication given by the intermediate people's court in its letter to the basic-level court was actually more delicate. It pointed out two questions (whether it was "common ownership" and the market price of the cattle when in common ownership). It actually implied another possibility—"co-ownership by shares." Due to the difficulty in obtaining evidence, or simply the judge of retrial did not understand the implication of the higher court, in a word, the judge of first instance adopted "common ownership" which was more simple and convenient.

systems and can set a complete criminal law code, from which the basic task of criminal justice is to find appropriate charges for actions that should be punished. This kind of formatted way of thinking has been extended into the justice of civil law and other laws in China. For Chinese judges, especially basic-level judges, one of the most important tasks when dealing with factual disputes is to arrange and even squeeze out a proper place for those unfit facts in the current conceptual system of stipulated law. If we understand this point, it will not be difficult for us to understand the phenomenon of "cutting out the facts" by Chinese judges discovered by Jiang Shigong and Zhao Xiaoli in their research.[14]

This shows that so-called legal facts are actually not born naturally. Geertz points out that "legal facts are made, not born, they are socially constructed, … everything from evidence rules, court room etiquette, and law reporting traditions, to advocacy techniques, the rhetoric of judge, and the scholasticisms of law-school education raises serious questions for a theory of administration of justice that views it as consisting of a serious matching of fact configurations and norms."[15] This remark is right; however, if we carefully observe the factors that Geertz raised to construct legal facts, we will notice that his argument of legal facts constructed by society has been limited to his local imagination. What he mentioned was mainly some procedural legal factors, and his judgment obviously had strong features of American judicial system he was in.

It is true that many times, legal facts, especially when borrowing evidence to construct the "truth" of past events, are often limited by rules, such as exclusionary rules. There are also many times where evidence and the facts and truth constructed based on the evidence are influenced by local imagination. For example, the ordeal only had a strong evidential weight only on the people of this primitive, rural society; things such as DNA inspection have unquestionable evidential weight only to modern society. But if we just change the context of this evidence, due to a network of local significance, people's imaginations will make evidence lose evidential weight in different contexts. The evidential weight and related facts all occur and only occur in a network with local significance.

This cattle case has demonstrated that apart from factual disputes related to the truth of the case, and whether or not many specific facts related to disputes do exist, China's basic-level judges in the first instance have to deal with another kind of factual disputes, which are considered as more important. This kind of fact is closer to "legal fiction" (the original meaning for fiction is "made up"). Whether or not these facts exist is not based on empirical evidence, but rather on some key

---

[14]Jiang Shigong: "Legal Knowledge, Legal Practice and Legal Feature." The abridged edition of this article: "Judicial Practice in the Rural Society: Knowledge, Technology, and Power" published in *Strategy and Management*, Issue 4 of 1997, pp. 103–112; Zhao Xiaoli: "Relationship/Event, Action Strategy and Legal Narrative"; both of the articles have been included into Wang Mingming (edited): *Authority of China's Folk Society*, China University of Politics and Law Press, 1997.

[15]Clifford Geertz, *Local Knowledge*, Basic Books, 1983; quoted from Liang Zhiping (edited): *Cultural Explanation of Law*, SDX Joint Publishing Company, 1994, p. 80.

words from the stipulated law, especially substantive law. Those key words have, first of all, created in the hearts of jurists and lawyers a "shell" composed of many conceptual features with the legitimacy of stipulated law. They then use many empirical materials to construct a fictional entity that is in line with this concept in real life, such as the "partnership" and "common ownership" mentioned in this article, the "intention of crime"[16] which Foucault used to analyze, as well as "negligence"[17] in the common law. It is only after this that related laws can carry on legitimately and normally in the judicial process. Once the judge fails to construct this kind of correspondence between a word and an article that the legitimacy of his decision in the current legal knowledge system and judicial system will be questioned and even be endangered, which is caused by the specific standard of judicial legitimacy requested by the judicial system in which China's basic-level judges are in. This kind of specific legitimacy is based on the superstitious belief in this kind of conceptual entity by the current legal system and legal knowledge system, and its essence is book-worship, essentialism, legalism, or conceptual jurisprudence. This phenomenon is relatively prominent among jurist circles and judges of second instance.

As my analysis has demonstrated, this kind of attention is not attention to facts, but to legal concepts (key words) and legal professional discourses. When people have a basically consistent evaluation on behaviors of other people in the real world, the determination of "facts" will not necessarily influence the actual function of law or practical division of rights. Just as the two divisions of property in the cattle case demonstrated, no matter whether it was determined as a "partnership" or "common ownership," the determination of "fact" does not change the basic judgment of the judge as "villager A should share more in a proper way." It is the process and specific details (villager A had been feeding the cattle alone for 9 years) of their social life that are not included into the legal conceptual system that really guides the judge's decision. Seeing from this level, what was the relationship between the plaintiff and the accused? The so-called fact determination had no real significance to the judge of first instance and parties involved.[18] Only when people had disputed evaluation on people and events in the real world, such as Wang Hai's judgment differences regarding "knowing to buy fakes," that fact like whether or not Wang Hai is a "consumer" is meaningful to the disputing

[16]Michel Foucault: "'Dangerous Individuals' in the nineteenth century," translated by Suli, *Forum of Social Theories*, Issue 5 of 1998.

[17]After the Hand Formula (B < PL), especially through the analysis of Economics of Law, the so-called negligence in the Tort Law is nothing but a legal setting to implement or exempt legal liabilities, instead of a description of mental status of infringers. Please refer to Richard A. Posner, *Economic Analysis of Law*, 4th ed. Little, Brown, and Company, 1992, pp. 163–167.

[18]The "meaning" I determine here is pragmatic. Whether or not a thing or an opinion is meaningful depends on and only depends on whether it makes a difference in the real world. In Holmes' word, "to live is to function.".

parties.[19] What people actually argue about is not whether or not Wang Hai is a consumer, but whether or not Wang Hai should be protected as a consumer. This is not an issue of fact, but an issue of value or policy judgment. In this sense, I think that studying intensively on this kind of "fact" cannot provide any professional training for judges; such practices can only make judges more accustomed to discern policy or value judgment as fact judgment, making a judgment more authoritative and unquestionable.

People may point out that this kind of attention to "nature determination" can reduce the discretion of judges and be conducive to the rule of law. But the analysis of this case has demonstrated that this kind of limitation is false. In the cattle case, the change of "nature determination" did not change the basic judgment of the judge. Nor did it limit the judge's discretion. If the judge, not out of comprise to villager B, or the respect to the court of second instance (he should at least save their faces after all), or confirmation of evaluation and legitimacy of the significance of his job (retrial), had made the property division in the retrial exactly the same as that of the first instance, I would have not seen anything illegal or irrational in such a decision. This kind of property division is still at the discretion of the retrial judge. I personally believe that the property division made by the judge of first instance has truly demonstrated his attention to specific facts: He calculated the due proceeds of each party based on the deserved reward of 120 yuan that villager A should have earned each year by feeding cattle (hay, stocking, tending, and even risks). This kind of division is not only pragmatic, but with little discretion. If there were a dispute, it would be easy to judge whether or not this division is fair. For example, you could argue that 120 yuan for each year is too much or too little. But the practice of only giving a new legal label to constructed event and dealing with it "according to law" is, on the contrary, actually a practice to do things carelessly and to try to deceive everybody, as well a way to be indolent in one's duty and ask the judge to do the same, which actually increases a judge's discretion. We should think about the famous saying of Holmes, "we should think about the events not the words."[20] We should make more observations and evaluation of the related details of the case, not just concept analysis.

6.5 The Social Format of Events

Taking a moderate attitude of analysis and critique, the above analysis has demonstrated that the dealing of facts in the basic-level administration of justice in today's

[19]For this reason, as for cases of Wang Hai knowing to buy fake in order to claim for double compensation, the majority of people—whether supporters or opponents—are discussing about the definition of customer or of consumption. But as far as I see, the truly key issue, which has been deliberately avoided, is whether or not to confirm the result of judicial practice of Wang Hai as a customer.

[20]Oliver Wendell Holmes, Jr., "Law and the Court," in *The Mind and Faith of Justice Holmes: His Speeches, Essays, Letters, and Judicial Opinions*, The Modern Library, 1943, p. 389.

China—nature determination—is actually more of the construction of facts under the guidance of the law, which is, simply speaking, intended to "label" case facts. It has also demonstrated that as far as the cattle case and related cases as dispute settlements are concerned, we do not need complicated analysis of legal concepts. I am not saying that we should reject fact construction by law and I don't deny the social significance of this kind of construction. In order to unify the rule of law (which certainly includes the unification of legal concepts and terms), to encourage the formation of a legal community, the law must have some kind of construction regarding unformatted reality. The point of giving Qiu Ju the explanation she desires, and taking on the mindset of "not kicking an area of his body which might kill him" as common legal rules are not as incompatible of fire and water, but at least can be coordinated through an institutional division of labor. The court of first instance deals with the cattle case in the view of "partnership," which may not be in line with the definition of partnership in the General Principles of the Civil Law, but even if we do not recognize the legitimacy of "judges making law," I still believe that the court of second instance may well support the judgment of first instance as "harmless error." This does not harm the governance of rules requested by the law.

The reason I take this position is because the above case and analysis have fully demonstrated the difficulty of China's basic-level justice (including judges, litigants in China such as Qiu Ju and the parties concerned in this case). The difficulty lies in the fact that it is difficult to include a large number of disputes in China's basic-level rural society into today's transplanted system of legal concepts (but not laws), and to go through the conceptual analysis of legalism. But this does not mean—and I have never tried—to emphasize the distinctiveness of Chinese culture or legal culture and conceptual systems from an abstract cultural standpoint.[21] As a matter of fact, the level I have repeatedly emphasized is the basic-level court and people's court in the rural society. I have explicitly realized and seen that when functioning in China's urban areas or rural areas with developed industry and commerce, the same legal conceptual system will be relatively effective and convenient. Why? My answer remains to be historical materialism. This kind of difference is mainly due to the difference of social production modes and related social living conditions, as well as the differences of people living under these kinds of conditions and their behavior patterns. If we simply compare this cattle case with an ordinary dispute of commercial contract, we can see the difference.

> Party A saw Party B's advertisement to sell steel and indicated to Party B that he wanted to purchase 50 tons of a certain kind of steel at a unit price of 2400 yuan. After negotiations, both parties agreed that Party B provide Party A with 50 tons of steel at the CIF price of 2500 yuan per ton. Party A agreed to pay Party B half of the cost in advance, and the other half upon the goods' arrival. Having received the advance payment, Party B immediately dispatched the goods to Party A. However, Party B soon received a notice from Party B, telling them that the goods did not satisfy his needs and that he had already

[21]But many readers have this kind of misunderstanding. About my position, please refer to Suli: "Contexualism—A kind of Approach and Method of Legal System Research," *Peking University Law Journal*, Issue 1 of 2000.

returned the steel and demanded the return of advance payment. But Party B, through investigation, found that Party A had actually purchased 50 tons of similar steel at the price of 2400 yuan per ton from Party C. Party B refused to return the advance payment and claimed that Party A had deliberately broken his promise and planed to give a lesson. At the same time, in order to avoid possible loss, Party B found a new customer and sold the steel at the price of 2450 yuan per ton. Party A took action, demanded the return of the advance payment, and provided corresponding documents (records of telephone conversation, tax, and emails) and other related commercial documents.

In this kind of case, even there was no official contract signed, it would not be difficult for the judge to determine that the contract had been completed through actions of both parties. Party A's actions were a serious breach of contract and should have been punished; but the judge would also feel (based on judgment of intuition) that the "lesson" given by Party B was too much. Based on a regularized remedy that had already been formed, and according to the specific market situation of steel and other policy considerations, the judge would not be difficult to find out or judge what kind of remedies that Party A should get. If from the perspective of encouraging market competition and speculation, the judge could only compensate Party B's anticipated profits lost due to Party A's default (=50 ton × 2500 yuan + Party B's extra transaction fees—50 ton × 2450 yuan. In order to ensure the transaction order and intensify transaction rules, the judge might be able to deprive Party A of all profits from this speculation and give them to Party B. Based on this, Party A could get a remedy of ([2500 − 2400] yuan × 50). The judge could also compare these two practical numbers and choose one which would be more beneficial to Party B or both parties. The judge could make some other choices based on other considerations.[22] In a word, the court would not have much difficulty in dealing with such a case.

The reason that this case is easily handled in a judicial way is not totally because the facts are clear (it is actually a case I have deliberately made up, since no matter from ontology or from epistemology, can have clearer facts than the cattle case), even though many readers are prone to believe so. What I want to ask is which factor made the facts of this case clearer in the justice. The main factor is that the significance and result of related facts in this case or this kind of case has a relatively explicit social definition in its social context from the very beginning.

First of all, this transaction is one of many transactions conducted by both parties on their own accord. Their contact was not the continuance of the multidimensional and longtime contacts. Their relationship was based on a transaction from which both sides previously believed they could make a profit. Although the relationship could go on due to benefits, it does not necessarily do so, since there are many opportunities to choose from in the modern market or the urban life. They do not have to accommodate each other too much. Once there is a problem, it can be clarified through all kinds of exchanges and even can be settled through lawsuit without worrying about the problem of how to go on with their contact.

[22]For example, the judge could provide remedies to the lost sales of the seller based on market demand.

Moreover, even if both parties continue to maintain their relationship, it normally is restricted to commercial business (single-dimensional).

Secondly, since it is a transaction between strangers, the property rights of both parties have been made clear or presumed to be clear before the transaction happens, and either party will not have such questions like "is the property you use for transactions with me yours or not?" If this kind of question was asked, the transaction would never happen. Even when there is this kind of problem, it has nothing to do with the transaction, legally, but is only related to each other in facts.

Thirdly, this kind of transaction is not mainly for the needs and convenience of existing daily life, which are profits that are hard to quantify, but instead for some future, and mainly monetary, benefits which are easy to calculate and predict. If there is a dispute, it will be easy for the judge to decide.

Fourthly, since the interests involved in the transaction are relatively large with big risks, the contact between both parties is bound to and usually conducted by lawyers or people with commercial experience. Due to the specialization and professionalism of those people, both parties must have and normally do have relatively clear and careful consideration (which is an advantage of specialization) of the social and legal results of their behaviors. Otherwise, they will be kicked out of the game in the competition. And the result is that people left in the game are more specialized, which requires and even forces people entering the transaction market to have higher professional abilities from the very beginning. This kind of cycle makes social transactions in urban areas and markets increasingly standard.

Fifthly, due to the exposure to and requirements of the commercial or urban life experience, as well as the longtime and abundant engagement with words, those involved can understand and grasp the significance of those words and behaviors with a stake more carefully and sensitively[23]; the exchange of words makes parties consider more carefully or understand more clearly the meaning of words and languages.

In addition, there are normally a series of relevant institutional organizations in urban life, such as banks and insurance companies, which help to reduce the risk of transactions institutionally; there are some other institutions which limit transaction risks in advance, such as limited liability, and corporations. I am not going to list one by one and analyze in detail all those factors—this is the job of the sociologist. But from those features I have listed, we can see that although commercial activities in the city are highly free with many choices, the institutions as social background have actually, from the very beginning, "formatted" the result which might be produced by a transaction. In this kind of process, people's intentions also (and even more frequently) change, their behaviors are adjusted, and unpredictable accidents happen, but justice can easily relate relevant legal liabilities to

[23]As for this point, theoretically speaking, the opposite argument can also be made; but from large amount of historical experience, the emergence of such words will help people to express their ideas and feelings more carefully and exquisitely. This point will be demonstrated most typically in evolution of literature in which studying and using words are themselves a kind of training.

those key events by sticking to moments, words, and deeds that said to be the keys for meaning. It is just in this kind of environment that the law continuously reshapes itself and accommodates itself to the society with more transactions among strangers.[24]

In comparison, the cattle dispute case (and many other cases mostly dealt with by China's basic-level judges) has some other features. First of all, the dispute was caused not by a certain highlighted contact of ordinary markets (such as borrowing or joint operation), and the dispute was gradually taking shape through a series of events from monotonous daily life. From borrowing money to buy cattle, joining feeding and using the cattle, and reselling the cattle, to the calf being born and sold, and the cattle finally being led away and sold, which led to the breakup of the relationship. This series of actions lasted for more than 10 years. We could pick out some cause–effect relationships judging afterward, but if we judged in advance, those cause–effect relationships become highly uncertain, and the parties concerned could barely anticipate such occurrences before conducting certain transactions. The significance and the result of those individual events did not have a predetermined social definition during the whole process of the dispute. If we just cut out certain period of life as "one" event for legal analysis and judicial handling, though there are some ambiguities, it could be ok. However, due to the unclear social definitions of the significance and the result of those behaviors and events in advance, every event afterward can, to some extent, be regarded as re-explanation of one previous event, then it would be extremely difficult for you to resolve (not analyze) the whole process as "one" case in the whole.

Secondly, the parties of dispute were relatives and villagers of the same administrative village. These given conditions made the identities of both parties in the transactions very uncertain, since people would always consider identities of transaction partners to determine transaction modes and to make clear transaction clauses. When your brother borrows money from you, you may not think of asking him to write you an IOU at all; if a colleague does, you may not necessarily ask him to do so, but the possibility is much higher, especially when if the amount he borrows is rather large. In addition, the property and the scope of "transaction" markets in rural areas and the limit of the "goods" (in this case, the transaction is actually adhered to the right to use the cattle; the partnership in using the cattle must be in the neighborhood) in regard to the transaction itself, to a large extent, determines that there are very few objects of transaction to choose from for both parties, and there are even not many other choices. From the perspective of economics, the cost–benefit cannot be calculated without choices, and thus there is no need to have a strict calculation of cost–benefit analysis. For this reason, from the very beginning, there was no clear definition of property rights adhered to the cattle, and the transaction's parties

[24]This does not mean that commercial transactions are inevitably transactions among strangers. I just say that the character of commercial transaction makes commercial disputes more formatted and easier for justice to handle. As for commercial transactions among acquaintances, please see Stewart Macaulay, "Non-Contractual Relations in Business: A Preliminary Study," *American Sociological Review*, vol. 28, 1963, pp. 55ff.

were definitely "shortsighted." Due to those above two points, there is an old saying among the people that "even an upright official finds it hard to settle a family quarrel." Here, "family quarrel" should be understood as an academic concept.

Thirdly, the transaction aimed for the convenience of production and life at least at the very beginning and was not conducted as a profitable business; thus, the significance of some specific events was not explicit in law. For example, it would be hard for you to determine the nature of reselling the cattle three times. Although estimated in money, villager B did not earn much by reselling the cattle; on the contrary, they paid an extra 20 yuan instead. But, in a certain sense, this was not necessarily an unprofitable business activity—otherwise, why would he want to resell? As a matter of fact, villager A said in the hearing that without the resale, the cattle he bought in 1984 would have been "too old to use"; his actions had maintained and increased the monetary value of the cattle and produced yields. But on the other hand, he really did not have the purpose of making profit in a general sense, and his purpose was more about using the cattle long term, and yields were almost an "accident" to him. We cannot "polish" (in Wang Shuo's words) those facts clearly enough, label them with concepts of legalese, or give those facts the so-called essential meaning with language.

Fourthly, since the event keeps happening, and the society of modern China transforms rapidly, all these have continuously provided those events which previously happened with a new context for understanding and enabled not only parties concerned but other people (including the judge and the author of this book) to possibly make new but similarly reasonable and justifiable explanations for previous events—and to even go further to demand or at least allow amending previous relationships and bring about new legal definitions. For example, in the perspective of the judge or onlookers when the case was filed in 1996, the fact that villager A resold the cattle three times alone was nevertheless a supplement of certain meaning to the cooperative relationship between villager A and villager B in 1987. It was more likely that the villager B got the right to use the cattle; on the contrary, if the nature of cooperation between villager A and villager B in 1987 had been determined in advance, then this event would have had new understanding for villager A's behaviors of reselling cattle and selling the calf alone. But the problem is that we cannot ascertain which fact between these two has priority in understanding, in explanation, and in law? Take another example, the birth and selling of the cattle, the strengthening of market economy factors from the 1980s to 1990s in China, and the promulgation and implementation of relevant laws that will make people review the profit opportunities they have not realized in advance (the so-called awareness of markets is raised, which make both parties concerned desire for and also likely review and self-determine their property right of cattle from their present situations, consciously and subconsciously give new explanations to relevant disputes of product rights which are more in line with their present interests and resort to legal reasons and legal bases, which were impossible to get in those years but are now available (e.g., there is only "partnerships," not "joining feeding," in the contemporary laws) to justify their present desires. In this fast-changing social context, the original social meaning of an event has already changed and shifted in a series of events happening afterward and has new possibility of explanation in a bigger context. Even those originally meaningless events are probably given meanings by interpreters in this context, or given some kind of farfetched but not completely inconsistent interpretations. For example, in the busy season, both parties were in an urgent need of the cattle, but due to the inconvenient exchange of information (they were not living in the same village and had no convenient communication methods to arrange in advance), there was friction in the arrangement of using the cattle jointly. Such kinds of frictions originally did not have any meaning, but in the context of litigation, both parties would regard those unavoidable disputes as displays of the other party's plot to seize the property.

After these simple comparisons, we can see that in judiciary, whether or not a case is clear in fact does not depend on how much knowledge people have about the details of the facts. What is important is whether or not the society has clear and stable definition for those facts and has provided all kinds of necessary social conditions and restrictions for the understanding of those facts and reaching consensus. And those conditions and restrictions themselves are a kind of format, which is one of the most basic preconditions of formatted judiciary.

6.6 The Document Format of Events

No matter in life or in law, another factor that is closely related to the social format of disputes and extremely important to formatted judiciary is "evidence," especially those various written records which are regarded as reliable and credible in the existing knowledge system. Weber has already pointed out that modern ruling by law (roughly as rule of law) has been conducted through official documents.[25] This is very obvious in the formatting operation of modern law. The court is an important component of ruling by law in modern society. If we regard written record materials as formatted documents, and courts, especially courts of appeal as file processors, then we could really feel the importance of the document format of events to whether the basic-level courts in modern China can effectively handle factual disputes.

As for contextualized information records, I'm not simply referring to the documented evidence regulated in all kinds of procedural laws in today's China, such as testimonies of witnesses and records of question, but also evidence that is decisive, hard to be mistaken, and demonstrated in all kinds of text formats seen from the standard of modern science and technology development in the current legal system. For documentary evidence, if it is the written record of recollection of parties concerned, then it is not that reliable, even if the person who recalls it is honest. It can be used as evidence of procedural law, but not necessarily meets the requirement of formatted document I put forward here. But a telephone record

[25]Max Weber, *The Theory of Social and Economic Organization*, trans. by A. M. Henderson and Talcott Parsons, ed. by Talcott Parsons, Free Press, 1964, p. 332.

registered based on timelines, even a report from the telephone exchange on call times and persons are likely more reliable formatted document. Indeed, the DNA test report of contaminants on Monica Lewinsky is a reliable contextualized record (since it was presented to the judges finally in words, like Starr Report). As an American judge of first instance once said, "Contemporary documented evidence has more power than oral testimony."[26] The documented evidence here must have a generalized and legal understanding.

According to this standard, in the fictitious case of commercial contract dispute mentioned in the above paragraph, it is not difficult to obtain evidence and testimonials in justice. Even if there was no contract officially signed by both parties, there are faxes, telephone records, and e-mails coming and going, as well as bills of payment, waybills, bills of lading, insurance policies and other related receipts or stubs, which would be enough to support judicial operation. But in the cattle case, these are all hard to obtain, or even impossible to obtain at all. Firstly, farmers are not much literate. Secondly, but more importantly—as Mr Fei Hsiao-tung has pointed out in his "Sending Words to the Countryside"[27]—the main function of words is to have exchanges across time; but in an society of acquaintance, the majority of exchanges are conducted face to face with no need for official words. In this case of selling cattle, whether it is reselling cattle or selling a calf, as well as other normal exchanges, it does not have any contextualized record which is completely reliable from the point of law in modern society to support this justice.

It is true that in the trial of this case, the parties concerned did put forward many kinds of documentary evidence. For example, villager B provided a proof issued by the village committee after the litigation that the property right of the cattle was to be divided in half, as well as documented evidence from other witnesses. But such kinds of evidence were produced for the ongoing litigation after the case happened, not the original records of scenes in that very year; they were mostly a recollection of certain normalized scenes in the daily life of that year. How could documented evidence of such kinds convincingly prove the true situation of the events that happened in that year? They were likely a fabrication of life in that year. To hear this kind of case, apart from facts recognized by both parties, judges would find it hard to find other trustworthy, simple, and cheap evidence. In fact, no matter whether in the first instance or retrial of this case, judges had only given one piece of fundamental evidence as the basis of "nature determination" of this case. That is, both sides acknowledged that villager B had invested 300 yuan, though there was still a dispute between the plaintiff and the accused on the manner of investment; as for the basis of property division, apart from this 300 yuan, what the judges depended on was that both sides acknowledged that villager A had fed the cattle on his own for 9 years, the calf was sold for 1000 yuan, and the cattle was sold for 1400 yuan. The judge did not use any of the documented evidence

[26]William G. Young, *Reflections of A Trial Judges*, Massachusetts Continuing Legal Education, Inc., 1998, p. 185.

[27]Fei Xiaotong: *Rural China*, SDX Joint Publishing Company, 1985.

provided by both parties which were said to be according to the distribution rules of the burden of proof in Civil Procedural Law, although I did not see some "documentary evidence" provided by both sides when reading this file. Facing a large amount of "documentary evidence" of this kind, the trial record marked it with formalized classification of "to be verified," but immediately following the "to be verified," the judge declared that the debate was over and started mediation and judgment. The documentary evidence which was promised to "be verified" by modern law would have to wait to be verified forever, like the Goddess Peak in the Three Gorges!

It is not because the judge is irresponsible, but that many facts are unverifiable in a large number (not a small number) of cases tried by the basic-level courts. Some are unverifiable in the sense of epistemology (who is capable of restoring history?), but more in the sense of sociology, which I put emphasis on. Theoretically speaking, in the cattle case, in order to determine the market price of the cattle at the time of the "partnership" (the intermediate court used to make such direction when sending a letter to the basic-level court), the judge could go to check—for example—the seller who sold the cattle to villager A in 1984, as well as the buyer who bought the cattle from villager A in 1988. The judge could also study the prices other villagers paid to buy cattle at the same year to verify. This kind of method has been used a lot in many trials of modern commercial cases (to study the prices of similar products at that time). Could the case trial by the basic-level court borrow this method? In the rural society, this practice is still not applicable.

If we have this kind of research in the villages, it is still mainly about evacuating materials from people's memories; even when memories are accurate and honest, since these kinds of transactions are relatively few and decentralized, the related data obtained by research are not necessarily typical. In this modern urban and commercial society, these kinds of data are normally kept for a long time in all kinds of documented forms. And due to commercial competition, such data usually reflects the market price of that time rather truly. The materials, such as information carrier and their reliability in rural society are quite different from those in commercial society, though they are all a retrospect of history. The former are records of the time, while the latter are recollections after the event (another conquering reconstruction of history).

Certainly, recollection of events will demonstrate the original status of life within a certain limit. But we need to remember the limits of resources and cost benefit. This case is only a case with monetary value of 2400 yuan, among which there is only about 1000 yuan in dispute. As a rule, is it necessary or possible for a society to demand that many of these kinds of cases faced by the basic-level courts should "be taken seriously as a communist usually does" (remark by Mao Zedong)? The problem here is not about what the judge's moral sense is and whether he has any feelings toward farmers, but about whether there is any society able to realize this "substantive justice" universally and for a long time. From the point of economics, justice has it cost or opportunity cost (even when you are not considering the cost), and the effectiveness of resources consumed to realize justice will also display a marginal diminishing trend. For this reason, there is no society that is possible to resolve a dispute of 2000 yuan with a social cost above 2000 yuan in a regular and common way, unless there are some other major benefits. Just think about it, why is the standard of evidence obtainment in American civil procedures so hugely different from that of the criminal procedure?[28] The most fundamental reason is that different standards of evidence obtainment mean different costs of evidence obtainment and testimonials, as well as different consumption of social resources.

There may be people saying that you have proposed a rather good principle, but it is not business that should be the concern of basic-level judges. The state has paid the court to make sure that the judges should act "meticulously" and "based on the fact." We must therefore understand what the actual disposable resources of the basic-level courts are based on our experience. As a matter of fact, the resources of basic-level courts are very limited. When doing research in the people's courton the cattle case, we noticed that the only direct means of communication for this court with the people's court of the county, which is located several miles away, was by telephone. The telephone was locked in a wooden box whose key was controlled by the court director. Only when there was an incoming call was the box allowed to be unlocked and the phone used. It could not make outgoing calls—obviously in order to reduce telephone charges. Their only means of transportation were their two legs—bicycles could not be used in such a mountainous area. In this kind of area, to collect evidence extensively would not only consume funds, but also influence the hearings of other cases. In comparison, a case in an urban area with rather advanced economy will not only involve greater interest (or otherwise, what is the point of being engaged in a lawsuit? Only if there is motivation of other interests or from other interest groups), and because commercial units or other banks and units of transportation and communication have rather available records and sometimes the total amount of research costs arc rather big, judging from the ratio of cost (monetary and non-monetary) and profit, the cost of urban courts is much lower than that of basic-level courts in rural areas.

This kind of life style and economic reasoning also explains why the stipulated laws have always paid more attention to commercial lives and urban areas. Even under the banner of the universality of citizens' rights, the law sometimes has tinges of the language of the wealthy, although it romantically claims itself to be the friend of the poor and the weak. In the traditional agricultural areas, all societies are, to some extent, "beyond the reach of modern law."[29] It is very difficult for modern justice that is mainly based on text information processing to deal with disputes in a society where information is passed on through word of mouth. It cannot function effectively at least.

This does not mean that the modern legal system has not yet entered or been able to enter into these areas. But it has entered into these areas, particularly in terms of criminal cases and some major civil, economic, and even administrative cases. When

---

[28]The former adopts the principle of preponderance of evidence and the latter adopts principle of rest assured.

[29]Robert C. Ellickson, *Order without Law: How Neighbors Settle Disputes*, Harvard University Press, 1991.

dealing with those cases, judges rely more on other official documents which are relatively more reliable to record situations when events happen: autopsy reports, injury assessment reports, fingerprints, footprints, receipts of medical charges, as well as other receipts and certificates related to criminal cases. Modern rule of law needs formatting and this type of formatting "does not read" non-text-based materials.[30]

6.7 Counterevidence?

People may ask whether the example I have raised is typical or not. It is really easy to raise questions against research of individual cases, although my previous analysis has tried best not to only stick to the facts, but rather reveal general truth from individual cases. For this reason, I think it is necessary to report and analyze briefly the types of cases from basic-level courts we have researched and the proportions taken by each type of case. I must also briefly analyze whether or not such case types are similar to the cattle case which I have analyzed above.

According to the deputy president of a certain county court, the cases tried by the civil court (including the people's court) in this county in recent years are approximately as follows: the number of normal cases (i.e., not cases with "sources deliberately developed," but lawsuits filed by farmers on their initiative) does not exceed 800, among which 40 % are divorce cases, 25 % are tort claims cases, 5–10 % are support cases, and the rest are disputes over property, inheritance, private lending, mountain forests, land, and water. The types of cases provided by other courts or judges we have studied are extremely similar to this, but due to different local situations, cases of such types take up different proportions.[31]

Judging from the types of those cases, we can find out that the majority of cases happen among acquaintances (divorce cases between husband and wife, support cases between father or mother and children, inheritance cases among brothers and sisters, as well as disputes among neighbors and people with adjacent lands) whose relationships are long-term and unavoidable. The occurrence of conflicts and disputes has often brewed for a long time. Their relationships often develop from intimacy to conflict. Even in the case of tort claims, there are usually

[30]This point even gets into the retrial judgment of the cattle case. I have read carefully all the files, especially the trial records and the final judgment. I notice that the judge does not put the history of contacts between the two parties into the judgment. The basic facts that the judgment relies on are facts recognized by both parties, such as the conversation about "joining" in 1987, fact that Villager B paid 300 yuan, and the sale of the calf and the cattle. The testimonial of the village committee as well as recollections of other acquaintance which are presented in text have been refused by the retrial judge as long as there are no other evidence to support them.

[31]For statistics of civil cases, one can refer to the summary of civil cases of 1987–1997 published by *Law Year Book of China*. One can also refer to the website of the legal information center of Beijing University under the category of judicial institutions which is http://www.chinalawinfo.com/fljg/fltj/.

infringement cases among villagers (e.g., children are hurt due to fighting, or employees are injured, rather than accidents of product liability or car accidents taking place in the cities). Since cases based on this kind of relationship are very similar to the cattle case and they cannot provide much credible evidence based on text, they usually have to rely on their neighbors for bearing witness. Although I can't provide a piece of evidence to prove how many cases have the same or similar features with the cattle case analyzed in this chapter, I don't think it necessary to put forward typical problems. I still believe that this kind of case takes up a rather large proportion, since three types of cases of divorce, non-support, and inheritance already take up the majority of all civil cases, and other cases are basically not far-removed from this type.

It has been claimed by this vice president other judges that since the court proposed to "hear cases outside the courtroom" and "find more cases" in 1987. In the court where the vice president works, there were only 264 "civil" cases in 1985, and the number increased dramatically to 2860 in 1988 while the number of cases in all types reached 4999 in 1996. In addition, there are tens of thousands of small cases "not seen as court cases," The increased cases can be divided into two categories: One is debt cases to recover agricultural loans and credits and the other is debt cases concerning "withdrawal and retaining of public accumulation funds, public welfare funds, and collective management fees—and arrangements of fees regarding family planning, compensation to disabled service men, militia training, road construction in rural areas, and non-government funded education." But these two types of cases have one common feature which is obviously distinguished from "normal" civil cases, that is to say, having explicit text documents, and cases being clear and simple with relatively clear rules. According to the vice president, he has handled more than 300 cases concerning "withdrawal and retaining of public accumulation funds, public welfare funds, and collective management fees, and arrangements of fees regarding family planning, compensation to disabled service men, military training, road construction in rural areas, and non-government funded education" in a certain village within one week and was praised by the provincial court; his experience was spread among courts within the province. He claimed that the handling of those cases was as follows. Based on the situation of land ownership, income, and family members of different families recorded in the village, the village committee filed a lawsuit, and the accountant calculated expenses and revenues. Then, the indictment was written with the seal of the village committee and handed to the court. The court would call in every defendant to check whether the numbers were correct, whether they were willing to participate, and when to hand in the indictment. Finally, the case would be closed by mediation or court decision. Judges of other courts have also mentioned and confirmed this type of case-handling.

It is true that the civil cases of rural societies are very simple and they far exceed the so-called ordinary civil cases in number. This fact cannot and does not overturn my previous analysis. First of all, this kind of justice is in name only, and as a matter of fact, it is more like "administrative law enforcement," although there are the so-called legal procedures and the cases are heard by judges which have become a branch of law enforcement. The reason the court takes part into this kind of enforcement is because, on the one hand, justice is said to be centered on "reform and opening up," but on the other hand, the bigger and more concrete motivation is the economic interests of the court. Courts that suffer from insufficient funds and judges with relatively low life benefits can increase the revenue of legal costs and obtain economic resources to improve their living environment (in both work and life). During the interview, many ordinary judges have raised fundamental doubts and sharp criticisms against and even complete disapproval of the legitimacy of this kind of "justice." Even the vice president, I have mentioned who has been praised by the High People's Court of the province also totally disapproves of the history he has created under the banner of "providing services for the reform and opening up," and believes that "this road is a dead end," since the practice violates the basic ways of functioning justice. He bitterly said that judges must stick to "sitting in the court to handle cases." Since the central government has put forward a requirement that the judicial system must "be supported by the government," I seriously doubt whether this kind of situation can last long in the basic-level courts. In addition, those judges themselves do not see the handling of this kind of cases belonging to "normal" justice. Even if we take one step back, we still need to see that the important reason this type of case can be handled by the judiciary rapidly, by certain fixed procedures, in large numbers, and in streamlined processes, is that the feature of those "cases" has been clearly defined by the society before the trial. They are very simple (although may not necessarily be legal or inline with central policies) and have relevant text documents as evidence. This has exactly confirmed my previous analysis and argument from another perspective.[32]

[32]This chapter has only observed two aspects of judicial formatting. There are many other important factors. For example, I don't provide any lawyers for observation in this chapter. Lawyers are actually an important factor that makes disputes of social lives formatted so that they can be effectively handled by the modern law. As long as they are decent lawyers (not "lawyers" who rely on building connections), they will, at different levels, format complicated and variable disputed questions of real lives according to existing laws. For example, they will put forward appropriate petition which can be found in law before the trial, exclude those plausible evidence, and focus on discussing the disputes of this case as well as laws applicable in this case. Those activities are actually formatting of cases. Due to the presence of lawyers, there must be even more official documents; and due to the factor of adversarial system, the evidence will be made more accurate in terms of forms at least, so as to facilitate the handling of disputes by judiciary. This point has not been yet given importance in the research of the judicial system in China. Many researchers emphasize the adversary relationship between judges and lawyers, but do not see that judges and lawyers are actually in the same boat in terms of judicial language and practice (in academic terms mutualistic or complementary). But the analysis of this chapter is enough to point out this approach and it is not for smart readers to draw conclusions implied in this chapter. Secondly, lawyer issues have been emphasized in practice since recent years, although the methods and approaches of demonstration are different. If we continue to discuss from the approach of this chapter, it is possible that it is more of an issue of knowledge, but not of direct practical meaning of many years ago. I will leave this issue for readers to slowly understand themselves or to speculate on the academic market, which may be more interesting. The last factor that I discussed about the issue of lack in lawyers in the basic-level society in other papers, and thus, it is not necessary to deliberately create this problem here.

6.8 Epilogue

From one winter to another, the efforts made by Qiu Ju have finally been given a confusing "explanation" by Weber's judicial vendor. As part of this judicial vendor, the judge of first instance for the cattle case complained to us "because of this case, my year-end bonus—300 yuan—is gone. They say the case has been misjudged!"

But I seem to hear those cases saying:

> … I have finally led a decent life which I have long admired. … I have created a clear image in front of other people and the image even charms and amazes me myself, no matter whether people like it or not. If we say that it is somewhat a natural image at the very beginning, then during the process of its final establishment, I was influenced by many kinds of complicated mentalities. I can ignore those whom I hate losing their temper, become more stubborn and secretely feel happy myself, but I can't fail the expectation and encrouagement of those whom I love. It is just like water becoming beer before it turns finally into vinegar.
>
> I guess I should be honest.[33]

I think we should be honest!

First draft on November 21–30, 1999.

Second draft on December 23.

Appendix: Judiciary as Formatting Tool and Process

This chapter has analyzed a specific issue of basic-level administration of justice. But to many Chinese readers, to simply put forward this issue is not enough. They also want answers, even if they are not truth. They may also want your opinion (as a matter of fact, I have already announced by opinion, "I think we should be honest"), even though the opinion itself does not solve any problem. The mentality of moralism has penetrated and spread around our daily life and even our academic life.

There is one thing that should be made clear. Although I have analyzed that there exists a problem of ill-matched format between social lives and judicial practice and emphasized that the social mode of production and the reform of the way by which our society is organized are of significance to the formatting of disputes and administration of justice, I must also emphasize that the administration of justice itself is one of the tools and powers of social life formatting. The intention of this chapter is not to deny formatting of the administration of justice (orientation of moralization), but only to carefully study judicial formatting (orientation of empirical research). The case analyzed by this chapter includes judicial activities that have shaped the social reality of China in different aspects and to different degrees and created certain new conditions of formatting for the judiciary's next encounter of life, no matter if the judicial results of this case are fair or not.

---

[33]Wang Shuo: *The Animal Is Fierce*, in *Wang Shuo Collection* (Volume of Innocence), Hua Yi Publishing House, 1994.

First of all, judicial activity has set an example for the community where a dispute takes place. No matter what the final result is, people will understand some legal and judicial knowledge because of this. From this case, they will see that their operations or transactions may have legal "loopholes" and "defects," and therefore will amend, adjust, or make clear their original relations to different degrees. They may make property rights even clearer, enter into an agreement, and make clear that the so-called joining agreement is a kind of "partnership" in law. And as far as the "thing" in the "agreement" or "partnership" is concerned, the person joining the agreement not only has a right to use, but also ownership. The new interests brought about by this thing during the partnership will be distributed equally as "yields." They may think about their future more and, with a clearer picture, define their potential proceeds in advance, or make an extra effort to define their own benefits instead of distributing their benefits to unfamiliar government officials or judges or other third parties whom they cannot rest assured when something happens. They want to take control of their own destiny and grasp their own profits. For this reason, when rather big interests are involved, it is not impossible that they will look for lawyers or legal workers and learn to use a kind of unfamiliar and even strange language to plan their originally very familiar expected interests. As long as they can get enough interests which exceed their costs from this arrangement, they will do this. Thus, the law has penetrated deeper into the village with their pursuit of interests.

The result of the trial of the cattle case has formed a pattern which has more or less constituted a certain realistic restriction on judges to deal with this kind of issue in the future. Although China is not a common law country and does not have stipulated requirements of stare decisis, judges sometimes change their own practice due to personal convenience or social/legal pressure. As long as social restrictive conditions do not have major changes, everyone will, to a certain degree, repeat their previous behaviors, perspectives, and ways to analyze and understand issues from the perspective of biology. Otherwise, they will demonstrate multiple personalities, which are definitely unaccepted by society. As a matter of fact, even a person with high degree of creativity is, to a large degree, a person of self-repetition, since people can only find out whether one person has creativity or not from his or her process of self-repetition. Otherwise, the person will be seen as inconsistent and unpredictable. Even the judges with the most creative power must demonstrate certain basic patterns or tendencies in their changeable behaviors and repeat themselves to a certain degree.

To the parties of both sides, no matter what the result is, the judicial settlement of their disputes is a lively legal education. They will have to reunderstand their behaviors and words and understand what kind of result their words and behaviors will have in law. In the past, they have tended to understand the words and deeds of the other party and their own within the standard context of traditional rural life, as well as the rights and duties of the other party. But now, they have to understand all these things in the context that has been changed or is changing. They can no longer rely on mutual accommodation among villagers. Nor can they be too willful or light in their words and deeds. They must learn to examine their words and deeds themselves and try to get a grasp of their own future instead of being controlled by others, not only on the cattle issue, but on some other issues that may cause disputes. They must connect their familiar concepts in certain aspects to concepts recognized by law, and use their familiar concepts to enrich and supplement legal concepts. They even have to give up some concepts not recognized by law (such as "joining a partnership").

The changes of global concepts is not only internal, it also brings about a series of changes in appearance and behaviors. For example, someone may refuse the practice of "joining a partnership"—a normal arrangement of property rights—since this kind of cooperation cannot be explained clearly in law today and is not recognized by law, which may bring about more disputes and wrangles. As long as there are enough financial resources, he can buy cattle on his own. Although costs are increased, there are fewer troubles and investments are thus more guaranteed. For this reason, he will give more emphasis to self-sufficiency and their own duties and therefore become more prone to individualism, rationality, and strategy, and more often guard against being harmed. He will think more about the future, not the past. It is to build a personality.

At the same time, each involved party will and have to rebuild a system of self-protection, since changes have made the words and deeds with explicit meaning in traditional society unclear in the formal laws of the country. When interacting with other people, there are more emphases on certain legal formalities (in the social sense), such as notarization and registration. There must be certain actions (such as signatures), certain words which are not customary (such as "joint possession"), and certain activities which are regarded as having real and regulated meaning by modern society or law. Active citizens must strictly determine meaning and results of activities in advance, instead of letting activities or life themselves play through. Such activities are just as Karl Marx said—they cannot express themselves without prescriptively being expressed[34] and can only be expressed by written word and statutory formalities.

Villagers cannot expect judges to decide things for them, as previous generations of rural people used to do. Today's judiciary requires that they complete the duty of testimony. Their security depends on whether they are willing and able to cooperate with the judicial institution to a large extent. Moreover, they cannot cooperate only through honesty or personality. In traditional society, the personality of a villager in his or her village (whether good or bad) would be, to a certain degree, recognized by a traditional judiciary or institution in a dispute settlement. It might even serve as a kind of evidence. But things are not the same any more. Personality no longer serves as a kind of evidence. They must retain evidence which can be handled and identified by a modern judiciary. Life without evidence has become dangerous.

---

[34]Karl Marx, "The Eighteenth Brumaire of Louis Bonaparte," *Collected Works of K. Marx and F. Engles*, vol. 1, People's Publishing House, 1994, p. 678.

In addition, today's evidence needs not prove "personality" or "moral quality"—which is important in rural society but rather the "intention" of one's previous words and deeds, as well as the significance of those intentions in regard to social activities and law. It is important not to underestimate this point. It means that the operating system and value system of traditional society is being scrapped while a new non-moral social operating system is being constructed. In law, the world is no longer a world which is modified and enriched by the process of life itself. It must be a predetermined world (though it can be modified by procedures recognized by other laws). In this world, people's daily activities withdraw from the stage and become more like a kind of background to explain concepts and propositions in line with legal statute, as well as those key words which are easy for the judiciary to handle. This world is more like a drama, in which law becomes the script or synopsis and everybody performs as certain characters. Life is no longer what Aristotle has said—being imitated by drama, but on the contrary, will imitate the drama. With less "spontaneity" and "arbitrariness," continuous reproduction of legal language, which is conquering new territories and human communities all the time, this world will be formatted and reformatted. This world of law will become a network mainly connected by abstract symbols, concepts, or propositions, instead of a network mainly connected by social activities, as it once was.

During this process, many people will be given more legal freedom gradually as they become able to utilize more skillfully the strength of this kind of language and logic in order to push forward their own interests. But on the other hand, they may realize that they are losing their freedom day by day, since they now must and can only guarantee their own interests or obtain new interests in this manner. They even notice that they are already unable to do things in other manners or speak other kinds of language, as there becomes less scrutiny toward the legal results of their daily words and deeds—eventually keeping people from understanding the inherent legal significance of their words and deeds. This process will grow rapidly and give rise to the process of continuous rationalization as talked about by Weber. The scope and speed of rationalization and normalization will be expanded and intensified especially due to the development of the market economy and the market continuously expanding its sphere of influence in rural societies with a certain degree of self-sufficiency in previous times.

This is only a kind of logical analysis, and this logical process will not be completed in an instance without going through experiences and lessons of Qiu Ju in which there may be blood and tears involved. If a person does not want to be mocked by law and become disgraced every time they go to court, and if they still want to use law to fight for some interests, then he or she has to accept this logic. They must format themselves in order to fit in the judicial model and furthermore must keep the format updated. In the age of Microsoft Office 2000, one cannot rest on Word Star.

In facing this whole picture, people will make their own judgments. Some will see its rosy beauty in the modernization of rule of law. But there are also people who will see the color of blood in the roses (such as Weber and Foucault). I am not going to make any comment regarding the nature of these crimson hues. If society develops in this way and demonstrates this color, then no matter how people see it, it will not change the color. Here, I only want to say that the fighting among the judiciary and legal definitions in the cattle dispute are not without significance beyond dispute settlement. The activities of the judges or the judicial process demonstrated by the judges are reformatting China's society—in which parties concerned and judges are firstly reformatted, and thus, people and the complicated social relations among them also become reformatted.

Modified on December 7, 1999, in Cambridge.

Chapter 7
Between Statute and Custom

The substance of the law at any given time pretty nearly corresponds, so far as it goes, with what is then understood to be convenient; but its form and machinery, and the degree to which it is able to work out desired results, depends very much upon its past.

—Oliver Wendell Holmes, Jr. (Oliver Wendell Holmes, Jr., *The Common Law*, Little, Brown, and Company, 1948, p. 2).

7.1 The Significance of Customs from the Perspective of Judiciary

In a paper about societal customs, I came to notice, from statistics, that in modern China, both legislators and jurists tend to ignore customs, and thus, customs are underestimated in statute, although due to the demands of the modernization of society, this kind of underestimation is rational in a certain way.[1] However, since the detachment of words from objects has become common in modern times,[2] the legitimate standing of customs in statute is certainly not in line with its actual position in judicial practice in any country. In the judicial practice of modern China, do customs fail to or hardly work and can they be replaced by statute, as expected by legislators and jurists? If customs do work, how do they work? What factors facilitate this action or inaction? These questions cannot be answered through the text of statutes, but instead by observing judicial practices of modern China. Only by doing this can we see the actual role of customs in laws of modern

[1] Suli: "Custom in Law of Modern China—Perspective of Statute," *Law Review*, Issue 2, 2001.

[2] Michel Foucault, *The Order of Things: An Archaeology of Human Sciences*, Random House, 1970.

© Foreign Language Teaching and Research Publishing Co., Ltd
and Springer Science+Business Media Singapore 2016

S. Zhu, *Sending Law to the Countryside*, China Academic Library,
DOI 10.1007/978-981-10-1142-9_7

China in a more practical and complete manner. In addition, if we observe customs and statutes from this angle, it will be of more significance to ordinary Chinese. For ordinary people, laws are forever specific. They do not care about the customary words and papers that jurists pay attention to. Nor do they care about the wording of statute in a "normal" fashion.[3] They pay more attention to the results of justice and law enforcement, which is actually the law they can see and feel and has direct impact on their lives.

In this chapter, I plan to study an individual case of a judicial institution at the basic level in China's rural areas. I came across this institution in an attempt to observe the customs of judicial practices in modern China. Yang Liu provided initial and rather insightful analysis and discussion on the case that this chapter focuses on.[4] However, since we have different broad focuses and perspectives on the same case, it is absolutely possible that we have different but compatible and complementary research results. The main focus of Yang Liu's paper is the technique used by the judge in dealing with the case. My focus is the impact of customs on judiciary. This chapter will demonstrate that although legal statutes in modern China have certain depreciating and sometimes even explicit denial toward customs, customs still fight their way into judicial practice and have major impacts on the process and results of judiciary, and even replace or rewrite statutes. This chapter will then discuss further what channels and manners that customs may influence the judiciary. The latter point may be of no significance to ordinary people and even legal academics who normally care about the result of cases, but I will demonstrate that it is of very special significance to jurists, legislators, and others concerned with rule of law in China.

Is this case typical, and do its result have any validity? Incredulous researchers will naturally put forward such questions. There are strange things in every description in this world, and you can probably prove any conclusion. It is just because I have foreseen those questions that I mentioned before that I *came across* instead of *collected* or *found out* about this case. In the field research, we had no intention to "hunt for novelty" or to deliberately collect some unexpected anecdotes. Nor did we intend to seek certain cases to verify our judgment (as a matter of fact, we do not have any conclusion or detailed expectation in advance). We even try not to question certain popular opinions or propositions. We only want to get an idea of the actual situation of China's judiciary. In this sense, we do not have any specific goal fixed in advance, nor do we put forward any grand theoretical outline. We just "come, see, and think about" those phenomena and

[3]This issue is complicated and requires more careful empirical research. Normally speaking, ordinary people always care about actual legal restriction and pay more attention to the actual legal results with which they are closely related. However, theoretically speaking, stipulation of statute can still provide a certain justifiable basis for the people's proposition, the stipulation of statute therefore can still influence judiciary, and people will thus still care about the proposition of stipulation of statute with a precondition that the channel of legal information keeps clear.

[4]Yang Liu: "Indistinct legal products—observation at two cases of mediation at basic-level court," *Peking University Law Review*, vol. 2, Issue 1, 1999.

problems. To use this case to analyze customs comes later. Frankly speaking, cases similar to the one analyzed in this chapter are very common at the basic-level judiciary of China. Every judge of the people's court can, without any "collection" or "investigation," talk freely about many "things" (not "stories") he or she thinks are ordinary, with little hesitation. The key is whether they have a sentimental heart and a diligent mind; most importantly to jurists of modern China, who are busy with national policy of rule by law, willingness to see the grassroot level of the justice system is important.

7.2 The Whole Story of the Case and Its "Legal" Treatment

In the 1940s, Mr. Fei Hsiao-Tung mentioned an example of conflict between law and local customs in his book *Rural China*. The story goes like this: A rural man committed adultery with a certain married woman and was caught by the woman's husband, who beat and injured him. However, adultery is not a crime while beating and injuring someone is. The injured adulterer went to the courts to sue the husband and demand protection from the law, but continued the extramarital sexual relationship with the woman.[5] By using this example, Mr. Fei Hsiao-Tung sharply, specifically, and vividly illustrated the separation of the law from the social customs and culture at that time and also pointed out that during the period of social reform, law was more often used by sly people to pursue their interests, which destroyed social order. In Mr. Fei Hsiao-Tung's own words, "the benefit from the order of the rule of law is nowhere to be seen, but the disadvantage of destroying order of propriety comes first."[6]

The story mentioned by Mr. Fei did put forward a series of complicated legal conflicts as seen in an abstract way: Does this kind of extramarital sexual relationship constitute harm to the spouse? How should and can the nation's statute deal with this harm? Can the victim demand the judiciary to have some kind of punishment against the person who infringes upon his or her marital relations? What is the limit of this punishment? In many societies, whether in the past or nowadays, one of the punishments against the spouse (especially the female) who has extramarital sexual relationship is to allow the victim to ask for a one-sided divorce. In ancient China, a wife being "licentious" had always been one of the seven circumstances that a husband asked for a divorce in, and this was beyond the limitation of the "three rules" to prevent husbands from divorcing their wives.[7] In many Western countries, the precondition for asking for a divorce is that the other

[5]Fei Xiaotong: *Rural China*, SDX Joint Publishing Company, 1985, pp. 53ff.

[6]Same as note 5, p. 59.

[7]Qu Tongzu: *Laws in China and Chinese Society*, Zhonghua Book Company, 1981, pp. 124–128.

party must be at fault, and adultery is always the first among all faults.[8] In some other countries with strong traditions of Catholicism, divorce is never an option in any circumstances. But since Catholicism strongly condemns adultery, the religion actually plays the role of the law in the society (instead of against a certain person). In addition, these countries usually have criminal or civil sanctions upon adultery.[9] Throughout history, an adulterous wife is usually punished more seriously than an adulterous husband is.[10]

There is no uniform law around the world on how to punish a "third person." Until modern times, or before the emergence of modern nation states, the punishment for a "third person"—especially the male—around the world seemed to be more prone to a certain kind of "illegal punishment" used by the injured spouse apart from community pressure and public opinion sanctions. Once the adulterous person was caught, he was beaten to leave him with a memory. But after that, the injured spouse could only let it pass. However, since sexual impulses are an extremely strong biological instinct in human beings, in some cases, this revenge can lead to deadly results.[11] In a time and space in which the authority is

---

[8]Please refer to Mary Ann. Glendon, *Abortion and Divorce in Western Law*, Harvard University Press, 1987; Richard A. Posner and Katharine B. Silbaugh, *A Guide to America's Sex Laws*, University of Chicago Press, 1996. Normally speaking, the reasons for fault divorce are adultery, abandonment, and violence, among which adultery ranks the first.

[9]For example, although France eliminated the crime of adultery in 1975, Article 222-7 of French Penal Code (translated by Luo Caizhen, China People's Public Security University Press 1995) stipulates that "the sexual assault crime (mainly adultery—my word) is sentenced to 5 years of imprisonment and a penalty of 500,000 franc." Italian Penal Code (translated by Huangfeng, China Politics and Law University Press, 1998) still keeps Article 559 and 560 about adultery punishment, although these two articles have been confirmed by the court as a violation of the constitution and thus not be executed any more. Spanish Penal Code of 1971 (translated by Pan Deng, China Politics and Law University Press, 2004) has a special chapter on "crime of adultery" with especially detailed stipulation in which adulterous men and women will be sentenced to a short-term imprisonment of 6 months–6 years. In the USA, laws of almost one third of the states, including Washington DC where the capital is situated, still stipulate that adultery is a minor offense, although those laws can be applied to nobody and thus become "dead words" (quote from a secondary source, Richard A. Posner, *An Affair of State: The Investigation, Impeachment, and Trial of President Clinton*, Harvard University Press, 1999, p. 35.

[10]For example, Italian Penal Code and Spanish Penal Code stipulate that for an adulterous husband, only when he publicly marries a concubine or has casual sex can he receive punishment equal with an adulterous wife. French Penal Code in 1810 stipulates that an adulterous wife will be sentenced to an imprisonment from 3 months to 2 years, while a man keeping concubine will be sentenced to a penalty of 100–2000 franc. As for situations in France, please see Antony Copley, *Sexual Moralities in France, 1780–1980: New Ideas on the Family, Divorce, and Homosexuality: An Essay on Moral Change*, Routledge and Kegan Paul, 1989, p. 87.
But this seemingly "discrimination" has its reason in biology. For a woman having illegal love affair, she might get pregnant and give birth to a baby, which will give her husband not only a burden of raising other person's child but also an opportunity cost of possibly losing his own child. However, a husband having illegal love affair will not bring about such cost to his wife normally. Please refer to Richard A. Posner, *Sex and Reason*, Harvard University Press, 1992, pp. 183–186.

[11]See Posner, *Sex and Reason* for theoretical analysis, same as the previous note; the story is more common in literary works. Mr Shen Congwen has this kind of description in his novel *Xiao Xiao*.

far away and national laws are unable to find themselves in day-to-day rural life due to many restrictions, this kind of extreme case may not be seen by people and may not have written records. The law can only treat such cases with the mentality of "out of sight, out of mind." But with the authority of a modern nation expanding comprehensively through society, social lives at the basic level are increasingly regulated and disciplined by centralized power. The criminal laws on adultery in different countries not only punish the male "third party" explicitly, but sometimes even excuse the radical actions of a male punishing a "third party," which is actually law enforcement in the hands of private persons.[12]

Since the beginning of the twentieth century, China has continuously embarked on a journey of "modernization" regarding this issue and others.[13] It has been 50 years since Mr. Fei wrote this article, and in these 50 years, Chinese society has gone through huge social reforms and transformations. As far as marriage, family, and related sexual relationships as mentioned by Mr. Fei are concerned, China's Communist Party and the Chinese government are pushing forward marriage autonomy including the freedom to divorce and the protection of women's interests, which has greatly changed the social status of women. "Women can hold up half the sky" has become a notion of common sense. In regard to criminal law of the People's Republic of China, adultery is no longer a crime. It is not an unlawful act in the sense of statute (in this sense, China's law is very liberal in this respect, from which the affiliation of ideology dominating the statute of modern China can be seen). Judging from modern mainstream knowledge discourse and legal texts, we can see that the family, marriage, and the intersexual legal relationship has changed tremendously; while voluntary extramarital sexual relationships are not attacked by law, they are not appreciated in society. But is the situation really like that?

[12]For example, Article 516 of US Criminal Code in 1910 stipulates that adultery between a married female and an unmarried male constitutes an adultery crime for both the male and the female. Adultery between a married male and an unmarried female, the male commits the crime of adultery. For another example, French Criminal Code in 1810 stipulates that if a husband deliberately kills an adulterous male who conducts adultery with his wife at home, he should be excused from the crime of intentional killing.
Please note that there is another kind of "discrimination" with reasons in biology and economics, which is severe punishment against male third party. It is demonstrated in the stipulation that when an unmarried person and a married person have extramarital sexual behavior, the unmarried will be given criminal punishment if he is a male, but will not be punished legally if she is a female (and will be regarded as victim of seduction). The reason is that from the biological perspective, the male normally more active on the issue of sex, while the female is often more proactive (especially for young females); and from the perspective of economics of punishment, restraining the activeness of males can more effectively reduce this kind of extramarital sexual behavior.

[13]An important example is the argument about "adultery with an unmarried woman." Please see Zhang Guohua, Rao Xinxian (as chief editor): *Outline of Legal Thoughts in China*, the second volume, Gansu People's Press, 1987.

In a certain municipal court at the county level on the Jianghan Plain, we witnessed a case as follows: The husband M of woman Q in a certain village went to the city to work and was there for many years. Seduced by another man W in the same village, Q had a sexual relation with W for more than a year (which was claimed by Q as "adultery after rape"). When the husband returned to the village learned about this, he was very furious and said that he "no longer had the face to live in this village." He fought W many times and even threatened his family, including a threat on the life of W's son. The village committee mediated this conflict. W took initiative and said that he was willing to pay M 7000 RMB as "compensation for psychological and reputational damage," but he wanted M to promise that he would no longer threaten him and his two sons after "settling the case in private." M refused this offer and continued to pester and threaten W. W contacted the party secretary of the village for help, who advised him to file a lawsuit against M at the local people's court to demand the cessation of M's attacks on W.

Until now, the story is basically the modern version of Mr. Fei's story. Apart from the moral standing of this "third party," the story line and its characters are roughly the same, although the "terms" used by narrators are different. Mr. Fei used was "adulterous man" and "adultery," while I refer to them as "the third party" and "extramarital sexual relationship" in order to be politically correct (the change of "terms" reflects the delicate but important change of morality and legal ideology in modern Chinese society). The following situations are different: In the face of W's lawsuit, M was unusually furious. Without any legal foundations that can hold water, M responded with a countersuit. He believed that the behavior of the plaintiff had caused "psychological harm and reputation loss," and he further demanded that the court should ask the plaintiff to compensate him 10,000 yuan (this is an example of mainstream legal ideology creating another "legal illiterate").

In face of this kind of delicate case, the court neither easily accepted W's claim, nor readily refused M's claim. It impartially mediated this case. During the process of mediation, the court, on one hand, persuaded W into accepting the decision of holding him in custody while, on the other hand, requested that M should make a concession as an exchange for M's detention. After working on both sides, the court finally had reached a reconciliation agreement. The agreement provided that: 1. W gives M 8000 yuan as a "compensation" for psychological and reputational harm; 2. M stops threatening and harassing W and his family, and neither side should provoke dispute (for W, it meant that he should never "go to see" the woman again); 3. The legal costs of this case were 600 yuan, among which W paid 400 and M paid 200. On the day when the agreement was reached, W, who had been put in jail for 13 days, was finally "released." W had no complaints against his detention, but on the contrary kept thanking the judge who chaired the mediation. M soon left the village and went to the city to work together with his wife.

From the legal point of view, this is a strange case. To most Chinese, the result of the case is seemingly perfect for everybody, but if we consider it carefully, we can see that almost all those involved in this case, including the judge, seemed to give up the foundation of statute, and the whole case seems to proceed on "a river without a[legal] navigation mark."

First of all, M's fury is well understood by everyone,[14] but his fury and his series of actions and demands did not have any legal ground. In China's Criminal Law, as it is currently in effect, adultery is not a crime and there is no explicit legal stipulation on this act.[15] On the other hand, even though M has everyone's sympathy, his harassment and threatening of W and his family are actions that should be punished according to the Public Security Administration Regulation and even Criminal Law.[16] In this case, both parties had never thought of the situation this way, and it had never been the expectation of their behaviors. The judge of this case thought about such legal issues, but he did not think seriously in this way either, nor did he plan to act strictly following the logic of the related statute. Strictly abiding by law is only a bargaining "chip" of judges who want to have a judicial result that can be acknowledged and accepted by all parties involved. Please see the following the dialogue between the judge and M.

> Judge: (propagates law knowledge), whether [the relationship between W and your wife] is rape or not should be investigated and settled by the public security committee. What is [your] reason to ask for money from [W] and threaten him?
>
> M: I have too huge a psychological pressure to undertake. I no longer have face to live in this world.
>
> Judge: Legally speaking… you don't have any ground to ask for money from him. The plaintiff demanded that you stop harassing him and you should immediately stop with unreasonable infringements against [W].

Although the judge mentioned the "legal perspective" here, his focus had nothing to do with law at all. He did not intend to apply statutes to M's case. Raising statute was only a tool to frighten M and force him to accept a certain result. During a conversation between another judge who is more senior in the court and M, this point was especially obvious.

> I can understand your mood and rash behaviors, you have been hurt psychologically and your reputation have been harmed, … W should pay a certain economic compensation, … things have been like this, so you should come around and think about the future. You should not have too much demand and your words and deeds should not go to extremes. According to the practicality of the situation, a compensation of 10,000 yuan is too high. Please think carefully, your wife was at fault too, … after [W] filed a lawsuit, you should not have fought with him. [If you] continue with radical words and deeds, you will be punished according to law.

---

[14]This is not only about Chinese. I once asked a middle-aged American woman for her opinion on this matter. According to her, even in America, this kind of issue of fighting out of fury can be understood and forgiven by the society and the judge will let him go, as long as he does not go as much as M in this case.

[15]Another important collateral evidence is that the Marriage and Family Law (draft) under the consideration of modification has already aroused many objections in the intellectual circle in China or at least related to law only due to the consideration of having certain legal restriction against the issue of "a third party."

[16]Such as Sect. 7.2 of Article 22 of Public Security Administration Regulations of the People's Republic of China (1994) and Article 238 of Criminal Law of the People's Republic of China.

Obviously, law is not evidence for cases, but instead a factor to force M to accept an agreement. Having held W in custody for the sake of protection, the judge then turned around and said to M: "Now W has been punished by law." Here, the judge explicitly defined W's behavior as illegal. The wording here certainly had the intention of comforting M, but the judge was not saying that only to comfort M. It reflected the judge's mentality.

In face of W, who aroused the dispute, the judge also clearly demonstrated his mentality of "having no consideration of law (statute)." The following is the judge's persuasion to W:

> Donot complain about the other party. ... You are the origin of the conflict. Your behavior was against law and seriously affected the other family and feelings between spouses, creating a harmful impact on society. ... You should see [your own] circumstances in the perspective of the law, and ultimately see the results. You should bear the main responsibility. You have undertaken a more serious violation of law.

In this short conversation, the judge went so far as to publicly criticize W's behavior as illegal three times. Legalists would believe that the judge's words were completely lacking general legal knowledge and that his words and deeds were unlawful, since W's behavior only violated certain moral laws at most (for some other people, this does not violate moral laws or even the universal values they believe in and practice). But this poor village sentimentalist had neither modern legal awareness nor proper social consciousness. He went so far as to accept the criticism completely. He not only accepted the court's decision of holding him in custody, which was obviously in violation of statute, but even expressed his heartfelt gratitude toward the court—he went as far as saying "the court holding me in custody is good for me."

7.3 The Spread of Customs and Their Wide Recognition

From the perspective of empirical law, the handling of this case is definitely lawless (without any derogatory sense). However, if a modern Chinese person comes to such a conclusion, then he or she must be wrong, bookish, or ignorant of worldly affairs. Typically, a Chinese person will think that the result of this case is generally reasonable (perhaps they may feel there was too much "compensation"). But for what reason is this reasonable? Why does this result make people feel as though this is justice?

If we observe carefully, we will find that all people involved in this case have actually approved such unwritten customary laws; for example, if a man has sexual relations with a married woman, then he has incurred certain "injury" to the husband of that woman. This does not constitute tort injury on statute for which the victim can put forward prosecution requirements, but to ordinary people, this kind of injury is not only wrong in moral sense, but also entitles the injured spouse to raise a certain kind of proposal. As long as the proposal does not go too far, the man having sexual relations with the women can pay this "debt of tort" in one or several ways.

We can see the attitudes of different people.

First is the woman. We have read all the files of this case and found that the so-called rape described by women Q is not that much different from the "adultery" described by W. The only difference lies in who took the first step, and whether Q had any refusing (not resisting) words when the man W first propositioned her. Neither side denies that since after the first time, they had a relatively long-term and non-compulsive sexual relationship. According to the descriptions of both sides and other indirect evidence, people can affirm that this was still certainly an adulterous act. However, this woman insisted on labeling her relations with W as "rape" even though she did not deny those facts or evidence. As for the argument of labeling this behavior, this is not only a product of woman Q being too shy to discuss her sexual demands. As far as I'm concerned, the most important consideration is that she tried to alleviate her guilty conscience toward her husband by this kind of labeling. For her, as long as this kind of sex relationship was not demanded by her or a result of her initiative, but instead was forced, then the behavior would injure her husband less.[17] If this judgment is correct, it would imply that woman Q see her extramarital sexual relationship with another man as an injury to her husband. This way, she does not see her sexual demands or sex as completely independent. On the contrary, she believes that marriage had made her bear certain responsibility toward her husband. Whether this responsibility holds up to a moral or legal argument, we should not make judgment from the position of ultimate truth. Nor should we see from the perspective of legal definitions. We should try our best to stand in her shoes. At least in her mind, this responsibility is legal; even when it is a moral responsibility, and it can be turned into a legal responsibility under certain conditions. In real life, legal responsibility coincides with moral responsibility on many issues, although this may not always be the case.

Now, we turn back and look at W and M, the two main parties of this case. All their words and deeds demonstrated recognition of the above moral responsibility and customs. Although the statute has not given M any legitimate rights on this issue, the reason why M felt so wronged, behaved so radically, and put forward all kinds of demands was that he felt a kind of moral injury. For him, a really reasonable law would give him more protection, instead of protecting the "bad guy" who stole his wife, which is a kind of expectation given to him customs. I'm not going to discuss whether he should or should not have this kind of feeling (or whether woman Q should feel guilty toward her husband), or whether his feelings meet the standards of the modern society. What we observe is a factual dispute—why he has such behaviors and what the basis is for his behavior? If we can get hold of

[17]On this point, we can criticize that this woman "lack the consciousness of subject," "lack independent personality." This kind of criticism can hold water, but if we observe further, we will see that this has constituted a kind of moral restriction on the sexual behavior of the husband to a certain degree. In this sense, sex loyalty, whether as ideology, or as a social practice, is actually often infiltrated with the conscious and unconscious right operation of sexual loyalty toward his or her sex partner.

this point, we will see that his behavior was also based on the above customs. It was also because of this that he could no accept settling the case privately with the 7000 yuan. The money could not help him let things go, and it even made him feel as though he was losing face in his village. He wanted to see that the state judiciary organ representing justice was standing by his side and that the cheater was punished in a way he felt more like a punishment. Only when the cheater "goes to prison" and is subject to national laws can he feel he is winning back his face and venting his anger.[18]

Now let us look at the third party, W. I have not met this rural cavalier yet, but I believe that his cowardice was not because his physical strength was not a match to M. As a matter of fact, when this event took place, he was around 40 years old and a "robust laborer." He did not seem to use money, or special social status, or any violence to attract woman Q to him. He was brave enough to "eat the grass nearby" (while at the same time, any ordinary person should have expected that once such a thing is exposed, there would be many disputes); however, he was not a wretched man as far as I can gather. Under other circumstances, if he had been bullied like this, he would have been willing to fight to his death, just like a villager willing to die for water in a drought. However, he was coward and avoided conflict in every possible way when the affair was exposed. The fundamental reason for his cowardice was the moral and customary laws he knew true in his heart. He actually admitted that he had done something against his conscience and he was in the wrong. The customs of rural society are a part of him. It is just because of this mentality that he took the initiative to offer to pay M 7000 Yuan in order to settle the conflict that he himself felt ashamed of. It is also due to this mentality that he had no complaints against his detention and even said that "the court holding me in custody is good for me." It must be pointed out that the so-called good for me was mainly because his detention actually ensured his personal safety. But on the other hand, and not unimportantly, during his conversation with the court, he said that the court's handling of this case, including the detention, was a "legal education" for him and that he would strictly abide by the "law" in the future. The "law" he mentioned here was actually not the national statute, but a kind of customary set of rules and behaviors shared among people in rural society.

What the judge accepted and truly approved of emotionally was actually the same customary rules. Only in this way can we understand why the judge not only showed too much lenience toward M's behavior, which threatened the other party's personal security (please consider this, if there is no adultery—the antecedent and background of M's behavior—would the court have so much patience

[18]In this sense, I don't agree with the summary of this case by Yang Liu's paper (same as previous note 4) and other researchers: adultery and racketeering. Considering the public pressure from the rural community, I believe that the fury of this husband is real. What he has done is not to blackmail (the amount of "compensation" he has finally got is lower than the amount he originally could get), but to humiliate W. Even if he cannot subject W to the sanction of statute, he must subject him to the sanction of customary law.

and lenience toward M's behavior? In other circumstances, he would have been immediately punished in a certain way), but the judge also clearly and repeatedly expressed that he could understand M's behavior and emotion. What is more important is that the judge did indeed take certain legal measures that were not clearly defined but were obviously not lacking in punishment features, and he informed M of this message in order to comfort him and calm his anger. When treating the third party, W, although the judge was fully aware that W was entitled to legal protection, what the judge provided to him was "detention" which was obviously punishment in the eyes of villagers and jurists (please think about it, if the life and property of another ordinary person were threatened, would the court provide this kind of "protection" and would it be enough to do so?), who publicly criticized that W's behavior was against the law and stirring disputes. The judge's measures, words, and behaviors were clearly not the occasional mishandling of a case or a poor choice of incorrect words. In the conversation, he blamed W three times for violating laws unconsciously, which fully showed the values held deep in his heart. Certainly, you can say that it is a slip of the tongue, but this is a judgment from the perspective of legal positivism, or a lawyer's perspective. If we change perspectives, this is absolutely no slip of tongue at all. This truly reflects the laws that the judge believes in or the moral laws as said by Kant.

Up until now, we have noticed that this case's handling, which could be seen by the positivist as lawless, is actually supported and guided by a relatively strict set of customary rules. Participants of this game have first of all accepted this basic rule to different degrees, so that the game can go on, and everybody can feel that this game is normal and the results are accepted.

If we go one step further, target the analysis and understanding toward ourselves, and ask ourselves this question: How will we—the city dwellers who have received higher, and even legal, education—see their words and behaviors, including those of the judge, as well as the results of this case? As a matter of fact, the other researchers and I, to different degrees, thought that the results were basically reasonable, at least at that time. I also believed that the majority of—if not all—readers would think that the words and behaviors of these parties were approximately reasonable. This means that we approve of these basic customary rules at least in principle (which does not mean that we approve of the way the trial was handled or the results. This kind of dispute actually comes from our different experience pertaining to life), and some are actually not able to accept the order of such a statute.

I don't want to sanctify this kind of customary rule approval, which definitely comes from specific social environments, or to mark this kind of customary rule as the pedigree of a certain kind of "natural law" because of this (although I believe that there is a long-term and stable biological factor of humanity playing role in this)[19]; however, this analysis has demonstrated that this rule is deeply rooted in modern China's customs in a way that is far beyond our expectations. Only when

[19]Please see Posner, *Sex and Reason*, as previous note 10.

we dissect society and the laws of modern China with the kind of passionate coldness of a surgeon can we distance ourselves from customary rules and find out whether this case handling is "unlawful" or not. This case demonstrates how powerful customs can be. One of the reasons that I quoted the story told by Mr. Fei 50 years ago at the beginning of this chapter is to show that even after 50 years of time, and through the great reforms of modern Chinese society, the rule of customs still has not fundamentally changed the customs rooted deeply in the soul and body of Chinese.[20]

Readers may say that we have just analyzed one custom; even if we are right, one custom cannot say many things. I need to point out that although I have concentrated analysis on one custom, careful readers should notice that the other behaviors and responses of parties in this case were strongly influenced by other customs. For example, the male M was especially furious when knowing that he had become a defendant while W had become the plaintiff instead. The main reason is because people in rural areas at least and even in urban places in modern China are accustomed to believe that the plaintiff should have more legitimacy morally.[21] Just think about the condemnation implied in the people saying: "the villain took the initiative to bring about a suit against his victim."As another example, the reason woman Q kept on emphasizing that her relationship with W was "rape" was because of another custom people widely recognize. It is not wrong to be forced to have sexual relation, which could potentially injure the spouse much less. There are more examples supporting this. The measure taken by the court against W was a punishment to all parties, not because the measure was itself punitive in nature,[22] but because in the context of rural society, "detention" is customarily defined by people as a kind of "punishment." If only from the perspective of physical and psychological pressures, W had a rather easy life in custody and

[20]I must point out that I use this example only to stress how powerful customs are and their influence toward case handling by justice, but not to justify this specific custom (though I personally approve it consciously and emotionally). I even oppose putting this custom into statute and I'm more willing to let this custom live among the people to play its role and change gradually. If these simplified anti-feudalists or radical feminists want to use those words as their attacking target, they must be careful enough not to hurt themselves!

[21]There are another two examples. At the beginning of the 1980s, I was an intern at a certain district court in Beijing. A male university graduate asked for a divorce because he had a new love, and the wife finally agreed with tears in her eyes. But her only formal request was that the court changed her into the plaintiff who wanted to sever the marital relationship. It looked like some black humor or the story of Wang Shuo's novel (it is actually very unfair to Wang Shuo who wrote novels like *Losing My Love Forever* and *Lady Flight Attendant*). But once we deeply understand the rules implied and reasons behind the rules, we can no longer laugh about it. Please see note 27 for another example.

[22]In Western society, once the weather gets cold, there are homeless people violating the law in order to get into a place to keep out the cold. He knows the goodness in it. When I served in the army in those years, I even thought that "confinement" is fine because I was too tired and desperately wanted to rest. And I could never understand why "confinement" was considered a punishment at that time!

this did not constitute punishment from the perspective of common sense. However, just because of the customary acknowledgement of a certain symbol, this kind of detention became a punishment. It is also because of a custom that the judge believed that he could play a trick on those involved and get away with it. Just in this single case, we can see that customs' influences on society and judicial practices in modern China are widespread and pervasive.

7.4 Interaction Between Statute and Customs

The above analysis has proved that customary rules are commonly seen as powerful in modern Chinese society and, furthermore, have strongly influenced judicial practices. This point is actually not that important. I'm not going to analyze whether these detailed customary rules are justified or reasonable—I don't think that is important. As far as this chapter is concerned, at least to me, what is more important is to analyze how these customs have entered into the judiciary and constituted "a vague legal product," as described by Yang Liu.

It is true that villagers file lawsuits according to the customary rules they are familiar with and believe in, and this is the paramount condition with which custom enters into the judiciary. Another important condition is that judges unconsciously approve and share folk manners and customs with the villagers. However, if we only analyze from this perspective, we may draw a wrong conclusion as far as I see—that is, parties and judges of prosecution, or cases, become locked up in a huge cultural structure—and they become so completely limited by this cultural structure or custom that they lack creativity and initiative. This conclusion can further imply that all our daily activities are in vain and the only possibility of China's transition of rule of law may be to imbue those opinions coming from above, which we believe to be modern, into the people and impose modern laws according to them. I oppose this conclusion, but my opposition is mainly not because I attach importance to customs, but because this conclusion may encounter another trouble which cannot be explained: Why can we and people who are powerful enough to imbue and impose modern opinions and institutions upon the bottom of society be free from the influences of this kind of cultural structure, even when we are living in the same social and cultural structure? I clearly can't accept this conclusion, and I must find more convincing explanations.

As for this point, I have demonstrated and pointed out in my other paper that, at least in China, there is no single system of cultural structure. There are always plural systems of legal rules in society. Even single rules can be utilized selectively or competitively by people—all stakeholders will choose to apply certain rules or explanations on rules to obtain legal results most beneficial to themselves.[23]

[23]Suli: "Legal Evasion and Legal Pluralism," *Chinese and Foreign Law Studies*, Issue 6 of 1993.

If we review this case carefully, we will notice that even these two male characters keep on choosing customary rules and national statutes guided by their own interests to different degrees. For instance, both sides have abided by customary rules, but when "the third party," W, found out that he could not meet the demands of M, and the safety of him and his family was threatened, he flatly chose statute to safeguard his interests, and he ultimately opted not to stick to the customary rules blindly and "settled the case in private."Victim M obviously borrowed the precedence of "mental and reputational harm," which has gradually become popular in China's urban areas since the 1990s, to support and justify his feelings and proposals, which are supposed to be expressed according to traditional customs, either due to his work in the city, or transmission from TV,[24] or his life in the Jianghan Plains where there is relatively developed exchange of economic and cultural information. Today's villagers not only put forward their own rights and proposals according to traditional customs, but also live in this fast-changing real world; they either actively or passively adapt to this world, or put forward their wishes and demands (what we call today as rights) by selectively choosing the most beneficial rules and using most "legitimate" language as we as jurists do.[25] It is just through this kind of choice that customs gradually enter into the judiciary. The tradition and the customs here are completely unlike what many jurists have said is hindering development toward consciousness of agricultural rights or civilian rights. On the contrary, what I have seen is that customs are one of the channels to develop rights and consciousness, and at times, the main route relied upon by the right to obtain judicial protection.

But we must be careful. Because even villagers or citizens have put forward rights and proposals according to customs, and this kind of proposal may not be able to enter into the judiciary and be recognized by the judicial system. Due to all kinds of reasons, the "explanation" demanded by Qiu Ju at that time could not enter into the judicial institution even though she had demanded it many times.[26]

---

[24]This point has become increasingly important. In many places, especially when villagers fight against all kinds of taxes in all kind of ways, they will always use the principle and the spirit of document or law from the central government which has been transmitted by TV and has greater legitimacy. This is actually the customary practice of urban people. The convenient information exchange in the modern society has greatly changed the knowledge sources and patterns of custom transition.

[25]Wang Liming believes that the right like "right of personality" is hard to grow from the "native resource" (Wang Liming: "System of China's Civil Law Code," Lecture on The Review of Legal Studies of the twentieth Century, December 27th, 1999). This is a conclusion hastily drawn without empirical research. Villager M might not use the vocabulary like right of personality, but when he claimed that he "couldn't live in the village any more" and demanded compensation on "mental and reputational harm," what he demanded was dignity of a person or man or husband. The fact that the villager M did not use the word does not mean that he does not have this kind of emotion or instinct. On the contrary, only when there is demand of this kind of emotion and instinct that an introduced legal category can be really rooted in the society.

[26]Suli: "Qiu Ju's Puzzle and Grandpa Shangang's Tragedy," *Rule of Law and Native Resource*, China Politics and Law University Press, 1996. Feng Xiang: "Qiu Ju's Puzzle and the Civilization of Vega," *Wooden-Leg Justice*, Zhongshan University Press, 1999.

As far as the judiciary is concerned, the judge is the only person who can refuse measures or admit customs within a certain limit and modify and replace national statute. If they are not willing or able to find a convenient and relatively safe entrance, then even if one party wants to influence the judiciary according to customs and puts forward a request of prosecution and rights proposal, he may still be refused by the judge finally. It is therefore in this case that we have one important question: Why will these judges allow this kind of custom to enter into the judiciary?

One of the explanations comes down to the judge's personal preference. Just as is criticized by current popular discourse, basic-level judges are not that high in quality and lack a modern legal viewpoint and attitude of strict law enforcement. It is true that most basic-level judges are born local, and have been living in the grassroots area for a long time. They do not know that "the world outside is excellent" and have not received the systematic training of law school. But this does not mean that judges do not know the consequences of breaking the law. The statute is there, and many years in public office and/or judicial practice have made them feel that they are different from ordinary people. As judges, they must exercise their official duty as judges and neither totally ignore W's request of personal protection nor let M do as he wants. Otherwise, it is a breach of their duty and they will be punished. We also see that even judges share the customary rules asserted by the parties concerned in this case, they have completely different circumstances from the parties involved. As far as this case is concerned, since the judges do not have many immediate interests in this, it is not worthwhile for them to take the risk of "breaching of law." They do not have to approve the customary rules in rural areas or at least do not have to approve them right now. As for this, if starting from personal interest, it seems as if they should deal with this case according to the simplified regulations of existing statutes so that it is totally justifiable for them to do so. Strict law enforcement is the most simplified and most risk-free practice implemented.

Another possible explanation is to romanticize the judge's practice or traditions and to believe that this handling has demonstrated the judge's compassion toward the villagers or his or her approval of the villagers' culture. This is also wrong. I don't deny that every judge has his or her cultural approval and has certain compassions. But as many thinkers have pointed out, altruism's role has its limited scope and extent,[27] so this practice has exaggerated many judges' moral sense. In addition, just as with the previous saying, we have underestimated the approval of

[27]About limited altruism, it was possibly the Confucius who had pointed it out earliest. It was the so-called view of "Love has its difference." Later, Mencius fully expressed this point and emphasized extending affection. In the West, The Holy Bible stresses that you should first of all love your neighbors. Adam Smith and David Hume also demonstrated this point. Please see: Adam Smith: *The Theory of Moral Sentiments*, translated by Jiang Ziqiang and etc., the Commercial Press, 1997; David Hume: *A Treatise of Human Nature*, the second volume, translated by Guan Wenyun, proofread by zheng Zhixiang, the Commercial Press, 1980, vol. 3, Chaps. 2 and 3.

modern culture by basic-level judges, their familiarity, and understanding of statute, as well as their intelligence. Judges would not give silence to or approve of interference, modify or even replace national statute, or make jokes regarding their careers only because of their feelings toward the land or the villagers or their approval of the Confucian School (do they know about traditional culture that much?). The judge did indeed feel that W's behavior was annoying and that M deserved sympathy, but is this enough to make them accept the customary rules proposed by the villagers? What has forced and pushed them to do this? Were they fully motivated their practical wisdom? Did they make an effort to go between statute and custom? Did they try their best to handle the case perfectly and to obtain approval in regard to tolerance and acquiesce of different parties? Did they even dare to take the risk of violating statute and receiving punishment?

In this case, judges had always been conscious of the presence and the demand of statute. They were privy to the rules of this set of games and the possible interest to judges if they did not obey the rules more or less than the parties concerned in this case. Before deciding to "detain" the third-party W, a senior judge had a conversation with W. Before releasing W, they had another time-consuming talk which seemed to be indirect. The main theme of these two talks was that there was a hidden meaning that was not in line with the stipulation of statutes that "we detained W, but we had to do this under such circumstance; you have to understand us and not to accuse us of detaining you illegally which violates law and discipline." This senior judge could not openly say this, however. He spoke indirectly and slightly touched on the point in order to reach a tacit agreement with him; what's more, he could not behave like he had a guilty conscience in the case for W, who did not plan to make accusations, or felt he had an advantage to take. The following conversation is a typical example:

> "We took those measures initially because you didn't have the right attitude. If we hadn't done that, we couldn't have guaranteed the safety of your life and property for you and your family. We do actually feel for you in every aspect and want to ensure that you get protected for abiding by the law."

He did not say "detained," but instead "took measures," "abiding by law," and communicated that because "you didn't have the right attitude" the purpose was to protect W. Those seemingly common words were full of rhetoric in which there were many judicial strategies concentrated. He redefined the measures and reconstructed causal relations. With both stick and carrot, he coaxed and cheated W. There was not only condemnation with justice, but also meticulous consideration. If we only see this practice as the judge's rhetoric, strategy, or management technique from above without considering the specific circumstances in which the conversation took place, it is not appropriate either.

For a judge in modern Western society, or a judge who utilizes judicial power under ideal conditions, he or she indeed does not have to yield to customs apart from the situation when a statute is obviously not fair. He does not need those strategies or this kind of method or rhetoric which is "against law and rule" but seemingly high-sounding. But the problem is that judges in Western society have many resources to use and after long-term and stable development of society and the statutes and social customs of their country have been able to get on relatively well with each other, unlike China which is in a period of transition where laws and customs are seriously disconnected. But what's more important is that in Western society, ordinary people will normally not rise up only because judges have taken coercive measures against M; and even when there are disturbances like this, the judges will not "lose their jobs" because of it. They do not have a "misjudged case investigation system" or "individual case supervision by NPC," which is currently under preparation. They have enough authority and resources to mobilize police and protect even a person like W who has moral defects.

For judges in China's basic-level courts, those conditions are not there or not sufficient at all. If Chinese judges had seriously abided by the law and taken certain coercive measures against W and provided certain protection for him (not to mention whether the judge was capable of mobilizing the police force and whether there were enough police for the judge to mobilize at the basic level to protect a plaintiff who might be considered a "bad guy." After all, they can hardly protect good people![28]), it would have been absolutely possible to cause a disturbance in the local area and even arouse ordinary people to besiege the court. The municipal party committee and government and even the people's congress would have been able to accuse the court and judges in the name of the people. The judge undertaking the case might have lost his or her job and his or her duties might have been suspended (or the people's congress might have relieved him or her of his or her post). He or she might even be attacked by the press from different places with words such as "the adulterer was guarded by the police, while the victim was held in custody" or "monstrous absurdity."[29] We also cannot eliminate the possibility that the judge himself or his or her family could suffer personal attacks. They could even refuse taking on this kind of case because there is no such stipulation in law (this can also cause disturbance in the press or even murder case). It is under this kind of pressure that when facing this kind of case, judges have to take the risk and go between the statute and customs in order to achieve a compromised result that both sides can accept.

The analysis here has demonstrated that judges allow customary rules to enter into justice by choice; they modify or replace statute, neither because they lack understanding of formal laws, nor because of approval of certain culture, nor cultural structure (cultural approval only decides which rule should be applied to

[28]Please refer to Chap. 5 of this book "Dispute Settlement and Governance of Rules": the old-aged mother who was beaten by her son could not get protection from the police.

[29]This is not just my speculation. As a matter fact, about three years ago, the Jiajiang County Court in Sichuan Province accepted the administrative litigation of a fake product manufacturer against a person who cracked down on fake products. The case itself was no more morally sensitive than the case mentioned here, but it aroused cries of journalists in the CCTV's Focus Interview: "Fake product manufacturer accuses person who cracks down on fake products instead."

modify and replace statute when there are many kinds of rules with same interests existing), but mainly because of many kinds of limiting conditions which involve their own interests (including considerations of duties and responsibilities). On this point, they are basically the same as the villagers. At least in some cases, only by utilizing this kind of knowledge and in this way can judges make themselves safe in basic-level society and the institutional environment of modern China. Those judges indeed use strategies, but not strategies of administering state affairs, nor governance. They are strategies more of individual survival.

This analysis aims to demonstrate, even from the perspective of judges, that customary rules are able to enter into and influence justice. This phenomenon is mainly connected with a series of institutional restrictions of economy, politics, and society in modern China, but is seldom related to cultural factors. It is just because of this that we can further review and understand the important role and seemingly awkward status in some senses of judges in China's basic-level courts and more broadly in China's modern rule of law.

7.5 More Conclusions

I have claimed in the previous text that customs have a strong vital force and will indomitably make themselves seen in the judicial process, which is not equal to the assertion that customs are free from influence of statute. As I have repeatedly pointed out in a series of articles, the customs or civilian law of modern society can no longer maintain their so-called protogenic situation formed before the emergence of national states in modern times. It must keep on rebuilding itself with its interaction with national laws.[30] We have seen similar situation in this case. When statute is replaced or distorted by customs, and if we change a point of view, we will see that custom itself is changing due to the pressure of statute. In this case, the "third party," W, was given a kind of protection from state power, however unpresentable it was. But the furious M decided to let him go under the persuasion, threat, and lure by judges. The judges themselves could not take the law totally for granted. They pointed out that M's behavior "went too far" and used legal authority to frighten M into accepting these conditions. They still could not let W "suffer from his own actions." If one has to judge from an ideal situation of strict law enforcement, I admit that the judges have submitted to customs. From the point of view of pragmatism, as well as people's creativity, we should see that the judges are rebuilding and reforming customs through their concessions (although they themselves may not recognize of this). All parties concerned have obtained a certain experience which is not conducive to adhering to national statute in this case.

[30]Please see "Legal Pluralism and Legal Evasion" and "On Legal Evasion again," both from *Rule of Law and its Native Resource*, China Politics and Law University Press, 1996; and "Custom of Modern Chinese Law—A Perspective on Statute," *Legal Review*, Issue 2, 2001.

We cannot simply believe that after this short encounter with statute, the space of customs has been squeezed out, and the space of national statute has been pressured; thus, we deduce that national statute will and should ultimately replace customs. Although it is easy for some legal scholars to draw this conclusion, I don't think it would typically go like this. If one sticks to this kind of view, they are just viewing customs with essentialism and realism, a changeless viewpoint and a viewpoint that one must choose good from bad and between customs and statue. "Customs" in legal science is just a substantialized word. Any custom in reality has always formed under different kinds of limiting conditions, and it is impossible for some customs to rid society of violence or power of this or that kind. In modern society, national power, whether it has pressured customs in legal or other forms, or leave customs a more vast space, is just the pattern adjustment of different factors which limit the growth, development, and manifestation of customs. Even if we presume that, during the growing process of customs in the past, national power was not present at all (but there were many other forces present, such as the force of family or the patriarchal clan), nowadays we can only say at most that there is one limiting factor which may be more powerful. The custom will continue to exist and will keep on adapting and changing with people's pursuit of their own interests. As long as the human race goes on, and all other social conditions keep on changing, then new customs will continue to be produced, which will forever be a restricting background for the operation of national statute (as long as there are still national states) and other administrative orders, and influence the practice and implementation of statutes.

As a matter of fact, even in those Western developed countries, the judiciary has always taken customs as one of the origins of laws. At many times in history, there was the explicit stipulation that customs must be obeyed if there is no stipulation in the law (statute), and in many commercial laws, there was even clear stipulation that the law (statute) was to be applied only when there was no pertinent custom.[31]

---

[31]For example, Article 1 of Swiss Civil Codes stipulates: In the absence of a provision, the court shall decide in accordance with customary law and, in the absence of customary law, in accordance with the rule that it would make as legislator. Article 2 of Japanese Law stipulates that customs that do not go against public order or good customs, and only limited to those recognized by laws and regulations or items without stipulation in certain laws and rules, have the equal effect with the law. Article 1 of Japanese Commercial Code stipulates that about commercial issues, in the absence of a provision, customary law shall be applied; in the absence of customary law, civil law shall be applied. In addition, when explaining contents of a contract or supplementing flaws of a contract, customs shall be applied first. In absence of applied customs, discretionary legal norms shall be applied (please note that this kind of sequence is a kind of custom itself, but it has certain kind of normative). Please see Shi Shangkuan: *General Principles to Civil Law*, self-published by author himself in 1980, p. 423, "The way to explain the declaration of intention should take the purpose that the parties concerned want to achieve as the first order, the custom as the second order and the random legal norms as the third order." However, in the Anglo-American law system, at least in terms of criminal procedures, "Some informal, beyond law customs that restrict justice process are as important (as US Constitution and The Bill of Rights)." Please see Richard A. Posner, *An Affair of State*, as previous note 9, p. 59.

Not only were customs allowed to play a more important role in judiciary, but judges were given jurisdiction and power to apply customs as well. This is not accidental. It is not only because statute cannot rule everything in life, and words cannot describe everything, but whether people admit it or not, customs will always be there—growing, developing, and influencing law in some way. Customs are forever a basic background that legal scientists or law makers cannot forget when analyzing and understanding the operation and effects of statute.

This is also the most important reason why I opposed making customs into statute in my previous paper on custom. Any custom, as long as it is included in the statute and put into words, will more or less lose its own vitality as a custom. This is not to say that statute has no vitality—it usually gets its vitality through a judge's interpretation, like the Constitution of the United States. We must clearly see that the vitality of statute is often more controlled by people grasping all powers, including the power of words (including legal scientists), while the vitality of customs is demonstrated by the actions of ordinary people in pursuit of their different interests. In addition, the interpretation of statute is always influenced by customs. When the Constitution of the United States was formulated in the eighteenth century, "men" in the sentence "all men are created equal" did not include black people according to the customs of that time, but when American judges interpret the Constitution of the United States today, black people can no longer be excluded. This is not because the law has changed, but because social conditions caused a change in the customary understanding of the definition "men" by the whole of society, which has forced law makers and judges make a new interpretation of the definition of "men" in correspondence with modern customs. It is just in this sense that we should and can understand the profound message implied by the famous saying "custom is the mother of law," but not like some scholars who see this as a conservative belief.

First Draft, dawn of November 6, 1999
Second Draft, November 18th
At Cambridge

Chapter 8
Delivery of Judicial Knowledge of Basic-level Judges

"The tunnels of each village all have many kinds of brilliant ideas..."

—Transcripts from movie *Tunnel Warfare*.

8.1 Relationship Between Judicial Knowledge and Judges

Due to the specific institutional space, courts of first instance, as well as time and space locations, China's basic-level society, where China's basic-level judges are at, and the knowledge and skills they need are different not only from those of ideal-type judges, but also from those of judges of second instance. For this reason, China's basic-level judges need judicial knowledge and skill training especially designed to their needs in order to improve their professional qualities.

This conclusion is not wrong in terms of practical judgment. From the point of analysis, it may lead to a wrong judgment—that is, the knowledge and skills of judges are only the result of knowledge input, and thus, the activity and creativity of judges are completely ignored. Within this one-dimensional cognitive framework and the resulting research framework, judges are seen as a kind of negative object receiving so-called judicial knowledge, instead of the subject producing judicial knowledge (which actually justifies a knowledge/power relationship in which jurists dominate judges). Then, we should ask one question: Where does the judicial knowledge taught by jurists come from? It is true that judges are no longer "declarers of God's will" (William Blackstone). But what about those jurists? How can they have obtained "God's will"? This seemingly right and reasonable knowledge/power relationship could not answer the question: Where does judicial knowledge originate from? Even though people who are in favor of this viewpoint in today's China deny the empiricism of judicial knowledge in principle, it is still easy for them to generalize currently popular knowledge produced and accumulated by judges of a particular

© Foreign Language Teaching and Research Publishing Co., Ltd
and Springer Science+Business Media Singapore 2016

S. Zhu, *Sending Law to the Countryside*, China Academic Library,
DOI 10.1007/978-981-10-1142-9_8

judicial system or certain institutional level (such as foreign judges or second-instance judges)[1] and to eternalize "judicial knowledge" which is actually very local. However, on the other hand, based on the knowledge/power relationship which is now widely accepted, it is absolutely possible that the certain kinds of experience and skills produced and gradually accumulated by Chinese judges during their judicial practice which can be of reference and guidance to the judiciary be excluded from the existing system of judicial knowledge. This will further separate "judicial knowledge" from judicial practice, which is not beneficial to either legal research or judicial practice. This has been obviously demonstrated by China's efforts of improving professional qualities of judges. On the one hand, jurists have justifiably and necessarily emphasized the significance of judges' professional training and education, but on the other hand, China's existing legal education and knowledge system very much disrespect the role of judges as knowledge producers.

As a matter of fact, since the jurisprudence came into being, especially since the development of jurisprudence in modern times which is centered on the judiciary, many jurists have emphasized the specialty of judicial knowledge in different forms. A kind of consensus has been reached that jurisprudence is a kind of practical rationality[2]; it cannot be passed on mainly through teaching, but can only be gradually grasped through a large amount of practice.[3] The strong argument of Mr. Hayek of judicial knowledge points to criticizing planned economy fundamentally, but it also shows that production of knowledge cannot possibly be and should not be monopolized by scholars. The "order" put forward by Friedrich A. Hayek has a tint of romance, but it also shows that it is absolutely possible for people to accumulate knowledge which is beneficial to them in a particular social and living environment, and thus, the system is formed gradually.[4] These viewpoints may provide some enlightenment for us in studying and understanding China's basic-level courts.

Based on interviews, surveys, and research of China's judges of basic-level courts, this chapter intends to initially sum up their knowledge and skills that have actually been formed during the trial process. The judges themselves may

---

[1]Please refer to the simple analysis of the currently popular judicial knowledge genealogy by Chap. 4 of this book: Courts of First Instance and Appellate Court.

[2]In Anglo-Saxon countries, this tradition can be traced back to the 15th century, when Sir Edward Coke put forward Artificial Reason. Another well-known saying is "the life of the law has not been logic; it has been experience" by Oliver Wendell Holmes, Jr. in the nineteenth Century. This kind of elaboration by modern jurists is more common. Please refer to Richard A. Posner, *The Problems of Jurisprudence*, Harvard University Press, 1990, Chap. 2. This idea can be traced back to Plato. In his kingdom run by philosophy, there were no places for jurists.

[3]For this reason, we can understand why the Anglo-American legal education, which is led by judicial practice, is more a kind of professional training, while only a very small number of students educated by the European continental law system, which has more qualities of a liberal education, prefer to enter into the job of judiciary. Before they enter into the judiciary, they need to go through all kinds of judicial training which gives more emphasis to professional skills.

[4]Friedrich A. Hayek, *Law, Legislation, and Liberty*, vol. 1, University of Chicago Press, 1973.

not necessarily pay enough attention to knowledge and skills, but they never live without them during the trial. However, I have to declare in advance that this kind of work, from the very beginning, is destined to be incomplete, with major risks, no matter how hard I try. The most fundamental reason is that judicial knowledge and skills as practical rationalities fundamentally reject systematic and organized description. This kind of knowledge has been produced when judges themselves encounter particular life situations. Normally, practitioners would not reflect much on the skills and knowledge used in their daily life, since their mind is not focused on the "knowledge," but instead on life itself. In addition to that, there are no effective definitions or propositions provided for discussing this kind of knowledge nor skills in China's law community. There is even no justification for discussion in today's China. As a result, the knowledge and skills of basic-level judges are always in their original nature and have not been incorporated in the existing, formalized body of legal knowledge and language yet.

This chapter must overcome the above two obstacles at the same time, while maintaining the identity of legal discourse to seek legitimacy. For this reason, I will mainly use existing legal discourse and definitions, which are admittedly, relatively abstract, to detour into the topic I am to discuss. I will keep referring to individual cases analyzed in previous chapters and hope that this style of writing, similar to internet links, cannot only make sure that the theme of this chapter will not be drowned out by a tedious description of cases, but also wake up the academic sensitivity of readers who pay attention to case details. This may bring about troubles to readers who are not familiar with those cases. Since there are no perfect things in this world, what I can do is make a choice based on practical rationality.

The next section will first discuss the basic institutional and social conditions for knowledge of Chinese judges to appear. The two following sections will analyze some skills which I believe are very critical to a basic-level judiciary and will divide the knowledge and skills into two parts, namely dispute settlement and rule observation. Please do note that here I do not have any intention to list out and describe knowledge and skills of Chinese judges at basic-level courts. The purpose of this chapter is to simply enter into instead of comprehensively demonstrate or outline this area or study.

8.2 Main Constraints and Resources of Knowledge Production by Judges

Knowledge is produced for people to tackle all kinds of practical problems in their real life. In a different time, space, and location, people face different ordinary problems. Some common knowledge, systems, and skills are gradually formed to tackle those problems in any specific time and space. They are, all in all, the so-called culture of a place.[5] This is also the case for judges. When answering ordinary questions from the society they are in, judges do not have many cultural differences from an ordinary person. However, since they are judges and have a different profession, the problems they face everyday are different from those of other professions in society. All the kinds of knowledge and skills required by this profession cannot be taught—either through verbal instruction or by personal example these skills are gradually formed, and some professional distinction is constituted. In this sense, what makes judges different from others is not their profession itself, but the knowledge they produce, accumulate, and personalize during their concrete works and the system they rely on (even though occupational division of labor facilitates them to obtain this kind of professional knowledge and rely on this system).[6]

This can somewhat guide us to understand the knowledge production of China's basic-level judges. First of all, since any knowledge and skills can be produced by people within certain restrictions, we must discover what the common problems and fundamental restrictions of China's basic-level judges are. As far as I see, there are mainly two major restrictions to the professional career of a basic-level judge in China. One is the large number of disputes in the basic-level society, especially in rural areas, which are not yet formatted and thus cannot be dealt with by some prescribed or regulated method.[7] In facing this kind of world, judges and courts must solve problems in a practical way; otherwise, they will lack the reasons for people or organizations of dispute settlements to exist. In their daily life, people always refer to people or organizations that can handle issues and solve problems in order to help solve their personal problems. If judges or courts can'not help, people will give up or even intentionally avoid them[8] and seek other

[5]Some knowledge can be produced even in extreme circumstances. Take this story from the warring states period as an example: The King of Chu had a special taste for women with a slim waist, and thus, many court maids starved themselves to death in order to have a super slim body. Those court maids had all been on a diet to win the King's favor. This kind of strategy or specific skill might not be common for ordinary people (I use the word "might" here because in some developed countries including some developed areas in China, there are a quite number of women who are actually following or adopting this knowledge or skill intentionally or unintentionally only for some specific or unspecific "King of Chu" in their mind), but for court maids at that time, it was a kind of knowledge and skill responding to specific living conditions. In this sense, there is no system that may completely suffocate people's creativity. However, this kind of creativity may be a kind of opportunistic behavior from the very beginning, but as long as this kind of restriction is long term and stable, this kind of adaptability of opportunism may and must be accumulated and thus become a kind of invisible and intentional knowledge or skill that can only be passed on by word of mouth.

[6]It is true that it must be pointed out that in many modern societies, this kind of occupational division begins not only from employment. Depending on different occupations, the training of occupational division starts in universities or vocational schools. This has been demonstrated most obviously in occupation-oriented education of post-graduates in law schools, business schools, and medical schools in the USA.

[7]Please refer to Chap. 6 of this book: "Inbetween Facts and Laws."

[8]Please refer to Suli: "Evasion of Law and Legal Pluralism," *Peking University Law Journal*, Issue 5, 1993.

ways to solve problems instead, such as appealing to administrative officials or higher authorities for help, or opting for closed-door settlements. We can roughly say that no judges nor organizations would like to be weeded out in this way.

There is another huge restriction to basic-level judges, which is that rule governance required by modern development as well as the discussion format of modern nation states. It must be emphasized that there is a huge (not the only, and not even the most important) difference between modern judges and dispute settlers in traditional society. The reason that modern judges have a right to settle disputes comes, first of all, from their location in the political system of the modern country, as well as the political authority attached to their position. In this sense, modern judges are mainly not part of the administrative organization of the community they belong to, but one of the parts that constitute the legal–rational ruling government of a modern country. Their authority and legitimacy mainly come from the use of violence being monopolized by the state, which uses the threat of violence as the last resort to guarantee that modern judges can exercise their duties of dispute settlement. If they do not or are unable to follow the requirements of legal–rational ruling state machine to exercise their function, their power and identity as well as related revenues and benefits may be deprived (which may come in the form of dismissal or suspension from one's duty in China, and resignation, impeachment, or recall in the USA). However, the duty of judges is not exactly dispute settlement, in the common sense. The state does not entitle judges the right to settle disputes by all methods which, in their belief, are convenient and necessary, but demand that they, as part of a modern governing machine, should settle disputes regulated by methods determined to be legitimate by the legislation. If those fundamental principles of modern governance are violated, the power that belongs to them as judges will be deprived.

Theses two kinds of basic restrictions should be in line with each other in principle and can support each other from time to time. In practice, they are not always in line with each other. Simply speaking, this is a contradiction between special cases and common rules. Even in developed countries, judges sometimes have to change certain rules in order to solve a problem, but in some other cases, judges have to sacrifice certain interests of parties concerned in order to maintain the rules, which is the so-called sacrifice of substantive justice in support of procedural justice.[9] Judges of first instance will feel this kind of contradiction and conflict more strongly, since they face the reality more directly. In China's basic-level society, since there is a lack of formatted works in the rule of law, the

[9]If some well-known American cases must be raised, the case which can represent the former is *Brown v. Board of Education,* which overturned the precedent of "separate but equal" that had lasted for almost 60 years, with the purpose of solving the problem of racial segregation and discrimination. The case that represents the latter is *Marbury v. Madison*, which adheres to regulations of the constitution and believes that the Supreme Court has no jurisdiction of first instance on the Marbury case, although Marbury's rights have been infringed unlawfully.

contradiction between law and reality is even more outstanding.[10] For this reason, the tension between demands of these two factors has created a special space for knowledge production and reproduction by judges of China's basic-level courts and thus has become the matrix to produce their knowledge and technology. Under these two main restrictions, judges are trying their best to pursue all kinds of material and non-material benefits of their own. During this process of benefit pursuit, they have unintentionally created and accumulated knowledge and skills which are of significance to their existence.[11]

There are two points I need to make concerning this kind of knowledge. First of all, we shall never conclude that this knowledge must be rural or traditional only because it has been produced by ordinary judges who live in basic-level society for a long time in the process of settling disputes coming from rural society. Even if the basic-level judges are components of the modern state system, their salaries and careers, to a greater extent, depend on the modern country. Just as I have analyzed in the previous chapter, even if judges approve of certain rules of rural society emotionally, they would not take the risk of disciplinary sanctions for the benefits of others.[12] This kind of knowledge has been, as a matter of fact, gradually formed and accumulated by judges in order to survive and conduct their work more effectively. It has been branded by the mark of modernization. It may not always be in line with the teachings of current legal textbooks, but it is nonetheless very useful and necessary to them.

In addition, this kind of positioning of basic-level judges will not destroy the legitimacy of basic-level justice. Just as what the well-known "invisible hand" of Adam Smith implies, it is absolutely possible that every one's pursuit of personal interests (which does not necessarily exclude the pursuit of ideals and justice) can increase social public welfare. A judge's pursuit of maximum self-interest is not necessarily against the judicial justice (with a system where embezzlement and bribe-taking by judges can be effectively discovered and cracked down upon, judges who pursue maximum self-interest will not consider embezzlement and bribe-taking as their maximum interest. Within a system where impartial justice can be recognized and awarded, judges who pursue maximum self-interest may pursue impartial justice as their maximum interest), which is similar to lawyers

---

[10]In the most severe circumstances, rule restriction can actually disable courts from settling disputes by the power it has. There are cases of this kind in our research. It is easy for court to make decision on cases of delinquency, but debtors may refuse to execute court decision by all kinds of means. Since law regulates that violent compulsory methods are not allowed to be used, it is easy for legal judgment to become a mere scrap of paper. For this reason, there come into existence some dangerous social organizations which prefer to use extreme violence to implement court judgment. It roughly goes like this: After the plaintiff wins the lawsuit, he or she does not apply for the court to execute the judgment.

[11]Cf., Richard A. Posner, "What Do Judges Miximize?" in *Overcoming Law*, Harvard University Press, 1995.

[12]Please refer to Chap. 6 "Inbetween Facts and Laws," and Chap. 7 "Between Statute and Custom" of this book.

who can maintain judicial justice for their own monetary interest. Apart from that, this pursuit of interests by basic-level justices does not influence the value of the knowledge they create. The knowledge of the market economy has been accumulated actually by business people during the process of pursuing their self-interest, but it does not obstruct the knowledge to be passed on to students in MBA courses today. Just as Mr. Foucault has pointed out that knowledge never occurs for no reason.[13] Thirdly, such positioning of judges is actually more in line with the spirit of modern rule of law, which has changed the image of ideal judges who attach too much emphasis on individual morality created and pursued by the judiciary in China. We do have this kind of judge, but there is a limited number, and they cannot be found or duplicated in a large quantity. For this reason, if we try to analyze and understand Chinese judges in basic-level courts based on the above assumption, we will, in theory, pay more attention to institutional law (rule by law), instead of personal behaviors and wisdom (rule of men).

8.3 From the Perspective of Substantial Dispute

As opposed to judges of second-instance courts, judges of basic-level courts, especially of people's tribunals, directly face a large number of concrete cases almost everyday,[14] from divorce cases to disputes of mountain and forest lands, and from supporting seniors to liability for minor injuries. There are not only material issues directly involved, but, and even more importantly, other non-material factors are involved as well (such as a wife's sexual relationship outside marriage will bring her husband a feeling of "being unable to lead a life in the village any more"[15]). In addition, just as I have pointed out previously, the majority of these disputes happen among acquaintances and genuine, credible evidence is therefore hard to get; there are no lawyers available to clear up and format lawsuit disputes; there is a lack of credible materials in the form of official documents; and parties concerned are not familiar with requirements of modern laws (such as evidence or procedural justice).[16]

Under this kind of circumstance, the priority of a judge is to settle these cases effectively and rapidly. For this reason, dispute settlement is the major concern of basic-level judges. They are sometimes confused and restricted by all kinds of materials and procedural rules, such as "natural determination"[17] of civil cases, but

[13]Foucault: "Nietzsche, Genealogy, History," translated by Suli, Issue 4 of *Review of Academic Ideas*, 1998.

[14]An article once says that "people's tribunals nowadays include 70 % of all cases dealt by courts around China and 80 % of cases dealt by basic-level courts." Please refer to "Tribunal Management is a Big Subject," written by commentator of *People's Judicature*, Issue 12 of 1994, p. 7.

[15]Please refer to Chap. 7 of this book: "Between Statute and Custom."

[16]Please refer to Chap. 6 of this book: "Inbetween Facts and Laws."

[17]Please refer to Chap. 6 of this book: "Inbetween Facts and Laws."

dispute settlement always ranks first to them at any time, and they must get things done. The most common saying for basic-level judges is "to solve problems for common people," which is also what judges normally do to make an effort. This does not reflect that judges have a strong feeling toward the community, care about people's pains, or remember their purpose of serving the people, but because dispute settlement is their legal job, which they have to fulfill, no matter what. If they fail to execute this duty effectively, they will probably be removed from their post or lag behind their peers in terms of salary, job titles, or positions due to their unqualified work. They may be criticized and seldom receive praise either by parties concerned or their bosses. Furthermore, they will receive less bonuses than others, and their word will not matter at all in court and they will receive no respect.

For this reason, basic-level judges normally hope that their cases can be settled with mutual satisfaction no matter what, which means that parties concerned are all relatively satisfied with, or at least accept the judgment or results of the conciliation and will not lodge an appeal against this judgment. Once there is an appeal, there is more of a possibility that the judgment will be amended or that the case will be remanded for a retrial. This is exceptionally evident in China's judiciary. As far as the situation of our research and to our understanding is concerned, at least some courts of second instance have set the minimum requirement for second-instance judges to amend judgments or remand cases for retrial in order to demonstrate the performance of second-instance judges or to prove that their existence is really necessary.[18] In addition, second-instance judges sometimes amend the judgment on the amount of compensation or debt without adequate legal reasoning or even without any reasons, just to calm down the dissatisfaction of appellants with the results and to close the case. Judges of basic-level courts normally see amendments or remands for retrial as a kind of negative evaluation on their intelligence and capability. Some courts even see cases that have been remanded for retrial as "misjudged cases" and will cut the bonus of the presiding judge. Basic-level judges will avoid this kind of contingency, and the key is to settle the case successfully.

The other hope of basic-level judges is to close the case as soon as possible so that they can deal with more cases and/or have more leisure time. This motivation is from the following two aspects. One is that institutionally, court leaders normally see the number of cases dealt with as one of the standards to evaluate a judge's capability. At the time of our research, as well as in the previous 10 years, case number has

[18] I felt it very ridiculous and almost beyond understanding when hearing about it for the first time. But later, I came to realize that this system is not entirely without a reason or benign intentions behind its apparent disadvantage. It wants to avoid the situation that first-instance judges and second-instance judges reach some kind of secret agreement by all kinds of proper or improper methods (which really prevails nowadays. According to information, many first-instance judges or judges of lower level courts tend to "flatter" direct judges of second instance in all kinds of ways), and tries to make second-instance judges discover problems and encourage them to think independently. But I have serious doubt on whether this system can achieve the function intended by the system designer. I even feel that second-instance judges may strengthen their improper influence on first-instance judges by selective methods. However, this needs further empirical investigation.

always been connected to judge's "economic benefit" to some extent. It is almost to all judges' hope that they can solve more cases so that their personal income will increase. The second aspect is more personalized. When faced with a large number of trivial cases of similar types day after day and year after year, judges of basic-level courts are easily bored by this kind of repetition. It is impossible for them to go to the basic-level court for research from time to time and have academic sabbaticals like jurists. They have some intellectual interest in cases but will not think about or elaborate on them over and over again as a scholar's thesis intends to do. It is true that judges are somewhat different on this point due to their different responsibilities, but in general, judges hope to spend less time and energy to settle disputes.

Judges of basic-level courts have accumulated some basic technology and knowledge from this.

We must first of all consider that cases must be settled with a relatively fair result. The "fair" here is not justice regulated by the statute, but it is more based on the public opinion of the community, as well as the approval of both parties. For this reason, in the case of "sexual relations outside marriage" in the last chapter, the judge should protect the "third party" whose reputation and possibly health and life were threatened according to the statute, but the court as a matter of fact provided "protection" by means of "detention," which has a connotation of punishment. The important reason is that this kind of settlement is more in line with legal and moral evaluation of the community, both parties, and the judge themselves. Once the parties of both sides feel that the result is basically fair, there is no likelihood that an appeal will be lodged and judges will not likely face a risk of losing out on benefits due to instances of appeal.

Judgment precedes application of law, analogy of law, and demonstration. This is the inevitable result guided by justice. In this sense, the judicial judgments of judges are often based on common sense, intuition, the standard of the community he or she is in, many years of judicial experience and upbringing, and many other factors, which can be called judicial quality. This kind of judgment is always prior to judicial reasoning and the application of law. At least at the level of a basic-level justice, application of law and legal reasoning is the product of judicial judgment, instead of the opposite. However, this does not necessarily mean that judges will insist on their prior judgment. During the process of legal application and reasoning following judgments, judges will also modify their prior judgment as long as they maintain enough sensitivity on the evidence and case details of the trial and have enough self-reflection, especially when legal rules conflict with intuitive judgment of the case. Take the nature determination of the "cattle case" mentioned in Chap. 6 of this book as an example. The first-instance judge firmly believes that it is a "partnership" just because there is no regulation of "joining as a partner" in the General Rules of Civil Law.

To get hold of the key dispute, it requires that justice should be the guidance and that cases be dealt with perfectly, which means that judges must solve the substantial disputes of the cases whenever possible instead of temporary mitigation of the dispute. It is like "taking away the firework under the cooking pot," as the Chinese saying goes, so that no appeal will need to happen. Judges of basic-level courts normally do not strictly apply the judicial principle of "no trial with complaint." They sometimes intervene in some problems as long as those problems are of significance to dispute settlements. This method of problem solving is especially important to judges of basic-level courts. Disputes that happen between acquaintances are normally composed of a series of minor events that have accumulated over time. The legal dispute itself is often a tip of the iceberg. Settling an appropriate dispute does not mean that conflicts among parties concerned are truly solved. On the contrary, a seemingly simple and strictly legally binding judgment often works like a painkiller. Since parties of both sides will still live in the same village or even the same family, if the key dispute has not been truly settled, the problem will emerge repeatedly but in a new form. Thus, it is difficult to execute the principle of "Ne bis in idem" in the judiciary in China's basic-level society. A simple and easy judgment at first sight may actually costs more time and energy for judges in the future. It is therefore very important for judges of basic-level courts to demonstrate and effectively settle real disputes instead of partial or temporary settlements. In Chap. 5 of this book, when a judge failed to permanently solve the problem of a son beating his mother, they suggested the lady find a husband to protect herself. This method seems to be detouring and not up to a judges' discretion, but as long as the primary contradiction has been caught hold of, secondary contradictions will be solved readily.

To determine the facts based on instinct, and to avoid those "facts" which are hard to determine and investigate even if time and energy are spent, for those facts do not affect the situation as a whole even when investigated. In the trial of the "cattle case" in Chap. 6 of this book, the judge's statement of the facts in his judgment uses only the verbal agreement between the two parties from 1987, as well as the facts approved or denied by both parties in certain ways. It completely avoids all other disputed facts on which each party sticks to their own argument but which are not necessarily without clear conclusions after careful investigation. Instead, it adopts a kind of attitude which neither denies nor affirms explicitly. This is because, on the one hand, the human resources, material resources, and time resources judges of basic-level courts can mobilize are very limited, and on the other hand, cutting out the facts can make those originally irregular and unformatted cases relatively regular. This does not only facilitate legal settlement (e.g., the negotiation between the two parties in 1987 is more like an instant offer and acceptance, as mentioned on legal textbooks). In addition, this kind of legal cutting-out and packaging is more easily employed to win over the legitimacy of legal terms for a specific settlement and judges can protect themselves more effectively without getting into trouble.[19]

Normally speaking, parties litigant in China's basic-level society at least pay more attention to case outcomes nowadays, as well as questions like "How many years have you been sentenced" or "How much money has been asked for in this compensation." They do not care much about legal or evidence sources that lead to this outcome. This kind of expectation of parties litigant often enables judges to try their best to make their judgment meet the satisfaction of both parties. As long as there is no doubt on the

[19]Please refer to Chap. 6 of this book: Inbetween Facts and Laws.

legitimacy of judgment itself, procedures are normally not important or can accommodate the circumstances. In the "maintenance case" mentioned in Chap. 5 where parents sue their son, judges did not considered at all the following issue of procedural law: Whether the daughter of the plaintiff should be named as a defendant as well? In the cattle case in Chap. 6, after the judge announced that there was a series of documentary evidence to be verified, he does not conduct an actual investigation, but instead entered into court mediation and court judgment.

Escalation of disputes must be avoided. A large number of disputes in basic-level society, especially among acquaintances, cannot be settled in a timely fashion—and sometimes cannot be settled at all by judges due to all kinds of reasons. When this happens, judges may use all kinds of methods to deal with urgent cases, including mobilizing all possible factors in society to earnestly persuade parties concerned to prevent a "transformation of contradictions" (which was used by Chairman Mao Zedong in his "contradictions among the people themselves will be transformed into contradictions between ourselves and the enemy").[20] Just as pointed out by Zhao Xiaoli's research,[21] the most worrisome contraction in rural society is actually not the dispute that can be seen and enter into court proceedings, but the "escalation of dispute" which may result in such vicious events as murder, suicide, or large-scale clashes or fights with weapons. Once it starts to build, since there is a lack of police forces or public security resources that can be utilized, to ease or "deactivate," the conflict is usually the judge's first choice[22]—especially without major events or crises. We can therefore understand why judges often criticize and suppress both parties when dealing with cases that might arouse sharp conflict. They even take the risk of adopting methods which are somewhat "illegal" in serious but neutral means in order to achieve a kind of result roughly accepted by society.[23]

8.4 In Terms of Legal Disputes

As previously mentioned, in basic-level society, the parties concerned pay more attention or even pay only attention to the outcome of the cases instead of the law (either substantive law or procedural law). For this reason, judges of basic-level

[20]Please refer to Shi Zeng, Yue Lai: Anecdotes of People's Tribunal, *People's Judicature,* Issue 10 of 1991, pp. 45–46; please also refer to People's Tribunal of Gu County on the suburb of Changzhi City in Shanxi Province: "Promoting objective management with orientation in order to build standardized people's tribunal," *People's Judicature*, Issue 12 of 1991, p. 4, the 5th aspect of concrete objective concerning management with orientation.

[21]Zhao Xiaoli: *Through Legal Administration: Research on Basic-level Courts in Rural China*, doctoral dissertation, Law School of Beijing University, 1999.

[22]Please refer to People's Tribunal of Sancang in the City of Dongtai in the Province of Jiangsu: "To deal correctly with the relationship with party and government departments in the area of administration to do a good job in people's tribunals," *People's Judicature*, Issue 12 o f 1991, p. 7.

[23]Please refer to cases analyzed in Chap. 7 "Between Statute and Custom" of the book.

courts pay attention to law and order mainly to deal with the issue of whether the judgment is justified and to implement the judges' decisions. The justification of law here has at least two effects. For one, this kind of justification can be used to exert a certain kind of pressure on parties concerned, to enhance the authority of the tribunal on mediation and judicial judgment, and is conducive to the actual implementation of court decisions. The reason is mainly that the law enforcement in basic-level courts is very weak.[24] If the law is enforced only by the coercive power of the state, the judicial effect will be reduced largely and the courts will probably be at a loss for what to do. As a result, one can often achieve better and substantial effect when making full use of traditional and symbolized understanding of the "national law" by ordinary people (mainly as criminal law or punishment), as well as the close connection between the laws in its traditional concept in China with state violence. There is another aspect in which judges attach importance to law, which is getting increasingly important, that is, to achieve self-protection through making judgments legally justifiable, either against possible dissatisfaction with the judgment by parties concerned, or against the legal trials held by superior courts, which are usually more critical.[25]

Related to the previous point, judges often deliberately exaggerate the severity of legal punishment or the serious legal consequences of a certain disputed behavior. It is true that there is a traditional factor of "punishment unknown and authority unpredicted" in this, that is, through this kind of legal rhetoric, to try to achieve a kind of tactical effect of psychological compulsion under the precondition that ordinary people have no or not much understanding of many concrete rules or statutes, as well as the fact that rural areas have no lawyers that are good at using legal rules. What is more important is that this has left a bigger leeway for judges' seemingly "generous" judgments. After all, judges also want to dress themselves as very understanding and reasonable, merciful, and having a human touch to save face for parties concerned. Thirdly, this kind of practice has a strong trace of "dealing with official business in a private manner," which is to make such public affairs as the judiciary process personal and individual, paying parties concerned a lip service. This kind of practice is very important in Chinese society, which pays great attention to personal relations, and in which people prefer to understand public affairs from the perspective of personal relations. Such practices can better meet the expectation of parties concerned, and it is therefore more easy to win over their approval. Furthermore, although it is easy to leave the impression of "dealing with official business in a private manner," on another level, the actual result of this

[24]In the court of a certain county, we came to know that there are altogether only 6 people working in this executive tribunal, with a single pair of handcuffs as their only equipment. At a people's tribunal, the judge told us that when a circuit court was held, the judge would sometimes sit in a chair with the chair back facing forward in case parties concerned resorted to force the judge was unprepared for. By doing this, the judge could easily use the chair to protect himself once the parties concerned resorted to force.

[25]Please refer to Chap. 1 of this book: Why Send Law to the Countryside?

kind of practice has enabled parties concerned to distinguish judgment of judges themselves and their decision based on the law, which gives rise to or enhances the impersonality of law objectively, and prevents head-on confrontation with judges by parties concerned who are unable to accept judgment. For this reason, judges can gain more of a sense of security. This point is more important in circuit courts where judges are totally unfamiliar with a place and the court lacks protection from judicial policemen. In the case of the judge going to the village to collect a debt mentioned in Chap. 1 of this book, the judge emphasizes to parties concerned repeatedly that it is a "debt collection according to law" and is a uniform action in the nation. He emphasizes that they would get more severe punishments if the judge abided by the law strictly, but instead gives a rather understanding punishment in reality. This can be seen as a kind of application and extension of such traditional "political and legal" tactics as "strict criticism with a lighter sentence."

Judges try to apply mechanically legal provisions as far as possible. As is mentioned in last section, in most cases for the basic-level judiciary, judges normally have a basic judgment in advance and then look for relevant laws. It seems rather different from the "trial after judgment" or "trial after decision" models. It is an indispensible step to look for relevant laws. During the process of looking for laws and understanding laws, the initial judgment of judges is indeed sometimes influenced or changed. Generally speaking, however, looking for laws is not intended for regularized dispute settlements and thus will normally not influence judges' basic judgments or settlement of disputes. It is only intended to provide a legal foundation or package for detailed dispute settlement. In the "cattle case" analyzed in Chap. 6 of this book, the General Rules of Civil Law have different definitions for "partnership" and "joint ownership of property." This difference does not actually influence the basic judgment of judges or the actual split of rights and duties, but is only an issue of "nature determination" of a case. However, using more proper legal provisions as a basis will make this judgment more like a "judicial" result. This result is more legitimate at both superior and lower-level courts. The determination of compensation on personal injury by basic-level courts is also included. Basic-level courts deal with many civil cases of personal injury and even death. However, relevant laws do not have any rules on compensation calculation, which has brought about much inconvenience for judges to determine compensation according to the law. It is certain though that cases cannot remain unsettled. To make the compensation of their judgment legitimate, judges keep telling us that they determine compensation according to relevant rules of Measures to Deal With Road Traffic Accidents issued by the Ministry of Public Security in 1991. However, this kind of practice is quite far-fetched from the perspective of legitimacy and from the perspective of strictly according to legal theory. Nonetheless, this kind of contrast does indeed provide a kind of possible reference for judges at basic-level courts. This kind of practice is not only fairer than refusing compensation based on the reason that there are no legal rules, but on the other hand has provided an alternative basis for this kind of compensation, since then, at least, no one can complain that the compensation of judgment is completely baseless. During our interviews and research, many judges felt puzzled as to why there are no decent rules and regulations for civil compensation for damages and hope that the legislature of the state can, in a timely manner, formulate detailed rules for compensation to which judgment can refer.

To make proper use of evasion of laws, as well as the flexibility and uncertainty of legal language to fight for a better outcome desired by the judge, and to spare all efforts to avoid bad outcomes that are obviously unfair are the ultimate goals of basic-level judges. This is exceptionally evident when dealing with divorce cases in rural areas. In a large number of cases, one party wants a divorce while the other does not, and the party who wants to divorce will usually have violated their marriage's agreement in advance. In the current circumstances of Chinese society, it is difficult not only for the other party to conduct an investigation, but also for the court to investigate due to a lack of manpower.[26] If abiding strictly by relevant rules of Marriage Law, the judge should grant a divorce when their relationship does indeed break down and mediation fails. It still causes trouble, not only because judges themselves feel unfair to certain parties concerned sometimes, but murder cases may even occur as the results of these disputes. For this reason, judges have to do a lot of work on words like "whether their relationship does indeed break down" and "whether their mediation fails." It is impossible for anyone to give a fair judgment on the previous question, and different people will have different views. The second question can only be answered when mediation (perhaps many times) has already been done. This does not mean that judges insist on not divorcing, but that they use discretionary measures to force the party who is more eager for a divorce to make a greater concession on property division or in some other aspect, and to be willing to follow any rulings the court makes, which will save all kinds of court resources. From the judge's point of view, the actual result of this kind of treatment may be fairer in rural areas. Another example of legal evasion is the different nature of determination of property by first trial and retrial, and the application of different laws in the "cattle case" in Chap. 6. My analysis points out that this kind of change does not have any substantive meaning. Its main purpose is to avoid discussing the relationship between the two parties concerned and to transfer the focus to the nature of the disputed property.[27]

To make full use of current legal rules, procedures, and systems to protect judge's self-interests is surely a tactic basic-level judges employ. This is especially demonstrated when the legal system is not appropriate or when there are social disturbances. Then, judges will take the initiative to use the existing legal rules and systems to protect themselves. In recent years, the ever stricter and even excessive "misjudged case investigation mechanism" will enable many judges to take the initiative to bring some "indecisive" case to the trial committee for discussion and

[26]Article 25: "When one party of a couple demands a divorce, one can ask for mediation from the department concerned or file a lawsuit of divorce directly to the people's court. When hearing a case of divorce, the people's court shall conduct mediation first. If the couple's relationship has indeed broken down and mediation fails, divorce shall be granted."

[27]Please refer to Chap. 6 of this book: Inbetween Facts and Laws.

decision.[28] For another example, when local parties and political departments are involved in the justice process improperly or due to the trouble caused by a small number of people, judges will normally tend to share possible legal responsibilities and protect themselves by using a trial committee. This includes resisting interference from local party and political departments as well as preventing criticism from courts of second instance.[29]

Collective decisions on legal application after research are important to aid in judicial decision making. Apart from official legal systems and rules, judges adopt some other unofficial systems inside the court to reinforce the legitimacy or justification of post-legal applications. This includes judges asking and discussing among each other when encountering difficult cases. A collective office makes the collective discussion of judgment on difficult cases a natural component of a judge's decision.[30] Apart from that, such non-statutory systems as examination and approval by tribunal heads and the president of the court in charge, as well as asking for approval from a superior court, have, to a certain extent, constituted part of the judge's self-protection system.

Another factor related to law is execution of rulings. Even though execution of rulings does not belong in the decision-making process of judging a legal dispute, judges of basic-level courts will often consider the factor of execution when judging some cases that are difficult to operate (instead of being difficult intellectually). Judges often emphasize the attention to whether the legal judgment can be actually executed. It has become an issue that a judge has to consider or even give priority to when choosing a method of legal remedy. A good judicial decision has to be fair and, most importantly, easy for execution. If without actual execution, or with a high cost of execution, this judgment is actually neither fair nor problem solving. For this reason, during our interview, judges always emphasize execution. In rural communities, the circumstances of parties concerned and situations of the communities need to be given special consideration as well. In the "supporting case" in Chap. 5, the judge even pays attention to questions like whether the seniors are supplied with green beans, yellow beans, animal fat, vegetable oil, and other specifics. In the "compensation case of a broken leg," the judge firstly considers the problem of who has the ability to pay the compensation of the judgment, as well as of how to make this person or organization be willing to pay. He also tries his best to create some condition to make sure that those plans can be earnestly realized.[31]

That is why courts or judges pay special attention to and even try their best to obtain support and cooperation from local governments and other related departments to mobilize all possible resources to solve problems. Many judges warn us

---

[28]Please refer to Chap. 3 of this book: The Judicial Committee System in Basic-level Courts.

[29]The Judicial Committee System in Basic-level Courts, same as the previous note.

[30]Special thanks to Mr. Lin Bin from the University of Beijing for reminding me of this point.

[31]Please refer to Chap. 5 of this book: Dispute Settlement and Governance of Rules.

that village heads and accountants should be consulted if one wants to know something about the parties concerned, even before looking for the parties concerned themselves. Things are much easier if the village head is present.[32] The execution of the judgment of the "compensation case of a broken leg" mentioned in Chap. 3 obviously required huge cooperation from other local departments.

8.5 Practical Significance of Knowledge of Basic-level Judges

The above induction is not complete, and I myself have no intention to make it complete. They are not the words of judges themselves, but a conclusion and a kind of knowledge structure of a scholar after having studied some cases of the basic-level judiciary in China. In addition, I refer to them as "knowledge" or "technique," but this does not mean that I myself approve of such practices. I just hope that I can try my best to describe the real situations that I see or understand. The ostrich policy that I have adopted prevents me from seeing the true problems and thus disables me from solving the problems truly effectively.

Regardless, I want to emphasize that the knowledge and techniques demonstrated by basic-level judges when dealing with disputes between fact and law in their judicial practice are not without a reason. Some can be justified both in practice and in theory. For example, guided by fairness, they try to make sure that the result of judiciaries (either mediation or judgment) be accepted by both sides so as to reduce the possibility of appeal. Although the judge's pursuit is based on saving his or her own troubles and making sure that they are safe, which seems to be very utilitarian, his or her effort may actually give rise to justice and efficiency. From the perspective of economics, the transaction that both parties of a dispute want to accept is normally a win-win transaction where at least the status of one party does not get worse due to judicial involvement. The judgment or mediation result that both parties can accept is actually a new contract on rights distribution endorsed by the court and often can be more easily executed by parties concerned by their own will. This is good not only to the judge themself, but also to the distribution of social and judicial resources, especially under the current social conditions of the "difficulty to execute" in China. Thirdly, this kind of situation has actually changed the current circle of legal science, in which judicial litigation has always been emphasized and pushed forward excessively based on misunderstanding of the slogan "Fight for Rights" (or more like an influence from the model of thinking of "guided by class struggle" and "struggle philosophy"). This kind of judicial tendency of basic-level judges has enabled a large number of disputes to be settled in terms of a contract. However, the method of "settlement out of court" in which lawyers take the lead and which has been largely adopted in the USA has turned

[32]Please refer to Chap. 1 of this book: Why Send Law to the Countryside?

into a method of "settlement within the court" in which the judge takes the lead in China's basic-level society where there is a lack and even absence of lawyers.[33] It is also true that we have to realize that this kind of "settlement within court" in which the judge takes the lead has both advantages and disadvantages. Do advantages outweigh disadvantages or vise versa? and to whom are the advantages and disadvantages? These questions are still hard to answer.[34]

In basic-level Chinese courts, a judge's decision goes ahead of legal application and reasoning. This kind of practice seems not to be in line with teachings from legal textbooks, but judging from the research results of contemporary humanities and social sciences, this process is, on the contrary, more common. It is not only in line with a human's biological nature,[35] but also accords with the hermeneutic circle and laws of human knowledge and understanding.[36] But for a judge of a basic-level court, which draws his or her attention firstly, it is the lawsuit at the moment, instead of the legal nature or declaration of intention of a certain behavior from the party concerned. It is only because the legal requirement and regulation on their responsibility during the lawsuit that the judge begins to pay attention to the legal nature of a previous behavior of the party concerned or their declaration of intention. It is true and also essential that the judge of first instance should cut in from the dispute at present. What they are more concerned with is how to make judgment from their intuition or first feeling more reasonable and be more acceptable to both parties concerned as well as the communities and society they live in. Just as Mr. Holmes points out that a sound law should first of all respond to true feelings and demands of people in the community, no matter whether this kind of feeling or demand is right or wrong.[37]

But a judge is not an arbitrator in the general sense. They cannot give an arbitrary (not necessarily unfair) decision, but must be restricted and settle the dispute peacefully according to rules and procedures. Due to this requirement, a judge

---

[33]To answer why there is such a change, one important reason may be that there are not as many lawyers in China as in the USA and that the private cost for settlement outside court is much higher.

[34]One of the disadvantages is that since the cost of dispute settlement for all courts mainly comes from governmental fiscal expenditures, it will definitely give rise to the tragedy of abuse of "public goods" often mentioned by economists. As a matter of fact, the number of Chinese judges has been constantly on a drastic rise. Apart from the push from the mainstream ideology of rule of law, one of the important reasons is that the judiciary is a kind of cheap "public good." This notion still needs further empirical study.

[35]Richard A. Posner, *The Economics of Justice*, Harvard University Press, 1981, pp. 211–212.

[36]Hans-Georg Gadamer, *Truth and Method*, 2nd and rev. ed., by Joel Weinsheimer and Donald G. Marshall, Crossroad, 1989.

[37]Holmes went on to say that if law does not offer help, people will use actions outside law to satisfy their passion for revenge. When this happens, law will have no choice but satisfy the desire itself so as to prevent the bigger evil of personal revenge. At the moment, the judge, no matter as an individual or as a lawmaker, should encourage anything but this kind of revengeful passion. Please refer to: Oliver Wendell Holmes, Jr., "The Common Law," in *The Mind and Faith of Justice Holmes: His Speeches, Essays, Letters and Judicial Opinions*, The Modern Library, 1943, p. 57.

must sort out legal evidence of cause and effect from a series of original details of events which are in chaos under the condition of paying attention to legal rules. He or she must rearrange event details of the past, give them legal meaning according to the current necessity and possibility of dispute settlement, and reestablish the original intentions and behaviors of parties concerned based on the necessity of dispute settlement and available legal rules. In addition, all this must accord with the current legal discourse; he or she must emphasize and highlight words and behaviors that seem more meaningful in legal discourse while weighing down and even neglecting those that are not coordinating with legal concepts or definitions, so that the evolution of the series of events in the current legal discourse's logic is clear and apparent. In this way, he or she can fulfill a judge's promise to the judiciary and constitute a process of progress in line with legal discourse. This is actually a kind of legal afterthought and a conquering of history by legal discourse. Sorting out this line of reasoning is not because that this kind of reasoning will inevitably give rise to this judgment (please think about the David Hume's saying: "Reason is the slave to the passions"), but because the current legal system demands this kind of reasoning to restrict and guide a judge's decision.

Almost all judicial adjudication is this kind of undertaking to some extent. The judge's decision is never completed under the guidance of statute law in the first place, but is more like a kind of basic judgment based on the intuition they obtain from the community or career training (which is often referred to as natural justice or judicial quality). Then, it is easier for the judge to classify different cases before he or she looks for and finds out articles he or she believes to be suitable from appropriate laws and at the same time reflects on his or her intuition and makes necessary amendments.[38] This whole process may repeat itself several times; regardless, it is essential to have a basic judgment on the case before a case trial. This is the Hermeneutic Circle pointed out by Gadamer.[39]

For this reason, we can understand that "fact tailoring" is actually a quite normal phenomenon in the judiciary. History has always been the "history of the winner." Posner has used this sentence to summarize the generalization and description of facts by judgment of the court of appeal, which is really profound.[40] However, due to the issue of information, this kind of situation has been exceptionally evident and must continue to be exceptionally evident for judges of basic-level courts in China when dealing with unformatted cases in China's rural society. When the judge gets to know the basic situation of the case and has a basic judgment on

---

[38]Posner, *Problems of Jurisprudence*, as previously noted 2, pp. 131–134; please also refer to the experience, reflection, and philosophical criticism on suspension of all judgment in judicial trials by Angela Bartell, a judge of first instance in a county court in the State of Wisconsin in the USA. Angela Bartell, *Judicial Decision Making in the Trial Court*, Disputes Processing Research Program, Working Papers Series 8, Institute for Legal Studies, University of Wisconsin-Madison Law School, 1986.

[39]Gadamer, as previous note 36.

[40]Posner, *Problems of Jurisprudence,* as previous note 2, p. 210.

intention of settlement, it is natural for them to give different emphasis and legal significance to facts with uncertain legal meaning in order to have correct "nature determination" and support the judgment in law. As a matter of fact, among all trials, the so-called legal facts are actually facts tailored by the judge (by law).

But the problem is how should we analyze and understand phenomena not compatible with traditional legal theory? Can we simply deny only because this kind of phenomenon, which is in line with the research results of contemporary social sciences, is not compatible with the proposition and the hypothesis deducted from the political philosophy in the eighteenth and nineteenth centuries but never verified by experience? Or should we constantly amend certain previous propositions based on discoveries of social and scientific research which have been pushed forward and developed? If using natural science as a metaphor, this problem is almost like whether we should put forward a new theory of planetary orbit based on the elliptic orbit of the solar system observed or stipulate orbits for different planets in the solar system by the "perfect" circular planetary orbits in our imagination? The answer is self-evident.

Other issues such as avoiding escalation of disputes, grasping the principal contradiction, and giving preconsideration to the enforceability of judicial decisions will not be analyzed here in detail due to the space limit.

The knowledge and techniques demonstrated by basic-level judges on issues of legal disputes certainly have their rationality or unavoidability. For example, to exaggerate the seriousness of legal sanctions is indeed somewhat disgusting if only from the perspective of moral discourse. However, if we consider the circumstances of basic-level judges and the resources they can mobilize to ensure the execution of judicial decisions, especially the fact that a judicial decision which should be executed, but cannot be, is actually an absolute injustice for a party concerned, we may understand the necessity of this kind of technique used by the judge. As another example, a judge using the ambiguity of the boundaries of legal language to reject divorce seems to be a kind of intentional "violation of laws." I believe this kind of method is by no means only restricted to divorce cases. There must be judges using this method to seek their own private interest. But this problem cannot be avoided completely, at least at the present.[41] Do we really hope that judges turn into an automatic vendor machines if possible, since those judges would be the kind of judge without creativity, imagination, or ability to amend legal mistakes?

As for judges' self-protection in the current legal system, you can certainly state that basic-level judges care too much about their own interests. From another aspect, however, this reflects that our existing judicial system has not given enough institutional protection to basic-level judges. It normally requires basic-level judges sacrifice their own interests to protect social benefits. This kind of request is beyond reproach morally, but it is a demand to gods or saints, rather

[41]Please refer to Suli: "Revisiting the Evasion of Law," *Rule of Law and Its Local Resources*, China University of Political Science and Law Press, 1996.

than a normal judge. It can be a belief for a small number of judges, but a system cannot possibly work effectively for long putting forward unrealistic moral requests to most basic-level judges. For another example, the unofficial discussion among judges may affect the independent decision of a judge, but in the basic-level court where there is literally no private working space, what kind of conditions can a judge possibly have for silent and independent thinking during office hours? If we make a deeper inquiry, what kind of major damage can this kind of discussion bring about, apart from violating a judge's belief of independent judgment so that we must eliminate it completely? This does not mean that I myself advocate more exchanges among judges (certainly not the opposite either). What I want to say is that as a jurist, we should not stick to some practice as a kind of belief without asking why.

I don't want to simply understand and appreciate the knowledge and techniques demonstrated by basic-level judges, although this is a priority and necessity. As a matter of fact, I have been able to identify some major problems through this process of gradual understanding and appreciation.

As another example, in mobilizing all kinds of resources in order to ensure the execution of judicial decisions, it is easy to turn the court into one of the administrative agencies of a local government. It not only opens a channel for local departments to interfere with the court (why should the court ask for our help while refusing to help us?), but also turns a court from an organization abiding rules to settle disputes to an organization purely for dispute settlement. As a result, the non-professional activities of judges will be increased, which may restrict the accumulation of professional knowledge for judges, and it will be even less possible for judges to become highly professional and specialized.

It is true that the emphasis on mechanical application of legal texts may (but not necessarily, please refer to Chap. 6 of this book) play the role of restricting and training judges. However, if we do not take one step forward, and we continue to impose statutes on judges in accordance with more detailed classification tables or regulations, it is not good for the improvement of their ability of legal reasoning and analysis, as well as their policy consciousness. In addition, basic-level judicial activities will lack human judicial intelligence even more and judges will have fewer opportunities to think independently. This kind of mechanical application of law will also restrict existing judicial systems from effectively absorbing the judicial thought of basic-level judges and reject the creativity of judges. From the perspective of the legal system, it will also give China's judiciary more features of administrative bureaucracy. From the social level, this may not be conducive to attracting more law-school graduates who are eager for intelligent challenges into the court system.

Even the knowledge and techniques I have approved previously imply some serious problems. Techniques guided by fair results of individual cases are certainly important for dispute settlement, but even if every basic-level judge sticks to this principle, it will certainly result in the problem of dissonance of laws in the region or even in the entire country. A judicial technique which may lead to fairer results in part may well result in a legal system which lacks regularity and predictability as a whole. For this reason, the kind of technique and knowledge that has widespread rationality and necessity must also be restricted properly. As a matter of fact, the second-instance trial, especially the legal trial, has this kind of institutional restriction and the issue that legal trials attempt to settle is the universality of legal rules.

It is also for this reason that we can truly understand that the different divisions of labor between first-instance and second-instance trials should not be understood and implemented in practice by many jurists, as if adding one more branch of insurance or supervision of judicial justice. The main functions of first-instance and second-instance trials are the judicial division of labor, which is an essential division of labor based on the competitive advantages of knowledge. This point has major significance both in theory and in practice. It will at least break the superior–subordinate relationship between the first-instance trial and second-instance trial in a judicial system of bureaucratic administration. We may well and should reconstruct the relationship between first-instance trials and second-instance trials in definition and regulation from another dimension. It should not be a distribution of power but a division of labor, including the function of knowledge, system innovation, and competition.

For this reason, what I'm saying here is far more than a dichotomous approach or the commonplace talk of seeing things not only from its advantages, but also from its disadvantages. I do not deny that this is what I hope to achieve first—but it is indeed the first step only. What we should do next is to see that the knowledge and technologies demonstrated by judges of China's basic-level courts today are not something that is nice to have or is borrowed only when necessary. Other legal organizations of a country cannot provide this kind of knowledge and technology, which are hard to replace. So we must, based on this, gradually find, design, establish, and optimize systems which are complementary to each other, and which are similar to, but not limited to institutional division of labor between first and second instances of trial. Even the basic-level courts are expected to gradually optimize other systems. In addition, we should also be aware of the issue that the court system must complement other systems in the society and that all systems must be gradually optimized.

This is exceptionally important, since we are legal people. The biggest difference between legal people and moralists or traditional political philosophers may be that the former rely more on systems, while the latter pay more attention to various ideas and beliefs. In other words, the former do not base the system on ideas, moral criticism, or preaching, while the latter more prefer to resort to those things.

8.6 The Theoretical Significance of Knowledge of Basic-level Judges

I have almost finished my task for this chapter, which is to demonstrate knowledge and techniques accumulated and formed by judges of China's basic-level courts in their special institutional space and social space. But before analyzing the academic meaning of this chapter, there are two indispensable annotations that need to be mentioned here. Firstly, although I call them knowledge, techniques, or strategies, and hereby emphasize the creative activities of judges, this does not mean that they are products of ethics from sober-minded judges. Such terms as knowledge, techniques, or strategies, according to a traditional understanding, imply some kind of possibility of choice, since techniques or strategies are possible only when there are choices available. I call them knowledge, techniques, or strategies based on my judgment observed from my perspective as an intellectual.[42]

Secondly, what I have reluctantly demonstrated here is still part of the knowledge, techniques, and strategies of basic-level judges, and part of the cases I have analyzed, as well as part of the picture I can manage to describe in words that will be accepted by legal or other academic circles. There is a large amount of knowledge waiting there for people to observe, to seek words to describe, and to obtain qualities such as common knowledge or knowledge that are easier for communication. In this sense, the research in this chapter is only a road sign marking "road passable." It is a summary, instead of a conclusion of the knowledge, experience, and techniques of basic-level judges.

The significance of this chapter is, to a certain extent, a kind of development and supplement of the subjects that I have elaborated on in other chapters of this book or in other papers. The analysis of this chapter can further explain that the justice style of China's basic-level judges, which is guided by dispute settlement, is not a product of a lack of understanding in rule-based governance—nor is such a conclusion easily drawn when we determine the legitimacy of judicial philosophy and practices in our textbooks, as it is a product of a lack of knowledge, philosophy, concept, and beliefs. Instead, it is only another category of knowledge produced based on different requirements of institutional space and social space.[43] This analysis has also further positively illustrated a series of problems I will analyze in the next chapter. These questions include musings such as why China's law-school graduates do not want to work in basic-level courts? The reason from the perspective of judicial knowledge lies here.[44] A tribunal head who graduated from a formal law school and has been working in a people's tribunal for a long time even gives a dismissive remark as he "has returned almost all of the knowledge he has learned in school back to his teachers." We can criticize the policy measures of placing demobilized soldiers to courts from the perspective of judicial specialization and long-term development of Chinese society. At the same time, we have to realize that a large number of demobilized soldiers have executed the function of dispute settlement in basic-level courts and people's tribunals, and some have done the job excellently. This chapter has implied some answers on these seemingly connected phenomena.

We may as well answer the question of how we see this set of knowledge. From a long-term point of view, this is not a question that can be determined through

---

[42]About discussion on the nature of knowledge, please refer to: Henry Plotkin, *Darwin Machines and the Nature of Knowledge*, Harvard University Press, 1993.

[43]Please refer to Chap. 5 of this book: "Dispute Settlement and Governance of Rules."

[44]Please refer to Chap. 10 of this book: "Professionalism of Judges in Basic-level Courts."

evaluation or theoretical evidence. The destiny of such knowledge and techniques will be eventually determined by the demand, effectiveness, and market of the knowledge body.[45] If it is doomed to be eliminated, the research demonstration of this chapter will not be able to save it. But if it has its utility and can get things done, then it will be used and produced by people. Just as you can never make one love beer by demonstration, you cannot make legal knowledge and techniques lose their utility in practical life by demonstration either. We must realize the limitation of discourse, although it should not let us abandon analysis or forecast.

If only from the point of view of rule of law (rule-based governance), I believe that this set of knowledge is largely limited. China's rule of law is not likely to be implemented mainly based on this set of knowledge. To a certain extent and within a certain limit, it even contradicts the rule-based governance expected by legalist circles. However, as shown in previous analyses, this kind of knowledge is at least effective at certain times and at certain levels in modern China. It is irreplaceable and thus essential. In the period of social reform in China, it is not necessarily incompatible with the pursuit of rule-based governance.

If China is modernized further and modernized social life has "disciplined" people more in order, while the living world and people demand more for rule-based governance, will this kind of judicial knowledge lose its utility and become meaningless? It is not necessarily so. First of all, the living world will be rich and complicated forever, and it will not be possible to be fully covered by rules. It is especially impossible for development and change of the society to be covered by existing rules (just think about the tremendous challenges brought about by the internet to existing legal rules!). Modernized discipline will only limit, instead of eliminate, the irregular aspects of the living world. The courts of first instance in the USA still stick to the jury system in many cases, including many civil trials today, which should not be understood from the perspective of legal rules only. What is important is that this system has, to a large extent, helped to solve factual disputes that are difficult for judges of first instance to deal with. Even in Chinese society, which is getting more and more modernized, judges of China's basic-level courts or trial courts still do need certain knowledge formed by their trial experience when dealing with some cases. They may also adapt or change the knowledge to conform to new requirements. I don't think the knowledge of basic-level judges today will be doomed; on the contrary, as long as there is a need for it in society, it will continue to survive.

If we analyze further and assume that knowledge and techniques themselves will not produce mistakes, then it is still necessary for us to generalize this kind of special judicial knowledge. Although mistakes may occur when the knowledge is applied, getting to know it can also be a good teacher and conducive to the formation of rule-based governance. A western Chinese saying goes, it is easier to deal

[45]As for the issue of survival utility and social choice of knowledge to people, please refer to: Henry Plotkin, *Darwin Machines and the Nature of Knowledge*, as previous note 42, especially Chaps. 4–6.

with a familiar devil than a strange one. If we do not understand the existing kind of judicial knowledge of basic-level judges and adopt an ostrich policy, then it will only increase dangers and difficulties, instead of reduce and control them.

As a matter of fact, certain kinds of judicial knowledge and techniques demonstrated by basic-level judges are also shared by other judges (second-instance judges or foreign judges). This means that certain experiences of basic-level judges are more local in terms of its scope, but its market is not necessarily restricted to certain areas. Just as the research of transaction costs by the Ronald Coase Institute started from the research of manufacturers, the application of this definition and theory was not necessarily restricted to manufacturer research. We should not distinguish the knowledge of China's basic-level judges from that of other judges in terms of value. The judicial trial knowledge of China's basic-level judges is not necessarily short of a certain significance beyond the specified context where the knowledge is produced. To a certain level, it is the same as the experience summarized by US appeal court judges, which is a local knowledge that has the widespread significance of enlightenment within certain realms.

Indeed, the knowledge of appeal trial (second-instance) judges is often more universally applicable and their decisions are often more authoritative and therefore may be regarded as more correct due to this authority. However, we should not thereby conclude simply that the knowledge of appeal trial courts must be more superior in terms of morality or truth and that knowledge of basic-level judges should be neglected, ignored, and even canceled. My opinion is exactly to the contrary. These two sets of knowledge are both useful in their own contexts. Each has its irreplaceable and independent importance without any difference of being good or bad.[46] If we truly respect knowledge for the sake of solving problems in Chinese society, we must create a possibility in which these two sets of knowledge can coexist in China's judicial system and true knowledge can grow by itself. We should not let one kind of knowledge oppress the other or rank knowledge by its place of origin or trademark.

The situation of knowledge oppression is actually very serious. In the reports from many "lower-level" courts in today's China, the tones of "upper-level" courts are often copied (which is regarded as following suit in the speech patterns of the upper level). In the popular language of rule of law, thousands of people have the same expression and thousands of people use the same words. It seems as if it is highly unified and disciplined. However, when you visit the grassroots level, you

[46]In January 12, 1959, Charles E. Wyzanski, Jr., a judge of a district court in Massachusetts wrote a well-known letter to a Federal Senator who politically supported and nominated him when getting to know he had been nominated as a candidate for appeal judge. In his letter, he eloquently pointed out the importance and advantages of first trial judges. Please refer to Charles E. Wyzanski, Jr., "The Importance of the Trial Judge," in Walter F. Murphy and C. Herman Pritchett, *Courts, Judges, and Politics: An Introduction to the Judicial Process*, 4th ed., Random House, 1986, pp. 108–110. Although judges of basic-level courts in China are very much different from judges of district courts in the USA, we may gain some enlightenment from them and see some new possibilities for studying China's judicial problems.

will find out that this is actually not the case. There are people "brave" enough to tell the truth occasionally, but it is usually during a face-to-face talk and will be over once said. Sometimes, the truth is revealed in the intervals of mainstream discourse and people without basic-level experience cannot realize its significance at all. Other times, the truth will be expressed in a kind of moralized language so as to fight for the legality of its practice. In Chap. 5 of this book, a judge's settlement of the case of "breaking-up of mother–son relation" might be championed as a "good deed" by the judge in a period when "helping people out" is given special attention.

This kind of knowledge oppression and situation where the words of the people with humble positions have little effect does remain serious in the law circle. The place of origin of the legal knowledge (imported knowledge is superior than local brands, knowledge from Beijing is better than from other provinces, and knowledge from urban areas is better than from rural areas) has almost become the only standard for jurists to decide whether the legal knowledge is good or not. I used to frankly speak to many friends and students that if I hadn't returned from my overseas study in the USA and had been to Xinjiang instead of Peking University, I wouldn't be who I am today. Please note that I mention this not out of complacence, but just to warn myself not to be complacent.

It is true that the difficulty related to discourse has reflected the aggressiveness of mainstream discourse, but it has, moreover, reflected the fact that Chinese jurists have not been able to provide the discourse space for those disadvantaged discourses. They have not provided elementary propositions, definitions, and terminologies for effective exchanges, nor have they provided a theoretical framework or knowledge system which is "perfectly justified." This is a subject that upon which we as Chinese jurists should make profound self-criticisms. However, what is more important is that we should change or at least improve this kind of situation through our creative works. If there is no such situation in which respecting knowledge might be different from what is popular now, and if we do not let local knowledge which might be at the lowest level and of the most original nature come into our view, then it will be impossible for our judicial research to have real vitality and creative force. Law professors may be complacent with the connected world of discourse and like to quote from Holmes, Posner, and Hart (whose words are often quoted by me). They may be able to win a few applauses or support from students who have just entered into the university. But what's next? What is your contribution? This question is still unavoidable. The judicial experience of Chinese judges, to modern Chinese scholars, must be and should be the main resource from which we extract and purify China's judicial theory and even legal theory.

First draft at Cambridge on December 3, 1999

Part III
Judges and Legal Personnel

Chapter 9
Legal Personnel in Rural Society

The first thing we do, let's kill all the lawyers.
—William Shakespeare (*Henry VI*, Part II, 4. 2. 63).

The study of China's basic-level judicial system certainly cannot be separated from the study of judges, and it is even necessary to focus on judges. This section will make an effort of this kind. Centralization will not cause people to forget about the margins, nor replace the definition of "basic-level judicial system" with the definition of judges. For this reason, as an opening, I will introduce some people and cases that could be easily neglected or even totally not seen in the traditional and standard judicial system study which centers on the court (or prosecutors) and the meaning of the people involved as well as the context of the cases. This is the pretext for the following two chapters which especially address judges. This chapter is not going to concentrate on discussing certain particular judicial issues, but instead I hope that the following introduction will make readers think about problems that are actually worth thorough studying and provide a research vision or framework that is as vast as possible for researchers of judicial systems and legal theorists in the future.

9.1 Summary of Legal Personnel in Rural Society

As I have said previously, modern judiciaries actually emphasize the "formative" process of dispute settlement and give it more emphasis day by day.[1] For disputes among people, the judiciary needs judges to be able to actually go through this judicial process. But it is not enough to have a judge—a person to apply rules and decide verdicts on disputes only. It is already impossible for modern judiciary to act like Ma Xiwu who, as a person with enough charisma combining the referee and politician within

[1]Please refer to Chap. 6 of this book "Inbetween Facts and Laws".

© Foreign Language Teaching and Research Publishing Co., Ltd and Springer Science+Business Media Singapore 2016

S. Zhu, *Sending Law to the Countryside*, China Academic Library,
DOI 10.1007/978-981-10-1142-9_9

him, made decisions in accordance with justice, human feelings, and state laws based on his virtue and wisdom.[2] Being liked or not, this ideal judicial character has gradually disappeared and been seldom seen in the process of modernization, professionalization, and specialization.[3] As a kind of judicial model, it may be refused forever. For today's judiciaries, and even for China's judiciary, which is not at all perfect in the eyes of either Chinese or Western legal scholars, it belongs to modern judiciary fundamentally. When I say modern judiciary, I mean a professionalized working process completed by many legal people cooperating with each other. It is more like an industrial assembly line. The judge's job is only part of this process while the job of the first instance judge is only part of the systematic function of the court. In this sense, the judge is a "screw" for the modern judiciary's function, although an indispensible one.

If we do not consider contemporary and modern China before the Chinese Communist Party took power, this judicial transition process has gradually progressed since 1949 as a matter of fact,[4] although the Cultural Revolution interrupted this process. Since the end of 1970s, China's judiciary has increasingly emphasized specialization. In particular since the 1990s, China has conducted important reforms on hearing methods—having more and more dependence on and requirement for specialization. As far as the basic-level judiciary is concerned, the most important principle may be that of "he who proposes must give witness" and related reforms on hearing procedures. Court hearings and mediation have become specialized narratives for day-to-day court function, and these are more difficult for ordinary people to access without the help of people who understand the law. It is under this background that a series of law-related professions (such as lawyers and notaries) has become popular in urban areas. It is already impossible to avoid the discussion of these systems when studying the contemporary Chinese judicial system. In order to study the judiciary of China's rural society, even the civil judiciary, the aspect that we have to pay attention to is a series of related people who guarantee the function of this judicial system in rural society.

In the 1980s and even early 1990s, all people related to this system belonged to the government. A definition familiar to the Chinese at that time and now is China's "political and legal system." This system includes public security organs, procuratorates, courts, and judicial organizations; now, judges, procurators, notaries, and individually practicing lawyers are increasingly becoming separated from government organizations. "Political and legal system" is a political category with a basic perspective on social control via the government. However, due to the emergence of lawyers and legal workers as discussed below, the change or transformation of social identity of these people, as well as the enhancement of professionalism and specialization of judicial

---

[2]Please see Zhang Xipo: *Ma Xiwu's Judical Method*, Law Press China, 1983. Ma is not only the ideal judge for Chinese people, but is also or used to be the ideal judge in the eyes of American people. The judge has styles of both legal people and politician. About the ideal lawyer and judge in America, please see Anthony T. Kronman, *The Lost Lawyer: Failing Ideals of the Legal Profession*, Harvard University Press, 1993.

[3]Kronman, *The Lost Lawyer*, same as previous note. In the eyes of Kronman, this happened only 30 years ago.

[4]Please see note 8 in Chap. 1 "Why Send Law to the Countryside?" and related text.

activities, it is now difficult to effectively and appropriately understand and analyze the structure and function of the Chinese judicial system through political and legal systems. From the perspective of social life, law is more of a social profession now, and the demand on this profession is already transferring to being privately specialized from previously being political. From the perspective of social research, a new definition which may cover more meanings and be more analytical would be "legal personnel." This definition emphasizes the professional quality of these people. On this level, although the majority of professionals previously belonging to "political and legal categories" may fall into the category of legal personnel, many governmental officers working as "political and legal committees," and even drivers, secretaries working in the public security bureau, procuratorates, and courts may not be regarded as "legal personnel." Lawyers possibly regarded as fighting against political and legal organizations have now become one of the key opponents of legal personnel.

If we observe from the perspective of politics and law, at the county level in today's China, the public security bureau, procuratorate, court, and judiciary (in some places, bureau of civil affairs and bureau of immigration also fall into the category of politics and law; we will see later that this kind of classification is reasonable to the civil administration at the village level at least) have their own extension and a relatively complete system. But there are some changes at the village level.

Procuratorates have different functions at the village level according to different situations. In the majority of counties we have researched, there are no working staff of procuratorial systems at the village level, and some counties (and cities) have established procuratorial offices based on "areas" (usually covering several villages). This kind of institutional setting is in line with reality, since regarding legal regulations[5] on

[5]Article 6 of Public Procurators Law of the People's Republic of China stipulates that the functions and duties of public procurators are as follows:

- to supervise the enforcement of laws according to law;
- to make public prosecution on behalf of the state;
- to investigate criminal cases directly accepted by the People's Procuratorates as provided by law; and
- other functions and duties as provided by law;

Article 5 of Organic Law of the People's Procuratorates of the People's Republic of China stipulates that the functions of duties of People's Procuratorates at different levels are as follows:

(1) to exercise procuratorial authority over cases of treason, cases involving acts to dismember the state and other major criminal cases severely impeding the unified enforcement of state polices, laws, decrees and administrative orders.
(2) to conduct investigation on criminal cases directly handled by themselves;
(3) to review cases investigated by public security organs and determine whether to approve arrest, to prosecute or to exempt from prosecution; and to exercise supervision over the investigatory activities of public security organs, to determine whether they conform to law;
(4) to initiate public prosecutions on criminal cases and support such prosecutions; and to exercise supervision over the judicial activities of people's courts, to determine whether they conform to law; and
(5) to exercise supervision over the execution of judgments and orders in criminal cases and over the activities of prisons, detention houses and organs in charge of reform through labor, to determine whether such execution and activities conform to the law.

responsibilities and duties of procuratorates and procurators includes the works of procurators at the most basic level, which are at least making contact with county courts. They have nothing to do with the people's courts dispatched by the county court to be stationed in the village. The establishment of procuratorial offices is only to facilitate related investigation and supervision. The official business of prosecution is still concentrated among basic-level procuratorates at the county level.

In the public security system, there are local police stations and permanent police officers in every village. Below the village level, there are usually several administrative areas, each of which has at least one official armed "police force" with a national salary. In some places, there are a small number of "public security and joint defence members" employed from local rural areas, who are not state civil servants, but rather "paid" by the village government. Their salaries are paid by local residents and dispatched to them by the county government. They wear purchased police uniforms, and in the eyes of the people, they are exactly the same as ordinary police officers. Nominally, they assist official police forces to guarantee the public security and sometimes take part in solving disputes, but they are often mobilized as an official police force. Generally speaking, those people in the procuratorates and public security organs at the village level can be counted as "legal personnel" in rural society, but their main responsibilities and duties are to safeguard social security and they have nothing to do with the judicial settlement of a large number of daily disputes in rural society.

The third group of legal personnel in rural society belonging to the political and legal system is civil administrative officials. They are the working staff at the most basic level in the civil administrative system. At the village level, their duties and responsibilities include formalities of marriage registration and divorce by consent, social welfare and remedies, disaster relief, households enjoying the five guarantees, emplacement of demobilized and transferred soldiers, giving out pensions to families of martyrs and soldiers, as well as social insurance work in recent years. The majority of this kind of work is related to administration. It is only with cases of divorce that the works of civil administrative officials are related to the judiciary. When a couple demands a divorce, and the village level mediation committee fails to mediate the case, the village will provide a mediation suggestion and ask both parties to go to the judicial assistants in the village for further mediation. If the judicial mediation fails and all parties agree to a divorce, then the couple then goes to the civil administrative official for divorce formalities which mainly involves a property distribution agreement and child support agreement, as well as the issuance of divorce certificates. If divorce by consent fails, then one party will go to the people's court to "file a lawsuit of divorce." In this sense, the works of civil administrative officials actually take on a quasi-judicial quality. As far as dispute settlement in line with rules is concerned, this civil administrator can be regarded as legal personnel in rural society, but they have no direct relation with the judicial judgments of the court.

Apart from judges, the legal personnel in rural society most closely related to the judiciary in the political and legal system is the judicial assistant (in some places, there are even established judicial bureau or judicial office in the village).

The judicial assistant's relation with the judiciary is getting closer. He or she is part of the judicial administrative staff with regard to basic-level authority, and they work under the guidance of leaders from the village and county governments and county judicial bureau, as well as the people's court at the basic level. His or her main responsibility is to manage the mediation committee, as well as rule of law publicity and education.[6] Specifically speaking, his or her substantial work is in dispute mediation. Apart from divorce mediation, he or she also mediates other kinds of disputes, from fights and scuffles to disputes regarding mountain and forest borders and other cases. When the dispute is solved, he or she issues a judicial agreement and then notarizes the agreement. Nowadays, however, one of the most important jobs of the judicial assistant has been transferred to providing legal services to villagers. He or she is called a "legal worker" and actually serves as a "lawyer" in rural areas.

In the following section, I will introduce some "legal personnel" more directly related to the judicial process in detail.

9.2 Legal Workers

After the Cultural Revolution ended and the Department of Justice was re-established, China's lawyer culture and legal system have gradually recovered. However, lawyers in China are actually practicing mostly in urban areas, with their services mainly covering urban areas and urban issues. How to provide good legal mechanisms and legal services for villagers to settle disputes has now become an issue.[7] In the beginning of the 1980s, there initially appeared village legal service organizations in Guangdong, Fujian, Liaoning, and other eastern areas with relatively developed economies. These organizations have been promoted around China since February, 1985.[8] In 1993, the Department of Justice conducted a series of reforms on legal services at the basic level, and the services were expanded from villages to "streets" in the cities.[9] By the end of 1997, China had

[6] *Judicial Administrative Work in Today's China*, Contemporary China Publishing House, 1995, p. 59; *Judicial Administrative Yearbook*, Volume 1996, Law Press China, 1997, pp. 20–21.

[7] "China's existing law firms and notaries are established in urban areas and county towns. They are generally understaffed with heavy tasks and it is therefore difficult for them to go deep into the grass-root to provide legal services for village enterprises and people. The problems that it is not easy for village people to hire lawyers, notarize and look for legal service especially stand out." *Judicial Administrative Work in Today's China*, pp. 463–464.

[8] For the early history of village legal service bureau, please refer to *Judicial Administrative Work in Today's China,* same as previous note, pp. 457–462. Please also refer to Li Ming: "Conference on Village Legal Service in China", *China Law Yearbook,* China Law Yearbook Press, Volume 1988, Law Press China, p. 715.

[9] Please refer to Jin Jueming: "Conference on Reform of Legal Service at the Basic Level," *China Law Yearbook*, Volume 1993, China Law Yearbook Press, pp. 141–142 for details.

established nearly 35,000 local legal service offices (among which at least 32,000 were village offices) and nearly 115,000 legal workers (among which 100,000 were village legal workers).[10]

The main scope of work in legal service offices includes the following: (1) Providing legal consultation, writing legal instruments, serving as a civil agent ad litem and non-litigation agent, and being employed as legal counsel for village enterprises, institutions, and rural lease-holding households; (2) Notarizing on behalf of parties; (3) Mediating economic disputes; (4) Legal publicity; (5) Assisting judicial assistants to mediate civil disputes and guiding or managing dispute mediation in local areas. Legal service offices practice the principle of "providing paid services and charging appropriate fees."[11] After that, according to stipulations of certain statutes, the legal service office no longer belongs to the government system and has become a kind of service institution. It now practices the mechanism of "Independent Management, Sole Responsibility for One's Own Profit or Losses, Self-discipline, and Self-development" with regard to business, human resources, and finances.[12] Our research has confirmed this point.

The legal service office is an institutional organization that does not hire national civil servants or use administrative funds or expenses. At the village level, the legal service office has a deep connection with the village government since the very beginning. In the villages where I conducted my research, legal service offices and judicial offices were "two organizations hiring the same staff." The post of the director of the legal service office was usually held by the village judicial assistant. The judicial office is a national judicial administrative organization established in the village's government and is the resident agency of the county judicial administrative organization. The judicial assistant is the judicial and administrative working staff of the basic-level authority, as well as the nerve ending of China's judicial administrative organization. In the eyes of the village people, and even the legal workers themselves, the status or identities of the head of the legal services office, and legal workers he or she hires, are not that clear. They are usually semi-official and can be both official and civilian at the same time. When villagers have disputes and go to the village government to settle disputes,

---

[10]Han Lihui: "Legal Service at the Basic Level," *China Law Yearbook*, Volume 1998, China Law Yearbook Press, pp. 180–181. About village law office and number of legal worker, please refer to Xu Xifu: "People's Mediation and Basic-level Legal Service," *China Law Yearbook*, Volume 1993, China Law Yearbook Press, p. 141; and *Judicial and Administrative Yearbook*, Volume 1996, Law Press China, 1997, p. 18.

[11]Provisional Regulation on Legal Service Offices in Villages and Towns (1987), *China Law Yearbook*, Volume 1988, Law Press China, pp. 586–587. The Department of Justice promulgated Detailed Rules and Regulations on Legal Service Operations in Villages and Towns in 1991, and Article 3 refined these 5 kinds of works into 8 kinds, namely serving as legal counsel, civil agent ad litem and non-litigation agent, mediating disputes, providing legal consultation, writing legal instruments, and assisting notarization. They are almost the same with the original one.

[12]Department of Justice: Opinion on Reform of Legal Service Work at the Basic Level (1992), quoted from Liu Guang'an, Li Cunpeng: "Civil Mediation and Right Protection," *Towards Time of Rights*, Xia Yong and etc. (edited), China Politics and Law University Press, 1995, p. 291.

it is usually up to the judicial assistant to mediate and settle the dispute. His or her identity at this time is a village government official, and his or her words count. Sometimes, the judicial assistant or director designates certain legal workers hired by the office to "deal with" disputes, and the legitimate identity of this legal worker presiding over the mediation is not clear. This is not necessarily important to both parties of the mediation. At least in the eyes of ordinary people, the identity of legal workers has a certain official color, just as "the members of a joint defense team" equals to "public security" in the eyes of ordinary people.

When this kind of mediation fails, the role of legal workers will change. He or she may provide certain relevant legal services on the basis of extra fees, including legal consulting, and writing indictments. When the people's court accepts the lawsuit, those legal workers, the judicial assistant included, will appear in court to participate in the litigation as the "lawyer" of one party upon the request of the party concerned. In addition, in daily life, the office hours of the legal services office always follow the working hours of governmental organizations. If villagers have certain unpleasant cases, or go to town for shopping or other issues, then they will drop by the legal services office for "consultation."

In the village site of my research, every legal service office has 2–3 staff members, one of which is the judicial assistant. He or she can be counted as a staff member of village government worker and is paid by the government. Others are hired by the director and are not the official workers for the village government. Their income depends on the revenue of the legal services office, but their salaries are fixed, so in this sense, they are also paid. In addition, some legal services offices need to pay back certain revenues from legal services to the village financial department.

Since they are all stationed in the village, legal workers at the village legal services office are very familiar with judges or other workers in the people's court. They have rather close relations with official legal personnel and know each other very well. Although I didn't see them contact or inform each other, I felt that they all knew who was or was not "at home" (office), where they had gone, and when they would be back. It is completely a society of acquaintances, although somewhat different from the society of acquaintances among villagers. In a certain village, the legal office service is located opposite to the court, and people working there visit each other quite often. It is quite normal for someone to go to court, and the judge to ask him or her to go to the legal services office to have a complaint written up and to be informed of the cause of action in a lawsuit.[13] My research has also confirmed some reports: The circuit court "puts most of its energy into guiding and training judicial assistants while it tries cases. The circuit court takes advantage of all opportunities and occasions to have systematic training for judicial assistants. First of all, judicial assistants will be asked to present or take part in the mediation when the case is tried, and they are taught by example in terms of

[13]Please refer to the first case in Chap. 5 "Dispute Settlement and Governance of Rules"of this book.

mediation skills and trial procedures; secondly, two joint conferences are held each year in which judicial assistants are organized to learn new legal regulations and judicial interpretations in order to get hold of the development trend in a timely fashion; and thirdly, the judicial assistants are gathered when the administrative meetings are held, when they can use leisure time to exchange information and study difficult cases."[14] Another report has mentioned that a certain newly appointed judge of the people's court "took the initiative to go to the judicial office to help when he did not have any cases to deal with while the judicial office was extremely busy."[15]

The legal workers in my research did not have any experience studying in law school; their legal education was just a half-month or ten-day training class organized by the county judicial bureau or a legal awareness training class. But this does not mean that legal workers do not have any experience in law. In a certain county-level city we researched, we met a judicial assistant whose surname was Liu in a village only 4 km away from the town center. Mr Liu was regarded as "Master Lawyer Liu" by local villagers, judges, and village government officials. He used to be a student at a technical secondary school studying to be a veterinary surgeon. When he returned to his village, he became a judicial assistant somehow. While he was in office, he provided legal services and studied law by himself. A few months before we visited his village, he had just passed the national unified examination for lawyers and become an official lawyer. He dealt with cases not only in his village, but also in the town, and he even accepted cases beyond his village or his county. When I visited his legal services office, I was told that he was dealing with a case in the Xinjiang Autonomous Region and would not be back for a few days. But I was also told that this "Master Lawyer Liu" had reached an agreement with a certain lawyer's office in the town center. He would soon resign and leave the village government to join a lawyer's office and work in the city. This was the only lawyer I met at the village level. The famous words of Shakespeare are unnecessary in the rural society. There is no need to kill anyone here since all lawyers will disappear naturally.

In this same legal services office, I also met a graduate of the local politics and law school (which is a technical secondary school) who was just 18 years of age and came from a different village in this same county. He was an intern in the legal services office and planned to work here after graduation. He was very serious about his job and behaved both careful and warmheartedly when receiving visiting villagers. He told me that his (most practical) role model was this "Master Lawyer Liu," who studied completely by himself and would soon work in the city. He hoped that he would one day fulfill this dream through self-study. As will be demonstrated in the next chapter, legal talent does not stay long in rural society, even for those young and junior intellectuals such as this secondary school graduate.

---

[14]Please see Chun Sen, Meng Tian: "Going with the Waves," *People's Judicature*, Issue 9, 1994, p. 35.

[15]Please see Chen Haifa: "'Kettle Director of Tribunal'," *People's Judicature*, Issue 1, 1991, p. 3.

But the situation here is not totally the same as that of the basic-level court that cannot keep law-school graduates.[16] The most fundamental reason for villages being unable to keep young people who have a certain amount of legal knowledge is that the market economy has created more opportunities for young people. It is not because they have no place to use their knowledge or that the basic-level judicial offices have no need for or reject those intellectuals. When I chatted with some local judges, they all said they hoped that legal workers or lawyers would participate in the court trials or mediations. Their reason is very simple: If those lawyers take part, then the judges will have a rather simple judicial trial (including mediation). It is easier for them to follow legal procedures and the trial will be more formatted.

First of all, judges can use more concepts of statutes or other legal words and languages to communicate with legal workers, based on which legal workers will communicate with their parties. This will give judges more convenient means to make decisions. At least, they do not need to frequently use excessively popular and even inelegant language ("during the debate, arguing is allowed while swearing is not) to explain to the parties concerned concepts that in our eyes should be naturally understood by people.

Secondly, judges can avoid the conflict between professional requirements and social morals. One judge said that sometimes judges must show a certain partiality, or otherwise their judgment will be against reason and nature. For example, in the divorce case, one party may not agree to a divorce, but he or she does not understand the specific stipulation of the law and relies on the judge, whom he or she believes will help him or her out. When putting forward the divorce scheme, the judge may have his partiality toward that party and hope that he or she can be allocated a little bit more property, but the party concerned may still not agree to a divorce no matter how the judge mediates. Normally, the judge can only make a "hard decision," the result of which will likely be more unfavorable to the party. At this point, the judge will find themselves in a very difficult situation, since he or she cannot totally give up the legal ideological requirements of a judge at the moment, which is to remain "neutral" and to care about the specific legal stipulations at hand. However, the judge cannot explain to the party which he or she has partiality with the stakes either in law or in him or herself, and cannot give more help to one party ("there are things that can be done rather than be said"). The judge says that under these types of circumstances, if there is a lawyer or legal worker present on behalf of the party, then he or she will help the judge to explain clearly all stakes, and free the judge from the conflict between law and conscience or emotion and law.

Thirdly, the judge I consulted said that due to the presence of lawyers or legal workers, the judge can avoid direct conflict with the parties concerned. The modern judiciary does not and cannot decide the case totally according to the rights and the wrongs of traditional rural society. The result of the judge's decision may

---

[16]Please refer to Chap. 10 of this book "Professionalism of Judges in Basic-level Courts."

therefore conflict with the expectations of the parties concerned. Take the divorce case in the previous paragraph as an example. As long as one party all along insists on a divorce, the judge can only make a judgment of divorce. Although when making this judgment, the judge has already given "Qin Xianglian" more benefits by discretion, "Qin Xianglian" may still believe that the judge has been brought out by "Chen Shimei" and thus may be angry with the judge. Since the law in her eyes is still a moral regulation in rural society, and the good judges in her eyes are still moral models who punish evil and praise good deeds according to their authority and cannot stand any sand in their eyes. If the judge does not follow Judge Bao Zheng's road, and allows the "heartless" one to divorce, then it only means that the judge is also heartless. In this situation, the judge says that if there are legal workers or lawyers serving as their legal counsels, they can explain to those angry parties concerned why they make such judgments and thus reduce conflict between judges and the parties concerned.

This judge's statements are all true. From my observation of the trials conducted by basic-level judges, I also deeply feel that these legal workers have played an enormous role in ensuring the formatted function of the judiciary, either in writing the complaint, or putting forward related remedies, or ensuring court procedures or participation in the court debate. It can be said that without these legal workers, the trials of some cases would not proceed, or could not proceed as efficiently as they do now. An example I used to witness was when a judge asked the party concerned (a senior of about 70 years of age) "do you want to apply for withdrawal." The old man did not understand what a withdrawal was and answered with a customary "yes, I do" (I think that in his memory of rural life, "apply" is always connected to "remedy money" and "remedy food" and it shows the "customs" mentioned by Bourdier). The "lawyer" at his side immediately said "no, he doesn't" and sent the old man away with a few words (I think that the old man still did not understand what withdrawal was, but he may have believed that his "lawyer" would not deceive him). Here is another example. Sometimes when a heated court debate turned into a "swearing match," even the judge could not properly perform his duties, I could see that the legal worker would try and tell his client to calm themself.

But we should not approach these personnel as if their purpose is only to ensure that the trial can proceed normally; from a broader perspective, this is a real "legal education," a civil education in modern society, a training of individuals, a teaching opportunity, a new style of manner, tone, vocabulary, attitude of speaking, an identification of authority and evidence, a new life and personality shaping, and an individual drilling.[17] This kind of influence will far exceed any lecture of examination of "legal education" supported by material rewards.

This drilling of court and judicial procedures will have influence not only on the parties concerned, but also on the legal workers. According to our research, the majority of village judicial assistants (legal workers) have been selected from

[17]Cf., Michel Foucault, *Discipline and Punish: the Birth of the Prison*, trans. by Alan Sheridan, Vintage Books, 1978.

educated villagers, most of whom are basic-level cadres or intellectuals in the village. These people have not received legal training or even a modern bureaucratic education. They just have been living in the village for a long time. Through settling disputes, they have gradually fostered a kind of capability of making judgment and settling disputes according to the nature of justice, human feelings, national laws, and policies. There are also a few judicial assistants who have joined the people's court in all kinds of manners to work as judges. In some mountainous areas and poverty-driven areas, it is difficult for county courts to send judges to the people's court in the village for much time.[18] They have to recruit judges of people's court from local judicial assistants or other official workers in the village government. Those staff members in the village government, such as judicial assistants, are also willing to work as judges since they are tired of their endless duties in the village and prefer a quieter life. They therefore will join the court through examination. For the judicial assistant, the experience of taking part in this kind of trial will be one of the main channels for him or her to understand and learn of judicial trials before joining the court.[19]

Fourthly, even if those judicial assistants or legal workers cannot join the people's court, the procedures of the judicial trial will have a huge influence on their dispute mediation skills or even on their administrative decisions on behalf of the village government. When visiting a certain village, I randomly took out a few files from the dossier of dispute settlements by judicial assistants to have a look. I originally planned to look them over only, but they surprised me. The procedure of dispute settlement is extremely similar to those in the files of the court. The dossier included "my requests" which were similar to indictments, "research records" and "discussion records" similar to judge's inquiry records, served documents and receipts similar to court summons, "mediation records" similar to trial records, and "settlement decisions" similar to verdicts. In addition, there were relative evidence materials, including oral and written testimonies. More than court dossiers, they had some memos of field research and discussion records, as well as sketches of division of land boundaries. These extra parts reflect that this kind of administrative decision attaches more importance to field investigation than the courts, and they focus more on "substantial justice" instead of "who advocates bearing the burden of proof." This situation surprised me and accompanying researchers. It is apparent that the judicial procedures of people's court have provided a new basic format for dispute settlement in an administrative way in rural society, but this kind of format has in turn supported or is expected to support the judiciary. It shows that as an "art of governance," the model of "rule of justice" is indeed penetrating into the grassroots, and the village people's court is an important channel

[18]This phenomenon is quite normal in the whole country. "It is really a test for court cadres to work in the court. Some people are not willing to work in the court even there will be more allowances for them each month." Please see Dai Jianzhi: "To Sing the Song of Nan Niwan Again," *People's Judicature*, Issue 11, 1994, p. 44.

[19]Please see related text in the second section of Chap. 10 of this book "Professionalism of Judges in Basic-level Courts."

or window. It has made me especially feel the power of documented rule of law in modern society, and also made me further understand the words of a judge who used to work as a judicial assistant for a long time. He generalized the features of works of both judges and judicial assistants as "one has procedures while the other has not."

9.3 Legal Instrument Server

In a relatively wealthy area on the Jianghan Plain, we inspected a few people's tribunals and discovered that the number of staff members in the tribunal was obviously higher than the number they told us. Upon inquiry, the judge told us that every tribunal has hired two to three young men to especially serve all kinds of instruments on behalf of the court and also to help with some other issues related to tribunal work, such as assisting case execution. Those legal instrument servers are normally veterans or some rurally educated young people, and their "salaries" are paid out of the "revenues" of the tribunal. To my regret, I forgot whether these workers had official titles or forgot to write down what judges called them. I have fabricated a title here and call them "legal instrument servers."

Why do tribunals have to hire this kind of worker? The judge told us that in this area, they have relatively more disputes because the economy there is relatively developed and the population flow is rather large. For this reason, the tribunals have loads of judicial works and judges usually do not have time to service related legal instruments themselves. Secondly, if judges or clerks serve legal instruments themselves and then hear the case in the tribunal a few days later, it will seem rather strange (please remember that distance will create authority and beauty).

Thirdly, and most importantly to my belief, the majority of judges have settled down in the county town, they have better living conditions in nearly every aspect and are provided with cars by the tribunal since the economy there is relatively developed and transportation is convenient. They go to work early in the morning and come home late at night or are stationed in the rural tribunal on weekdays and go back to the county town on the weekends. This kind of living condition has made those judges increasingly unfamiliar with specific conditions in the villages. Villagers no longer have the judges of the people's tribunal from old times who still live in the village and are familiar with the village. Many judges told me that villages are not like cities. In villages, villagers' residents do not have streets or addresses. Communication is inconvenient (it is impossible to make appointment), and instrument service becomes a toilsome task. Sometimes you go to serve an instrument only to find that the door has been locked and the person has gone to the market. There is even possibility that the server passes them by in the street without knowing that he or she is the person they are supposed to serve. One judge said that since the judges of the people's court now live in a different community, the tribunal needs someone who is familiar with the local community to serve instruments. The judge can then tell the local representative which person in which group of which village the instrument needs to be served to, and he can definitely fulfill the task. They normally know almost every adult in the village and will not miss anyone if meeting them in the street. With those people working in the tribunal, the judicial trial will be more normalized and more effective.

This is somehow unexpected to me, but also enlightening. First of all, I feel that modern social and economic development demands judicial specialization. The large number of disputes demands a more efficient organization structure of the judiciary. In this process of social development, even the works of people's tribunals are undergoing certain revolutionary changes quietly and attaching greater importance to the specialization of work and bureaucracy. The development of society is now reshaping tribunals and judges in the villages, including their lifestyle, knowledge, and the way the judiciary functions. Secondly, although I have learned of the political and judicial sense of space moving toward modern social organization form Durkheim and Foucault,[20] it is only here that I have seriously felt the verification of the modern Chinese experience: Spacial organization does indeed have influence on political life. (I think this could be another good subject for a doctoral dissertation.) Those judges certainly have never heard about or do not care about Durkheim or Foucault, but their instinct and experience on issues of rural judicial practices have clearly made me feel a kind of analysis which might be ridiculed by others as "post-modern," and I see the significance of space in social control. It is true that if you do not live in this kind of environment, you cannot feel the difficulty the judiciary has in entering rural society in the villages. The difficulty does not lie in knowledge or philosophy only. It is not about money either. It involves comprehensive reorganization, structuring, and integration of society and relates to issues such as addresses and street districts, as well as reforms of road networks, telephone services, or other communication methods. Here, I have seen what Foucault meant when he said that the discourse mechanism of rule of law must rely on a series of very specific non-discourse mechanisms. I feel that we, as jurists, who stay indoors to "do academic research" tend to view the practice of rule of law too simply and often regard it as an issue of ideas.

Apart from the demand of this kind of effective "social control," those servers play some other roles in the tribunal, such as a role similar to court police. If the judge needs to go to the village to execute cases, then he will often bring legal instrument servers to take part in the compulsory execution of the judicial process. Their role is similar to that of guards. While the judge returns to his home on the weekends, the people's tribunal will be guarded by these local representatives. Their existence has resulted in a more meticulous division of labor in the tribunal. In comparison, tribunals here are obviously more similar to modern tribunals than the people's tribunals in mountainous areas where there are only two to three judges stationed in the village.

[20]Please refer to Emile Durkheim, *The Division of Labor in Society*, trans. by W. D. Halls, Free Press, 1984; Michel Foucault, *Discipline and Punish, the Birth of the Prison*, trans. by Alan Sheridan, Vintage Books, 1978.

The appearance of such people has also encouraged further changes among judges. The main change is to force judges to distance themselves further from the acquaintance-based society of the rural areas and to make the judiciary more independent of social ties. First of all, judges come to deal with disputes among villagers as an outsider (instead of a member in the community). They are influenced more by urban lifestyles and less by life standards of rural society, and thus, the Judiciary may follow procedures and rules more strictly, instead of focusing only on dispute settlement. Secondly, judges become gradually less dependent on the village government. Thirdly, villagers may gradually separate tribunals from village governments, which is conducive to the social awareness of judicial independence. Fourthly, due to the social philosophy that "foreign monks give better sermons," the increase of distance between judges and parties concerned may enhance the authority of tribunals and judges. Fifthly, from the perspective of possibility, this kind of change may encourage some law-school graduates who have joined the basic-level court to go to the people's tribunal to work in the future, although at the moment, there are almost none or only a few law-school graduates in county-level courts. It must be noted that my analysis here seems to be positive, but it may not necessarily turn out fine. The changes may as well bring about a series of new problems. What on earth will the result be? We need careful and long-time observation to draw conclusions.

However, even if we assume that those changes are desirable, people's tribunals must have their own private funds or be able to guarantee the salaries of those "servers" from all kinds of charges or nationally allocated funds in order to do this. At the moment, the changes of those tribunals happen only because the local economy is relatively developed and there are many disputes which produce income for the court. Only in this way can tribunals afford using several of those "servers."

But how do people's tribunals in those faraway deserted and rather poor areas deal with issues of service? In a people's tribunal in a mountainous area, I found that the judge answered this kind of unformatted issue of space in other ways despite that tribunals were too poor to employ "servers". First of all, in those areas, fewer disputes are settled in tribunals. It is either because the society is more closed up, and the population density is rather low so that disputes themselves are relatively fewer, or because the area is poor and transportation is not convenient, and thus less disputes are settled in tribunals. Secondly, the judges are basically stationed in the locality for a long time and are familiar with local situations and inhabitants. When they talk about parties concerned, they will normally not refer them by their names, but by someone in some village who lives next door to whom, or someone living at the foot of a hill (this kind of "GPS" can only be possible in places with low population density). Thirdly, judges normally serve related information of tribunals by using local administrative systems. On the day we arrived at the tribunal, the judge made the phone call to the village committee and asked the director to inform certain parties to go to the tribunal to take part in the litigation. Because population mobility is relatively small, the village committee normally can find someone that can ensure information is transmitted. Fourthly, once the information is passed on to the parties involved, the judges or clerks will serve the instruments. This kind of situation again demonstrates that even the specialization and independence of the judiciary are directly or indirectly related to the development level of social and economic development. At the same time, I have seen the influence of economic and living conditions on knowledge accumulated by the judges and the working methods of the court.

9.4 Judges as Lawyers

Although I will not discuss judges at the basic-level court in detail until the next two chapters, I want to discuss briefly another social function often played by judges at people's tribunals in villages and rural counties. It is the function of lawyer, which has been neglected by all researchers until now.

It has been initially shown in the previous text (though not through the reasons spoken of by Shakespeare) that there are usually no real lawyers in the jurisdiction of a people's tribunal[21] in the basic-level court. It is not only difficult for ordinary villagers to have access to lawyers from the city (they may have to walk tens of miles to get to their home), but they are also unable or unwilling to pay the relatively high fees. But the villagers do have many disputes demanding legal services. In the vast rural areas of China, there is a kind of institutional demand for legal consultation. It is just this kind of demand that produces legal service offices in the villages and promotes growth. But in the eyes of ordinary people, there is no strict distinction among courts, village governments, or judicial assistants. As far as they see, all of those organizations are places for them to reason things out. Secondly, the legal services offices charge fees as well, so some villagers therefore often skip the legal service offices and go to the court directly to file a lawsuit, especially for cases that are "perfectly justified" in the eyes of villagers (such as divorce or other standard legal procedures. People who have interest in this can do an analysis research on causes of actions stipulated by statutes as well as "causes of action" in the eyes of villagers, which would be a perfect subject for doctoral dissertation). Under this social background, judges of people's tribunals have actually played the role of the first lawyer to a large degree.

In Chap. 5 of this book, I mentioned a "case" like this. A son wanted his mother's money but failed, so he abused his mother many times; the mother went to the court to sue him and demanded to "be freed from their mother–son relationship."

[21]In the county of our survey, there is roughly one people's tribunal in each village; in China's East and Middle Region, one tribunal for one village has been realized in the end of 1980's. In some relatively poor region in China, due to finance, personnel and other reasons, there are also situations that one people's tribunal for several villages (please see Li Jianhua: "Dealing Local Cases to Ensure Local Security," *People's Judicature*, Issue 12, 1994, p. 41); there are also places in which two or more tribunals work together due to the lack of appropriate working conditions (Dai Jianzhi: "Sing the Song of Nanniwan Again—What I have seen and heard in the people's tribunal in Nanniwan," as in previous note 18, p. 44).

Under this situation, the judge told her that there was no such regulation in the law and thus, she was not allowed to do so. This was the first consultation and answer on legal issues. After that, the judge considered the actual situation of this mother and provided her with the best legal advice in his eyes—to divorce her husband who had left home and been without any contact for 20 years, and to find another husband to protect her. This was the second legal consultation provided by the judge—to design a safer future for the parties involved. Then the judge asked her to write her complaint in the legal service office opposite to the court, and told her how to write it and what the cause of action was. He even led him to the legal services office himself. This was the third legal service provided.

At least, the first two services, strictly speaking, should be the responsibilities of lawyers or legal workers. But they are often undertaken by judges in China's rural areas. Strictly speaking, judges not only do not have any obligation to undertake those responsibilities, but they should not and even should be prohibited to undertake them in law. For this reason, the judge actually "made judgments after decisions" as far as this case was concerned—if the woman really had followed the judge's advice and took relative action in the court, would the judge have made any other judgment? Certainly, this case did not involve many serious problems. But imagine, if the woman had followed the judge's advice, and took action against her son on charges of abuse (the judge did not give such advice, but only considered the possibility), then the case would have had a huge prejudice from the very beginning, which would have been unfavorable to her son. The judge's practice was in conflict with the professional ethics of the judiciary no matter what procedural law or traditional legal principles we apply to the situation.

Judges not only often play the role of lawyer before the prosecution, but also often actually do or even are forced to play the part of lawyers when the parties have not hired lawyers or legal workers to represent them in their hearing (including the mediation). This was demonstrated during the interviews, when many judges talked about their cases. Take the divorce case as an example again. The husband wants a divorce and even is willing to pay more money to express his guilt. However, the wife still does not want to divorce no matter what. Because the wife lacks related legal information, and no lawyers would represent the parties to give advices; if the judge maintains judicial "neutrality," the wife will often be misguided by decisions without complete information. At this time, the judge will often inform the wife what kind of settlement would be best for her and sometimes there is even suspicion that the judge exceeds his duties, meddles in parties' affairs, and makes decisions on behalf of the parties. It is actually the judge playing the role of lawyer here. Some other examples in other chapters of this book (such as in the "case of supporting the old man," where the judge made related arrangement on food and edible oils;[22] in the "case of compensation on broken legs," where the judge made arrangement on compensation on damages[23]"), as

[22]As previous note.

[23]Section 7 of Chap. 3 of this book "The Judicial Committee System in Basic-level Courts."

well as some reports on judges of people's tribunals[24] have all demonstrated that judges have played the role of lawyer on many occasions.

I don't want to raise more examples, but I do want to discuss their social and legal implied meaning.

First of all, this shows that there is indeed a huge demand for legal services, lawyers, and legal workers in China's rural areas. This is an enormous potential market for legal services. An important aspect of whether China' rule of law can be established is whether the villagers' demands of this kind can be met.

Secondly, we must also see that this potential market has not and even will not in a short-term turn into a practical market for legal services. This kind of demand is only a demand for those whom do not have capability to make payments. Frankly speaking, the reason that lawyers do not go to rural areas is that villagers cannot afford to pay the lawyers. As far as I see, apart from the lack of knowledge by villagers on the difference of these two systems, one of the very important reasons for villagers often turning to judges directly instead of consulting legal services offices is that the legal services provided by judges after listening to the appeals is a free lunch. The court will not charge fees until villagers hand in appeals and agree to be registered. Villagers are smart in this aspect, and they know how to save their cash.

On the other hand, the existing legal knowledge system is not able to provide effective legal services. That is to say that when producing existing products of legal knowledge, producers do not give enough careful consideration to whether they actually meet villagers' demands. At the moment, the legal knowledge provided by China's law schools is more suitable for commercial and industrial society and urban life and attaches importance to rules—rules to which villagers give little care and caution. Due to constraints of production and living conditions, as well as organizational patterns of society (it is a society of acquaintance), the required legal knowledge is hugely different. The legal remedies needed by villagers are often exceptionally specific and meticulous and have local features. It is essential that the parties concerned on the opposite site have the ability to execute remedies or that the judicial organs have the ability to actually implement such remedies. The lawyer can ask for very high compensation amount and the court can also make such judgments. However, if the party of the opposite side has no ability to pay at all, then all efforts made and services provided by this lawyer will amount to nothing. The definition of legal service needed by villagers must have its context and be refined when in practice, and should not be replaced by the theoretical definitions of jurists.

Due to these two constraints, we can see that the demand of legal services among Chinese farmers cannot be met at the institutional level. At the same time, it is the institutional demand of legal services of farmers produced by these two

[24]Please refer to Chen Haifa: "'Kettle Director of Tribunal'," *People's Judicature*, Issue 1, 1991, p. 3; Chen Nianhua: "'Peasant Household' Zhang Kaidi," *People's Judicature*, Issue 1, 1994, p. 42. In the first report, when this tribunal director took this office, there was no case for trial, so "he asked to offer help in the village judicial office when he found that the judicial office was too busy to handle cases."

constraints that forces the professional character of judges in the basic-level court, and especially when the people's tribunal changes or shifts subtly. He or she is not only a judge, but also a legal worker who spreads legal information which farmers care about, and they provide relative legal services. It is also just because of this practical social function of basic-level judges that I feel it necessary to include the judges of the people's tribunal who exercise this function into the analysis of this chapter as the legal workers of rural society. This kind of classification is not only due to convenience but also includes sufficient reasoning.

Starting from this function of judges in the basic-level court, especially the people's tribunal, we can further understand the special role they play in China's rural society. Many people claim that the professional quality of judges in the basic-level court, and especially the people's tribunal, is rather low and that judges lack the temperament and capability of the ideal judge (jurist/statesman), as well as the neutrality of the ideal judge. Those criticisms are not only accurate, in a way, but also unreasonable in some circumstances. If one goes to the village level in China and takes a look at what those basic-level judges do every day, the parties they receive, the problems they face, and the choice they have to make between textbook legal professional ethics versus real practical life, one will see that this kind of role deviation is unavoidable and even justified. Even so, my expression is too intellectualized. In their working and living environment, only when they have such behaviors can they behave impartially, and avoid bringing disgrace to the expectations of people toward "judges."

We may therefore need to review the abundant connotations and definitions of "judge" again. The definition of "judge" certainly should cover judges such as Sir Edward Coke, Oliver Wendell Holmes Jr., Albert Cardozo, Learned Hand. But judges are not only like Sir Edward Coke and Oliver Wendell Holmes Jr. They should include judges of people's tribunals in China or magistrates in the USA, UK, and Australia. An outstanding figure should not become a standard definition of the category to which he belongs. Otherwise, we Chinese jurists cannot be called jurists any more in front of the likes of Oliver Wendell Holmes Jr. and Richard Posner. If this was the case, which professor in China's law schools would dare to call him or herself a jurist professor?

In the end, the phenomenon of judges working as lawyers also demonstrates that the professionalism of judges is unavoidably connected to the local economic and social development level, at least in the basic-level courts of modern China. Considering the situation of other legal persons discussed earlier, we may even be able to say that legal personnel needed in these places cannot be too professional. Too much professionalism toward rural "clients" may mean more disadvantages than advantages. Here the same sentence works: To seek truth from facts and to study problems case by case. This is an old sentence, but after reading the above introduction and analysis, have we really been touched intellectually?

Now it is time for a more detailed observation on judges of basic-level courts.

At Cambridge, December 29, 1999

Chapter 10
Professionalism of Judges in Basic-level Courts

Present Situation, Origins, and Ways out

In this world, things are complicated and determined by factors of many aspects...
—Mao Zedong ("About Chongqing Negotiation," *Mao Zedong Collection* (one volume edition), People's Publishing House, 1966, p. 1055).

10.1 "Demobilized and Transferred Soldiers Working in the Court"

Shortly after the New Year in 1998, He Weifang published random thoughts and writings titled as "Demobilized and Transferred Soldiers Working in the Court."[1] He raised criticisms about the election and appointment system of Chinese judges, especially the general views of society and the government on works of courts and judges behind this practice. His basic view, as far as I see, is completely correct. That is, today's court is already different from the courts of New China about 30 years ago (which he called a "tool of proletarian dictatorship"). Today's court is an institutional organ with strong professionalism which settles detailed disputes (realizes judiciary/justice) according to common rules and acknowledge rules in dispute settlements. The emphasis on styles, temperament, and the strict sense of organizational discipline of soldiers has reflected that the understanding of judges and courts by society has already left behind the demands of the times and no longer accommodates the requirements of modern courts and even the development of rule of law in China. If some decision-making officials in central and local

[1]He Weifang: "Demobilized and Transferred Soldiers Working in Courts," *Southern Weekly*, Jan. 2, 1998.

© Foreign Language Teaching and Research Publishing Co., Ltd and Springer Science+Business Media Singapore 2016

S. Zhu, *Sending Law to the Countryside*, China Academic Library,
DOI 10.1007/978-981-10-1142-9_10

governments still insist on traditional views and pushing forward arranging demobilized and transferred soldiers to work in courts as a policy which is conducive to the establishment of rule of law, it may go against the development of specialization and professionalism of courts and judges.

This short essay of 2000 words requires an attractive title, vivid description, and strong views, so it is difficult to say every word that he wanted to say. Furthermore, He's essay made "mistakes of common sense" (e.g., he confusingly and mistakenly believes that all demobilized soldiers and army cadres are arranged by the state). Even so, I still believe that He's basic idea is right. He reasons through the subject using facts instead of only sticking to reporting the facts.

Because this critical reasoning uses facts, some people related to the "facts" may be unhappy with the results. In particular, on one hand, the Chinese government at that time announced disarmament of another 500,000 soldiers, and many military officers faced problems of "being laid off and seeking reemployment," and, on the other hand, China's reform has made supply and demand of labor more market-oriented. This originally simple issue and reasoning has thus tuned sensitive under such circumstances. Soon after, another essay with the title "Why can't demobilized soldiers work in courts" was published first in *PLA Daily* and then in *Southern Weekly*.[2] The author, Cao Ruilin, was an officer in the active services who received legal education and worked as a journalist for a certain military newspaper. We met once.

Both of the two essays talk about transferred soldiers, but strictly speaking, this essay pays attention to and discusses problems which are completely different from He's article. They have only some overlapping areas or connections on certain problems. Approximately speaking, Cao Ruilin thinks that modern society requires every job be specialized, and thus, transferred servicemen shall ultimately return to society. But where should they return to? He also claims that "the experience of soldiers is [...] an invisible fortune. They study hard, forge ahead with determination and tenaciously strive to succeed. Those kinds of spirits and practices are enough to make them into competent people's judges."

The previous problem of Cao Ruilin, the employment of servicemen, is a problem that needs to be resolved. However, this is not the problem that He's article discusses. Today, when the socialist market economy increasingly develops, to my view, this issue is definitely decided more by markets and participants in market activities themselves and will be decided completely by the market in the future, although at present, it cannot and should not be only decided by the market. However, Cao's article later assumed that transferred soldiers "study hard, forge ahead with determination, and tenaciously strive to succeed." Can anyone not become a judge if they can do all this? Why do transferred soldiers have priority? This kind of argument, based on assumption, is not convincing, in my view. In addition, it is not convincing enough to only claim that soldier's experience

[2]Cao Ruilin: "Why Can't Demobilized and Transferred Soldiers Work in the Court?" *PLA Daily*, Feb. 10, 1998.

is a kind of invisible treasure. Since everyone has his own experience as long as he is alive, the experience is an invisible treasure to him at the very least. It is a kind of common sense that everyone treasures his own experience. And it does not mean that the soldier's experience must be a kind of invisible treasure in judicial practice.

Up until now, my conclusion seems to be obviously in favor of He Weifang: Soldiers are not judges, and the long-term policy that courts are to be used as the main place to employ soldiers is obviously deviating. However, I'm saying this neither because I'm cold toward soldiers who have devoted their life to national defense (actually I used to be a soldier myself. Although I am not working in the court—it doesn't mean that I can't work in the court—I "entered a law school as a demobilized soldier" as He Weifang joked about.), nor because I believe that soldiers are destined to the battlefield and cannot work in the court after being demobilized and transferred, or become competent judges.[3] The problem lies not in whether China's transferred solders can work in the court, but what is the actual basis for their qualifications to work in the court and what kind of job they can do in the court?

This question is simple in logic: Soldiers do not equate to judges. But this chapter is not going to discuss issues only on this level. As far as I see, what is important is to understand the circumstances of China's judges, what has produced these situations, and what kind of improvement can we put forward on this basis. We have a series of questions that need to be understood. For example, what on earth is the situation of judges in basic-level courts of modern China? How many demobilized or transferred soldiers or, roughly speaking, people without

[3]As a matter of fact, Oliver wendell Holmes, Jr., the most famous jurist and Chief Justice in American History used to serve in the army for many years and took up official post. Having been injured three times by gunshot wounds, he was also a famous wartime hero. But his contribution to American jurisprudence and law is widely recognized around the world. In 1902, when President Theodore Roosevelt appointed Holmes as the Chief Justice of the Supreme Court, an important factor was his "remarkable military experience" (please refer to Max Lerner, "Holmes: A Personal History," in *The Mind and Faith of Justice Holmes: His Speeches, Essays, Letters and Judicial Opinions*, The Modern Library, 1943, p. xxxi). Even out of the present (1999) 9 Chief Justices of the Supreme Court, 3 of them used to take up official post in the military (National Guard). Apart from the present two female Chief Justices, 43 % of them have military experience. And this percentage is not the highest. I have studied all 21 males Chief Justices of the Supreme Court in the last 35 years, 11 of them had military experience and the percentage is beyond 50 % (material and date source: http://oyez.nwu.edu/justices/justices.cgi). Lord Denning, the famous Lord Chancellor of the UK who was also familiar to the law circle in modern China also had 2 years military experience (please refer to Edmund Heward, Lord Denning, *A Biography*, Weidenfeld and Nicolson, 1990, pp. 10–12). I use these facts not to prove that soldiers are good judges or only those who have military experience can become good judges. Nor can I prove this. As a matter of fact, those people entered court and became remarkable judges not because they used to be soldiers. They used to study in law school before or after their military experience and had outstanding academic results. These examples can at least show that military experience is not incompatible with legal or judicial knowledge, and military service is not opposite to judicial trial. I will have detailed demonstration later.

law-school education are working in the courts? Can they effectively exercise the duties of judicial trials, and for what reason? What kind of judicial duties do they exercise? As far as undertaking the job of judicial trials in basic-level courts is concerned, do law-school graduates do a better job compared to their less educated counterparts? Why? Are there quite a number of graduates with modern legal training that want to work in the courts? What kind of court do they want to join? Do demobilized soldiers and other people without professional training take up the place of law-school graduates if they work in the court? Or what kind of places do they take up? What kind of knowledge do basic-level trials require? Is it true that "jurisprudence" knowledge labeled by existing subject structures is definitely knowledge of judicial trials or useful to judicial trial? What kind of knowledge does modern China's legal education teach and what is useful to conducting trial and what is not enough? If there are not enough competent judges, can demobilized soldiers replace them in the court? Is there any better replacement? Are military experience and other social life experience compatible with judicial trials in court? On what aspects are they incompatible with each other and on what aspects are they compatible? We even have to ask whether all judges need to have the same working knowledge. And under the social conditions of modern China, how can we make relatively better choices from practice to the relatively ideal status of rule of law. All these questions need to be given careful observation and analysis. We cannot make simple inference logically, nor can we answer all questions according to logical inference or definition analysis.

There are many questions to address, and some of them are big questions with a sense of philosophy. However, the author of this essay does not study such questions in pursuit of philosophical meaning, but accidentally or unavoidably touches on those philosophical issues in order to study the questions. It must be pointed out that the research of empirical issues is not only in regard to material collection. As far as I see, it should be at least the same (if not more of an) intellectual challenge. Due to all kinds of restrictions, however, I cannot give clear or confident answers to these questions. For this reason, this chapter tends to focus on observation of present situations of judges in China's basic-level courts and the materials I use come from research and interviews in the basic-level courts of Hubei Province. However, what I want to emphasize and what is clear to me but may not be clear to readers is that just because of the limits of my research materials, the conclusions of this chapter have drawn are restricted to the basic-level courts of rural China. Some conclusions may be inspiring to problems of other levels or other courts, but we cannot extent to other problems without limit and research.

10.2 The Rough Situations of Judges in Basic-level Courts

I will start from the present situation of judges in basic-level courts of modern China. Firstly, I need to define the term "judges," as used in this chapter, which I define as staff workers in the courts with titles beyond clerk. Why make such definition?

First of all, during the research, I noticed that clerks, especially in the people's tribunal, actually played the role of assistant judge at many times. They often took part in case discussions and decisions. Judges and assistant judges would not only listen to their opinions and often asked clerks to put forward their own views. This kind of practice certainly has the "democratic" factor of China in the old days, but also has a factor of "teacher and pupil" training. As a matter of fact, at least at the basic level (I believe it is more or less the same in courts of higher level, since as I will discuss later, judicial experience cannot be taught at school. To use a fashionable philosophical definition, it is a kind of "practiced rationality"[4]), the majority (if not all) judges are trained through this kind of "semi-teacher and pupil system." For law-school graduates, if they really want to become a judge, they must go through this kind of internship to different degrees.

Secondly, at least up till now, most of the clerks will be gradually promoted to assistant judge or judge and officially take part in and preside over trials as long as they continue to work in the court without causing big problems and accumulating trial experience. On the contrary, some staff workers who have the title of judge from the very beginning may never take part in any kind of trial. Nor do they have the capability to take part in the trial. For example, a person has a title of judge only because he or she "has been working here since the court was established."

Thirdly, in the eyes of many ordinary people in grassroots society, the distinction between clerks and judges is very vague. Even in the eyes of staff workers themselves in the basic-level courts, the distinction is not important. It is roughly only a problem of "rank," not a problem of "occupation" distinction. For this reason, when observing situations of judges in basic-level courts, if we exclude those people only because of titles, it is obvious that we start from labels and definitions and do not understand China's "market situations."

From the interviews with more than 100 judges, as well as the situations of two county-level courts of our field research, we have discovered that, first of all, today's judges are truly far away from the ideal or imagined judges (where does this ideal judge come from? It deserves research of knowledge pedigree. As I quote Feng Xiang's words, "lawyers are not required to have law-school education background in the USA until the early stage of the Imperialism"[5]) in law circles at the cultural level. Although many lawyers have obtained diplomas or even bachelor's degree via all kinds of methods (college entrance examination by self-education, correspondence teaching, part-time university on law, TV education, and studies at party schools), most of the judges do not take such academic degrees too seriously themselves, apart from a few judges who have obtained academic degree by passing the college entrance examination based on self-education. They publicly claimed that they are "unqualified goods." Their academic degrees were born

[4]Please see Richard A. Posner, *The Problems of Jurisprudence*, Harvard University Press, 1990, Chap. 2.

[5]Feng Xiang: *Wooden-legged Justice*, Zhongshan University Press, 1999, Preface, p. 7. As a matter of fact, for American judges, they are not required to have law-school diploma, although all judges have graduated from law school nowadays.

through mass production based on conspiracies of leaders of higher levels and the judges themselves in order to meet all kinds of requirements. As far as they see, the most invaluable education is the past-time university of law organized by the court itself.

As far as legal professional training is concerned, judges of basic-level courts have seldom received law-school education beyond an official bachelor's degree of law. In a certain county-level city on the Jianghan Plain with a relatively developed economy, its court has two law-school graduates. However, in a certain county court located at the E'xi mountainous area where the economy is relatively lagging, there has never been a single official law-school graduate up till now, nor a single graduate from an ordinary university. What has proved this indirectly is that among the 100 judges from Hubei Province whom I have interviewed, and among the judges who have attended judicial training class organized by Zhongnan Politics and Law College for seven sessions since the spring of 1996 (about 60 per session), none is a law-school graduate.

If one must make certain distinctions (I will provide criticism on this kind of classification), China's basic-level judges have approximately three origins at present: firstly, graduates from normal universities and colleges who study law or other majors, with a bachelor's degree or college degree. The number of this kind of judge is very small, less than 10 % in most of the courts. Secondly, people were recruited locally or transferred into courts from other government departments. They account for about 30 %. Others are demobilized and transferred servicemen, as mentioned at the beginning of this chapter, which account for more than 50 % of the total. According to a deputy director of a people's court in a certain county (he himself is also a demobilized soldier, but has been working in the court for nearly 20 years), about 70–80 % of people in their court have military experience.

This kind of classification does not have much meaning, unless we take the position of essentialism. Because among the demobilized servicemen, a few are military officers with diplomas from standard universities; many demobilized servicemen found a job in their local area before they entered the court through all kinds of channels voluntarily (through examination) or involuntarily (being allocated to work in the court). During the interview, I can't feel which judge has chosen his team according to this classification. Nowadays, the game rules of the court are not much different from those of other professions. What is important is not "what kind of family you are from" or "family status," but your professional ability (as far as today's university professors are concerned, who would care that he used to be "school graduates," "workers," "cadres," or "demobilized soldiers"?). The distinction of judges is completely created by a few people in legal circles, and it does not have much value for analysis, at least in the basic-level court.

In addition, people working in the court are not necessarily engaged in the trial even if they have the title of judge or assistant judge. Many people are engaged in administrative affairs for their whole life after being transferred to the court, no matter whether they are demobilized cadres or local cadres. They work as drivers, court policemen, or dispatchers, or are engaged in the works of part-time university, disciplinary inspection, logistics, reception, trade union, and even works related to lawsuits, complaint, execution, and medical expertise, which can be accounted for as legal business.

But it must also be pointed out that as long as you work in the court, no matter what kind of job you start with, it is not impossible that one day the president of the court may agree to let you join the trial, so long as you are competent and make enough efforts (mainly making strong requests instead of studying judicial business). One may one day become a real judge and even a good judge. For this reason, we can discuss in detail the situations of judges temporarily based on this classification, and our purpose is to "get rid of the bridge once crossing the river" and to finally get rid of this kind of classification.

10.2.1 Demobilized Soldiers

First of all, we must notice that demobilized soldiers are completely different from transferred cadres. It is a kind of carelessness and misunderstanding to put them into a same category. Demobilized soldiers are normally enlisted when they are 18 or 19—or even older—and it is their duty to serve the army for 2–3 years at least or for 5–6 years at most. They return to their hometown when they are discharged from active military service. If their original registered permanent residences are rural places, they are regarded as so-called rural soldiers, the state does not have responsibility to arrange their jobs, even though some of them have learned certain kinds of skills in the army such as driving, and it is possible that they will be "recruited." Before the 1990s, the state had the responsibility to arrange a few "urban soldiers" to be employed as workers. They normally did not work in the court since their identities were workers instead of cadres. Even when there were a few demobilized soldiers recruited by the courts, they worked as workers or staff workers (such as drivers and typists) and would not become judges directly. It is true that some of them would become judges after being recruited by the court, but they had to pass the examination for cadre recruitment or go through a certain kind of self-study to pass the college entrance examination and become a judge after graduation. For example:

> Judge A, female, born in 1960. She was sent to rural area to work for one year after having graduated from middle high school, and was enlisted as a soldier when she was 18 years old. Two years later, she was discharged from active military service and entered into the court to do "internal business" (receiving and sending documents, typing, and taking care of files) for 10 years. During this period, she graduated from university through self-study and turned to work as a judge in a criminal tribunal. She is now taking the examinations necessary for bachelor's degree.

> Judge B, male, born in 1961. He was enlisted in 1979 and was a driver in the army. He was discharged from the military service in 1983. Since the criminal tribunal court needed a driver, he was recruited as a driver in the court. He became a cadre in 1995, firstly took part in trials in criminal tribunal, then worked as a clerk, and is now an assistant judge.

Judge C, male, Miao ethnic minority, born in 1958. He joined the army in 1978 and was discharged from military service in 1982 when he entered the judicial bureau to work. A few years later, he was transferred to the political section of the court and later to an administrative office where he was engaged in legal publicity, file arrangement, and document receiving and sending.

Judge D, male, born in 1954. He joined the army when he was 16 years of age. Three years later (when he was 19 years of age), he asked to be demobilized since his father died and he had to take care of his mother, brother, and sister as the eldest son of the family (he was regarded as "future cadre" in the army and was going to be promoted to military officer). When he returned to his hometown, he joined the court to work. Starting as a clerk, he used to work as the head of the people's tribunal and head of the civil tribunal. He is now the vice president of a county-level city court. He is extremely familiar with works related to the court and knows well the cases that the court used to try in the past (e.g., during the interview, he mentioned without referring to any record that "the total number of civil cases tried by the court in the year of 1985 was 264, while the number was 2860 in 1988, which increased by 10 fold"). He had a thorough analysis of the courts and sharp and deep criticism against the malpractices of the current systems of the court. In 1986 and 1987, he took the initiative to propose court reform and suggested "hearing cases outside the court and exploiting case resources." The result was good, and the court was rated as the most outstanding court of the whole province. During his interview, he criticized himself by saying that this road was a dead end and "cases must be heard in court." I would like to note that he is exceptionally intelligent:

I should say that these people are no different at all from other people who have no military experience but have entered the court and gradually become judges—I will talk about this later. After their many years and even 20 years of working experience in the courts, it is hard for you to define them by their military experience or use essentialism to describe them, as if it is hard for you to use "company commander" to describe Holmes. I often regard myself as a soldier, but the Central Military Committee would never consider giving me the military rank of air vice-marshal.

The so-called problem of demobilized soldiers entering court is actually the problem of demobilized army cadres entering the court. All these people are army officers with all kinds of posts demobilized to local places which are normally in their hometown or the hometown of their wives (it often depends on which place has better living conditions or other conditions). The state has a responsibility to find a place for those people. When they get into the court, they are normally given a certain administrative post according to their previous administrative level in the army (in the past 10 years, it has been usually the case that they are given place lower than their actual level); and what's more to our research is that they are given a corresponding judicial post. As far as we know, in the basic-level court, it is normally the case that platoon leaders are arranged as clerks, company commanders as assistant judges, and people above battalion commanders as judges. These demobilized soldiers are actually a kind of burden to court system.

But if you analyze carefully, the reason that the court sees them as a burden is not because these people used to be soldiers and could not undertake internal works of the court. After all, works inside China's court are versatile, instead of being just trials alone. The main burden is actually that those people have to share all kinds of resources inside the court system which are originally very rare and most of which are administrative posts, operational posts, and other symbolic resources as well as other accompanying material resources. The second is that demobilized army cadres who have occupied operational posts cannot exercise or exercise effectively corresponding responsibilities (e.g., they have the title of judge but cannot try cases independently). For this reason, if the president of a certain court refuses demobilized army cadres to enter the court, it does not mean that he or she is open-minded or that he or she welcomes law-school graduates. He or she may just not welcome anyone who wants to share the existing resources of the court. We must see through this kind of worldly, practical, wisdom-based lens.

Do demobilized soldiers want to join the court? We have interviewed several judges and covered this issue, but there was no final conclusion. The main reason is that the situation in modern China changes so fast. A judge who went to the court to work in the mid-1970s before the end of the Cultural Revolution said that they did not have much choice at that time and was assigned to work in the "team of political works."[6] Because their business was related, he went to the court to work. After the mid-1980s, with China's disarmament of 1 million troops, a large number of army cadres were demobilized to local places and it was then that demobilized army cadres became an issue. Certainly, if demobilized cadres had specialties or techniques, choosing a job was basically not a problem. They normally could be assigned to a job which is close to their original specialty. The problem is that the majority of demobilized cadres could not find a specialty which fit in with their vocational training (not that they have "no specialty" as we are used to imagining, but they only had experience leading soldiers). Under such circumstances, it is said that only a few demobilized army cadres were willing to go to work in private enterprises. To them, they would not ever be signed to enterprises with profits. If they went to enterprises with no good performance, it would mean that their jobs were not stable. Moreover, it would be difficult for them to demonstrate their talents in enterprises. At least until the beginning of the 1990s, the first choice of the mobilized army cadres was party and government organizations, especially those like the department of organization, which is in charge of human resources and has real power. The second choice was administrative and law enforcement agencies like those in charge of industry, commerce, and taxes, which not only have certain power, but also are relatively well paid. Those ranked rather far behind were public security organs, procuratorates, and courts. Even in the "political and law system," courts are normally not the first but the last choice, since courts are not as powerful as public security organs and their works are not that similar to those in the army. For some interviewees, at least until the beginning of the 1990s, demobilized army cadres who had entered courts generally had

[6]During the Cultural Revolution, local governments were taken power and a "Revolutionary Committee" was established under which "team of political works" was a main administrative with huge jurisdiction, including the department of organization, department of propaganda, public security, and court system of today's party committee.

few local acquaintances, nor were they well connected. Certainly, this kind of situation may have changed in recent years. There may be more demobilized army soldiers who are willing to work in enterprises or courts.

10.2.2 University or College Graduates

Before the 1990s, university or college graduates who worked in courts were basically assigned by the state. In recent years, since it has become a two-way selection for university graduates to find a job, it is usually the case that graduates contact courts themselves and courts accept their applications. There are also a few university or college graduates who have been transferred to courts from their original jobs, and they are seldom law graduates.

The basic-level courts of areas with different economic and cultural development levels have different ratios of such people. In a certain county-level city court on the Jianghan Plain as mentioned above, there were only 2 people there who were law-school graduates. One graduated from the department of criminal investigation of a certain political and law college and later became director of a certain people's tribunal. When we went the court where he worked to do research, the president highly recommended his tribunal for us to see. This showed that the court attached great importance to him. During our conversation at his tribunal, we saw clearly that he was a rising star in the court. The other one was a female who graduated from the department of law of a certain political and law college in 1992. In the spring of 1998, when we conducted our research, she was already the deputy head of the civil tribunal of the court. The civil tribunal is usually the most important tribunal (not one of the most important tribunals) in basic-level courts, since it actually undertakes the responsibility of guiding the trial of people's tribunals which scatter across different villages, and is very similar to "the instance of appeal" of different people's tribunals in some sense. During the interview, the head of civil tribunal regarded her as the "talented lady" of the court, since she was the only one who had published two "papers" in the whole court. Obviously, she was also given an important role in the court.

We did not study other university graduates who had transferred from other professions or were demanded by judges in those courts. Among judges in our interview who received trainings at Zhongnan Political and Law School, several were transferred from other professions. We got to learn of some basic situations from the following four judges:

> Judge A, current vice president of the court, judge. Born in 1951, he was a worker-peasant-soldier student and began to study at university in 1975 (started work). After he had graduated and returned to his hometown in 1978, he worked in the county party committee office and first became a clerk, then a secretary, and later an office administrator of the county party committee. In February, 1997, he was transferred to be the vice president of the county court in charge of finance, administrative affairs, and human resources.

The reason for his transfer was that "there had never been anyone retiring from the office of county party committee." According to him, persons of his age normally do not have prospects for promotion in the county, and he has to be prepared for his retirement. At the same time, he learned some real business practices in the court.

Judge B was born in 1972. He graduated with a degree in political education in 1995, when he should have reported to the county educational committee and been assigned to work in the village middle school as a teacher. However, he managed to get into the court himself. In the spring of 1997, when we were conducting our research, he had already become assistant judge (in less than 2 years). His father was then the vice party secretary, but he claimed that he was not on good terms with his father and his father didn't help him in getting the job. He didn't deny, however, that his ability to get this job in the court and his promotion weren't somewhat related to his father's position. At least, "other people may think like this" he commented. He didn't often agree with other judges. During our conversation, he repeatedly called other judges as "they," but approved of us researchers and referred to us as "we." In addition, he said he was alone in the court and couldn't find anyone to talk to. He repeatedly stressed that his "personality" was different. He mainly worked in the court since he didn't want to teach.

Judge C, assistant judge, born in 1966. He graduated from a certain mercantile marine college and worked with an ocean shipping company in a certain metropolitan area. Because his family needed him to take care of (but I guessed that what was more important might be his personal problem of marriage, since it was extremely difficult for seamen to get married; he claimed that he "got married in less than two months after he was transferred back to his hometown"), he was transferred back to his village in 1992. He first worked for the county government, and then passed the recruitment examination for the court and became the deputy head of a certain people's tribunal, where he was actually in charge of the tribunal (the head of tribunal would soon retire). He was efficient, smart, honest, and was very familiar with laws which were often applied in rural society and was familiar with local conditions. It was said that he couldn't attend training based on his present professional level and he "fought for it." When we asked why he wanted to work in court, he said: "works in court are simple while works in the county are miscellaneous."

Judge D was born in 1962. He joined the army in 1980 (enrolled by the military academy) and worked on an island base after graduation. In the end of 1990's, he was demobilized and returned to his hometown where he worked as deputy head of the administrative tribunal. He was demobilized because he and his wife lived separately for too long a time and he was working on the sea island where there was little chance for promotion—but why did he choose to work in court? He didn't give a direct answer on this, but he said that "(at that time) only a few demobilized military cadres wanted to work in enterprises where jobs were not stable and their working experience in the army couldn't be used."

As far as university graduates are concerned, except from higher academic degrees, they do not have any advantages compared with demobilized soldiers on their familiarity with courts and trials. Some of them are demobilized soldiers themselves.

In addition, there are also some technical secondary school graduates who can be included in this series. Despite their small numbers, they are still young—and most are clerks or assistant judges. They are quite satisfied being able to work in the court, and at the same time, they are full of fairly realistic ideals. Some of them are able to work in court since they have certain kinds of special relations.

10.2.3 Judges Transferred to Court from Other Places

This can be divided into two categories. The first are those that have been gradually transferred to work in court from other jobs related to law. The following two judges are relatively typical examples:

Judge W, born in 1955. After he graduated from senior high school, he returned to his hometown to work on the farm. He used to work as a production team leader and secretary for a local CPC branch on a production team and on the production brigade from 1976 to 1979. In 1980, he was recruited as a cadre and worked in the community as a judicial assistant (with the main responsibility of mediating all kinds of disputes) for one year. After that, he worked as a semi civil affairs officer (with main responsibilities including formalities like marriage registration and divorce agreement, as well as promoting rural social insurances. In China, at least at the district and county level, civil affairs departments are sometimes put under political and legal system covering public security organs, procuratorial organs, judicial affairs, civil affairs, and immigration [in the Three Gorges Dam area or other places receiving sizable immigrant populations, there are immigration bureaus], and thus courts are slightly related. From 1990 to 1995, he worked as a CPC committee member in charge of organizational work in the village (equals to rural minister of organization without this same title). Starting in June, 1995, he worked in the people's tribunal and was formally transferred into the court system in October when he was appointed as a judge. He worked in the people's tribunal in his village and maintained his original administrative rank, but wasn't given any administrative position in court. When asked why he wanted to be transferred to court, he said that he thinks that the profession of judge has dignity, and that jobs for the government are too miscellaneous for him to have private time, while the works of a judge are rather simple. He also said that serving as a judge allows him to attain professional knowledge and do some real business in court.

Judge X, born in 1962. After he graduated from senior high school, he worked on a farm in his hometown, where he was eventually elected as village committee director. In 1985, he took part in the recruitment examination and became a cadre for the village. In 1990, he was transferred to work in the local people's tribunal. He graduated from a part-time university where he studied law. After several promotions and transfers, he now works as the head of certain people's tribunal.

Judges in the other category have been transferred to the court as leaders and work as the president or vice president of court. The above-mentioned judge A is an example. Another two examples are as follows:

Judge Y, born in 1958. He was enrolled in the public security school after graduating from senior high school in 1976, and then worked as a public security officer after graduation when he "did almost everything" until he worked as head of the department for preliminary inquiries. Later he was transferred to the party school of the municipal party committee (at the county level) as a teacher. In 1987, he was transferred to the judicial bureau as a deputy director and was in charge of law popularization for "the second five years." He was transferred as vice president of procuratorate in 1989 and as vice president (the 4th president in charge) of his court, as well as judge, in 1994 where he was in charge of the administrative tribunal, executive tribunal, and trial supervision tribunal. He is very familiar with works in the public security organ, judicial bureau, procuratorate, and court, and has all related regulations and systems at hand. He has lots thoughts and ideas on many issues regarding the court, and is candid and extremely smart.

> Judge Z, born in 1950's. He has always worked at the grass-root level, starting as a production team leader for the village CPC committee secretary. His village was the wealthiest village in the county. It was said that even the county had to "beg him" for money, and that he was the most prestigious village CPC committee secretary in the county. He didn't have any experience in law or the judiciary in a narrow sense. He was transferred to the court as president in 1994 mainly because the prior president held a position at the vice county major level and he was promoted in this way. Other judges we had interviewed all believed that he was very capable and that his arrival had greatly elevated the position of court in the county, since it became easier for them to ask for money and people from the county. In the people's congress, the report of the court received the highest degree of satisfaction and other organizations normally didn't dare to interfere in the case trials of the court. Several judges, a law school graduate included, claimed to us with rough meaning that "it is not necessarily bad for the court to have its first hand be a non-legal professional."

Apart from these two categories, there is actually a category of people transferred to court from other jobs locally. In the words of some judges, these people have been "squeezed" into the court under all kinds of names and titles, since they are rather well-connected in the local area and even in the court. Those people could not stay longer at their previous jobs either because their "professional level was too low," or because the social benefits were not as good, or because they were handicapped (certain policies of the "International Day of Disabled Persons" had to be implemented), or because they were relatives or children of certain leaders. Because the court is not independent—either in human or financial resources, or because the court had to look for help and did not dare to offend their backstage supporters, it had to accept to recruit those people. Every court had a few of such kinds of people, but no one was willing to say who they were, so we could not get interviews on this.

I didn't follow a strict methodology or have strict sampling when I introduced these judges, but I still believe that they roughly represent the ordinary situations of the basic-level courts in the Province of Hubei at present. As far as the national situation in China is concerned, due to imbalanced development of economy and culture in different regions, judges of basic-level courts in eastern coastal areas may have higher cultural and professional qualities, while judges of Western regions are typically lower. Roughly speaking, there is not much difference. For this reason, I believe that the description here is representative of the general situation of China's basic-level courts. Moreover, considering reasons I will talk about later, it may be difficult for this kind of situation to undergo much change in recent times, and even within the past 20 years. We can thus take this as the basis for further analysis.

10.3 Where Have All the Law-School Graduates Gone?

If comparing the above situation with the ideal judge or court,[7] established based on an incomprehensive understanding of Western judges and courts at present, we have to admit that judges of China's basic-level courts are not satisfactory either in

[7]Please refer to notes 24–26 and their contexts.

their cultural qualities or in their professional level.[8] But what has caused this situation? We can trace this back to the indifference to the law and the rule of law by the Chinese government and governing parties before the time of reform and opening up, as well as insufficient education and training of legal talents. However, it has been 20 years since China started its reform and opening to the outside world, and it has been only 20 years since legal education in China was resumed comprehensively.

According to official statistics, which are obviously not sufficient; since the mid-1980s, the total number of university or college graduates majoring law in China each year has exceeded 10,000. Since the 1990s, China's law education has been developed at an unprecedented speed. Speculating from the enrollment numbers of law school in ordinary universities in 1996, the number of law graduates from universities may reach 37,000 in 2000.[9] The number of law graduates from correspondence and night universities has also been on a dramatic rise since the mid-1980s, which reached 10,000 annually by the end of 1980s. Today, the number

---

[8]Please note that I don't exclude that cultural quality may be related to professional level and integrity, but up till now, I haven't seen any research, home, or abroad that has demonstrated that they have cause-and-effect relationship. It is for this reason that I can't draw the conclusion that corruption issue of China's court system is related to judges' cultural level. In today's China, ethics seems to be often regarded as an issue of knowledge. As a matter of fact, passed experiences (e.g., Qian Zhongshu and Wang Shuo spoke ironically about intellectuals in their novels) and a large number of empirical studies have led to opposite conclusion, "Exposure to moral philosophy may lead educated people to behave less morally than untutored people. … moral reflection does in fact undermine the capacity for moral action" (Richard A. Posner, *The Problematics of Moral and Legal Theory*, Harvard University Press, 1999, p. 7). In his book, Posner has taken a lot of efforts to analyze many related pieces of empirical research which have illustrated this point. One research which may be most touching is that only 70 % of freshmen in the Harvard Law School have expressed that they will be engaged with law related to public interests, while only 2 % of juniors have this same wish (Robert Granfield, *Making Elite Lawyers: Visions of Law at Harvard and Beyond*, Routledge, 1992, p. 48). Posner therefore thinks that the moral education we often talks about is completely useless in terms of improving the morality of students. Morality has nothing to do with knowledge.

In addition, the professional ethics of judiciary in America is actually a kind of law or semi-law. It is a kind of institution and has nothing to do with morality. On the contrary, this kind of professional ethics only aims to tell lawyers how judges will be engaged with certain immoral or morally suspicious action legally. We can see that this kind of professional ethics is put into practice in the press conferences or televised speeches by President Clinton. People asked whether Mr. Clinton had even taken mariguana, and his answer was "I have never violated American law" (later people came out to testify that he used to take mariguana when he studied in the U.K.). Later he said that "I didn't inhale, but just took a little of it." In front of all American viewers, Mr Clinton declared that he "had never had a sexual relationship with Monica Lewinsky). Technically speaking, it was true, since the definition of sexual relationship by American statutes is contact of sexual organs. But the oral sex between Mr. Clinton and Monica Lewinsky obviously belongs to sexual behavior in the eyes of ordinary people.

[9]Department of Planning and Construction of the National Education Commission of People's Republic of China (compiled): "Statistics of Law Students from Regular Institutes of Higher Education," *Educational Statistics Yearbook of China* (1988–1996), People's Education Press, quoting from a secondary source Law Education of China Law Information Center in Peking University, http://www.chinalawinfo.com/.

of those graduates has reached 20,000 each year.[10] This number may not include graduates from higher institutes of politics and law subordinate to the Ministry of Justice and Ministry of Public Security, of which the amount averaged 10,000 people annually.[11] If we assume that an average of 30,000 university and college law students have graduated annually in the last 20 years, then the law students educated by China's law schools are estimated to be among 500,000–550,000. Assuming a quarter of them have entered the court (the rest have jobs related or unrelated to law), then among China's so-called army of "judges" with titles above clerk (court police not included) should amount to about 250,000 people today,[12] at least half of them should have a legal education background from a university or college. According to my estimates, the number of judges in basic-level courts takes up at least 2/3 of the total number of judges in courts around the country, which is about 160,000.[13] Assuming that among the 80,000 judges from above the court of appeals, 2/3 have a formal "academic background" in law (others have an academic background or do not have an official academic background), then there should be at least 60,000–70,000 university or college graduates in law entering China's basic-level courts, which means that in the basic-level courts, at least 1/3 of

[10]"Statistics of Law Students in Correspondence Department of Regular Institutes of Higher Education and Night Universities," same as the previous note.

[11]"Statistics of General Information of Higher Institutes of Politics and Law," same as previous note.

[12]There are no more recent statistics. According to *China Law Yearbook* 1991 and 1992, the total number of judicial people above clerks in people's courts around the country was 182,000 in 1990 and 188,000 in 1991. The number of judicial people above assistant judges was 144,000 in 1990 and 151,000 in 1991. Even considering all factors, there are approximately 250,000 "judges" in China's courts (quote from Judicial Institutes of Peking University Law Information Center http://www.chinalawinfo.com/). Another braver estimate is from the end of 1995, and the total number of court system personnel would reach 292,000 people; please see He Weifang: "Realizing Social Justice through Judiciary", compiled by Xia Yong and etc.: *An Age towards Rights*. This number has been confirmed and *Guangzhou Daily* on October 26, 1999, gave a number of 300,000 judges. But He's estimate includes court police and emphasizes "total number in the court system." If we only calculate the number of judicial people above clerk, then He's estimate is almost the same as mine.

[13]According to Statistics of Administrative Regions Around China (http://www.chinalawinfo.com/), there are 1740 counties and 414 county-level cities in China, and the total number is 2154. If there are 10 people's courts in every county, and 2 judges or assistant judges, 2 clerks in each court, plus about 40 judges, assistant judges, and clerks (3–5 court presidents and vice presidents; 4–7 court reviewer in civil, criminal, economic, appeal, execution, and administrative tribunals; 1–2 people in charge of forensic test, part-time university, disciplinary inspection, and administrative affairs in county courts), then the total number of "judges" in basic-level courts may be 150,000 people. According to some county or court leaders we interviewed in our research, the number of people in basic-level courts is about 100–150 people. Excluding some workers and court police, this estimate is not far from the real situation. Please refer to "Court Management is a Big Topic" *People's Judicature*, Issue 12, 1994, p. 7. This article claims that there are 18,000 people's tribunals around China, and the "cadres" in tribunals take up almost a quarter of "cadres" of courts around China (with total number of 250,000 people). *China Law Yearbook* 1998 (p. 138) claims that there are 15,000 people's tribunals in urban and rural areas.

judges are university or college graduates in law. If this is really the case, the legal training and professional qualities of judges in China's basic-level courts should be far beyond the situation we ended up seeing during our research.

I have, many times, heard people complaining that the current situation in the courts was only because people with formal training in law institutes cannot get into courts and the procuratorate system, while demobilized soldiers have taken up the jobs of law-school graduates. Is this really the case? It does happen occasionally, but the question is whether this is a common case? Or is this a common case in basic-level courts? These questions must be examined. According to my understanding, this kind of situation often happens in relatively big cities and rather developed regions. It is also more common in bigger cities and wealthier regions, and at least in courts above the intermediate level.[14] In the basic-level courts of our field research, there is none that falls into this category. During the interviews, at least some vice presidents in some courts claimed that the courts were "looking for talent" and hoped that graduates of law would go to work in their courts and they were vexed about not having graduates from regular law schools.

What they said was not untrue, since at the time when the leadership was required to be professional, knowledgeable, and young, there must have been some young members with rather high academic backgrounds in the leadership, which is a political requirement from the CPC Central Committee. Otherwise, the leadership cannot get approval from the higher authorities. As for what is mentioned previously, there were only two graduates from regular academies or politics and law in courts of our research and both of them were put in an important position. It seems that to people of their age with no regular legal training in those courts, this requirement is very important. The so-called situation that the court pushes law graduates aside does not exist as a kind of normal situation at least in the basic-level courts. It is absolutely fabricated and out of imagination.

Thus, the question remains: Where have all the law graduates been?

We must analyze and discuss this problem in detail. My basic view is that in the past 10 years, due to all kinds of interests in a broader sense, law-school graduates normally refused to work in the court system, especially those basic-level courts in the central and Western regions, unless they had no other choices. The basic logic of analysis is that as the labor market is becoming increasingly open, as well as the elimination of the system of planned work assignment, law-school graduates, and other graduates who have already worked in court have more options, which have better interests compared with jobs in basic-level courts, and the difference is quite big. It is just this enormous difference in income that has made law-school graduates, old and young, move toward the big, coastal cities, with higher income and better professional prospects. During this process, the basic-level courts have lost

[14]Nowadays, it is even difficult for PhD graduates whose native hometowns are not in Beijing to enter into court. Last year, a graduate with master degree from Law School of Peking University could only find a job in the government of certain village but he wanted to work in Beijing. I can't and would never look at the whole country from the same perspective, although people usually deduce situations of the whole country from things happening before their eyes.

their advantages. They are not only unable to attract new law-school graduates, but, even without other reasons, they cannot keep those graduates who are already working in the court (please note that the two law-school graduates we found in the county-level courts entered the basic-level court before the "socialist market economy" was proposed).

We can give some detailed analysis. First is the income. Law-school graduates will have higher income if they work in courts of big and middle sized cities than in basic-level courts. The income difference may not only come from the file wages of the state, but more importantly comes from the benefit and bonus inside the court, as well as "tributes paid" by courts of "lower level" in all kinds of ways. Judges of courts of "higher level" sometimes receive gifts given by judges of courts of "lower level." In addition, it has never occurred to me that courts above provincial level ever delay paying wages to judges. But among judges of our research and interview, since some counties have very tight finance, there are complaints about delaying paying wages. Some judges in certain counties even have not received the full amount of their wages for 9 months in a year.

It is the same from the perspective of promotion. Law-school graduates will have more opportunities for promotion and development prospects if they enter into courts with levels higher than the High Court, due to China's administrative level system. If they work in the Supreme Court, they will soon become officials of the "section leader level" and then in 5–10 years reach the director level. If they work in the basic-level courts, even after a lifetime of busy work and attaining the position of president of their court, they are still only of the "deputy director" level. This is the career summit for many law graduates who have entered into basic-level courts. More than that, the opportunities of promotion in higher courts are not exactly the same as those in the basic-level courts. In the latter, this kind of symbolic resource is more rare and with fiercer competition. A "tribunal director" in the basic-level court, who is not really a junior government official in our eyes, may have to wait for 5–10 years before attaining a promotion, and it also depends on opportunities. Some judges complained to us that judges of higher courts are only "born in a better family" and thus become senior judges. Economic benefits are also related to job titles. In face of those two choices, it is natural that law-school graduates will choose to work in Beijing, provincial capitals, and cities where there are more prospects for promotion, or choose those places with more developed economies if the conditions are the same, whether they have to work in the basic-level courts or not.

Under the conditions of the modern market economy, the court is not the only access point for employment for law-school graduates. Through the civil service examination, students can enter into the party and political institutions at all levels from the central authority to local areas and are engaged in research regarding related politics and law or other professions. They will have a better chance at promotion and higher incomes compared to judges in basic-level courts. Alternatively, they can go to universities or institutions of scientific research (in recent years, legal education has become quite popular. There are law faculties everywhere and are normally located in central urban areas) where they do not have very high income or prospects of promotion, but they have more leisure time and freedom. By having a part-time job as a lawyer, they will have higher monetary and non-monetary incomes than law-school graduates in basic-level courts. Even if they do not work as a lawyer, they still can indulge themselves in self-admiration and enjoy the freedom of not keeping office hours. If they do not like politics or teaching, law-school graduates can also work for private enterprises. In many places with relatively developed economies, they can also work in foreign enterprises with a monthly income 5–10 times those of judges in basic-level courts. Even excluding influences of the consumption level, it is quite normal for their incomes to be 3–5 times higher. Nowadays, law-school graduates can also be self-employed, either as a lawyer or a businessman. Although the work is tiring and requires asking for help from time to time, it has relatively more freedom and higher income than judges. Their incomes can be hundreds of times higher than judges of basic-level courts.

In addition, there are other non-monetary or non-promotion-related factors, such as the cultural lives in medium-size cities and regions with developed economy, and education for children. Those intangible benefits are forces that attract law-school graduates.

In comparison, there is almost nothing attracting law-school graduates to basic-level courts. Factors related to idealism among law graduates are decreasing steadily, if not dramatically. Please note that I'm not saying today's students have no ideals or that graduates of the past had more ideals, nor am I speaking highly of ideals of university graduates in the 1950s and 1960s. In my eyes, even in the ideals of the previous one or two generations, there are also motivations of cynical benefits apart from a little romanticism, such as the determination to do something that is really outstanding, or to change the features of a certain village's circumstance, which can also be regarded as plans motivated by personal interests. This kind of personal plan may help law graduates and other talents to move toward the basic level of China's society objectively. However, this kind of motivation mechanism of devotion for ideals is almost gone or has become really weak nowadays. Today's interest allocation mechanisms are not at all in favor of law-school graduates who go to the basic-level courts and stay there. Moreover, I will later analyze from the perspective of knowledge as to why law-school graduates won't stay in the basic-level courts long, even if they occasionally enter them.

My analysis here is not simply a kind of coarse deduction of utilitarianism, but is supported by many non-systematic empirical facts. For example, among my classmates, there is none working at the basic-level courts, and only one is working as a chief procurator for certain intermediate procuratorates today. Others are working in Beijing and other capital cities or metropolitan areas such as Shenzhen or overseas. Most of them are engaged in professions such as lawyers, businessmen, government officials, teachers, scientists, or researchers. Among students who graduated from the Law School of Peking University between 1996 and 1999 and found a job after graduation (others went to graduate school or went to study abroad), 59 % of the 1996 graduates and 55 % of 1999 graduates stayed in Beijing. None of 1996 graduates went to work in courts below district level, while 7 of the graduates in 1999 went to work there. 80 % and a higher percentage of the 1999 graduates went to work in the central or local government departments, national, private, or foreign enterprises, or law firms. Only 3 of the 1996 graduates (only 3 %) and 9 of 1999 graduates (only 9 %) entered into the public court system.[15]

In the two counties of our research, the situations are similar. In the downtown of certain county-level city on the Jianghan Plain, we were told that among 40 lawyers, only 8 were graduates from regular universities of politics and law, and one of them was the husband of a woman judge who worked as the deputy head of the civil tribunal. According to this female tribunal head, her husband was working in the court originally but later quitted his job and became a lawyer. For her, one found an "external" job which was not reliable but had a high income, while the other worked in the court with a reliable job and an opportunity to take care of home. This is a good combination. In a certain county in the west of Hubei Province, although there were only 8 lawyers in the whole county, one of them was a law-school graduate from the law faculty of the South-Central University for Nationalities. However, the court system of this county did not have even one graduate from a regular university.

The vice presidents of other courts also told us that even at the end of the 1980s and early 1990s, law graduates who were allocated to work in the basic-level courts also resigned and chose to "take on adventures" in Shenzhen, Hainan, Wuhan, or other big cities one after another. Starting in 1992, when the reform and opening up commenced and the socialist economy was being built, many of these "adventurers" "did quite well."

Those situations have demonstrated to us that the fundamental problem nowadays seems not to be that there are not enough law-school graduates (it is certainly possible that there are still not enough), or they are unable to go into the basic-level courts, but that even when they get into the basic-level courts, those courts still do not have enough resources to keep those graduates. This kind of situation exists in many medium- and big-sized cities and in courts or other government departments of Beijing. As far as I know, many postgraduates and PhD graduates from the Law School of Peking University only have a chance to enter into Beijing municipal courts and procuratorates, or even districts and county courts, and procuratorates, and the competition for entering into those institutions is fierce. What is more important is that many of them are not going to devote themselves to the profession of judicial trial wholeheartedly from the very beginning, but see those positions as a transition or a springboard for staying in Beijing or switching to another job. It is also a best place for their internship toward legal practice after graduation. This phenomenon commonly exists in other places with relatively developed economies. For those graduates, their plan is to work for a few years in the court first, and after getting acquainted with legal practices, they will, in their own words, "go out" and become a lawyer and find another job.

---

[15] I would like to thank two teachers Gong Wendong and Han Liu for offering me those related materials.

It is just because they have suffered this kind of "loss" so many times that courts and procuratorates in Beijing and other cities, as well as many party and political institutions, now are more cautious in selecting law-school graduates who apply for jobs. They also set out tougher conditions and requirements. Many law-school graduates who are looking for jobs thus have a feeling that courts do not want "law-school graduates" and then make an inaccurate judgment that demobilized soldiers have taken the jobs of law-school graduates. As long as those graduates put themselves in the position of courts and other government institutions, observe their own motivations, and be a little more just, they will notice that this kind of situation has been caused by themselves (or strictly speaking, by the previous law-school graduates) to a certain degree.

I'm saying this not as a complaint, but as an observation. Under the circumstance of market economy, everyone has the right to choose or change their profession. From a long-term point of view, this kind of freedom of choice is good for society. However, we must understand that the choices of the market have always been and should be two-way. Academic background has never been and should not be the only standard of choice. Loyalty, faithfulness, devotion to profession, stable expectations, as well as knowledge and skills required by the employers are important standards for choosing labor force in the market, and they will become increasingly important. In summary, what I want to emphasize is that judge is not necessarily a very attractive job for the majority of law-school graduates in today's China,[16]not to mention judge in basic-level courts. In China, judges are not officials; they are another kind of civil servant.

Where have all the law-school graduates gone? The answer is that in today's reformed market economy, law-school graduates are pursuing jobs and opportunities which are more beneficial to their development and happiness. This may require us to adopt a series of actions to make law-school students return back to the courts or enter the courts more often. Even as those actions are taken, I assume that this kind of situation is unlikely to be changed within a short time.

[16]There is one example that can more or less illustrate this point. In 1998, as a gesture of reform, the Supreme Court openly recruited 10 senior judges from the society. It demanded "first class lawyers, law professors, law researchers and legal workers from legislature, political-legal organs, administrative law enforcement organs whose registered permanent residence is in Beijing, aged 35–50, with administrative rank above director level" ("The Supreme Court Openly Recruited Senior Judges for the First Time," *People's Daily*, March 2, 1999, p. 3). Although there are at least more than 1000 lawyers and legal professors who are qualified in Beijing, at the time when the scheduled registration period ended, there were 3 people that applied and all of them were from outside Beijing (thus, we cannot say for sure but there is still possibility that some of them want to use this job as a springboard for entering Beijing), and the Supreme Court had to prolong the registration period. It had become a joke, but it could demonstrate clearly and sharply how attractive senior judges in the Supreme Court to law-school graduates in today's China. The time that "wealth cannot match nobility" is ending, if it has not gone yet.

10.4 "Liberation Army as a School of Revolution"

It is against the aforementioned background that demobilized soldiers and others without any judicial experience have entered the basic-level courts to become a reluctant replacement for institutionally qualified court members. I will demonstrate later that before there were a large number of people with high-quality law degrees or judicial training to replace them, these displaced soldiers were not a bad replacement for the basic-level courts in today's China.

During interviews with some court leaders, they all said that they hoped there would be more university students with regular legal training working in the basic-level courts (I'm not sure whether this was a gesture toward researchers, but I don't believe so considering they often face order-like requirements from their superiors to educate leaders in waiting and arranging leadership). However, when there are not any students and other conditions are roughly the same, court leaders are more willing to have Demobilized army cadres or demobilized soldiers instead of personnel from county CPC committee, county government, or other departments.

One interviewee (vice president of court) mentioned three reasons for this willingness almost without thinking: demobilized army cadres have strong sense of organization with little relation to local areas and, thus, do not cause problems; secondly, their qualities and standards are higher than local cadres; thirdly, they are more willing to learn professional knowledge and devote themselves to intensive study. Normally speaking, they are competent enough to do the job after working in the court for one and a half years.

Such an answer is somewhat unexpected to me. I originally have one premise: People from rural society are more familiar with rules in rural society and may be more pragmatic, and consider local situations more instead of simply applying legal texts mechanically, whether they resolve disputes or just apply rules, but military experience attaches importance to organizational discipline and emphasizes obeying orders. Those features may be somewhat good in regard to strict enforcement of the law, but in terms of settling disputes in daily life, they are unlikely to have more advantages compared with cadres from rural society. After careful observation, thinking, and analysis, I have found that those three points are real and imply many meanings.

First of all, the majority of China's transferred army cadres and demobilized soldiers would return to their hometown when leaving the army, so they are all local (almost all judges of basic-level courts are locally born and raised, which can partially explain why local protectionism is relatively common in China's courts. I will discuss the disadvantage of this point later) and have all kinds of local connections. However, they have been out to make a living for a few years, and some even for ten to twenty years, which has made them separated and somewhat distanced from their local society of acquaintances for a relatively long time. Inside the armies of China, the relationships of acquaintances or of villagers are sometimes considered, but according to my experience in the army and the requirements to successfully run the army, Chinese armies nowadays have grown to be firmly against soldiers attaching too much importance on relationships of fellow countrymen. Every army will recruit soldiers from different provinces. When dividing classes, they will put soldiers from different regions together with an aim to break up the geographic or regional views of soldiers. In the army, as well as in the region where the army is stationed, soldiers must learn to associate with locals. This has promoted the exchange of information, which has, to a certain degree, changed the narrow views of different regions, as well as the general view of human relations. This is a kind of modern discipline which is very important. The impersonality of human relations is one of the most fundamental features of the modern rule of law, and it is also an important prerequisite social condition for modern rule of law to function.

The situations of local cadres are far more complicated. Many cadres have been in the modern government system for a long time and are willing to accept this modern discipline unconsciously, but in China's modern society, cadres have become less able to move around when it comes to the basic level. The more important the relationships of acquaintance are, the more difficult it is to get rid of them or to avoid personal consideration. In a county, almost every person is connected to one another, and this is even more so in villages. For this reason, generally speaking, cadres at the grassroots level have a strong sense of locality and an intensive network of relationships. As long as modern law gets into the network of acquaintance, it will be difficult for it to function.[17] In comparison, demobilized soldiers, especially transferred army cadres, have far more simple human relations and they would not be easily troubled by human relations. As a result, they at least appear to have a stronger "sense of organization," more stick to principle and have a higher level of regard for policy and law. Please note I'm not saying that transferred army soldiers are better in terms of moral quality or really have a stronger sense of organization. I'm just saying that because they have less of these local relations, there will be relatively fewer people asking for favors. Even if there are people asking for extra help, since the displaced military are not as deeply connected to them, it will be easier for them to refuse.

On the other hand, as previously mentioned, transferred army cadres who have entered into court usually do not have strong interpersonal relations in the locality they are assigned to. They have been gone from their hometown for many years, and they lack enough resources of interpersonal relations to take action. For this reason, they have to and usually do rely on leaders of the court more. For court presidents, those judges or cadres are easier to lead compared to people with complicated local relations and even backstage supporters. They would not cause accidents as often and thus have a strong sense of organization. This kind of strong sense may be related to synchronized goose-stepping, marching, and the strict enforcement of orders and prohibitions in the army—but they are not that closely related. For me, what is more closely related to this is the environment that "we

[17]Donald J. Black, *The Behavior of Law*, translated by Tang Yue, Suli, China University of Politics and Law Press, 1994.

are from every corner of the country" (Mao Zedong, "To Serve the People") in the army, as well as the interpersonal interactions in this modern "society of strangers." In this environment, he or she has to learn a way of association different from a society of acquaintances. This kind of unconscious nurturing has made soldiers accept the kind of modernization mentioned by Foucault somewhat more easily than compared to local cadres.

Second is the high quality of personnel. This is also very much related to the environment of army. In China's rural society, people stay in one place for a long time in order to get used to their local lives. This will make people able to concentrate on people and things in local areas. Things happening on the radio or TV are remote and seldom related to local life. For this reason, many intellectuals feel lonely when they work in the basic-level courts. This is not because basic-level rural society is actually lonely. Loneliness is the creation of loners themselves, as well as their unfamiliarity with the culture and experience of others. As a matter of fact, villagers, citizens in a small county, or even basic-level cadres have a whole set social system of their own, as well as their own local concerns. They will discuss somebody that "has an affair with someone," which couple had a fight last night, and other intimate subjects. Intellectuals are lonely only because the world they care about is not the world villagers or basic-level cadres care about. They have a different world of awareness. The intellectuals may care about the death of Princess Diana and the issues of privacy and freedom of speech (but rural people will ask, "Who is Princess Diana?"), the new measures of China's reform, as well as "in what direction is China heading?" (But for villagers and basic-level cadres, it may be how much money they have to pay or will receive this year's under the "Three Deductions and Five Plans" programs.)

The majority of soldiers in today's China obviously cannot pay attention to "big events" of the state, society, and world, as intellectuals do—at least in the manner of intellectuals. Upon taking a court position, they are removed from their previous environment of acquaintances. When they are surrounded by strangers, it is impossible for them to talk about things they used to be familiar with (conversation needs similar knowledge on background and topics. Old friends without contact for many years can only connect to each other through recollection of old memories apart from introduction of experiences after separation, for example); or they do not dare to discuss them at ease. In this way, the new and strange environment has not only blocked their previous channel of communication, but also deprived them of conversation resources. It seems as if they have been entrapped in a kind of "prisoner's dilemma" in which they cannot communicate. It is in this place and at this moment that a series of discourse mechanisms and non-discourse mechanisms (including military, political, and cultural experiences) in the modern Chinese army begin to play a role and gradually help them to cross the gap "from an ordinary person to a soldier"(by Mao Zedong).

Many people often emphasize discourse mechanisms such as political studies and ideological education in modern Chinese armies. However, this is not the most important in shaping modern people, as far as I see. The most important is actually a series of functions of non-discourse mechanisms inside the army which are connected to modernization. For example, according to the standards of a soldier in the army, a relatively important mechanism of competition begins to come into play. It helps to maintain some features or identities to their own hometowns which are very important to individuals living in specific communities to a certain degree. In the past, a hometown could be a cultural capital for a person, and it was quite useful. For example, an identity such as the son of a battalion secretary or the son of a village head has been greatly devaluated or even become worthless in the army. People whose surname is Zhang might be a minority in the village of Li and are told by their fathers not to make trouble and to give grounds to people whose surname is Li whenever possible. When in the army, however, apart from a tiny minority of sons and daughters of cadres at a very high level, this does not work. In the modern military, a set of institutional rules begin to play a role. There are almost no commodities here, but in terms of emphasizing the competition of personal abilities, it is very similar to the capitalist commodity society which cuts off all kinds of feudalist restraints, as analyzed by Marx and Engels in The Communist Manifesto.[18] Here, we emphasize the competition of personal abilities and specialties under military rules (whether one can shoot accurately, throw hand grenades far enough, keep an orderly queue, act fast enough, or use a computer well enough). Moreover, rules here are also common, and a modern strict hierarchy caste system is used instead of the "patterns of different sequences" in traditional Chinese society (as said by Fei Xiaotong). Even other dialects have become a real issue—you have to learn or at least understand mandarin, while still maintaining a local dialect. This is a brand-new system and social environment where there is actually a kind of training for a modern legal setting. According to military standards, a kind of personality or quality which is actually more similar to modern individualism (emphasizing personal abilities) is fostered here in the apparent collectivism. It is just during this process that modern Chinese armies, to many modern Chinese, are "a revolutionary school" as mentioned by Mao Zedong.

Another important reason that transferred army cadres have good qualities for court is that in modern China, the promotion system inside the army before the 1980s had been an important talent selection mechanism in modern China, especially among military cadres below the middle level. During the Cultural Revolution, since there were no other means of employment, it was one of the best (if not the best) ways-out for both urban and rural educated young people. This kind of special social status has enabled the army to obtain a large number of talented people who were outstanding, at least culturally and intellectually for quite a long time. After reform and opening up, due to the resumption of the college entrance examination system, there were more opportunities for employment in the city and the army therefore became less attractive to young and educated

[18]The bourgeoisie, wherever it has got the upper hand, has put an end to all feudal, patriarchal, and idyllic relations. It has pitilessly torn asunder the motley feudal ties that bound man to his "natural superiors," and has left remaining no other nexus between man and man than naked self-interest, than callous "cash payment." The Communist Manifesto, *Selected Collection of Marx and Engels*, People's Publishing House, 1994, p. 275.

people in the city. But to many educated people who live in villages, especially in the central and Western regions with relatively undeveloped economies that are unable to go to the college either due to failure on the entrance examination or due to a lack of financial resources, joining the army is still a rather important way out which may change their destiny. In this sense, it is still an important mechanism for selecting talent in modern Chinese society.

Since the army must be ready to face a ruthless war environment at any time, the selection mechanism of bold people and cadres is basically a kind of strict merit-oriented system. It may not necessarily be the best to select cadres only in terms of intelligence in the army, but it is normally the best in terms of the comprehensive demands of the army. Those basic-level army cadres selected for promotion are usually educated, rather smart and flexible, and must have certain abilities in regard to organization and handling business, as well as a certain charisma. They must also be rather eloquent and deterrent, enjoy good health, and even have rather handsome looks (I have never met army cadres who have wry mouths and are skew-eyed, stooped, or stammer). However, all these features are actually connected or compatible with certain qualities needed by judges who are engaged with trial and mediation in basic-level courts, as I will analyze in the next chapter.

I am not denying that there are also unhealthy or maybe even severe tendencies regarding establishing relationships inside the army, but compared with a society of acquaintances in a rural area, the army is basically a place where one can compete fairly according to the rules. This is especially the case in the field forces. It is just because of this that cadres selected from the soldiers, normally speaking, had qualities higher than ordinary demobilized soldiers before their status as cadre is fostered and selected by the military academy, although not everybody thinks it fair. It does not mean that the selection mechanisms and standards of the army are commonly applicable to other professions (as a matter of fact, it can be said that I myself am a person eliminated from this process, although this kind of elimination is not necessarily bad, either to me or to the legal research in which I'm engaged today). The army can only choose cadres according to its own standards. It is through this kind of selection that we must also recognize in the ordinary sense that soldiers and demobilized army cadres actually have more advantages compared to ordinary people when they have equivalent education levels. This kind of situation was already quite obvious when the Cultural Revolution had just ended. At that time, among students of liberal arts who studied in the university, those who were soldiers or had military experience largely outnumbered those who had been workers in the city or educated young people who went to the countryside. I recall that among the 60 people in our class, more than 1/3 were veterans or enlisted soldiers. I'm not singing the praises of the army, but analyzing why military experience at that time was enough for those relatively remarkable young people to stand out is a worthwhile question. Among cadres at the battalion or company level who were transferred to local courts in the 1980s and even the beginning of the 1990s, the majority entered the army during or at the end of the Cultural Revolution.

Even if we take one step back and assume that I'm the president of a court, when facing unfamiliar demobilized army soldiers and cadres who have been transferred from certain department of the county whom I'm also unfamiliar with, how can I make prejudgment? I can at least be sure that the demobilized soldiers will definitely have no serious disabilities or bad experiences (if there are, I will have reason to refuse them), or at least there will not be people who cannot speak clearly or are totally illiterate! This alone has reduced the expenses for collecting and confirming information related to the qualities of those two cadres.

Thirdly, transferred army soldiers are generally more willing to study legal knowledge than cadres transferred from local areas. Most transferred army soldiers were aged 35–45 when they entered the people's court at the basic level. After many years in the army, they were fully aware that they would be entering into a completely new and strange environment, where they were unfamiliar with people or places and there would be nobody or only a few people for them to rely on, except for those that they had some very strong relationship (but people with strong relationships would normally not be transferred to the court, at least before the mid-1990s). On the contrary, they had a feeling of depending on others or seeing others' faces for a living. Transferred army cadres also know that "things are complicated in local areas." Local leaders speak passionately upon their reception, but you cannot take their words seriously. Those in charge are more important than county magistrates, and you cannot make a living in a local area by following state polices targeted at "transferred army cadres." Transferred army cadres also know that things they have been familiar with for many years in the army will no longer work in local areas, and they must start again and can only live well once they become professionally accomplished enough. Finally, demobilization gives those people a feeling that they have started a new life. They were likely moved a lot in the army, where there is not really a home, since nobody can really stay in the army for a lifetime. Upon retiring, they finally settled down now and will likely not move any more. Even if they might not be happy staying in the army, they are now provided the opportunity to start again. Moreover, for people aged 35–45, they are not young, but still not that old—they still have time to strive for a better life and have plenty of social experience. It is because of this mentality of welcoming the big turns of one's life that transferred army cadres are more willing and even more eager to face the challenges of life and work.

One judge whom we interviewed has demonstrated this point. This judge joined the army at the end of 1972 and was engaged in political works for a long time. He used to take part in law popularization and organized law popularization in the army. In 1997, he was demobilized and returned to his hometown where he decided to work in the court. He felt pleased to be able to work in the court.

Q: Do you know that transferred army cadres are actually not that welcomed in this place?

A: I know I'm not welcome here. It takes time. But it is not easy for me to get along with others like this.

Q: You said it takes time. How did you manage?

A: I used to do political works in the army. When I entered the court, they asked me whether I wanted to do administrative works or my own profession. I had past experience in the army, and I had the opportunity to be promoted through my professional specialties. For this reason, I had to learn professional knowledge specific to the local place I was in. Whether one can obtain a firm footing in the court depends on whether he or she has a professional specialty. So I was determined to offer to work in the people's tribunal at the basic level. I would have fewer opportunities to return home if I worked in the people's tribunal, but there were all kinds of cases in the people's tribunal and I would be able to be familiar with—cases that employed both substantive laws and procedural laws within the first year. I would have learned nothing if I had stayed at the administrative office.

Q: Wasn't it difficult for you to handle cases in the people's tribunal if you didn't understand law at all?

A: I had to learn from the very basic level. For example, one case was about a land dispute and the notice of court sessions had to be delivered to the parties concerned. The job was often done by young people but I jumped at the opportunity. After that, I went to the spot to have a look at the land and began to understand things fairly well when dealing with the case. It didn't daunt on me when talking about evidence once in the tribunal.

Q: Is it enough to learn just like this?

A: I had to read books of course, and study at the part-time university of the court system. I also fought for my opportunity to attend training programs. In addition, I ask people a lot of questions. Whenever there is something that is unclear, I will ask others and even clerks. It is not shameful to ask questions now, but if I keep on asking people questions after a few years of working in the courts, it would be shameful indeed. When one has his professional specialty, he can be a lawyer if he doesn't stay in the court.

Frankly speaking, I felt somewhat saddened when hearing what he said. Here was a forty-year-old serviceman who used to lead several hundred soldiers that had such a solemn and stirring mentality of cutting all means of retreat and choosing desperate fighting. Even if you have never been a soldier, you can still feel sad for his loss. But this is not my concern. What I care about is what action or results this kind of mentality will lead to.

I must recognize that not every demobilized army cadre has such a strong entrepreneurial mentality and an open heart. I must also admit that, in comparison, most people transferred from local administrative offices to the court do not have such mentality or bearing. The main reason is that local mobility makes people "exhausted." If it is a normal job transfer, it would not cause such turbulence in one's mind. If it is a promotion, one will feel pleased for his promotion, and this will only be a transition (one rarely stays long in the court system). If one has been pushed aside to work here under somebody's nose, then it is not a place to restart one's career. At the county-level party and political system whose environment is very familiar, people are already relatively sure about their own destiny and thus would not have the courage and determination to work hard with high aims. After all, in a place like this, it is not possible to start afresh no matter how enormous efforts are that one has made. People often say "stand up from where you have fallen down." Please think about this: What is special about this sentence? The specialty is that it is difficult for an ordinary person to achieve this in a familiar environment. Only in the face of change which is under one's expectation, but is still impactful, and when one is completely free from a past network of acquaintances (the army)—and thus has the possibility to rebuild other's expectation of him or her—is when one is brave enough to change his or her destiny and a strong desire to define and create oneself can emerge.

Certainly, it is only the personal willingness of transferred army cadres. However, "willingness is infinite, but there are many obstacles to implement it. Aspiration is boundless, but one has to follow reality when taking action."[19] For this reason, my analysis cannot stop at simply the psychology of transferred army cadres, but must also investigate their actual situation. According to our research, almost all judges believe that as long as transferred army cadres work hard enough, they will be able to undertake normal judicial works within one year to one year and half. A graduate from political and law school also admits that transferred army cadres are able to handle cases within one year. "They have their own advantages." The majority of transferred army cadres have been approved by military institutions.

Although this chapter focuses on transferred soldiers, we still have to give a brief analysis on those from other party and political departments. Then, the analysis can be on the situation of judges at basic-level court instead of on transferred soldiers only.

We can see that among those transferred from other departments to the court, some are cadres who have, for a long time, been engaged with works closely related to law. For example, judge Y as previously mentioned went to the school of public security after graduating from senior high school. Following many years of working in the public security sector, he then worked as the deputy director of the Judicial Bureau and deputy chief procurator and later was transferred to court in charge of administrative trial. Although he had no experience working in the courts, especially trials, since he had been working in the "political and legal sector" for a long time, he was not an outsider, but instead considered a professional. Even in the USA where judge's qualities are very much emphasized, it is also natural for people like him to work as a judge.[20] Some other examples include Judge W. After graduating from senior high school, he worked, successively, as a production team leader and party branch secretary of production brigades. After he had been recruited as a cadre, he worked as a judicial assistant for one year and later as a civil affairs officer in the communes and villages for over 8 years, as well as a committee member in charge of organizational work for 5 years. He was extremely familiar with dispute settlements in rural areas. He finally entered into the people's tribunal. Although he does not have any formal academic background in law, he has been engaged in dispute settlement and rule application for most of

[19]William Shakespeare, *Troilus and Cressida*, Act III, Scene ii.

[20]Many federal judges in the USA started as procurators. Among federal magistrates and state judges, many also start as procurators and receive attention from the public and politicians through severe punishment of crimes in the name of "law and order." Of course, all procurators in the USA today must be law-school graduates.

his career. It can be said that rural life experience and work experience trained him to be a trial mediator of civil cases with relevant capabilities and experiences. As a result, when I asked him what the difference between what he does now and what he used to do is, he simply answered that "one has procedures, while the other does not (need) procedures."

Certainly, some people that are transferred to work as judges do not have any prior experience with law, such as Judge A and Judge Z, as previously mentioned. The former had worked in the administrative office of the county party committee for many years and knew nothing about judicial trials. He entered the court simply due to a "same level transfer," since he could not retire from the administrative office of the county party committee. The latter is a locally famous village party secretary who also had no judicial experience. How do we view such people? I myself think that the transfer of those people does indeed go against the improvement of professional qualities and the level of specialization. Moreover, once these people are transferred to the court, since the members of trial committees are always (instead of often) related to their titles, they will have a major impact on judicial works.

But not everyone comes to court at a disadvantage. To meet the demand of practical works, new judges do have to learn some legal and judicial knowledge. After holding their posts for a long time, they will be influenced by what they have seen and heard and will know something about judicial trials. Their working experience and policy level in the past will also help them to have a better grasp of the cases. Just as one judge said, those people who do not understand the profession but have relatively strong relations in the county and mean what they said are usually more "blunt" than the professionals. They are also more capable of using all kinds of power resources to resist all types of external disturbances or coordinating relations to facilitate solutions to problems they face.[21] Because they are not as professional, they show more affection to talents and respect professional cadres (this is actually quite a common social phenomenon; that is, people usually admire their subordinates who have capabilities which they lack while hate those who at the same level). It is in this sense that those people are completely negative toward the development of the court system.

However, even if we put all the advantages together and give adequate consideration to the benefits of having judges from non-legal backgrounds, I still believe that it does more harm than good. My reasons are, firstly, these people do not know the legal profession and thus cannot perform their duties as well as judges and court leaders, and they lack their own opinions. Even if they "love talent," it may turn out that they listen to only one side and are short of imagination and motivation regarding the long-term development of court. Although their personal authority in a locality may strengthen the position of the court in the local area,

[21]Please refer to Chap. 3 of this book "The Judicial Committee System in Basic-level Courts," especially the section of "Analysis of Two Examples."

it is still temporary. For judges in such places, the only thing they care about is how to make external pressure smaller. What we, as researchers, care about is not whether the leader is blunt or not, but whether the court can maintain the independent trial as an institutional organization and eliminate external interferences, no matter how reasonable and justifiable those interferences seem to be. This is the key to the institutional construction of the court. Secondly, due to their identities, positions, and experiences, cadres do not have as strong a desire to learn professional knowledge as transferred army cadres do, even though they may be of similar ages. Even if they stay in the court for a rather long time, it is still not possible for them to completely change their knowledge structure and working style which they have already formed, or to make efforts to adapt to the needs of the court. It is more likely that they try to shape the court in their previous working style. In the long run, it is not good for the institutional building of the court to let those cadres work in the court.

As a matter of fact, however, these cadres who have entered the court are not the worst. What is worse is that, due to all kinds of reasons, there are always some personnel who are "not capable at all" or "not capable of anything" entering court. We have not interviewed judges of this kind since the judges who came to study in the judicial training class were at least capable of being shaped or getting improvement. Even when we did research in the county courts, it was not possible for us to interview completely incapable "judicial personnel." Nobody forbade us to do so, but nobody reminded us to interview this kind of "judge" and nobody "pointed out" such judges for us (which could be highly offensive to those people). This kind of people would dodge as far from us as they could to avoid humiliating themselves. Many judges or leaders in court used to say anonymously that the court is usually forced to accept those people, some of whom could not work well in any department and were "made" to work in the court.

This is not to say that at the county level, the court is the only place to employ these people. As a matter of fact, in China and in almost all "units," from the center to local areas, from factories to schools, there are always some people that are "well provided for." In addition, there are also some people who have relatively strong backstage supporters or relationships, and the court has to accept them for the sake of convenience. These two types of people are the biggest headaches for the court.

In today's China, party and political organizations and even schools and scientific research institutions do not have real "staffing power," especially the power to fire or dismiss employees. As a result, once these people get into a certain organization, you do not have any way to deal with them unless you are able to "squeeze" or "drive" them away to other departments. So the real problem seems to be the cadre system of the iron bowl. These people are a kind of trouble no matter where they are. They not only cannot work, but they also bring about all kinds of troubles and become an important channel for people who have special connections to enter the court.

10.5 "Washing Our Face with a Basin of Water, While Still Washing Our Face with a Bucket of Water"

While reading this, many readers may doubt whether I have overestimated the capabilities of judges in basic-level courts. Is law really that simple? Can a layman really be competent to the judicial works at basic-level court after one and half years?[22] Is it true that the difference between legal trials and dispute settlements at the basic-level in rural society is really that the former has procedures while the latter does not? If people without formal legal training can try cases well, why on earth do we need university law schools? Should law schools be eliminated completely? I will answer these possible and justifiable questions in the following two sections. The answers to those questions cannot be deduced from definitions by sitting at home—they require field research. I believe that "one does not have the right to speak without research." I will observe the features of basic-level courts as well as the special knowledge needed by the judiciary of basic-level courts in this section. In the next section, I will examine what kind of knowledge China's law schools of today have actually provided and what kind of skills they are training. I believe that after observing and studying these questions, we will have some new understanding of the above questions, at least as long as we are not dogmatists or do not blindly insist on starting from definitions.

Nowadays, when we think about China's judicial system, we will start from very big definitions to a large degree. Indeed, the birth and use of formal legal definitions will make our lives more simple, but we have to recognize what Wang Shuo has said, "Thinking of questions from the level of definitions is like drawing a curve heading downwards and finally reaching the lower end" (in an intelligence, instead of in moral sense).[23] For example, when studying courts and judges, many researchers start from a conceptualized court and judge. It seems that as long as it has the name of "court" or "judge," it will do the same thing or they will be required to have the same standards. In real life, due to different conditions in environments and other aspects, the person, even though they have the title of judge, will face very different problems. As a result, courts of different levels will have different working situations and focuses and have different requirements regarding the knowledge and skills of judges; thus, different situations will call for different professional knowledge and skills.

For example, in first-instance courts and courts of the USA, the works of first-instance judges are very much different from that of judges of appellate courts. Judges of appeals do not care about fact disputes, but only taking care of legal

[22]Due to the distinctiveness of legal knowledge, there are scholars in the USA suggesting that the three-year law school should be changed into a two-year system. Please refer to Richard A. Posner, *The Problematics of Moral and Legal Theory*, Harvard University Press, 1999, pp. 281ff.

[23]Preface for Self-Selected Collection, *Wang Shuo Self-Selected Collection*, Huayi Press, 1997.

disputes. They normally have more than plenty of time to think about and analyze cases. When a legal dispute is not clear, judges of appeals have to give legal support of argumentation to their own judgment (most appeal cases actually do not have a demonstration or argumentation of a judgment, but only include the new judgment. Even when it is a question of dispute, if the judge thinks it is not that important, they do not have to answer, but only sign a court opinion). In particular for the chief justice of Supreme Court, it is very much different. They not only have huge power to choose the cases to review, but they can also, to a certain degree, completely disregard the significance of case results for the parties concerned. US Supreme Court Chief Justice Frankfurter claimed that "[The Supreme Court] only reviews cases which are of significance to the function of our federal system and thus demand a verdict. It is not enough that the results of cases are important to parties concerned." Chief Justice Vinson also declared that "the Supreme Court is not really concerned with correcting mistakes made by lower courts, and as a result, [its] function is to settle opinion disputes which are of wide significance to federal issues and to supervise lower courts according to the US Constitution, laws, and treaties."[24]

Judges in courts of first instance in the USA, which are normally local courts, must face factual disputes and legal disputes at the same time. Since it is not easy to make clear the factual disputes, different people may well—which is absolutely normal—have different identification of certain evidence. For this reason, the jury system has been established to deal with factual disputes which are difficult for judges to deal with and are prone to cause disputes.[25]Judges in courts of first instance must deal with numerous and complicated factual issues with relatively simple rules. In addition, for those judges to perform their duties well, there is a required kind of decisive judgment and reaction, commanding manner, and experience of presiding over trial—which are, in the eyes of Posner, not indispensible but actually very important. Such features, to Posner, are "not of vital importance to judges of appeals courts."[26] Posner also pointed out that in these two kinds of trials, the audience that are of the judge's concern is different. Judges of first instance in the US federal system do not care much about rules, and the purpose of their trials is to make their judgments "appear just, reasonable, safeguarding of the

---

[24]Quoted from Henry J. Abraham, *The Judicial Process: An Introductory Analysis of the Court of the United States, England and France*, 6th ed., Oxford University Press, 1993, p. 176.

[25]"As a matter of fact, I believe that one of the reasons for our practice of leaving problems with or without fault [to the jury] is exactly the most serious defect in its theoretical function: the jury will introduce a certain amount of—which is a large amount of as far as I see—public prejudice to its verdict, and thus make sure that the implementation o flaw is in line with the hope and feelings of the community." Oliver Wendell Holmes, Jr., *Collected Legal Papers*, Harcourt, Brace and Hows, Inc., 1952, p. 237.

[26]Richard A. Posner, *Federal Courts: Challenge and Reform*, Harvard University Press, 1996, p. 35.

authority of judges, and ensure everything is in order."[27] However, judges of appeal courts do not care about whether their manners or actions are appropriate or not (senior Chief Justices of the Supreme Court sometimes doze off and even snore during trials), since the main audience is other judges (especially judges of lower courts and judges of other courts at the same level) and lawyers (including professors and students of law schools). For judges of appeal, what is the most important is the quality of the judgment (i.e., the result of the case as well as the legal reasoning supporting this result).

In China, the boundary between the trial courts and the courts of appeal has never been clear. We can say that all courts are courts of first instance in a certain sense[28] (although this is very problematic and I will address this in an article to demonstrate why), but courts at the basic level are indisputably courts of first instance. For this reason, we should not simply put the ideal formats of US Supreme Court Chief Justices on China's basic-level judges: They are familiar with all kinds of laws and create judicial opinions, majority opinions, concurring opinions, and opposing opinions which are outstanding both in words and in reasoning. We must observe and study the features of China's courts of first instance, especially courts at the basic level with a spirit of seeking truth from facts. We not only should not mechanically apply the standards of US judges of courts of appeal, but we also should not simply copy China's requirements on judges of second instance. We should not apply modes of models of US judges of first instance either.[29] In fact, we must analyze features of China's courts of first instance from the standpoint of the problems they face, the communities they are from, their

[27]Same as the previous note, p. 36. In addition, Posner quoted in another area of this book the "working requirements" of another well-known US judge on judges of first instances. Judges of first instances must "fairly combine timely decision with result in the best way and settle cases through trial or reconciliation; and they have responsibility to demonstrate to ordinary citizens—parties concerned, witnesses, and jurors the quality of the federal judiciary." "For this reason, it may seem shocking, which means one can never make it perfect. However, the mission features of courts of first instance have defined the limit that the judge can realize this job. The decision of whether to verify the evidence is the most evident example. What is most important here is making decisions as soon as possible. Apart from this, I don't believe that the greatest judges of local courts will spend several months writing a legal opinion with new ideas and a spirit of complete devotion. And on this issue, the opinions of those judges are definitely not the final say." Henry J. Friendly, "The 'Law of the Circuit' and All That," 46 *St. John's Law Review* 406, 407 n. 6 (1979). Quoted from Posner, *Federal Court*, pp. 336–337.

[28]Please see Article 18, 19, 20, and 21 of Civil Procedural Law of the People's Republic of China (1991) and Article 19, 20, 21, 22, and 23 of Criminal Procedural Law of the People's Republic of China (1996).

[29]Upon introspection, I myself have this kind of tendency. When I studied in the US, I read was opinions of judges of appeal selected by textbooks from tens of thousands of Supreme Court judgments by a certain group of editors. It was easy for me to believe that all American judges of different levels are capable of making famous judicial judgment. This kind of overgeneralization happens not only with me, but also with many people who have received training in American law schools. I also don't exclude the possibility that some people have used this point deliberately in order to promote certain opinions or interests.

position in the community, their ability to act as a judge, as well as other restricting or supporting conditions.

Judging from this point, the primary feature of China's basic-level courts is to "get things done." As a matter of fact, this is unavoidable in courts of first instance in every country. Law is a subject which is very practical. No matter how extravagant it may sound, it must reach a result (not judgment only) which is roughly reasonable to ordinary people and all parties concerned. This is where the legality of any law finally lies. This kind of legality is not in any book or any First Principle. Neither is it in any big words such as "justice," "fairness," nor "human rights." It is in the heart of people. For this reason, in basic-level courts, an important thing for judges facing all kinds of strange things is to obtain a result which can be approved of by all sides by all possible means while understanding basic legal principles. On one hand, this result must be basically accepted by parties of both sides. Secondly, the result must approximately fit the moral value judgment of local people. Finally, judges have to consider whether this result is in line with the requirements of law or with other rigorous requirements that may be proposed by judges of appeal (second instance).[30] Trial judges have actually always been putting their talents to a good use to settle disputes in this small gap and adhere to these standards. This issue embodies the conflict between "dispute settlement" and "rule governance," which I discussed in earlier sections.[31]

This means that the concerns of basic-level courts and judges of people's tribunals are different from the concerns of judges of second instance and also different from the knowledge and concerns of legal scholars who have been educated either locally or overseas. To us scholars who have been formatted by knowledge systems of law schools, what we care about is systematic knowledge, justification, and legitimacy of rules, the justification of those rules in legal knowledge systems and legal power structures, as well as whether certain practices are in line with our definitions and knowledge systems. However, judges of first instance pay more attention to whether a specific issue can be settled, whether certain results are rightful and legal, and whether the result is compatible with heavenly principles and human feelings of local community as well as formal legal power structure systems. The difference in attention will cause a tremendous difference in mentality. For example, the research of Easterbrook believes that dispute settlement is actually backward looking and distributes gains and losses according to things that have already happened; conversely, rule verification is forward looking and aims to inform people of their situation and therefore change their future behavior.[32]

Although judges of first instance in every country have a tendency of "getting things done," China's situation is still very much different. The previous chapters

---

[30]As a result, Holmes believes that law is the prediction of a judge's decision. This is especially important to judges of first instance. Please refer to Oliver Wendell Holmes, Jr., "The Path of the Law," in *Collected Legal Papers*, Harcourt, Brace, and Hows, Inc., 1952, pp. 167ff.

[31]Chapter 5 of this book "Dispute Settlement and Governance of Rules."

[32]Frank H. Easterbrook, "Foreword: The Court and the Economic System," 98 *Harvard Law Review* 4 (1984).

have already provided relatively detailed discussion on this, and I will not say more than needed. Using the previously mentioned concepts, we can finally understand why judges of basic-level courts who have not received systematic and standard trainings—whether they are from the military, the basic-level court, or another government departments of the same level—can provided advantages to effective solution of cases due to their rich social experience. Their understanding of the ways of the world as well as the will of the people and the local sentiments and conditions, their credibility to parties concerned as an accomplished adult,[33] their efficiency and toughness—which can be fostered in the army or demonstrated (due to the chosen system) as a demobilized army cadre, their eloquence—which is more or less capable of effectively influence ordinary people—and ability to use language which is more popular (including dialect),[34] as well as their relatively handsome appearance and healthy body as a demobilized army cadre due to the army selection system has enabled former soldiers to become effective judges without any special training. These less-formally trained judges actually have an advantage over students who have just graduated. Certainly, such features of basic-level judges are not necessarily all advantages in the court of appeals. Judicial duties in the court of appeals require a policy-oriented mind and more consideration to the generalization and coordination of rules, and ultimately need more reflection.

---

[33]Feng Xiang used to say that suppose you are a young genius who has entered the university at the age of 13, do you dare study law? If you graduate from law school at the age of 17, who would be willing (or can be assured) to hire you to demand repayment of a loan, to obtain evidence, or to accompany fellow judges to eat and drink? Preface to *Wooden-legged Justice*, Zhongshan University Press, 1999, p. 6.

Although we have always been emphasizing specialized knowledge, as a matter of fact, age has always been a more important factor at least to trial judges. Judging from different countries of the world, people acting as a judge or playing the role of arbiter have always been a middle-aged man, or post-adolescent at least. "Young people cannot do things well" is a kind of typical generalization, but judicial trials are not only an activity of wisdom, they require life experience as well. Young people may be very experienced, but people often use age as an index of experience in order to save on information costs. A court president told the following story: A university student who had graduated not long ago mediated a marriage in a people's tribunal. After speaking for a long time, he still could not persuade the young wife of his decision. A juror who was a woman of 60 years also said a lot. But her last sentence was "My girl, I'm old enough to be your grandmother. If you don't listen to me, who else can you listen to?" This made the couple reconcile their issues. This made the young judge think a lot. Certainly, we cannot take this story too seriously; the effect of the last sentence of the old lady might be the result of previous mediation. It might be possible that the young wife had already changed her mind. Even so, the art of the last sentence is still important—it caused changes and thus saved a lot of time for all parties involved. The swiftness of decision is one of the main requests for trials of judges of first instance, and experience can help bring decisiveness.

[34]I once heard a story during my research. The judge told the party concerned that he has a right to argue, but the party concerned did not understand. The judge explained, "it means you can quarrel, but can't swear." This kind of language is not accurate, but roughly and effectively conveys a message. Even university students who have received more than 10 years of Chinese grammar training cannot say or even imagine the language. What's more possible is that after many years of training which always emphasize that language must be vivid—so they cannot think or speak like this.

We must also see that in China's basic-level courts, especially at the level of the people's tribunal, disputes are often both complicated and simple. They are simple in terms of rules—if a man worked far away from his hometown where he had a new love and wanted to divorce his old wife, it is very simple from a legal standpoint. That is, if one party is determined to divorce, he or she can get a divorce.[35] Is there anything here to learn? What is difficult in this kind of legal issue (I don't know why my professor spent so much time talking about the principle of "incompatibility," which is very simple but could not be defined accurately when I studied it in the law school)? One judge we interviewed says that if a couple has rough patches like this, it would be wrong to say that they are still compatible with each other. The real questions are, if you make such judgment, what can the divorced wife do? What is to be done with their kid? How is property to be divided? How can a judge check up on a series of preparations made by the man for divorce, including capital transfer? Divorce cases take up 40 % or more of the cases in China's basic-level courts. In addition, according to our investigation, at basic-level courts, 25 % of cases are personal injury compensation; 5–10 % are support cases; and others are cases of property, inheritance, and land disputes. Those cases are not very complicated in law, but they need to be dealt with well with little or no error. We must try our best to coordinate the potential conflict between "hopes and feelings of the community" proposed by Holmes and the legal texts, which requires lot of knowledge outside legal textbooks.

There are also a small number of economic cases in the civil tribunal and economic tribunal in county courts with just small amounts of money involved, since those with a large amount of money have been collected by courts of higher levels at present (the superficial reason is cited as differential jurisdiction, but actually it is about economic interest, since the standard of registration charges is based on the total amount of objects under litigation. Differential jurisdiction like this can help courts of higher level to obtain more legal fees). It is said that certain county courts can only try economic cases involving less than 300,000 yuan. Cases involving 300,000–1 million yuan belong to intermediate courts, and all cases with an object of litigation exceeding 1 million belong to the provincial high court. In this legal world faced by basic-level courts in which original jurisdiction has been divided up so seriously, frankly speaking, a person with moderate degree of education, a little responsibility, and common sense can well become a good judge as long as he or she is not greedy, pays attention to research and studies, and receives some legal training. After all, the judiciary is not comprised of purely rational activities, but is a practically rational activity as a whole. A senior tribunal director who has worked in the court for more than 20 years said that the most fundamental thing for a judge to have is a conscience. I do not totally approve of his view, which is universally moral and may play down specialized knowledge if applied across the board. However, if we view this perspective from the legal world where

[35]Section 10.2 of Article 25 of Marriage Law of the People's Republic of China: "In dealing with a divorce case, the people's court should carry out mediation between the parties. Divorce shall be granted if mediation fails because mutual affection no long exists."

he actually lives, in terms of the many cases faced by basic-level courts, the issue of rules is indeed not the most important issue of basic-level courts.

The majority of cases dealt with by basic-level courts are quite ordinary and insignificant. On this point, judges of China's basic-level courts have a major difference from judges of first instance and even magistrates in the USA. In the USA, cases that enter a court trial are more or less interesting legal disputes. This is because most cases, including 90 % of criminal cases,[36] and about 95 % of civil and commercial disputes,[37] as long as the facts are clear, will be settled separately in manners like plea bargaining and out-of-court settlement before they enter into court or during the process of litigation. This actually filters out the majority of normal and ordinary cases. The rest are cases which require trial by judges, and they tend to have more or less new legal disputes. This will make even the judges of first instance feel something new, interesting, and challenging when hearing court cases. Moreover, since original jurisdiction is general, which means that courts of appeal cannot casually deprive courts of first instance of the jurisdiction of trying all first-instance cases, we cannot exclude the situation that judges of first instance will accidentally meet some cases which are nationally eye-catching. However, in China, almost all cases have to be tried or settled by pretrial mediation once they have been registered in the court. Those bigger, more complicated—and therefore more interesting—cases belong to the jurisdiction of courts of higher level. Judges are not allowed to create law by discretion according to actual situations, and it is difficult for judges of basic-level courts to encounter some unique or interesting problem. It is all the more so for people's tribunals. For this reason, those "apprentices" are good enough to deal with problems in their life after their actual working experiences with their mentors, plus self-study and their life experiences in other aspects that they have accumulated previously. Based on this, we can understand why the above-mentioned judge W believed that the only difference between his works in court and his previous works as county judicial assistant or civil affairs director was simply that "one has procedures while the other has not." We are also able to understand why not only demobilized military cadres, but also students studying other majors can deal with cases independently after following their mentors for only a few years.

In an environment like this, these may be all the demanded qualities for judges of basic-level courts. Just like what was said by the judge during an interview, it is good for you to know a little more, but as "you can wash your face in a basin of water, you can also wash your face in the bucket." This kind of saying is actually in line with the mockery made by the famous American jurist Friedrich K. Juenger on the kind of judges of first instance who "have spent a decade on just one thing." Both of these perspectives provide insight for the judicial experience of judges of

[36]Please see Renstrom (edited): "Plea Bargain," *American Law Dictionary*, translated by He Weifang and etc., China University of Politics and Law Press, 1998, p. 190.

[37]"Beyond Litigation—an Interview with Robert Mnookin," *Stanford Lawyer*, Spring-Summer 1989, p. 5; quoted from Mary Ann Glendon, *A Nation Under Lawyers, How the Crisis in the Legal Profession is Transforming American Society*, Harvard University Press, 1994, p. 224.

first instance. We jurists who have spent our lifetime reading textbooks may find this kind of saying unpleasant to the ear, but "those who dare to make fun of philosophers are truly philosophers"![38] We should also have this kind of easy attitude toward judicial knowledge.

The more important problem is not what kind of legal knowledge or how much legal knowledge the judges have, but what kind of legal knowledge rural and basic-level society need. For a kind of knowledge to be useful in the world, it must be targeted.[39] Much mathematical knowledge has become theorem nowadays, but if we want to solve chemical problems, the mathematical knowledge is useless even it is correct. It may be one day that the knowledge available to basic-level judges must be updated and upgraded, but only because those villagers need a "full bath" instead of just a "face washing."

10.6 "What I Learned in School Has Already Been Returned to the Teachers"

This is a simple answer given to us by a graduate from a college of politics and law when he was asked what the uses of legal education to the practice of judicial trial are. He even had an expression of contempt in his eyes.

We certainly could not take his answer too seriously. First of all, he is a judge on a path of promotion in the court where he works. His decades of judicial practice in the people's tribunal may make him feel that knowledge in the textbooks is superficial and divorced from reality. When he entered the college of politics and law in 1979, the curriculum of law school was indeed very bad. Most of the lessons were so-called theories of jurisprudence and department law with contents of political discourses which were popular then. There was very little presentable legal knowledge, let alone knowledge related to judiciary. For example, among the jurisprudence, a controversial problem at that time was "the essence of law" or the relation between the class nature and the sociality of law. But was there any significance of this kind of content to a judge who had to "get things done" in real life? Didn't they know that the judge would not make any wrong judgments only because he had missed two words when writing down the essence or standard definition of law (while the teacher would find it wrong)—although it may be an interesting issue to those researchers of philosophy of law? The most important "theoretical problem" for law of economy at that time (and maybe even today) was the object of regulation of economic law—teachers talked about it for most of the semester. This kind of advanced knowledge has nothing to do with practical world of law. Many students who used to actively take part in this kind of

[38]Blaise Pascal, *Pensees*, trans. by W. F. Trotter, E. P. Dutton & Co., 1931, Sect. 10.1, §4.

[39]William James, Pragmatism's Conception of Truth, *William James Collection*, selected and edited by Wan Junren, Chen Yajun, Shanghai Far East Press, 1997.

discussion of legal theory in the school usually had a feeling of being deceived once they entered society and the professional world, especially when they gain access to judicial practice or issues of lawyers. It is natural that they will soon return the knowledge to the person it belongs to. But frankly speaking, the judge's answer may also imply a certain kind of non-confidence in face of researchers who are doctors and professors of Peking University. Even so, we still could not let go of answers like these, since when we talked with many of our classmates or schoolmates who are now lawyers or judges, they also often demonstrated the same kind of attitude, especially to people like me who are researching legal theories.[40]

A comment from another woman judge who graduated from a college of politics and law may be fairer. To her (deputy director of civil tribunal; we shall know that this position is very important), certain principles in the science of civil law, civil procedure law, and jurisprudence taught in the school are very useful, while others are not. She especially emphasizes that the moot court in college is "not real," nor practical at all. Although her words are relatively nice to the ears of us researchers, who come from these colleges and went through these systems, her answers are still worthy of analysis.

This judge graduated from the college of politics and law in 1992, so at the time of the interview, nearly 10 years had passed since the resumption of legal education. Civil law and civil procedure law originally have relatively strong academic foundation and never stray away from this foundation in practice (although there is no relative legislature). After the reform and opening up, it resumed its development with relatively strong academic knowledge. What is more important is that she is currently engaged with civil trial and responsible for hearing relatively complicated civil cases in the civil tribunal of a county court. She also has a duty of guiding all works of people's tribunals in the county (which basically deal with civil cases). For this reason, civil law and civil procedure law are at least fairly useful to her, no matter whether in terms of cases she faces or in terms of her working locations, or her legitimate responsibilities. Her position has made her judicial decisions a kind of "second trial" or "trial of appeal." That is, certain principle knowledge becomes important if one has to provide legal guidance for

[40]This kind of situation is also very common among American judges. Posner used to talk about this problem in *The Problem of Jurisprudence*. Since modern legal education became one of the conventional conditions for judges in the USA, some most well-known and greatest judges, such as Holmes, Cardozo, Hand, and Jackson, were not good students in law school. The only exception was Frankfurter. The other exception was Posner himself (a most outstanding student from the University of Yale who ranked first place at Harvard Law School and was the chief editor of the *Harvard Law Review*). Posner emphasized many times that it is not necessary to choose judges from the most outstanding students in law school. Ordinary students should also be included, since judiciary is not about a competition of wisdom (those with superior wisdom are usually not that reasonable), and judiciary is more about getting to know the feelings of ordinary people. Please refer to Richard A. Posner, *The Problems of Jurisprudence*, Harvard University Press, 1990, p. 452; and Richard A. Posner, *The Federal Courts, Challenge and Reform*, Harvard University Press, 1996, pp. 16ff for detailed analysis.

dealing with difficult cases of people's tribunals, or coordinate the legal practices of different tribunals. This has further proved the proposition I put forward in the previous section. Whether certain knowledge is useful or not is, to a large extent, related to the demands of the person who uses this kind of knowledge as well as the problem he or she has to resolve. Otherwise, the knowledge has to wait for the highest bid no matter how useful it is. It is like using antiaircraft artillery to shoot a mosquito. It is not that the artillery has a problem, but more that the problem and the method do not match.

Why is the moot court useless? The key point is that the basic design of moot court is to improve the ability of students to use law, including using legal knowledge and indisputable facts to determine the nature of the case. But it cannot improve students' ability to settle factual disputes. If there is a dispute in the facts and the facts are not clear, then the moot court cannot really be open. Please imagine, if it is made clear whether a person has killed another person or how he or she has conducted the killing, then how can the case be debated?

However, as I have mentioned previously, the most important disputes in the basic-level court may be factual disputes. For example, if there is fighting among villagers, legal disputes about gang fighting, human injury, and compensation are very simple. What is difficult is how to check out and identify facts. It has nothing to do how many books one has read, but is related to one's social experience. At the same time, the moot court attaches importance to procedural training. But in basic-level society or rural areas, there are no lawyers, or people cannot afford to hire a lawyer, so it is difficult for designed testimonial and cross-examination to function. The person who shares the burden of proof is never to the point and often talks about insignificant and legally trivial things which are, in the eyes of rural people, very important and will be repeated again and again. Since the litigation directly involves their own interests, the parties concerned often deliberately offer far-fetched argument on facts. It is not like in the moot court, where both parties have basically approved the facts and only have to strive for correct answers legally. This can be said to be the most fundamental reason why moot court training in law school is not useful to judges of basic-level court. When this kind of situation happens in real life, according to judges, it is impossible to check up on the case based on testimonials of both sides, and the case will get more unclear and more complicated as the investigation goes further. The causal relationship can be traced back infinitely, and it can be traced back to several years and even the last generation. The only method for the judge is to get to know the case directly instead of depending on testimonials only, and the judge will thus have his or her own insight. Moreover, it is in fact for the purpose of resolving problems to check up on and divide the responsibilities. However, if the conflict can be resolved (there would not be any disputes as long as medical expenses are covered and apologies are given in an injury case), sometimes it is not necessary to divide responsibilities so clearly, and sometimes they simply cannot be divided so clearly ("not even good officials can settle family troubles").

Some judges even emphasize that in the basic-level courts, the only expectation for many rural people is that the court can speak for them, especially for women in a divorce case. Under this circumstance, if the judge can be "impartial" and let parties concerned debate with each other, then the victim in the divorce case will be obviously discarded. It will not only be against the judge's own conscience, but is also against the expectation of the rural people. What is taught in law school is that there is "no trial without complaint."

Those words and reasons look simple, but to me, they are not the experience of basic-level judges in practice. Those judges have sharply pointed out the special problems basic-level courts must face and the special knowledge and skills they need. The necessary knowledge and skills are not taught, and cannot be taught, in law school. They can only be grasped through practice and study.[41]

We must also see the restriction of resources on basic-level judicial trials. For example, testimonial can be said to be the most important procedure for lawsuits in courts of modern developed countries, but it is very difficult in basic-level society in rural China. I myself have witnessed testimonies and witnesses provided by two sides of the lawsuit come from the same person, while the facts proved by these two evidences are completely opposite to each other (whether it was A or B who took the first action), and both "evidences" have fingerprints of witnesses. I did not investigate whether one piece of evidence was fabricated or why the judge did not look into the possibility of perjury. Those questions are not important here. I believe that those two conflicting pieces of evidence could indeed come from the same person. We still have to think about it: Is it possible that this witness refuses his or her villagers' request of providing evidence since they belong to the same village? He or she may not be able to read, and when others have written down the testimony and asked him or her to press his or her fingerprint signature on the document, can he or she refuse it? Will the court really plan to check the evidence just for this piece of "perjury"? Can the court lock up those people who can't read and don't know anything about legal severity regarding "perjury," while leaving the case on hand unattended? Probably, the only way is to settle this dispute fairly is according to a certain method which is not that particular. Doing this may not be in line with the basic judicial requirements of "clear facts, irrefutable evidence, and accurate applicable law." However, if the result of meeting those requirements is just a dispute settlement, then what kind of motivation or resources do judges have? Is it really necessary to spend originally limited resources on this? If the world is not regular itself, wouldn't this be analogous to the saying "to cut one's feet to fit the shoes" if we give to much emphasis on "regulation"?

Certainly, to legal researchers and even judges of second instance, it is beneficial to the future of China's rule of law if those little problems are treated seriously. Like everything else, rule of law has to start from very little thing and is accumulated bit by bit. But the problem is that we should not exceed our duties

[41]Please see Suli: "Classification of Knowledge," *Dushu*, Issue 3 of 1998. American scholar, Judge Frank used to propose that judges of first instance should be given special professional training. Please refer to Jerome Frank, "Special Training for Trial Judges," in *Courts on Trial: Myth and Reality in American Justice*, Princeton University Press, 1973 (1949), pp. 247–253.

and meddle in others' affairs. What we need is to build a kind of mechanism and social environment, in which those judges are willing and able to "verify the facts" seriously and meticulously. Can all this be resolved only by telling them the importance of "strict enforcement" or by explaining several principles and definitions?

Here is another point: Please note that apart from those important courses in law school mentioned by the female judge, we shall also pay attention to the courses she did not mention. We need to observe things that are not present.[42] For example, though she works in the civil tribunal, she did not mention anything about company law, financial law, law of negotiable instrument, securities law, laws to protect intellectual property rights as well as consumer rights and interests, and other laws which are relatively popular for students who are in favor of civil and commercial law. Why? It is actually very simple. There is hardly any problem like this in such a small place, if any at all.

We can thus find here another problem related to modern law-school education. Although there has been great development in legal education in recent years, honestly speaking, the purpose of law-school education at present is basically to cultivate talents for modern industrial and commercial society and cities. The so-called most leading-edge legal courses in law school, to a large extent, are not for the legal life order of China's basic-level society, but more for urban life and the upcoming social life order in China's developed regions. As a result, the knowledge studied by China's law-school students is separated from the demands of China's basic-level and rural societies to a large extent. We should also make clear that knowledge with legal labels is not equal to judicial knowledge. Readers should know clearly that I'm not implying any kind of criticism by saying this. I'm not saying that China's legal education should abandon attention to major problems of legal practice which are of growing applicability to the entirety of China under the banner of "focus on reality." I am just pointing out a reality, only for the sake of finding out the features and merits of (which may also be a weakness) our legal education at present, and in turn having a new understanding of the formidable tasks of China's legal construction and adapting our demands on qualities and professions of judges in basic-level courts appropriately.

It is also here that we can see why, when facing issues of basic-level or rural society, law-school graduates do not necessarily have more advantages over people coming from rural society, or over those demobilized soldiers who left rural society temporarily and then returned to work in the courts. The advantages of law-school graduates may be the following: (1) They are good at dealing with legal disputes but not at settling disputes or "dealing with" all kinds of relations in a complicated circle of acquaintances; (2) They understand comprehensively or even in advance the game's rules which are very important to China's modern society or the upcoming modern society. Among this knowledge, there is at least a

[42]Foucault, "Nietzsche, Genealogy, History," translated by Suli, Issue 4 of *Review of Academic Ideas*, 1998, p. 380.

large amount that is not that useful or even useless in the basic-level society, which is still not that modern at present.

As a result, even many law-school students may have great talents as well as ideals and aspiration to do something for the country and the people, but if their knowledge cannot play a role, then the vast space of basic-level society and China's rural areas is still quite narrow to them. Their encyclopedic mind will be wasted on a petty job. Not to mention that knowledge can never be used out of memory, but can only be remembered when in use. For this reason, it is not difficult for us to understand why that law-school graduate would say: "I have returned all I learned from the school to my teachers."

This is also why many law-school graduates quit their court-appointed jobs to become lawyers or businessmen after working in the intermediate- or basic-level courts, or sometimes even courts of higher levels, although they were full with passion and ideals originally. Money is certainly a temptation, but it is probably not the only reason. One of the important reasons is that the knowledge that these students invest in does not have significant day-to-day use in those courts. It is said that "men will die for those who understand them while women will doll themselves up for those who love them." Their skills and advantages cannot be used, but instead become shortcomings, and even a source of scoff. At the same time, there are other places where they can make use of their advantages; is there anyone who is willing to hang themselves on such a tree? In this sense, many law-school graduates prefer to leave basic-level courts and enter into the urban areas and regions with relatively developed and rich economies, where they can work as lawyers and are often engaged with business law. This is not because that they despise the poor and only care to serve the rich, but that they can make use of the knowledge they have learned in modern society and meet greater challenges in regard to knowledge and wisdom. This is exactly the demand function of a market economy. It is just in this sense that law-school graduates who have turned down the basic-level courts are significant of the development level of the economic and cultural society in China's basic-level courts.

10.7 "Becoming Spring Mud to Give a Better Protection to Flowers"—A Reflection on Demobilized Soldiers Entering Courts

I have to re-mention here the issue of "deteriorating and flushed rural areas," as proposed by Fei Xiaotong more than 50 years ago,[43] and reflect a little bit on China's modern law education. In the eyes of Fei, in traditional China, as talent fostered by rural society, scholar-bureaucrats would go to other places to take their jobs once they passed the imperial examination. No matter how high a post they reached, they

[43]Fei Xiaotong: *The Rebuilding of the Countryside*, Shanghai Observation, 1948, pp. 65ff.

still had to return to their hometown when they retired. After they returned, those retired scholar-bureaucrats would use the money they had saved or collected from the people to buy fields or lands and to build schools and develop the village. In their minds, this is how they paid the village back and created a condition for knowledge to spread (no matter how old and decayed some knowledge might be) for the next generation in the village. Their knowledge of self-cultivation and regulating the family, the country, and the whole world is the "hard currency" of society at the time.

In modern times, with the introduction of all kinds of new subjects and knowledge, groups of smart and curious rural children have travelled to cities to study. However, even though they are full of ideals and passions to serve their villages, after a few years of study, they become "rural children who can't go home,"[44] as mentioned by Fei. This is not only because of the temptation of rich urban lives and cultures, or because of changes in cultural attainment, temperament, and interest—the reason that is more important in my eyes but often neglected by others is that the more advanced, profound, and deeper their knowledge, the less useful it is in rural or basic-level societies. You can compare the first pages of children's books of different times, and you will have a few clues: "I love my great motherland. And I love Tian'anmen Square in the Capital." Comparing this with the knowledge of "people, hand, mouth, pig, cat, and dog," which one is more directly useful to China's basic-level and rural society? The answer is obvious. For this reason, in China's process of modernization, villages are not only squeezed and "exploited" by urban industrial economics, but what is most heavy and tragic in my eyes is the silent robbery of talent from villages through market mechanisms.

My comment here is just to point out a fact. From my personal judgment, which may prove to be wrong, if China wants to be prosperous and independent and make her people gradually attain wealth, she must take the road of modernization, stick to the reform and opening up, and develop market economy and scientific technology. In this sense, we cannot only avoid this situation, but make it imperative. The problem is that the grand undertaking of modernization should not conceal or submerge primary or basic demands of ordinary people. This does not mean that free Internet access is provided to places with no electricity—it is much deeper. On the issue of judiciary and law, a main problem faced by the basic-level and the rural courts in modern China is not much different from what was said by Fei 50 years ago—we need only change a few words: that is "how to input modern knowledge into the most basic production base of China's economy—the village. There must be media broadcasts to input modern knowledge. The basic problem is how to send intellectuals to the countryside to rebuild rural areas."[45] It is because of this point that we may need to re-examine the problem of quality and specialization of judges in basic-level courts, as well as the problem of a lack of talent in basic-level courts. It may be even necessary for us to re-examine the setting up of China's basic-level courts.

[44]Fei Xiaotong: same as above, pp. 70–73.

[45]Fei Xiaotong: same as previous note 43, p. 163.

I don't agree to the inflexible practice of forcing law-school graduates to go to the basic-level courts for "training" (it is certainly best if they choose to go themselves). It not only goes against the principle of human resource arrangements in the market economy, but more importantly, it results in a certain waste of talent and resources (educational resources) and is actually not practical today. If we say that the experience of the last 50 years, both positive and negative, has taught us something, then the most important one is people must be given more choices, and we should let the market do the choosing. The demand, supply, and flow of talents eventually depend on people's choices.

I have analyzed in other places that an important difference between the modern judge and traditional county governor, as well as between the modern court and traditional government office, in settling social disputes is "dispute settlement" and "rule confirmation/utilization," although they are not entirely different and have all kinds of connections. If we have this point in mind, when reconsidering many events in China's basic-level courts, especially of people's tribunals, we will notice that most works done by judges at basic-level courts are "dispute settlements" (please think about the statement that the difference between courts and judicial assistants is "one has procedures while the other has not") and even "legal consultation."[46] Those works are certainly very important, especially to the villagers.

Even in such developed countries as the UK and the USA, those works are not mainly done by courts or judges, but by justices of peace (magistrate justices) who rank between judges and ordinary people. These "judges" are ordinary people, usually without any formal legal training. Many of them only have education level of senior high school or have incomplete university education, not to mention law degrees.[47] They have integrity and common sense, uphold justice, and understand local situations. In trying "cases," they utilize comprehensively all kinds of knowledge with relatively considerable discretionary power. However, they do not have meticulous or strict procedures and only take dispute settlement as purpose. As far as I see, their works are very similar to those of judges in China's basic-level courts, especially people's tribunals. The similarity also lies in professional and cultural qualities.

Certainly, we still cannot copy examples of foreign countries, but instead have to make some institutional adjustment based on specific situations of China's basic-level society. For example, in Western countries, especially in the UK, magistrate justices are produced completely from the communities. However, if we need to make similar judicial adjustment in China, I would oppose selecting magistrate justices entirely from communities, either by election or by appointment.

---

[46]Please refer to the last paragraph of Chap. 9 of this book "Legal Personnel in Rural Society.".

[47]For situations of American magistrates of justice, please refer to Henry J. Abraham, *Judicial Process: An Introductory Analysis of the Courts of the United States, England, and France,* 6th ed., Oxford University Press, 1993, pp. 138-140 and Robert A. Carp and Ronald Stidham, *Judicial Process in America*, 4th ed., Congressional Quarterly Inc., 1998, pp. 67–68, 68–69. For situations of magistrates in the UK, those who prefer Chinese materials can refer to Wang Qianghua: "UK's Magistrates," *Democracy and Legality*, Issue 7 of 1999, pp. 21–23.

My main reason is that in those Western countries, due to all kinds of social conditions, even for people living in the same community, their interests are not that closely connected to the community they live in. Although people are familiar with each other in those communities, it is not a "society of acquaintance" in the sense of sociology (not to the degree of rural China, at least), but a highly individualized society where every person living in this community shares a greater social interest beyond the community to a greater extent and recognizes a greater society (nation). For this reason, the problem of bullying non-natives usually does not exist. But China's basic-level societies, villages, village towns, and even some counties are fairly closed in my eyes. The connections of the community, whether in terms of information or in terms of people with blood relationships, generational affinities, and other social contacts, clearly still exist in rural China. I believe that this kind of closeness is actually a problem which basic-level courts in modern China need to solve immediately. All forms of local protectionism and problems of low-quality judges are also closely related to this. In this social environment, if all basic-level judges are selected locally, it would be easy to intensify this kind of closeness of people and information in the local courts of today's China. In order to gradually reduce this kind of closeness, to encourage further circulation of information and talents, and to promote the development and formation of China's unified market, judges of basic-level courts and judges of people's courts must be selected from pools of human resources with a more open vision.

There is also a problem here: First of all, who is willing to leave their hometown to become this kind of judge at the most basic level in another place? As I have analyzed in the above text, law-school graduates are not likely to go to basic-level courts in large numbers voluntarily at a time when there are more and more opportunities in urban areas and especially when their knowledge cannot necessarily play a role in basic-level society. University students of other majors in other places are not necessarily willing to come (why on earth would they take the trouble to leave their hometown if they have to go to the basic level anyway?); they not only lack legal knowledge, but do not understand a basic-level society which they are not familiar with; even if they are willing to come, it may be difficult for them to execute the responsibilities of judges effectively. Again, we face another choice in which we cannot satisfy both sides at the same time.

We have not yet reached a dead end, however. It is just at this moment, I believe that it is possible for all kinds of students of colleges and technical secondary schools who have left their villages or hometowns to go to school and then come back to their hometown for all kinds of reasons, as well as demobilized professional soldiers with an education level above senior high school to fill this void. On the one hand, they were born in those places and are relatively familiar with local situations; if they choose to return, we can assume that they normally will feel at ease when living in their hometowns. On the other hand, they left this society of acquaintances at a time when they were relatively young, both malleable and eager to learn something, and thus cut off their connection to this society of acquaintances, at least partly or temporarily to enter into a "society of strangers." They have accepted the nurturing and training of certain modern institutional organizations[48] to a certain degree, which has expanded their vision and enabled them to understand that "the world outside is magnificent." This kind of training and experience for only a few years can also exert a certain influence on them, change their opinions and understanding of this world, as well as their ways to associate with strangers, and foster their abilities and experience to associate with strangers. Even if they return to their villages or small towns to these societies of acquaintance, things will be different after all. "A kind of entrance can never exit" (my old saying), and it is true from personal experiences. They will definitely bring certain fresh possibilities to their societies of acquaintance. This is why in many rural places nowadays, those demobilized soldiers can normally bring some new factors and features to the villages when they return, no matter whether it is regarding running township enterprises, or conducting private contracts, or even filing lawsuits or fighting against old-style marriages.

I have to frankly say here that I feel demobilized professional soldiers can play a bigger role in village judiciaries in this aspect. For one reason, they do not have a high level of academic achievement, and urban lives which attach importance to educational backgrounds and diplomas will thus discriminate against them and even refuse them to a certain degree. Most of their knowledge is given by social experience and may be more useful in dealing with disputes in basic-level society, rather than the knowledge learned by colleges or technical secondary school students. They are older than graduates from technical secondary schools, and it is therefore easier for them to gain a certain kind of trust in basic-level societies and to start working immediately (while graduates from technical secondary schools may need 3–5 years of internship, since they are too young).

At a broader level, this kind of system even may improve the cultural and ecological environment of China's basic-level society and can at least resolve part of that sharp question I put forward at the beginning of this section. They started from the basic-level society, left it, spent a few years in the world outside and then came back with some new knowledge and social practices. This kind of cycling, the "feeling of leaves toward roots," and the return to the land not only have a biological meaning, but also have a sense of aesthetic value as well. It reminds me of a line in a famous poem: "it turns into spring mud to give more protection to the flowers"—although it may be a bit too romantic.

[48]It may be possible that many jurists or university student unions will feel furious that I have confused universities with the army, as they typically do not "condescend" to associate with soldiers. However, if you know something about China's modern history, you should know that today's army is different from traditional army or Hunan Army or Jiangsu Army in history in regard to nearly every aspect. In China's modern history, the army is at least one of the first institutions to realize modernized systems, if not the very first. Its history of modernization spans a longer timeline than any other organizations in today's government or universities. It is more modernized and has always been connected to the world. For more systematic analysis of related theories which people find difficult in certain areas but feel obliged to accept, please refer to Michel Foucault, *Discipline and Punishment: the Birth of the Prison*, trans. by Alan Sheridan, Vintage Books, 1978.

10.8 "Things in the World Are Complicated"

From a sincere acknowledgement, some readers may discover that my investigation ends unexpectedly in a conclusion which betrays my friends. However, I still need to repeat the words I have said in some other places; that is, in general, China's judges have relatively low cultural and professional qualities. As a result, I don't approve of "demobilized cadres going to court" as a common judicial measure or policy, but I do approve further professionalism of judges. The problem is that professionalism is not simply about going to school more often and reading more books, as we imagine. From human history, the most fundamental way for professionalism to develop is to have further and more detailed division of labor according to the demands of social development.[49] The judicial development of the USA in recent years has also demonstrated this point.[50] As a result, to half-judicialize or semi-judicialize the people's courts of today's China is not in contradiction to the further specialization of the judiciary. On the contrary, they are compatible and even facilitate each other.

As a matter of fact, some intermediate courts in China are currently undergoing reforms of similar features or have proposed some suggestions on reform, such as to make the position of clerk a full-time job,[51] to separate judges from other staff in the court.[52] Those practices actually intend to non-judicialize those non-judicial people who are even working in intermediate or high courts and with an educational background in law. Through this way, we can encourage the true vocational judges to take shape and encourage them to feel to have this job, have a sense of responsibility, reduce corruption, and at the same time improve their working efficiency. A thing is valued if it is rare. Careful readers should have realized that the conclusion of this article seems to not be in line with the judgment at the very beginning, but the aims are the same. In this sense, my analysis and the central viewpoint of He Weifang are different in approach but the same in result. I am not willing to "seek" jobs in China's judicial undertakings for those comrades-in-arms whom I have never met before, only because I myself used to be a soldier and

---

[49] Suli: "On Specialization of Legal Activities", *Rule of Law and Its Native Resources*, China University of Politics and Law Press, 1996, pp. 129ff; Richard A. Posner, *The Problems of Jurisprudence*, Harvard University Press, 1990, especially its Introduction and Chap. 3 "Professionalism."

[50] Posner, *The Problematics of Moral and Legal Theory*, as previous note 22, pp. 190–206.

[51] For example, Xia Feng: "A Few Thoughts on Building Order System of Clerks," *Comprehensive Talks on Reform of China's Judicial System—Essay Collection of the Sixth Academic Seminar of China's Court System*, edited by Essay Evaluation and Selection Committee of the Sixth Academic Seminar, People's Court Publishing House, 1994, pp. 411ff.

[52] Such as Xin Shangmin: "Establishing progressive selection system of judges is a key to guarantee qualities of judges," *Comprehensive Talks on Reform of China's Judicial System—Essay Collection of the Sixth Academic Seminar of China's Court System*, edited by Essay Evaluation and Selection Committee of the Sixth Academic Seminar, People's Court Publishing House, 1994, pp. 432ff.

have always been and will feel proud to be a soldier, and have never regretted for spending my youth as a soldier. For me, it does not matter who enters the court. The real problem is who can get things done, do things for ordinary people, and be good for China's long-term development. What is more important is whether one can do that and how one can achieve that.

For this reason, the really important point of this article is not regarding my certain specific conclusion on judges of basic-level courts and a series of suggestions which I have concluded, which are extremely sketchy but cannot be refined, and may be seen as idle theorization. Through this series of analyses, which start not from a definition itself, but from experience I have put forward, and at least try to answer with logical problems which, I believe, are not given enough emphasis in the legal circles or the judicial circles of modern China. At the very least, we have once again discovered the reality that "things in the world are complicated" and that we cannot solve and cannot even really understand China's problems from any one definition or proposition.

Honestly speaking, I pay more attention to the series of problems gradually demonstrated through the analysis of this article. This includes the establishment issue of China's basic-level institutions—is it really necessary to include a people's tribunal in the official court system, and is it really necessary to use official judges? Is it necessary to ask them to maintain the qualification requirements of judges which are difficult to be fulfilled if the measure of planned economy is not adopted? Even if they are realized in form, do advantages really outweigh disadvantages? Or to whom the advantages outweigh the disadvantages? I have also implied some other problems in the court system of modern China. For example, the jurisdiction by levels in today's courts is not good for judges at the basic-level to improve their professional qualities, and the selection system of judges in today's China is likely to increase its dependence on local government and make the community of judges more closed. The implied meaning of these conclusions is that the selection of judges may have to be centralized properly if we want to gradually form jurisdiction based on division of labor or division of functions.

I have even put forward questions or a certain new possibility for the legal education of today's China, including its curriculum, its educational aim, and the positive or negative role it has actually played in modern society. It is not possible to raise these questions in a normalized and therefore comprehensively legitimized theoretical framework of modernized rule of law. It is true that these questions demand more detailed analysis and discussion, and I'm not sure, or insistent, that my answers or implied answers are correct, but I will definitely put forward these questions and give legitimacy to a thorough discussion. Moreover, I believe that, based on the discussions targeted at specific questions, researchers are themselves in charge of raising questions based on legal research and can real questions be raised instead of vaguely and generally discussing big, albeit useless topics.

Theoretically speaking, my analysis, in certain sense, has actually reobserved the role or the possible role played by China's demobilized soldiers as a special group in today's Chinese society in a broader and modernized social aspect. This kind of analysis is preliminary though its perspective is brand new and the conclusions it has drawn are beyond what I imagined when I started this chapter. For example, the Chinese army has created a society of strangers in a way relatively disconnected from society, and this "society" has shaped those young soldiers; it has shaped the modern sense of individualism or certain aspects of individualism in activities of collectivism. Although those analyses are very preliminary, it is absolutely possible to open up a new research field and provide a new research perspective for sociological research of these questions in the future.

My analyses and many conclusions may be once again inappropriate for readers who like authors that show their attitudes right away and give explicit conclusions, especially in today's "turbulent" (in its derogatory sense) tide of judicial reform. Many opinions seem to become the final conclusions of jurist circles or legal circles, and it seems as if I'm making some inharmonious voicings and may make those officials and scholars who seem to know all the answers take more time to reflect on their decisions which have been tinted by the popular colors of legitimacy. I myself often reflect on my inappropriateness and have no conclusion. Maybe I should avoid such Hamlet-style reflection and obtain peace of mind and confidence from the words of Chief Justice Holmes:

> I know I'm not God, so when people… do something and I can't explicitly prohibit them from doing so by quoting from the Constitution, I then say, no matter I like it or not, 'Go to hell and let them mess it up!'

First Draft on 7th to 12th November
Second Draft on 18th to 20th November
At Cambridge

Appendix: Magistrates and Magistrate Jurisdiction in the USA

Summary of Magistrates

(Henry J. Abraham, *The Judicial Process: An Introductory Analysis of the Courts of the United States, England, and France*, 6th ed. Oxford University Press, 1993, pp. 138–140.)

With rare exception, the lowest court at the state level—and there are those who would put the noun *court* into quotation marks in this particular connection—is the *Justice of the Peace*, originally a fourteenth-century Anglo-Saxon office. The officeholder is often, and sometimes irreverently, referred to as the "J.P." (standing for "Justice for the Plaintiff," in some eyes). The J.P. is also occasionally styled as *squire* and *magistrate* increasingly in many cities (e.g., New York). By no means are they necessarily a lawyer, this official is usually elected for a two- to six-year term in counties, townships, and towns, but sometimes he or she is appointed for a term of similar length by the executives in the cities. The office has an honorable and, indeed, ancient tradition that came to the colonies from England. It was initially designed to aid in the administration of justice in minor matters at the local level.

Today, the Justice of the Peace, who is usually also a public notary, still performs a modicum of court work, but many of the duties are quasi-legislative, quasi-judicial, and quasi-administrative, including, characteristically, the performance of civil marriages. Most of these tasks are undertaken on a fee basis—probably a regrettable practice in view of its close link to meting out justice. The J.P. does, however, retain at least the appearance of a court of first instance in minor civil and criminal matters. In the former, the jurisdiction normally extends only to cases involving less than $300; in the latter, it is limited almost exclusively to misdemeanors.

With notable exceptions, again usually confined to some urban areas—for example, New York City, where magistrates have a legal background, are appointed for ten-year terms of office, and receive about $86,000 annually, an unusually high figure for that office, which normally commands a far lower remuneration—the Justice of the Peace's lack of training and qualifications is exceeded only by a surefire penchant for convictions, which have averaged 96 % in civil cases and 80 % in criminal cases.[53] A study conducted in 1956 of a minor judiciary of North Carolina found that not a single J.P. in that state then had a law degree, that 75 % had never gone to college, and that 40 % had never even attended high school![54] A similar study in Virginia a decade later showed that of 411 past and present members of the Association of Justices of the Peace of Virginia, a mere four were lawyers, 71 % had never gone to college, only five of the 29 % actually graduated, and 18 % were not even high school graduates.[55] In Oregon, only nine of the seventy JPs surveyed had law degrees in 1966.[56] Even in such a cosmopolitan city as Philadelphia, only six of its twenty-eight elected magistrates held a law degree in 1968. All this represents an unfortunate state of affairs, and given the suitable attributes of integrity and proper qualifications, the Justice of the Peace might well still provide able and inexpensive adjudication and settlement of minor legal problems in the judicial process. But Philadelphia's then Chief Magistrate, Joseph J. Hersch, insisted in a 1961 interview, followed in 1968 by his successor, John Patrick Walsh, that the job of the magistrate is "more social then legal;" he decried the increasing clamor for the law degree, stating:

> A law degree doesn't make a magistrate more qualified. Living with people is more essential than going to a law library to find out what it's all about. … If you take Purdon's law books away from them [the lawyers], they're out of business.[57]

---

[53]In 1962 in Pennsylvania, of 63,040 criminal cases handled by the then 4305 J. P.s, 51,997, or about 83 % resulted in convictions, another 6375, or 10 % were bound over for court trial; and 4688, or about 7 %, were dismissed (XI *Horizons for Modern Governments* May 5, 1963, p. 4). For examples of conviction rates from 95 to 99.2 % in Michigan, Mississippi, and Tennessee counties, see Mitchell Dawson, "The Justice of the Peace Racket," in Robert Morlan and David L. Martin, *Capitol Courthouse and City Hall*, 6th ed. (Boston: Houghton Mifflin, 1981).

[54]Isham Newton, "The Minor Judiciary in North Carolina" (unpublished Ph.D. thesis, University of Pennsylvania, 1956).

[55]"Justice of the Peace in Virginia: A Neglected Aspect of the Judiciary," 52 *Virginia Law Review* 151 (January 1966), describing a survey conducted by Weldon Cooper of the institute of Government of Pennsylvania, 1956).

[56]*The Christian Science Monitor*, May 9, 1967, p. 5.

[57]Interview with author (Henry J. Abraham) on December 18, 1961.

Yet evidence of questionable judicial qualifications based on bench behavior that have continued to surface with some consistency is not likely to stop the drive for an end of judicial staffing in the local court's offices. However, as noted earlier, in 1976, the US Supreme Court ruled in a Kentucky case[58] that a non-lawyer jurist may preside even at a criminal trial involving possible jail sentences, at least when the defendant has an opportunity, through an appeal, to obtain a second trial before a judge who is a lawyer. In the case at issue, the lay City Judge, C.B. Russell, had not only proved himself incompetent, but outrageously so.[59] But following the US Supreme Court's holding, a number of state supreme courts (e.g., New Hampshire, Washington, Idaho, and Florida) upheld the utilization of lay judges in sundry cases.[60] On the other hand, North Carolina enacted a statute requiring all judges to have a new degree.

Trial Courts of Jurisdiction

(Robert A. Carp and Ronald Stidham, *Judicial Process in America*, 4th ed., Congressional Quarterly Inc., 1998, pp. 67–68, 68–69.)

Trial Courts of Limited Jurisdiction

Trial courts of limited jurisdiction handle the bulk of litigation in this country each year and constitute about 90 % of all courts in the USA.[61] They have a variety of names: Justice of the Peace courts, magistrate courts, municipal courts, city courts, county courts, juvenile courts, domestic relations courts, and metropolitan courts, to name some of the more common ones.

The jurisdiction of these courts is limited to minor cases. In criminal matters, for example, state courts deal with three levels of violations: infractions (the least serious), misdemeanors (more serious), and felonies (the most serious). Trial courts of limited jurisdiction typically handle infractions and misdemeanors. They may impose limited fines (usually no more than $1000) and jail sentences (generally no more than one year). In civil cases, these courts are usually limited to disputes under a certain amount, such as $500. In addition, these types of courts are often limited to certain kinds of matters: traffic violations, domestic relations, or cases involving juveniles, for example. Another difference is that in many instances, these limited courts are not courts of record. Because their proceedings

---

[58]North v. Russell, 427 US 328 (please see the first note in paragraph 21 in Chap. 2).

[59]See the description of Allen Ashman and Pat Chapin, "Is the Bell Tolling for Non-Lawyer Judges?," 59 *Judicature* 9 (April 1976).

[60]Thus, New Hampshire's Supreme Court, following North, upheld a similar arrangement for its state, which allows a denovo trial in the Superior Court following a lay judge court decision below.

[61]Harry P. Stumpf, *American Judicial Politics*, Harcourt Brace Jovanovich, 1988, p. 75.

are not recorded, appeals of their decisions usually go to a trial court of general jurisdiction for what is known as a trial de novo (new trial).

But another outstanding feature of trial courts of limited jurisdiction is that the presiding judges are often not required to have any formal legal training. As a matter of fact, many judges are part-time amateurs who are even not familiar with the most basic legal concepts.[62]

Those courts suffer from a serious lack of resources. Often, they have no permanent courtroom, meeting instead in grocery stores, restaurants, or private homes. Clerks are frequently not available to keep adequate records. The results are informal proceedings and the processing of cases on a mass basis. Full-fledged trials are rare, and cases are disposed of quickly.

Finally, we should note that trial courts of limited jurisdiction are used in some states to handle preliminary matters in felony criminal cases. They often hold arraignments, set bail, appoint attorneys for indigent defendants, and conduct preliminary examinations. The case is then transferred to a trial court of general jurisdiction for such matters as hearing pleas, holding trials, and sentencing.

Trial Courts of General Jurisdiction

Most states have one set of major trial courts that handle the most serious criminal and civil cases. In addition, in many states, special categories, such as juvenile criminal offenses, domestic relations cases, and probate cases, are under the jurisdiction of trial courts of general jurisdiction.

In the majority of states, these courts also have an appellate function. They hear appeals in certain types of cases that originate in trial courts of limited jurisdiction. These appeals are often heard in a trial de novo or tried again in the court of general jurisdiction.

General trial courts are usually divided into judicial districts or circuits. Although the practice varies from state to state, the general rule is to use existing political boundaries such as a county or a group of counties in establishing the district or circuit. In rural areas, the judge may ride from one town to another within the district or circuit to hold court in different parts of the territory according to a fixed schedule. In urban areas, judges hold court in a prescribed place throughout the year. In larger counties, the group of judges may be divided according to specialization. Some may hear only civil cases; others try criminal cases exclusively.

The courts at this level have a variety of names. The most common are district, circuit, and superior. As noted earlier, Ohio and Pennsylvania still cling to the title "court of common pleas." New York is undoubtedly the most confusing of all; its trial court of general jurisdiction is called the supreme court. The judges at this level are required by law in all states to have law degrees. These courts also maintain clerical help because they are courts of record. In other words, a degree of professionalism is evident at this level that is often lacking in the trial courts of limited jurisdiction.

[62]See, Allen Ashman and Pat Chapin, "Is the Bell Tolling for Non Lawyer Judges?" *Judicature* 59, 1976, pp. 417–421.

Part IV
Reflection on Research Method

Chapter 11
Power Resources of Legal Sociology Surveys

A Reflection on the Social Survey Process

"Power" is basically the ability of an actor or organization to influence the attitudes and actions of other actors or organizations.

—*Blackwell Encyclopedia of Political Science* (Deng Zhenglai (chief editor) trans., China University of Political Science and Law Press, 1992, p. 595).

11.1 Emergence of This Question

While this topic is big, it is a small event that inspired this chapter.

About a year ago, I went to Province H to conduct a field survey. It was there that I met a university mate who worked in the politics and law committee of that province. During our casual conversation, they talked about some anecdotes of the secretary of the politics and law committee and the director of the public security bureau of the province whom he used to work for. The director of the public security bureau was a loyal, responsible communist who cared about the sufferings of the people. He often went into the villages disguised to do surveys of the communities and the people, and he worked in a careful manner. For example, during one of his visits, he asked my friend several times to "report a case" to the local police office out of nothing, so as to observe whether local policemen really cared about the suffering of the people, as well as their manner when providing their services. When reporting the case, my friend did not disclose his real identity or say thanks to the policeman—at least not until the policeman walked out of the gate of the police office with my friend. This was to avoid making the policemen feel as though they were being fooled for too long. There were even some times when the director of the public security bureau would check his watch to see whether the policemen were able to arrive at the so-called case (such as robbery) location

© Foreign Language Teaching and Research Publishing Co., Ltd
and Springer Science+Business Media Singapore 2016
S. Zhu, *Sending Law to the Countryside*, China Academic Library,
DOI 10.1007/978-981-10-1142-9_11

within a set time after reporting the case on the telephone without disclosing his real identity. He did so to get to know the conventional response of public security officers. If they were not able to arrive in time, the director would seriously criticize the local department of public security and ask them to make corrections. Such stories are bound to be the perfect materials as "the main theme" for news reporters or directors of TV series, and, honestly speaking, have won my admiration and touched my feelings—but that is all; it all seemed to have nothing to do with my academic research.

After one year, those anecdotes accidentally came to my mind and I suddenly realized that those stories do actually have some academic significance. My interest lies in the following questions. Didn't this director of public security bureau use this method to conduct his empirical and experiential research, as well as in order to obtain "knowledge" which he cared about but he might not even call its knowledge? Can we adopt this "method" of survey and research as well?

At least in a certain sense, this director of the public security bureau was also obtaining a kind of real knowledge, and this was the kind that I myself, a researcher of legal sociology who cares about social lives in Modern China, want to obtain. Moreover, as compared with me going to the countryside to do surveys on courts, inspect the education level of policemen, case reception rates, and crime detection rates, just listening to their introductions about themselves and observing their case dealing, the practice of the director is obviously more effective and direct. At least in certain issues, the knowledge he has obtained on local "policemen, politics, and law" is more accurate, more convincing, and more directly related to daily lives of ordinary people. But it is obvious that I can't use this kind of method. The question is why can't I? People will say, if you do so, then you will be in big trouble. This is true. In better cases, we will be warned for reporting false cases to obviously disrupt public service, while in the worse cases, I may be detained, and even suffer some aggression if I meet some "unfriendly" policemen who feel like "resorting to violent manners."

However, I had never done that. I didn't do that not because of the consequences, but, honestly speaking, not because of fear but because I have never thought of using this kind of research method. My social life and experiences, status, and the education I have received on how to do academic research has shaped my habits and characteristics and at the same time deprived me of my imagination while conducting social surveys and research. Thankfully, I experienced this unconventional, yet effective, method. We may be unable to obtain the same kind of knowledge, although both of us are keen and eager to have specific knowledge out of different professional interests and aims, and I can't overcome the obstacles for obtaining knowledge with my authority, even though I have the same sincerity for understanding real situations. In a certain sense, we may well say that this knowledge indeed is there, but for my specific research, this knowledge is beyond my ability and it is therefore in this sense that the knowledge actually does not exist.

For this reason, I need to ask, what is the difference between me and the director of the public security bureau? What has constructed our different approaches and methods for obtaining knowledge? Obviously, it is power. This very simple example has at least made one thing clear, the power and the dominating relationship between knowledge seekers and the objects of knowledge seeking based on power are important conditions for obtaining knowledge. If this relation were absent, then it could not exist, and there would be willingness for seeking knowledge, all the while knowing that this survey, as an action, would be impossible.

Thus, I realize that the knowledge we can obtain is definitely limited. The limit here is not out of a general sense, or out of a limit in the efforts one can make, or even the degree that one can be smart and sensitive. Nor is it a limit of educational training, cultural difference, language difference, gender, or individual difference. It is actually out of the difference between the power positions among the power dominating relationship.

This conclusion is actually "not felt new today" in the sociological study. Foucault put forward an acute postmodern proposition on knowledge production—in a word, knowledge is the production of power. In a series of writings, especially in the discussion of *Discipline and Punishment*, he deals with this topic deeply.[1] Said adopt Foucault's ideal in his *Orientalism* and discuss the historical, social, and political conditions for the study of orientalism.[2] Both of them see power dominating relationships as one of the fundamental conditions for certain knowledge to happen. This has put forward a fundamental challenge for certain methodological propositions of sociology research. They have made the process of knowledge formation an object of the reflection and research of sociology.

This point is also in line with the reflection of sociology or "sociology of sociology" suggested in principle, although definitions, terms, and approaches used are very much different. If according to Bourdieu's view, we can see sociological survey and research as a field, within which the production of knowledge depends on the mobilization and utilization of at least three kinds of capital—economic capital, social capital, and cultural capital[3]—then the amount of capital and type of capital may influence the knowledge power of the surveyor, and thus influence the type, quantity and quality of the "knowledge" he or she may obtain.

The story at the beginning and the following casual thoughts must be further analyzed, polished, and illustrated to have significance on sociological surveys and research. In one aspect, there may be some people who will argue with the normative view that the knowledge studied and pursued by sociology and anthropology has its specialty which only cares about academics and genuine knowledge, while the surveys and research of sociology and anthropology just aim to eliminate this power and the power dominating relationship, since the power and the power dominating relationship—at least according to traditional views—are often

[1]Michel Foucault, *Discipline and Punish: the Birth of the Prison*, trans. by Alan Sheridan, Vintage Books, 1978.

[2]Edward W. Said, *The Orientalism*, Penguin Books, 1978.

[3]Pierre Bourdieu, Loic Wacquant: *Practice and Reflection—Introduction to Reflexive Sociology*, translated by Li Meng and Li Kang, Central Compilation and Translation Press, 1998, and Bao Yaming (chief editor): *Interview of Pierre Bourdieu—Cultural Capital and Social Alchemy*, translated by Bao Yaming, Shanghai People's Press, 1997.

(if not always) distorting the development of academics and impeding obtaining genuine knowledge. However, the story above has denied this viewpoint itself. What the director of the public security bureau obtained through his power was not an error, nor was it insignificant to academics (for example, if we want to get to know the responsive ability of an official legal organization in a certain region, as well as the manner and quality of the service provided by policemen to local people).

There may be some people who argue from an empirical viewpoint that although by analyzing the above example, we can conclude that power and the dominating power relationship is an important condition and even precondition for obtaining knowledge, this kind of power and power dominating relationship are only one of the preconditions for obtaining a certain knowledge and that this example is not enough to demonstrate that this kind of dominating relationship must exist and always exist in the field research of sociology or anthropology. As a matter of fact, many outstanding anthropologists and sociologists have been consistently emphasizing in their research reports and reflection on methodology that you must respect the objects you study (seek knowledge), respect different cultures, and hold a kind of humble attitude toward seeking knowledge. For this reason, this kind of power dominating relationship seems not to exist during well-conducted kind, sincere, scientific, and fair-minded research. Moreover, sociologists and anthropologists do not have the kind of power that the above director of public security bureau has at all. Based on this, people may argue or conclude that the problem illustrated by this example does not have common sense.

This means that to make this example have relevant and suitable sense of vigilance to my research, I must reflect further on my field research and observe whether the similar power and power dominating relationships always exist, what do they depend on, and how have they been constructed in my field survey. For this reason, I turn to reflection and observation in my field survey.

11.2 One Analysis on Power Relationships

My research is about the function of China's basic-level justice system; it is funded by the Ford Foundation. It is because of the sponsorship of the Ford Foundation that my research was possible. If there was no such money, or only the tiny amount of money for social scientific projects from a particular state, province, or department (50,000 RMB at most—less than 6000 USD), I and other researchers would not be able to conduct these field surveys. Please note that I did not say that I could not study basic-level justice without money. I'm just saying that it was just because of this money—not only because of money, as I will discuss later—that we could go to the field and observe the basic-level judiciary on site. We could pay relevant fees and try our best to lower the burden of courts, public security bureaus, and judicial units with which we conducted interviews. They did not need to spend anything, or perhaps spent less, by receiving us (we could rid off the suspicion of "cheating in order to eat and drink" and win a little dignity of intellectuals which has become especially sensitive in the field).

By doing this, we could win over their cooperation and make this kind of cooperation easier and more thorough.[4] In this sense, and at a certain level, it is this sum of research capital that has established and maintained this relationship of research and enabled us to obtain information about China's basic-level judicial situation.

As a matter of fact, many research projects cannot go on without money, which is admitted by almost all researchers of sociology, anthropology, and other disciplines, no matter whether they are about natural science, social science, or the humanities. It is true that money does not mean success, but to those scholars who are willing to do a little practical, empirically based research, money means that they have a possibility to establish this kind of dominating relationship with the question or object they want to study, a channel to obtain certain true or false knowledge, and a possible right of speech on this problem (such as attending certain meetings, submitting a thesis, and publishing research results). Here, money is both power and right. It can be said that there is a kind of "power for money deal," in a non-negative sense.[5]

Honestly, it is absolutely impossible to live without money, but as many people say today, money is not possible in every way. Money is not enough to guarantee the stability of this dominating relationship and can sometimes damage and hamper power dominating relations. For example, paying "wages" to interviewee can sometimes make them "actively cooperate" in an excessive way and cater to us intentionally. In today's China, some people may feel like they are treated as information channels only and interviewees with self-esteem issues may even refuse to cooperate. In certain fields, it is even more difficult for money to guarantee sincere and effective cooperation of respondents. This point is very prominent in my sociology research concerning the judiciary, if not outstanding.

The judiciary is a set of systems of the power function of the state, and it has its own internal institutions, both formal or informal. Such institutions make it difficult to enter for people outside this system, while people inside the system hold certain vigilance and suspicion and thus refuse to cooperate; this resists the kind of power dominating relation which we are trying to establish. For this reason, we should impose a certain influence on them and make them do things which they have abundant institutional or personal reasons to refuse to do without increasing

[4]It is very difficult for the basic-level courts which we visited to get full funding. They not only lacked work expenditures seriously, and some courts even paid their judges 80 % of their salary. In a poverty-stricken county, a judge told me that of the 12 months of the previous year, he received less than 200 yuan each month in 9 months and 3 months in which 100 yuan was delayed temporarily or deducted due to fees (such as poverty relief, "voluntary donation" organized by the court, fees to fight flood and deal with emergencies).

[5]In this sense, in today's China, many subjects which are supposed to emphasize empirical research depend their "research results" on copying other books and "fabricating books," including using ancient books. Why? Apart from the academic model of "elaborating the theories of the predecessors while having no original ideas of one's own," and the training lacking empirical research, one of the important reasons may be having no money to conduct empirical research. If this speculation is established, then judging from this perspective, the issue of money can even influence the general patterns of the academic development of a nation.

their economic burdens when this kind of influence does not exist,[6] and we must provide other resources to guarantee this dominating power relation as the precondition for us to investigate and understand situations.

Our research has encountered this kind of impediment. As a matter of fact, our research does not intend to obtain certain secret information. We do not attempt to spy upon the state judicial system's secrets or court privacy. What we want to understand are very ordinary situations. We know from our instinct that without the guarantee of certain power, we may well encounter cold faces. Since it is not necessary for courts and judges, we interviewed to associate with us strangers, and we do not have any relations with them and cannot bring about any direct interest—but may cause troubles. In order to break down this kind of obstacle and achieve confidence and cooperation from the courts and judges we visited, we utilized all kinds of resources.

We asked some political and legal departments of higher levels to notify in advance the basic-level courts in which we planned to conduct our research, either orally or by issuing a letter of introduction from political and legal departments of a higher level. Apart from this, according to the "rules," which are quite popular in China's society of today in which "public things must be dealt with privately while private things must be dealt with publicly," we borrowed the acquaintance relationships of students, teachers, fellow villagers, and others, while also giving previous notice to some people in the court, especially the president and the vice presidents. As a matter of fact, when choosing courts of research, we did consider factors of this kind, but did not think about the representativeness of sampling only—at a point, there were two basic-level courts with very similar situations, and why did we choose this one instead of that one? Was it only the issue of sampling? The courts observed in our research had students I used to teach[7] who took certain posts in the local courts or had a certain ability of activity (i.e., had certain dominating power).

That is to say in order to guarantee that they cooperate with us and give us convenience to obtain knowledge, we had utilized at least two kinds of resources. One was the official power of the court system or political and legal systems of higher levels, and the other was the unofficial power resources accumulated from my previous social contacts. It is true that the latter resource might only be possible in traditional or transitional China, and it was even more essential. These two resources, from the level of retrospection, strengthened our dominating power relationship with objects who sought knowledge.

---

[6]Please note that that this actually implies the most common definition of power in political science: the ability of actors or institutions to influence the attitudes and behaviors of other actors or institutions.

[7]In a court we visited, there were 4 students taking different posts who I used to teach. Apart from them, there was an alumnus of Peking University who was taking a senior post as well as a classmate of an acquaintance who worked as the president of the court. Our interview achieved the best results in the jurisdiction of this court.

The analysis here is abstract, but the field research is our actual experience. When the numbers of power resources we utilized were different, we achieved clearly different results during our field interviews. Certainly, I can't claim that it must have a uniform causal relationship or even symmetrical association. Even if the personal factors of interviewers remain unchanged, the number of times using such resources was not the only deciding factor for the results obtained. Due to the personal characteristics of interviewers themselves (some are more outspoken and candid while some are quite cautious during conversation), the dominating relationship formed and its depth and stability are not always the same even when the interviewer utilizes the same resources (I will explain later the implication here). However, how many times these resources are utilized is indeed related to the difficulty of obtaining relevant information. In a court of a certain county, there was only one student I used to teach working there. We neither utilized resources of the official court system (no introduction letter from court or political and law committee of the higher level or previous words from them), nor had or used other acquaintance relationships. We were received politely and properly with cooperation, but when we wanted to look into a case file mentioned during our interview with them, we encountered some trouble—and did not see the file eventually. Certainly, if I were them, I would do the same thing. Their caution was fully understandable. For this reason, the situations we wanted to get to know were unobtainable sometimes or unable to be supported with more evidence from original resources. In another court, we had used almost all possible relations, which were later seen as too adequate,[8] and we were given comprehensive cooperation, although the situations we wanted to know did not exceed those in the previous court.

11.3 Analysis Two of Power Relationship

We had not only borrowed relationships between superior and subordinate inside the institution, but also launched this relationship through private channels. However, the influence of institutional relationships was sometimes very limited at the very concrete level, especially because we had interviews and observation as our methods. The court of lower level could accept the instruction of the court of higher level or institution concerned to assist our academic research, but this could not guarantee that every interviewee in the court of lower level obey the instruction. Specific interviewees might do something perfunctorily, instead of accepting our interview with a positive attitude. It was not necessary for them to talk about their experience and internal feelings; it was their choice whether they could have talked more or less. It was not their responsibility. They might even dislike

[8] I only give one example here. When we arrived at the city, we noticed that there were even two departments sending people to meet us at the station, which made us feel extremely uneasy.

instructions from the superior level—they did not need to show or disclose this feeling publicly. At this time, the official power resources we utilized might play a negative role on the individual level.

In particular, when we studied the people's tribunals which ranked several levels below the court of the provincial level which we previously discussed, it was especially the case. There are sayings like "a field commander must decide, even against king's order," "a county magistrate cannot do better than the chief directly in charge," or "a dragon is not stronger than a local snake" from ancient China. As long as the instruction of "giving cooperation" is not from the chief directly in charge, judges of people's tribunals may well be ignored and do something superficially. Many judges of people's tribunals are posted in the villages, and they do not have much in regards to expectations (of either promotions or otherwise) from their superior. Theoretically, they have nothing to fear when facing us researchers. In this sense, it was impossible for the dominating relationship which was established based on the superior–inferior relationship of institutions that was necessary for obtaining knowledge with stability for a long time. It is determined to be like any other superior–inferior relationship in any other institution which is fluid and changeable.[9] Under this situation, I discovered in retrospect that in order to strengthen our dominating power relationship which was established by borrowing superior–inferior relationships, an important point was to build a kind of personal relationship at the individual level, especially a power relationship between us and the interviewee, which softens the superior–inferior relationship.

We can still resort to many kinds of resources through building this kind of personal relationship, but a resource which might be more important may be our identities and daily behaviors which may play a direct role in the interviews themselves. In review, our research actually used a large number of this kind of resources, especially my identity as the professor in the law faculty of Peking University. When I conducted interviews and research in a certain court, some interviewees emphasized many times that this was the first time intellectuals from the universities of the highest level in China had come and claimed that this would be marked in the local history (the speakers of which might be very sincere, but it was a kind of painful exaggeration for us). For another example, my teaching used to leave those students (judges) with very good impressions. It was practical and vivid, understanding difficulties and hardship of judges, and linking theory to practice. In addition, they came to know that I am a doctor who had studied in America for many years. All these factors made them feel that my research and interviews were a kind of earnest sign of concern about them. Although we repeatedly told them explicitly that interviews did not play to and could not bring any material benefits to them or improve their working environment—they still believed that it was a kind of recognition for them when their ordinary, routine, and practical work without any theories could draw attention of "scholars," especially "scholars from Peking University." When they knew that we lived in a hotel

[9]Foucault, as previous note 1 please also see section 3–6 of Chap. 1 of this book: "Why Send Law to the Countryside?"

in the village which was only 8 yuan per night, they even said that they made us suffer—although we had pointed out that we stayed here for only two days while they had to work here one year after another.

Honestly speaking, we did not have the mentality of using interviewees subjectively, but we still feel that due to the great disparity of "cultural capital," the gesture seen by the interviewees as "going deep into the grass root" enabled us to obtain a large amount of "symbolic profits," as mentioned by Pierre Bourdieu. This greatly increased the resources we could utilize and the interactive relationship, thus establishing a more of personal relationship instead of the power relationship between superior and subordinate. This facilitated our research and interviews, and actually strengthened the dominating relationship in terms of seeking knowledge, although it was a dominating relationship based on voluntary cooperation of both parties.

The identity of professor from Peking University and doctor who studied abroad was not always useful. Not all judges would "take" this identity. Although normally speaking, the difference of social status is more possible to bring symbolic profit for people with high ranking; to some people with individualist ideals, this difference makes them even more reluctant to cooperate. Some ordinary people in China do have a demeanor of celebrity, and there are more of them in my generation, or in another word (to my regret), left in my generation.

Among the judges of courts in different places, there are a certain number of former military-transferred cadres or demobilized soldiers. Some of them are quite good, in either their ability or wisdom. Due to the imbalanced development of social and economic development in different places of China, especially in urban and rural areas, they could only get away from rural areas by joining the army. In particular during the decade-long Cultural Revolution, joining the army was actually the best way out for young people with a certain degree of education at that time. After 1978, when the university entrance examination was resumed, they may not have been able to pass the examination or be permitted to take part in the examination because they were soldiers. Without diploma, switching to a new job without professional training, they surely feel somewhat lost and thus must have strong dignity. In addition, they have life experience—some of them even commanded "thousands of soldiers" themselves. It is therefore not easy to impress them with a certain identity (even of a celebrity). If they got to know me and my story, they would see me as a "lucky fellow" and put me into another category with an attitude of "staying at a respectable distance." My experience, staying in the army for over 5 years in the 1970s plus studying in America, would easily break their "classification." My "venturing out to rural areas to do field research" would no longer serve as a gesture to them anymore, but induce a real feeling of intimacy. During many interviews, I heard more than once that "you are different, and you are more pragmatic." I not only had gained more symbolic profits, but more, I was granted access to their true feelings regarding their work in the court. My rich experience not only created an affiliation effect toward demobilized cadres in the court, but as a matter of fact, was quite effective in establishing a bond with many court cadres in my age range.

I want to emphasize a few points. First of all, we definitely cannot equate this dominating relationship of knowledge seeking to the dominating relationship of human communication. The former is a dominating power relationship, limited to seeking knowledge established due to the difference between social structure and people's social expectations. Only when a relationship of equality in human communication, built on common sense, is established can a more stable and reliable dominating relationship of knowledge seeking be established and maintained. Secondly, the dominating relationship of seeking knowledge which is based on this seemingly equal communication relationship cannot be established only or mainly by certain expressions or efforts made by people. As my military career has demonstrated, the establishment of this kind of relationship must be based on certain convincing social experience, such as similar or closely tied life experience. Similar experience is very important in the in-depth research of sociology, especially in the mentality of research of modern China. Not many interviewees will "preach to deaf ears." Although it is no longer the case that a gentleman is ready to die for his bosom friends, it is roughly applicable in today's Chinese society that "when drinking with a bosom friend, a thousand cups will not be too many." Similar life and work experience is normally one of the prerequisites for this kind of "bosom friendship."

Thirdly, this kind of human relationship is established in the day-to-day actions of both parties, instead of being realized by elaborate plans or manipulation of any one party. For this reason, it is not certain whether this kind of relationship can be established or not. There are even possibilities of it being subverted. When we were trying to complete our research and leave a certain court, a judge said something to the effect of "we can see that you are not good at drinking alcohol, but you behaved honestly when drinking and did not play any tricks. All of you are honest people." We thus came to know that our words and behavior were also observed by them. "To take in the view, on the bridge stood the viewer."[10] We were also objects for research and investigation by the interviewees. If we had not been honest or "true," it is possible our research would not have been as conveniently gathered.

The problem is that our honesty and other efforts did not require any extra giving. Our behavior was just an ordinary and persistent way to deal with people and things. Why is it that because of this that I have a kind of feeling of guilty?! Due to social structures and perceptions, some ordinary actions enable certain people to obtain "symbolic profits" and thus further objectively guarantee a dominating power relationship with objects we want to know.

11.4 Inspiration

One anthropologist against my analysis claims it is "postmodern."[11] His reasoning is that a certain amount of anthropological research does not lead to analyses like these. He used his research in the aboriginal areas in Taiwan as an example.

[10]Bian Zhilin: "A Broken Stanza," *Carving Insects*, People's Publishing House, 1979.

[11]This is the opinion of Mr. Li Yiyuan when criticizing this article.

He described in detail how he had lived in the "field" for a long time to get familiar with all kinds of customs of the local people, as well as learn their languages. He even talked about how he pretended to be asleep while listening to local boys discussing and commenting on girls, and how he pretended to go out on business but recorded what he had seen and heard in places where other people could not see him. He said that with this methodology, there was no dominating relationship of power.

There are two different points here. One is the general proposition; that is, the power resource is not the only condition for research, to which I personally agree. The power resource is the necessary condition for the production of knowledge. However, this does not mean that the power resource is enough to obtain knowledge. As a matter of fact, many research projects have plenty of capital, and some of them have even got support from state government departments. Due to insufficient capabilities or carelessness of researchers, research results are usually too poorly measured to be of use and can literally be regarded as a kind of disrespect to the phrase "research results" (even if there is an "essence" of research results). On the other hand, some leaders cannot understand the real situations. Although they may have great power and specialized research institutions and can utilize power and all kinds of resources, and researchers that truly want to understand the real situation, it still may not work. Indeed, the above-mentioned resources are not enough for obtaining knowledge. Knowledge production requires the knowledge and capabilities of researchers themselves in the traditional sense.[12]

What I can't agree with are the real examples he used to support his proposition, nor the analysis and nature of determination in those examples. For me, the utilization of "research techniques" is also a kind of utilization of power resources, to a certain degree. Please note that the classic determination of power is "the capability of actors to influence other actors," which inevitably includes capabilities of actors to cover their behaviors in a certain way and to make other actors act normally. Through such methods, he has turned himself into—actually disguised himself as—a member of the group being surveyed or investigated and thus improved his capability of obtaining materials and knowledge. "The best assault on a fortress is to attack from the inside." Those familiar with the story of "Taking

[12]This point can be argued. Where is our knowledge-acquiring capability from? Many of our capabilities of observation and analysis, especially the theoretical framework for analysis, are not obtained naturally as we grow up, but are achieved in the long process of education, learning, and training. On the other hand, not all people, or people with the same intellectual potential, have the same kind of opportunity for learning and training. Those opportunities are actually connected to the family's wealth, social, and living environment of many individuals (please think about the sayings like "children from poor families share the household burden early" and "it takes three generations to cultivate a nobleman" which imply that wealth builds different capabilities of people). If we see part of this capability as a kind of deposited wealth, then the proposition about the utilization of power resource—at least in logic—still holds water for the formation of knowledge capabilities, though I'm not that sure this is truly so. Research and analysis in terms of esthetic interests of related questions can refer to Pierre Bourdieu, *Distinction: A Social Critique of the Judgment of Taste*, trans. by Richard Nice, Harvard University Press, 1984.

Tiger Mountain by Strategy" will discover that at the level of obtaining knowledge not available to researchers, anthropologists doing research in the villages are not much different than Yang Zirong, who was exceptionally brave and resourceful when he disguised himself as Hu Biao. This kind of analogy has no intention of depreciating or elevating researchers of sociology or anthropology, but just to build a kind of connection between two phenomena which may seem to have no relation, in order to achieve a shock of reflection.

To me, the key is not about whether there is an intervention of power resources in academic research, but whether this power execution has ever harmed people being investigated or studied. For whatever reason, in China, we have given a kind of morally derogatory connotation to the definition of "power." It seems as if power is always bad and is even equal to evil (although in real life, many people including myself act in a manner in which we are pursuing power), and once the power resource is introduced into academic research, the academic themself must feel morally shamed. However, this is not true for power, which can be constructive depending on how you use it. It is the same for the political power. Research from many scholars has already demonstrated this point[13] and there are a large number of examples in our daily life (the power execution of that director of public security as one example). I therefore don't want to speak more about it.

In addition, traditional power is not only always defined legally—as mentioned by Foucault—but also accustomed to be substantialized. It is often seen as an object and a kind of privilege which belongs exclusively to certain people. We therefore are not able to analyze the power function in a more detailed and complicated manner, or see power as a kind of structural relationship, as a network, and as a comprehensive effect. The analysis of this research has pointed out that in sociological and anthropological research, there are also intervention and mobilization of power resources, and this mobilization is necessary. I can't deny that our research has or must have power factors only because we are not officials and the purpose of our research is purely for knowledge. Whether there is utilization of power resources in sociological and anthropological research is not provided by the moral or immoral motives of researchers regarding whether to subjectively harm the objects being studied.

What is the meaning of pointing this out? First of all, it may help us to reflect on so-called research methods. The author has written much on field research of sociology and anthropology. Among these writings are many books, especially textbooks that often take field research as a method to obtain the knowledge which is "just over there" and a route to enter the established knowledge-seeking structure. We have been warned about many precautions to take while doing research, but most advice is just technical guidance, such as knowing local languages, taking part in observations, respecting local customs and habits, avoiding bringing about adverse consequences to people being investigated or letting them have any

[13]Apart from the above-mentioned Foucault, please also see Anthony Giddens: *Nation State and Violence*, translated by Hu Zongze and Zhao Litao, SDX Joint Publishing Company, 1998, p. 9.

unreasonable expectations of "making a profit," having reliable people who are aware of local customs—certainly important and essential pieces of the experience of research. With accumulation of experience, a research method of sociology or anthropology which is commonly applicable seems to be formed. Although there is reflection on such methods and there is sometimes even strict criticism, the basic presumption or presupposition discussed by the question is that as long as such principles are followed, reliable, definite, and complete knowledge can be obtained. This article is at least a question for this methodology. It shows that at certain level or targeting certain questions, due to different power resources that can be mobilized, people can obtain different knowledge. I don't have the power resources of the director of public security and therefore can't get the knowledge that he can obtain. Such an abstract sociological or anthropological research method that is easily or already generalized is questionable.

My reflection also shows that during sociological research, the power we use for knowledge is not the formal and legal power used by a director of public security, as mentioned earlier. The power we use is based on many kinds of power resources (but also includes formal power resources), and the dominating power relationship thus formed is also different. But this kind of dominating relationship has to exist. Simply speaking, we have to seize an object which is as stable and "true" as possible. Only in this way may you obtain information and knowledge which you think is important. It is just during the process of forming this predominating relationship that the learning objective from whom you want to pursue knowledge gradually emerges, disclosing its information and enabling you to obtain knowledge. The obtaining of knowledge here is actually a process that the dominating power targeted at the learning object from whom you want to pursue knowledge forms and plays a role with—a process of "conquering" and a process of breaking through barriers and building access.

Certainly, as we are talking about dealing with specific people, in this field, it is not only social researchers that have capital or absolutely superior capital—those being surveyed do also have certain kinds of resources, more or less. For this reason, it means that any sociological research must be a game between two parties based on the capital each owns and a war without the smoke of gunpowder. But in another sense, it can be said to be a game joined by both parties—a conspiracy. Since the process of gaining knowledge is also the process of practice to enter this field and to get to know the object of study and the process that this dominating power relation forms, during research practice, there is no such sequence that one must get in first to eventually acquire knowledge later.

It is also in the sense of practice that I even suspect that there are some methods or methodologies independent of the production process of sociological knowledge. Epistemology is in accordance with the methodology here. From this structural perspective, the formation of knowledge, whether it is cultural, social, or natural, is highly similar, if not the same. The only difference may be that researchers are facing cultural activities, human activities, or natural activities.

If this conclusion stands, we must therefore re-inspect the boundary of knowledge that we are able to obtain. Since a power dominating relationship based on capital is not as we imagined that it, as long as we pay attention to certain things and have a sincere thirst for knowledge, and since our power resources are limited either in terms of categories or in terms of the amount of resources that can be consumed (certainly supplemented as well), then the amount of capital or even kind of capital owned determines not only influences, but the category and amount of "knowledge" researchers can get. Usually, we are not able to effectively build a comprehensive dominating relationship targeted at the learning object, but can only construct this relationship within the scope of our power resource. For this reason, we can never believe that we have obtained the truth based on one piece of excellent research. For me, I may never be able to gain the knowledge obtained by the director of public security, as mentioned in the first section. Similarly, the director of public security cannot obtain the knowledge I get due to limits constituted by his power resource.

In addition, just because there is mobilization and utilization of power resources in some sociology research and some people surveyed tend to resist the power of surveyors, we should be more cautious in mobilizing and utilizing the power resource available and in obtaining knowledge through this method. We should also be highly cautious about the results that such research might produce. This is not only because there are at least some researches or surveyors that have adopted dishonorable methods which have indeed brought about some inconvenience and embarrassment in the people being surveyed, who do no harm to others while bringing huge benefits in different forms to researchers themselves,[14] but what is more important is that if we forget about the mobilization of the power resources of researchers and surveyors themselves, but only care about the so-called truth, "learning knowledge for knowledge and doing academic work for academia's sake," then we will find a kind of justifiable reason for our inappropriate and even improper utilization of power resources. Just like falsehood, truth is sometimes also deadly (to other people).

This chapter not only intends to give a seemingly moralist warning; if previous analysis stands and is pushed to extremes, we will see that the analysis of power resources may help us to re-understand the research features of many subjects.

In the natural sciences, such as research in physics and chemistry, since the learning object is usually lifeless, the establishment of dominating power resources needed by the researcher often does not employ social or cultural capital. Even if there is mobilization of this capital from time to time, it is usually for achieving economic capital (just like a doctoral supervisor can more easily obtain research grants). Social capital or cultural capital cannot have direct effects on its learning objects (a molecule will not be more cooperative in the experiment whether the researcher is a doctor or an undergraduate).

In the literature and history of research in the humanities, the learning object is mainly all kinds of texts (in broad sense, including historical materials). For this

[14]It is highlighted in some news concerning real people and events and some literature reports, such as disputes caused by *Report on Majiajun* (Zhao Yu, the China Federation of Literary and Art Circles Publishing Corporation, 2000).

reason, building the relationship of dominating power with texts does not require much social or cultural capital either. However, since the meaning of texts is determined by society instead of being inherent,[15] the social or cultural capital of researchers will then play a really important and often indirect role. Similarly, talking about the research results of Li Bai, if the researcher is a professor who has devoted his whole life to studying Li Bai instead of someone less prominent, then the research results of the former may be more respected by society and more likely to influence other readers who moreso want to read about Li Bai rather than someone else. It will, to a certain extent, change the common meaning of a text in its social life.

For social sciences, especially sociology and anthropology, their learning objects are often, although not always, living people and their lives. In comparison, they are a kind of object which is less easily dominated or asked to cooperate. Then, it requires more social capital and cultural capital to guarantee the formation and persistence of the relationship of dominating power. Under certain circumstances, even all of this capital is not enough to ensure the necessary dominating relationship or to guarantee that the learning object will cooperate. For those subjects, field work is thus unavoidable. In this sense, there is no reason that field work cannot be regarded as a method to remove the vigilance and resistance of learning objects, as well as to guarantee the establishment of a dominating power relationship, and to guarantee the cooperation of a learning object (please recall the metaphor of the previous example, the "Taking Tiger Mountain by Strategy" concept).

Certainly, many researchers do not belong to one certain subject neatly, such as the jurisprudence. A researcher not only needs to deal with texts (laws, legal precedents), but also has to deal with people (judges, lawyers, plaintiffs and defendants, and others). Even if it deals with texts, legal texts are different from literary texts.[16] For this reason, the analysis here is just preliminary and general. But this kind of analysis may be regarded as supplementary access to the feature study of different subjects, although it is not and should not be considered alternative access.

Second draft on July 16, 1988

Third draft on July 25 in Weixiu Garden, Peking University

[15]There are many books of this kind. Please refer Stanley Fish, *Is There a Text in This Class?: The Authority of Interpretive Communities*, Harvard University Press, 1980; for Chinese materials, please see Stanley Fish, *Is There a Text in This Class?: The Authority of Interpretive Communities*, translated by Qian Yan, edited by Sheng Ning, collected in *Latest Collection of Western Literary Articles*, Lijiang Publishing House, 1991. For opposite opinions, please see E. D. Hirsch, *Validity in Interpretation*, translated by Wang Caiyong, Joint Publishing, 1991.

[16]Please see Suli: "Difficult Problems of Interpretation: Looking into Different Ways to Interpret Legal Texts," *Social Sciences in China*, Issue 3, 1997. Please also see: Richard A. Posner, *Law and Literature: A Misunderstood Relation*, Harvard University Press, 1988, especially Chap. 5.

References

Chinese Works

Aristotle. (1965). *Politics* (W. Shoupeng, Trans.). Beijing: The Commercial Press.
Bao, Y. (chief editor) (1997). *Interview of Pierre Bourdieu—Cultural capital and social alchemy* (Y. Bao, Trans.). Shanghai People's Press.
Biwu, D. (1985). *Dong Biwu collection.* People's Publishing House.
Black, D. J. (1994). *The behavior of law* (Y. Tang, Suli Trans.). Beijing: China University of Political Science and Law Press.
Bodenheime, E. (1987). *Jurisprudence—The philosophy and method of the law* (D. Zhenglai & J. Jingwu, Trans.). Huaxia Publishing House.
Bourdieu, P., & Wacquant, L. (1998). *Practice and reflection—Introduction to reflexive sociology* (L. Meng & L. Kang Trans.). Central Compilation and Translation Press.
Cao, R. (1998). Why can't demobilized and transferred soldiers work in the court? *Zhongguo Guofangbao.*
Cardozo, B. N. (1998). *Nature of the judicial process* (Suli, Trans.). Beijing: The Commercial Press.
Chen, H. (1991). Kettle director of tribunal. *People's Judicature.*
Chen, N. (1994). 'Peasant Household' Zhang Kaidi. *People's Judicature.*
Chen, R. (1996). China's code of criminal procedure after amendment—Analysis from the point of international standard of criminal justice. *Modern Law Science.*
Chunsen, M. T. (1994). Going with the waves. *People's Judicature.*
"Court management is a big subject," written by commentator of *People's Judicature.* (1994).
Criminal procedure code of the French republic (Y. Shutong & Z. Xie, Trans.). Beijing: China University of Political Science and Law Press. (1997).
Dai, J. (1994). Singing the song of Nanniwan again. *People's Judicature.*
De Montesquieu, C. D. (1961). *The spirit of the laws* (Y. Zhang, Trans.) Beijing: The Commercial Press.
de Tocqueville, A. (1992). *The old regime and the revolution* (F. Tang, Trans.). Beijing: The Commercial Press.
Dershowitz, A. M. (1994). *The best defense* (J. Tang, Trans.). Law Press China.
Duara, P. (1994). *Culture, power and state* (F. Wang Trans.). Jiangsu People's Publishing House.
Economic Tribunal of Jiangsu Higher People's Court. (1999). Several thoughts on how to improve the quality of economic dispute judgement document. *People's Judicature.*
Educational Statistics Yearbook of China. People's Education Press. (1997).

© Foreign Language Teaching and Research Publishing Co., Ltd
and Springer Science+Business Media Singapore 2016
S. Zhu, *Sending Law to the Countryside*, China Academic Library,
DOI 10.1007/978-981-10-1142-9

Engles. (1994). Anti-Duhring. *Selected works of marx and engels* (Vol. 3). People's Publishing House.
Fei, X. (1948). *The rebuilding of the countryside*. Shanghai Observer.
Fei, X. (1985). *Rural China*. SDX Joint Publishing Company.
Fei, X. (1993). *Rural China and rural reconstruction*. Storm and Stress Publishing.
Feng, X. (1999). *Wooden-legged justice*. Zhongshan University Press.
Foucault, M. (1998a). Nietzsche, genealogy, history (Suli Trans.) *Review of academic thoughts* (Issue 4). Liaoning University Press.
Foucault, M. (1998b). *The archaeology of knowledge* (Q. Xie & Y. Ma, Trans.). SDX Joint Publishing Company.
Foucault, M. (1999). 'Dangerous individuals' in the 19th century (Suli Trans.). *Forum of Social Theories*.
Fu, D. (1999). Judicial profession and independence of Germany. In B. Song (Ed.), *Procedural, justice and modernization*. Beijing: China University of Political Science and Law Press.
Fu, Y. (2000). Function and style of civil judgement document. *Social Sciences in China*.
Gadamer, H. G. (1995). *Truth and method (I)* (H. Hong, Trans.). Shanghai Translation Publishing House.
Giddens, A. (1998). *Nation state and violence* (Z. Hu & L. Zhao, Trans.). SDX Joint Publishing Company.
Hamilton, A., Jay, J., & Madison, J. (1980). *Federalist papers* (F. Chen, Trans.). Beijing: The Commercial Press.
Hayek, F. A. (1997). *The constitution of liberty* (D. Zhenglai, Trans.). SDX Joint Publishing Company.
He, L. (1999a). On reasons of judgement. *People's Judicature*.
He, W. (1985). Realizing social justice through judiciary: A perspective on current situations of Chinese judges. In Y. Xia (Ed.), *The age heading toward power*. Beijing: China University of Political Science and Law Press.
He, W. (1997). Two issues of China's judicial management system. *Social Sciences in China*.
He, W. (1998a). Demobilized and transferred soldiers working in courts. *Southern Weekly*.
He, W. (1998b). *Judicial philosophies and systems*. Beijing: China University of Political Science and Law Press.
He, W. (1999b). A few comments on trial committee system. *Peking University Law Review* (Vol. 1). Law Press China.
He, X. (1999c). Amendment and production of retrial criminal judgement document. *People's Judicature*.
Hirsch, E. D. (1991). *Validity in interpretation* (C. Wang, Trans.). SDX Joint Publishing Company.
Hu, J., & Li, H. (1992). On self-management of court judicial administration. *People's Judicature*.
Huang, R. (1997). *China: A macro history*. SDX Joint Publishing Company.
Huixing, L. (1995). Legal protection and benefit balance of TV program previews. *Chinese Journal of Law*.
Hume, H. (1980). *Treaties of human nature* (W. Guan, Trans., Z. Zheng, Proofread). Beijing: The Commercial Press.
James, W. (1997). Pragmatism's conception of truth. In W. Junren & Y. Chen (Eds.), *William James collection*. Shanghai Far East Press.
Jiannan, B. (2000). Symposium on judgement document producing theory and practice was held in Beijing. *People's Judicature*.
Judicial Administrative Work in Today's China. Contemporary China Publishing House. (1995).
Judicial Administrative Yearbook, Volume 1996. Law Press China.
Law Yearbook of China (1988–1998). Law Press China, Law Yearbook of China Department.
Li, J. (1994). Dealing local cases to ensure local security. *People's Judicature*.
Liang, H. (1989). Review and interpretation on the case in which the employer contracted to tear down a factory building and led to the employees' death of infection. *Chinese Journal of Law*.
Liang, H. (1995). *The hermeneutics of civil law*. Beijing: China University of Political Science and Law Press.

Liang, H. (1996). Who is the creator of 'the adventure to the amazing source of the Yangtze River video'. *Chinese Journal of Law*.
Liang, S. (1987). *Highlights of Chinese culture*. Xuelin Publishing House.
Liang, Z. (1992). *Legal arguments*. Guizhou People's Publishing House.
Liang, Z. (Ed.). (1994). *Cultural explanation of law*. SDX Joint Publishing Company.
Liang, Z. (Ed.). (1998). *About legal interpretation*. Law Press China.
Liu, X. (1998). Mass words and elite words in legal interpretation—An issue raised from the modernity of law. *Studies of Comparative Law*.
Liu, G., & Li, C. (1995). In Y, Xia (Ed.), *Civil mediation and right protection, towards time of rights*. Beijing: China University of Political Science and Law Press.
Liu, Z., & Liu, P. (1999). A preview about law studies in China at the turn of the century. *Chinese Journal of Law*.
Lü, Y. (1996). Thoughts on Improving the working system of judicial committee. *Legal Science Monthly*.
Mao, Z. (1966). *Mao Zedong collection* (one volume edition). People's Publishing House.
Mao, Z. (1991). A single spark can start a prairie fire. *Collected works of Mao Zedong* (Vol. 1). People's Publishing House.
Marx, E. (1994a). The communist manifesto. *Selected collection of marx and engels* (Vol. 1). People's Publishing House.
Marx, K. (1971). *Preface and introduction to Political Economy*. People's Publishing House.
Marx, K. (1994b). The 18th Brumaire of Louis Napoleon. *Marx and engels collected works* (Vol. 3). People's Publishing House.
Marx, K. (1994c). The civil war in France. *Selected works of marx and Engels* (Vol. 3). People's Publishing House.
Max, W. (1997). *Economy and society* (R. Lin, Trans.). Beijing: The Commercial Press.
Meng, Q. (1996). My view on legal protection and benefit balance of TV program previews. *Chinese Journal of Law*.
Meng, T. (1994). Traveling around mountains—Notes of interview on Yong Ning people's court in Yi Ethnic group autonomous county, Yonglang, Yunnan Province. *People's Judicature*.
Nietzsche, F. (1992). *On the genealogy of morality* (H. Zhou, Trans.). SDX Joint Publishing Company.
Pan, J., & Sujuan, Y. (2000). Comments on the judical system reform in Japan. *Peking University Law Journal*.
People's Tribunal of Gu County on the suburb of Changzhi, Shanxi. (1991). Promoting objective management with orientation in order to build standardized people's tribunal. *People's Judicature*.
People's Tribunal of Sancang in Dongtai, Jiangsu. (1991). To deal correctly with the relationship with party and government departments in the area of administration to do a good job in people's tribunals. *People's Judicature*.
Qu, T. (1981). *Laws in China and Chinese society*. Zhonghua Book Company.
Renstrom, P. (Ed.). (1998). *The American law dictionary* (W. He, Trans. and Proofread.). Beijing: China University of Political Science and Law Press.
Richard, P. (1994). *The problem of jurisprudence* (Suli Trans.). Beijing: China University of Political Science and Law Press.
Sabine, G. H. (1990). A history of political theory (S. Liu et al. Trans.). Beijing: The Commercial Press.
Shen, K. (2000). Institutional change and judges' choice of rules. *Peking University Law Review, book 3* (Vol. 2). Law Press China.
Sheng, H. (1996). Public choice and judge verdict. *China social sciences quarterly* (Hong Kong).
Shi, S. (1980). *General principles to civil law*. self-published by author.
Shigong, J. (1996). *Legal transplant, public domain and legitimacy*. Law School of Peking University, Master Thesis.
Shigong, J. (1997). Judicial practice of rural society: Knowledge, technology and power. *Strategy and Management*.

Shigui, T. (1997). On judicial independence. *Tribune of Political Science and Law.*
Shizeng, Y. (1991). Anecdotes of people's tribunal. *People's Judicature.*
Shouxing, D. (1999). Increase the argument and reasoning in criminal judgement document. *People's Judicature.*
Shujie, Q., & Wang, J. (2000). Civil judical reform: An inspection of comparative law. *Peking University Law Journal.*
Smith, A. (1997). *The theory of moral sentiments* (J. Ziqiang, et al. Trans.). Beijing: The Commercial Press.
Song, B. (Ed.). (1999). *Procedural, justice and modernization.* Beijing: China University of Political Science and Law Press.
Suli. (1993). Legal evasion and legal pluralism. *Chinese and Foreign Law Studies.*
Suli. (1994). Thoughts on legal sociology of legal professionalism. *China Social Sciences.*
Suli. (1996a). Rationality and feasibility of modern rule of law. *The East.*
Suli. (1996b). The lawsuit of the *Story of Qiu Ju*, Qiu Shi's rat poison case, and freedom of speech. *Chinese Journal of Law.*
Suli. (1996c). *Rule of law and its local resources.* Beijing: China University of Political Science and Law Press.
Suli. (1997a). A few explanations on 'native resource'. *Graduate Students' Journal of Peking University.*
Suli. (1997b). Difficult problems of interpretation: Looking into different ways to interpret legal texts. *Social Sciences in China.*
Suli. (1998a). China's modernization and rule of law in the 20th century. *Legal Research.*
Suli. (1998b). *China's rule of law in the modern vision. Knowledge of China.* Jiangxi Education Press.
Suli. (1998c). Classification of knowledge. *Dushu.*
Suli. (1998d). How systems are formed? *Journal of Comparative Law.*
Suli. (1998e). Why send law to the door? *Sociological Studies.*
Suli. (1999a). Observation and thoughts on trial committee system of basic-level courts. *Peking University Law Review* (Vol. 1). Law Press China.
Suli. (1999b). Resolution of disputes and rule of rules in basic-level courts in rural areas. *Peking University Law Review* (Vol. 2). Law Press China.
Suli. (1999c). *How systems were formed.* Sun Yat-sen University Press.
Suli. (1999d). *Reading order.* Shandong Education Press.
Suli. (2000). Contexualism—A kind of approach and method of legal system research. *Peking University Law Journal.*
Suli. (2001). Custom in law of modern China—Perspective of Statute. *Law Review.*
The Supreme People's Court. (1999). Five-Year reform outline for the people's courts. *Gazette of the Supreme People's Court of the People's Republic of China.*
Vile, M. J. C. (1997). *Constitutionalism and the separation of power* (Suli Trans.). SDX Joint Publishing Company.
Wang, L. (2000). *Studies on judical reform.* Law Press China.
Wang, M. (Ed.). (1997). *Authority of China's folk society.* Beijing: China University of Political Science and Law Press.
Wang, Q. (1999). UK's Magistrates. *Democracy and legality.*
Wang, Q., & Zhang, D. (1989). On due attributes of judicial independence. *Science of Law.*
Wang, S. (1994). *Wang Shuo collection.* Hua Yi Publishing House.
Wang, Y. (not published). Court Independence and Its Dilemma.
Wang, Z., Sheng, N., & Li, Z. (Ed.). (1991). *Latest collection of western literary articles.* Lijiang Publishing House.
Wu, D. (1999). Where can we find the right solution when witnesses refuse to testify. *People's Procuratorial Monthly.*
Wu, H., Fei, X., et al. (1988). *Imperial power and gentry's power.* Tianjin People's Press.
Wu, Y. (2000). Thoughts on fact authentication in judgement document. *Political Science and Law.*

Xia, F. (1994). A few thoughts on building order system of clerks. In Essay Evaluation and Selection Committee of the Sixth Academic Seminar (Ed.), *Comprehensive talks on reform of China's judicial system—Essay collection of the sixth academic seminar of China's court system*. People's Court Publishing House.

Xia, Y. et al. (Ed.). (1995). *The age heading toward power*. Beijing: China University of Political Science and Law Press.

Xiancui, K. (1995). Legal guarantee mechanism need to be established to ensure the independent trial of people's courts. *Modern Law Science*.

Xin, S. (1994). Establishing progressive selection system of judges is a key to guarantee qualities of judges. In Essay Evaluation and Selection Committee of the Sixth Academic Seminar (Ed.), *Comprehensive talks on reform of China's judicial system—Essay collection of the sixth academic seminar of China's court system*. People's Court Publishing House.

Xu, G. (1992). *Interpretation of civil law principles—How to overcome the limitation of statues*. Beijing: Chinese University of Political Science and Law Press.

Yang, L. (1999). Indistinct legal products—Observation at two cases of mediation at basic-level court (not published).

Ye, Z. (1999). On verdict reasons. *Xiangjiang Law Review* (Vol. 3). Hunan People's Publishing House.

You, R. (chief editor). (1992). *History of foreign legal systems*. Peking University Press.

Yue, L., Chen, R. (1997). International standard of criminal procedural justice and criminal procedure law after amendment (I). *Tribune of Political Science and Law*.

Zeng, G. (writer and compiler). (1989). *Constitutions and governments of western countries*. Hubei Education Press.

Zhang, B. (1999a). *An introduction to law reasoning*. (Doctoral Dissertation, Renmin University of China).

Zhang, G., & Rao, X. (chief editor) (1987). *Outline of legal thoughts in China*. The second volume, Gansu People's Press.

Zhang, Q. (1999b). Law reasoning and judical justice. *Rule of law and judical reform* (Xin, C. & Li, L. Chief Editors). China Legal Publishing House.

Zhang, X. (1983). *Ma Xiwu's judicial method*. Law Press China.

Zhang, X. (1999c). Amendment and production of criminal decision document on commuted sentence and parole. *People's Judicature*.

Zhang, Z. (1999d). *Practice analysis on legal interpretation*. Beijing: Chinese University of Political Science and Law Press.

Zhao, X. (1997). Relationship/events, action strategy and narrate of law. In M. Wang (Ed.), *Authority of China's civil society*. Beijing: Chinese University of Political Science and Law Press.

Zhao, X. (1999). *Through legal administration: Research on basic-level courts in rural China*. (Doctoral Dissertation, Law School of Peking University).

Zhenglai, D. (chief editor) (1992). *Blackwell encyclopedia of political science*. Beijing: China University of Political Science and Law Press.

Zhou, W. (1996). Three policies of China's legislative reform: rule of law, institution and decision-making. *Xinhua Digest*.

Zhu, F. Thoughts on reform of administrative judgement document. *Administrative law review*.

Zou, H. (1996). Unjustified enrichment and pertinent problems in infringing people's rights and interests. *Chinese Journal of Law*.

English Works

Abraham, H. A. (1993). *The judicial process, an introductory analysis of the courts of the United States, England, and France* (6th ed.). New York: Oxford University Press.

Atiyah, P. S., & Summers, R. S. (1987). *Form and substance in anglo-american law: A comparative study of legal reasoning, legal theory, and legal institutions*. New York: Oxford University Press.

Bartell, A. (1986). *Judicial decision making in the trial court*. In Disputes Processing Research Program Working Papers Series 8, Institute for Legal Studies, University of Wisconsin-Madison Law School.

Black, D. (1976). *The behavior of law*. Orland: Academic Press.

Bok, D. (1996). *The state of the nation, government and the quest for a better society, Cambridge*. Mass: Harvard University Press.

Bourdieu, P. (1984). *Distinction: A social critique of the judgment of taste* (R. Nice, Trans.). Cambridge, Mass: Harvard University Press.

Carp, R. A., & Stidham, R. (1998). *Judicial process in America* (4th ed.). Washingto, D.C.: Congressional Quarterly Inc.

Danelski, D. J. (1989). The influence of the chief justice in the decisional process of the supreme court. In S. Goldman & A. Sarat (Eds.), *American court system, readings in judicial process and behavior* (2nd ed.). New York: Longman.

Danelski, D. J., & Jeanne, C. D. (1989). Leadership in the warren court. In S. Goldman & A. Sarat (Eds.), *American court systems, readings in judicial process and behavior* (2nd ed.). New York: Longman.

Durkheim, E. (1984). *The division of labor in society* (W. D. Halls Trans.). New York: Free Press.

Dworkin, R. (1977). *Taking rights seriously*. Cambridge, Mass: Harvard University Press.

Easterbrook, F. H. (1978). *Discipline and Punish, the Birth of the Prison* (A. Sheridan Trans.). New York: Vintage Books.

Easterbrook, F. H. (1980). Power/knowledge: Selected interviews and other writings, 1972–1977, (C. Gorden Ed.). New York: Pantheon.

Easterbrook, F. H. (1984). Foreword: The court and the economic system. *Harvard Law Review, 98*.

Eisele, T. D. (1997). From 'Moral Stupidity' to professional responsibility. *Legal Studies Forum* (Vol. 21).

Ellickson, R. C. (1991). *Order without law, how neighbors settle disputes*. Cambridge, Mass: Harvard University Press.

Fish, S. (1980). Is there a text in this class? The authority of interpretive communities. Cambridge, Mass: Harvard University Press.

Foucault, M. (1971). *The order of things, archaeology of the human sciences*. New York: Pantheon Books.

Frank, J. (1973). *Court on trial, myth and reality in American justice*. Princeton: Princeton University Press.

Friendly, H. J. (1979). The 'law of the circuit' and all that. *St. John's Law Review, 46*.

Fuller, L. L. (1969). *The morality of law* (rev ed.). New Haven: Yale University Press.

Geertz, C. (1983). *Local knowledge, further essays in interpretive anthropology*. New York: Basic Press.

Glendon, M. A. (1987). *Abortion and divorce in western law*. Cambridge, Mass: Harvard University Press.

Glendon, M. A. (1994). A nation under lawyers, how the crisis in the legal profession is transforming American society. Cambridge, Mass: Harvard University Press.

Glendon, M. A., Michael, W. G., & Christopher, O. (1994). *Comparative legal traditions*, 2nd ed., St. Paul, Minn.: West Publishing Comp.

Goldman, S., & Jahnige, T. P. (1971). *The federal courts as a political system*. New York: Harper and Row.

Granfield, R. (1992). *Making elite lawyers: Visions of law at harvard and beyond*. New York: Routledge.

Habermas, J. (1996). *Between facts and norms: Contributions to a discourse theory of law and democracy* (W. Rehg, Trans.). Cambridge, Mass: MIT Press.

Hanssen, F. A. (1999). The effect of judicial institutions on uncertainty and the rate of litigation: The election versus appointment of state judges. *Journal of Legal Studies, XXVIII*(1), 205–232.

Hayek, F. A. (1973). *Law, legislation, and liberty* (Vol. 1). Chicago: University of Chicago Press.
Holland, K. M. (1981). The federal rules of civil procedure. *Law and Policy Quarterly*.
Holmes, O. W., Jr. (1943a). Natural Law. In M. Lerner (Ed.), *The mind and faith of Justice Holmes: His speeches, essays, letters and judicial opinions*. Boston: Little, Brown, and Company.
Holmes, O. W., Jr. (1943b). Law and the court. In M. Lerner (Ed.), *The mind and faith of Justice Holmes: His speeches, essays, letters and judicial opinions*. Boston: Little, Brown, and Company.
Holmes, O. W., Jr. (1946). *The common law*. Boston: Little, Brown, and Company.
Holmes, O. W., Jr. (1952a). The path of the law. In *Collected legal papers*. New York: Harcourt, Brace and Hows, Inc.
Holmes, O. W., Jr. (1952b). Law in science and science in law. In *Collected legal papers*. New York: Harcourt, Brace & Howe, Inc.
Howe, M. D. W. ed. (1953). Holmes-Laski letters: The correspondence of Mr. Justice Holmes and Harold J. Laski, 1916–1935 (Vol. 1). Cambridge, Mass.: Harvard University Press.
Jacob, H. (1983). Courts as organizations. In K. O. Boyumand & L. Mather (Eds.), *Empirical theories about courts*. New York: Longman.
Kalven, H., Jr., & Zeisel, H. (1966). The American jury: Some general observation, In *American Jury*. Boston: Little, Brown, and Company.
Kronman, A. T. (1993). *The lost lawyer, failing ideals of the legal profession*. Cambridge, Mass: Harvard University Press.
Landes, W. M., Lawrence, L., & Michael E. S. Judicial influence: A citation analysis of federal courts of appeals judges. *Chicago Working Paper in Law & Economics* (2nd Series).
Larmore, C. (1996). *The morals of modernity*. Cambridge: Cambridge University Press.
Lempert, R. O. (1975). Uncovering 'Nondiscernible' differences: Empirical research and the jury-size cases. *Michigan Law Review*.
Lerner, M. (Ed.). (1943). *The mind and faith of justice Holmes: His speeches, essays, letters and judicial opinion*. Boston: Little, Brown, and Company.
Lessig, L. (1999). The prolific iconoclast, richard Posner. *The American Lawyer*, December 6.
Lithwich, D. (1999). Richard Posner, a human pentium processor has been assigned to settle the microsoft case. In http://www.slate.com/assessment/99-11-23/assessment.asp
Macaulay, S. (1963). Non-Contractual relations in business: A preliminary study. *American Sociological Review, 28*.
Mayr, E. (1997). *This is biology: The science of the living world*. Cambridge, Mass: Harvard University Press.
Mikva, A. J. (1988). For whom judges write. *Southern California Law Review, 61*.
Nietzsche, F. (1966). *Beyond good and evil: Prelude to a philosophy of the future* (W. Kaufmann, Trans.). New York: Vintage Books.
O'Brien, D. M. (1990). *Storm center, the Supreme Court in American Politics* (2nd ed.). New York: W. W. Norton & Company.
Pascal, B. (1931). *Pensees* (W. F. Trotter, Trans.), New York: E. P. Dutton & Co.
Plotkin, H. (1993). *Darwin machines and the nature of knowledge*. Cambridge, Mass: Harvard University Press.
Posner, R. A. (1981). *The economics of justice*. Cambridge, Mass: Harvard University Press.
Posner, R. A. (1988). *Law and literature: A misunderstood relation*. Cambridge, Mass: Harvard University Press.
Posner, R. A. (1990). *The problems of jurisprudence*. Cambridge, Mass: Harvard University Press.
Posner, R. A. (1992a). *Economic analysis of law* (4th ed.). Boston: Little, Brown, and Company.
Posner, R. A. (1992b). *Sex and reason*. Cambridge, Mass: Harvard University Press.
Posner, R. A. (1995). *Overcoming law*. Cambridge, Mass: Harvard University Press.
Posner, R. A. (1996). *Federal courts, challenge and reform*. Cambridge, Mass: Harvard University Press.

Posner, R. A., & Katharine B. S. (1996). *A guide to America's sex laws*. Chicago: University of Chicago Press.
Posner, R. A. (1999a). *The problematics of moral and legal theory*. Cambridge, Mass: Harvard University Press.
Posner, R. A. (1999b). *An affair of state: The investigation, impeachment, and trial of president Clinton*. Cambridge, Mass: Harvard University Press.
Richardson, R. J., & Vines, K. N. (1970). *The politics of federal courts*. Boston: Little, Brown and Company.
Said, E. W. (1978). *The orientalism*. New York: Penguin Books.
Satter, R. (1990). *Doing justice: A trial judge at work*. New York: Simon and Schuster.
Scalia, A. (1989). The rule of law as a law of rules. *University of Chicago Law Review, 56*.
Schwartz, B. (1983). *Super chief, earl warren and his supreme court: A judicial biography*. New York: New York University Press.
Shakespeare, W., *Henry V*.
Shakespeare, W., *Troilus and Cressida*.
Shapiro, F. R. (2000). The most-cited legal scholars. *The Journal of Legal Studies, 29* (pt.2).
Teubner, C. (1983). Substantive and reflexive elements in modern law. *Law and Society Review, 2*.
Unger, R. (1986). *The critical legal studies movement*. Cambridge, Mass: Harvard University Press.
Wapner, J. A. (1987). *A view from the bench*. New York: Simon and Schuster.
Weber, M. (1954). *On law in economy and society* (R., Max Ed. and Trans.). Cambridge, Mass: Harvard University Press.
Weber, M. (1964). *The theory of social and economic organization* (A. M. Henderson & T. Parsons, Trans. and T. Parsons Ed.). New York: The Free Press.
Wilson, E. O. (1978). *On human nature*. Cambridge, Mass: Harvard University Press.
Wyzanski, C. E. Jr. (1986). The importance of the trial judge, January 12, 1959. In W. F. Murphy & C. H. Pritchett (Eds.), *Courts, judges, and politics: An introduction to the judicial process* (4th ed.). New York: Random House.
Young, W. G. (1998). *Reflections of a trial judge*. Boston: Massachusetts Continuing Legal Education Inc.

Cases

Brown v. Allen, 244 U.S. 443, 540 (1953).
Brown v. Board of Education, 347 U.S. 483 (1954).
Marbury v. Madison, 1 Cranch 137 (1803).
Plessy v. Ferguson, 163 U.S. 537 (1896).
State v. Wester, 126 Fla. 49, 54, 170 So. 736, 738–39 (1936).

Index

© Foreign Language Teaching and Research Publishing Co., Ltd
and Springer Science+Business Media Singapore 2016
S. Zhu, *Sending Law to the Countryside*, China Academic Library,
DOI 10.1007/978-981-10-1142-9

The manufacturer's authorised representative in the EU is Springer Nature Customer Service Centre GmbH, Europaplatz 3, 69115 Heidelberg, Germany. If you have any concerns regarding our products, please contact ProductSafety@springernature.com

Printed and bound by CPI Group (UK) Ltd, Croydon, CR0 4YY
30/09/2026
02225436-0010